HOLLYWOOD AND THE LAW

Edited by PAUL McDONALD, EMILY CARMAN, ERIC HOYT, PHILIP DRAKE

palgrave

A BFI book published by Palgrave

CONTENTS

ACKNOWLEDGMENTS

Editing a book anthology, like producing a movie, is a collaborative endeavour. The editors wish to acknowledge the scribes, suits and grips who helped *Hollywood and the Law* move from development to post-production.

First and foremost, we want to thank the authors who contributed chapters to this anthology. Peter Decherney, Mark Bartholomew, John Tehranian, Jennifer Porst, Laura Wittern-Keller, Ross Melnick and Catherine L. Fisk all delivered chapters that exceeded our already high expectations. Beyond their clear writing styles and expertise, we are grateful for their professionalism and patience during the editing process.

In addition to the authors who directly contributed to the anthology, we learned a great deal from scholars who joined us on law- and industry-oriented panels at the annual conferences of the Society for Cinema and Media Studies and European Network for Cinema and Media Studies from 2010 to 2015. Our thanks go to Ian Christie, Jane Gaines, Nitin Govil, Tom Kemper, Shawna Kidman, Anne Helen Petersen and Ellen Seiter for pushing us to make this the best possible anthology. Thank you also to the six anonymous peer reviewers who offered valuable feedback at the proposal and manuscript-delivery stages of the publishing process.

We had a terrific experience working with BFI Publishing at Palgrave. Slowly revolving 360 degrees in a restaurant on the thirty-fifth floor of a Los Angeles hotel, we first developed the blueprint of the anthology with commissioning editor, Rebecca Barden, who shepherded us through the proposal, peer review and contract stages. In the latter stages of editing the anthology, we were grateful to work with the team of Jenna Steventon, Sophie Contento and Lucinda Knight at BFI Publishing and Palgrave.

We also thank the BFI for their generosity in permitting us to use photographs from their collection. The Academy of Motion Picture Arts and Sciences' Margaret Herrick Library and University of Southern California's Warner Bros. Archives were similarly invaluable for providing access to archival sources used by several authors in this anthology. Our thanks especially go to Val Almendarez, Barbara Hall and Jenny Romero at the Margaret Herrick Library, and to Sandra Joy Aguilar and Jonathon Auxier at the Warner Bros. Archives, for making the research process such a pleasure.

Selections from Eric Hoyt's chapter, 'Asset or Liability?: Hollywood and Tax Law', first appeared in his 2010 *Film History* article, 'Hollywood and the Income Tax, 1929–1955'. This material appears courtesy of Indiana University Press, all rights reserved. Selections from the chapter 'Doing the Deal: Talent Contracts in Hollywood' also appear in Emily Carman's forthcoming 2016 book *Independent Stardom: Freelance Women in the Hollywood Studio System*. This material appears courtesy of the University of Texas Press, all rights reserved.

Finally, we wish to thank our institutions for their support and our students for their diligence and assistance. Paul McDonald would like to thank the School of Cultures, Languages and Area Studies at the University of Nottingham for a period of research leave which enabled him to work on the book. Funding from the University of Wisconsin-Madison's Graduate School and the Dodge College of Film and Media Arts at Chapman University enabled us to hire three graduate students, Caroline Leader, Derek Long and Andy Motz, who helped us locate images for the book, together with harmonising formatting and citation styles between the worlds of film and legal scholarship.

Thank you to one and all who helped in the making of *Hollywood and the Law*.

Now, on with the show.

NOTES ON CONTRIBUTORS

MARK BARTHOLOMEW is Professor of Law at SUNY Buffalo Law School, State University of New York at Buffalo. His scholarship and teaching focus on intellectual property and law and technology, with an emphasis on copyright, trademarks, advertising regulation, celebrity studies and online privacy. He has published numerous articles on these topics and is currently at work on a book project, *Adcreep: The New Advertising and the Legal System's Failure to Respond* (forthcoming, 2016), investigating the social and legal challenges posed by modern marketing techniques.

EMILY CARMAN is Assistant Professor of Film Studies in the Dodge College of Film and Media Arts at Chapman University, where she teaches classes primarily on American cinema, film history and historiography. Previously, she has worked for various motion picture archives in Los Angeles, including the Warner Bros. Archives of the School of Cinematic Arts at the University of Southern California, where she was the curator responsible for the preservation of the collection and its research access. She is the author of *Independent Stardom: Freelance Women in the Hollywood Studio System* (forthcoming, 2016). Her research interests include the Hollywood studio system, film stardom and screen labour, film censorship, moving image archives and film restoration, and media industries. She has published articles in *Celebrity Studies*, *Quarterly Review of Film and Video* and *The Moving Image*.

PETER DECHERNEY is Professor of Cinema Studies and English at the University of Pennsylvania. He also holds a secondary appointment at the Annenberg School for Communication and an affiliation with the Center for Technology, Innovation and Competition at Penn Law School. He is the author or editor of five books, including *Hollywood's Copyright Wars: From Edison to the Internet* (2012) and *Hollywood: A Very Short Introduction* (forthcoming, 2015). He is co-editor of the journal *Critical Studies in Media Communication* and has testified before the Copyright Office of the USA and filed amicus briefs in several cases, including the Supreme Court case of *Golan v. Holder*. Professor Decherney has been an Academy of Motion Picture Arts and Sciences Scholar, a fellow of the American Council of Learned Societies and a US State Department Arts Envoy to Myanmar. He has won multiple teaching awards at Penn and he is a Forbes.com contributor.

PHILIP DRAKE is Head of the Department of Media and Professor in Film, Media and Communications at Edge Hill University. He has recently published research on film marketing and distribution (in *The Contemporary Hollywood Film Industry*, 2008), on 'reputational capital' and Hollywood independence (in *American Independent Cinema: Indie, Indiewood and Beyond*, 2012) and on creative talent and creative industries discourse in the UK (in *Behind the Screen: Inside European Production Cultures*, 2013). He has also written on image rights in Hollywood, on television and deregulation and on screen performance. He is a member of the Editorial Board of Media Industries Project (MIP) Research, is currently completing a book on the Hollywood industry and is conducting research for a Digital R&D Fund for the Arts project on independent film distribution and video-on-demand.

CATHERINE L. FISK is the Chancellor's Professor of Law at the University of California, Irvine, where she teaches courses on labour and civil rights law and on the legal profession. She is the Director of the Center on Law, Society and Culture. Fisk is the author of dozens of articles and four books, including *Labor Law in the Contemporary Workplace* (2nd edn, 2014), *The Legal Profession* (2014) and the prize-winning *Working Knowledge: Employee Innovation and the Rise of Corporate Intellectual Property, 1800–1930* (2009). Her next book, *Authors at Work: A Legal History of Writing for Hire in Twentieth Century Film, Television, and Advertising* – which is based on the archives of the Writers Guild of America – West, the J. Walter Thompson advertising agency and several production companies – examines struggles between writers and employers over attribution of authorship and control of copyrights between 1930 and 1960.

ERIC HOYT is Assistant Professor of Communication Arts at the University of Wisconsin-Madison. He is the author of *Hollywood Vault: Film Libraries before Home Video* (2014), co-director of the Media History Digital Library and lead developer of the open access media history research platform *Lantern*, which received the 2014 Society for Cinema and Media Studies Anne Friedberg Innovative Scholarship Award. His articles on the media industries, law and culture have appeared in *Cinema Journal, Film History, Jump Cut, Velvet Light Trap* and *BioScope: South Asian Screen Studies*.

LAURA WITTERN-KELLER holds a PhD in history from the University at Albany (State University of New York), where she currently teaches US legal and constitutional history. She is the author of *Freedom of the Screen: Legal Challenges to State Film Censorship* (2008), the research for which earned her the 2007 designation as the New York State Archives researcher of the year. She is also the co-author of *The Miracle Case: Film Censorship and the Supreme Court* (2008), published in the prestigious Landmark Law Cases series of the University Press of Kansas, and is a chapter contributor to *Silencing Cinema: Film Censorship Around the World* (2013). She splits her time between Albany, New York, and her home in Wilmington, NC.

PAUL McDONALD is Professor of Culture, Media and Creative Industries at King's College London. Before joining KCL, he was Professor of Cinema and Media Industries at the University of Nottingham. He is the author of *Hollywood Stardom* (2013), *Video and DVD Industries* (2007) and *The Star System: Hollywood's Production of Popular Identities* (2000), and co-editor of *The Contemporary Hollywood Film Industry* (2008). He jointly edits the International Screen Industries series from BFI Publishing, and he is a member of the founding Editorial Collective for the journal *Media Industries*. He established and is currently co-chair of the Society for Cinema and

Media Studies Media Industries Scholarly Interest Group, and founded and coordinates the Screen Industries Work Group of the European Network for Cinema and Media Studies.

ROSS MELNICK is Assistant Professor of Film and Media Studies at University of California, Santa Barbara. His most recent book is *American Showman: Samuel 'Roxy' Rothafel and the Birth of the Entertainment Industry* (2012). His research has been published in journals such as *Film History* and *The Moving Image*, and he has articles forthcoming in *Cinema Journal* and *Historical Journal of Film, Radio and Television*. He is currently completing his next book, *Screening the World: Hollywood's Global Exhibition Empires*, for which he received a National Endowment for the Humanities fellowship. Before joining UC Santa Barbara, Melnick was Assistant Professor of English and Cinema Studies at Oakland University and a Postdoctoral Fellow at the Fox Center for Humanistic Inquiry at Emory University. He has held positions in: theatrical marketing and distribution at Miramax, MGM, DreamWorks and Sony Pictures; as historian/archivist for Loews Cineplex Entertainment; as a curator at the Museum of the Moving Image; and worked in business development and marketing for digital media start-ups in New York's 'Silicon Alley'. He is the co-founder of the website Cinema Treasures and the co-author of the eponymous book (2004) with Andreas Fuchs.

JENNIFER PORST is a Lecturer in Visual and Media Arts at Emerson College. Her work has been published in *Film History*, *Studies in French Cinema*, *In Media Res* and *Mediascape*. Her current major project examines the struggle over the licensing and sale of Hollywood's feature films to television before 1955 as it relates to contemporary media industry convergence and disruption.

JOHN TEHRANIAN is the Irwin R. Buchalter Professor of Law at Southwestern Law School and has previously served as a tenured Professor of Law at the University of Utah and as a Visiting Professor of Law at Loyola Law School. He is a founding partner of One LLP, an intellectual property and entertainment firm in southern California, where he has litigated numerous high-profile lawsuits, including disputes involving Madonna, Don Henley, B. B. King, Bettie Page, Jimi Hendrix and Perez Hilton. *Variety*'s 2013 Legal Impact Report recognised John as one of the world's top fifty entertainment lawyers. A graduate of Harvard University and Yale Law School, John is the author of dozens of articles and two books: *Infringement Nation* (2011) and *Whitewashed* (2009). He has spoken at numerous conferences and has served as an expert witness in intellectual property and civil rights cases. His work has been widely cited, from testimony before Congress and decisions of Israeli and American courts, to briefs before the Supreme Court in such landmark cases as *MGM v. Grokster*, *Tiffany v. eBay* and *Golan v. Holder*, and in leading publications such as the *Yale Law Journal* and *Harvard Law Review*.

INTRODUCTION
ON THE LEGAL LIVES OF HOLLYWOOD

ERIC HOYT, PAUL McDONALD, EMILY CARMAN AND PHILIP DRAKE

Since the earliest days of cinema, legal instruments, processes and institutions have influenced the conditions in which Hollywood films are made, sold, circulated and presented. From the talent contracts that enable a film to go into production, to the copyright laws that govern its distribution, or the censorship laws that may block exhibition, the law shadows cinema at every step. Meanwhile, the Hollywood film industry has left its own impression on the American legal system through lobbying to expand the duration of copyright, providing a highly visible stage for contract disputes and representing the legal system on screen.

To study Hollywood *and* the law is to examine a relationship, the reciprocal exchange between otherwise seemingly distinct spheres. Exploring the instances and complexities of that relationship is the purpose of this collection. Yet problems arise from presuming such a separation, for the law becomes cast as somehow extraneous or supplementary to film and cinema as cultural form. Coming out of traditions of thought in the arts and humanities, film and cinema studies have frequently privileged attention to films as aesthetic or symbolic works, with the consequence that there has been a general lack of attention to how films are equally legal artefacts, often taking the form of properties subject to conditions of authorised ownership that are produced by contracted labour working in an industry supervised by numerous regulatory constraints. Only by assuming a separation between film and the law has film scholarship been able to largely ignore the legal existence of moving images. And yet, looking beyond Hollywood to intersections between the law and film more generally, Leslie Moran, Emma Sandon, Elena Loizidou and Ian Christie note 'law and film are not only produced as separate categories and phenomena, but also … are deeply implicated in each other, making law and film a problematic if not impossible distinction'.[1] It is therefore equally the purpose of this collection to move beyond the separation of the Hollywood and the legal sphere by interrogating how the presence of the law is fully integrated and implicated in the formation of film culture.

With previous studies of the law and film, the most prevalent approach has been to read movie representations as 'legal texts', interpreting how films communicate and construct the workings of law.[2] This collection, however, takes a different critical direction. Where studies of representation are concerned with the law *on* screen, looking at the law through film, here the purpose is to critically interrogate the law *of* and *off* the screen to trace how the industry and culture of film are shaped through legal frameworks. *Hollywood and the Law* seeks to question how law has *ordered* – both in the sense of commanding but also arranging – the conduct of Hollywood. While this suggests scrutiny of the regulatory or prohibitive rule-bound functions of law, it is equally the intention to see the law as a productive influence in the shaping of Hollywood. As Rosemary Coombe argues: 'Regimes of law are constitutive of the cultural conditions of production and reproduction of representations, providing both incentives to produce and to disseminate texts, regulating their modes of circulation and enabling some while prohibiting other forms of reception and interpretation.'[3] From this perspective, Hollywood and the law must be seen to be mutually constitutive, for statutes and legal doctrine have played a significant part in producing Hollywood, which in turn has had a hand in the production of the law itself.

Hollywood is situated here within a variety of legal frameworks, with individual chapters covering copyright, trademark, piracy, antitrust regulation, international exhibition, censorship, tax, talent contracts and labour. In each case, chapters discuss contemporary legal frameworks and cases while also taking a historical perspective in order to contextualise current conditions and practice. With these multiple perspectives, this collection is, therefore, centrally concerned with mapping what might be described as, to appropriate and adapt a phrase from Coombe, the 'legal lives' of Hollywood.[4]

Most readily associated with the emergence, consolidation and transformation of a small concentrated core of dominant American film production and distribution firms, 'Hollywood' is regularly used as the shorthand label for the 'studio system' that has dominated American cinema over successive decades. Media diversification, conglomeration and globalisation, however, problematise this definition. Diversification by the major film firms into broadcasting, theme parks and online media expanded the realm of Hollywood. Accompanying changes in ownership also brought media and entertainment operations under the same corporate parentage as other areas of business, which historically have included car parking, office cleaning, consumer electronics, energy and water supply and waste management.[5] Geographic extension by those firms into industries and markets beyond the USA also produced a particular tension in how Hollywood has come to be located across local and global space. As Allen J. Scott argues, Hollywood represents 'a very specific place in Southern California … a particular locale-bound nexus of production relationships and local labor market activities', but also 'Hollywood is everywhere, [for] in its realization as a disembodied assortment of images and narratives, its presence is felt broadly across the entire globe'.[6]

As these transformations have redefined the contours of Hollywood, they influence the parameters of this collection. With its attention to the historical trajectories of Hollywood's engagements with the law, this collection privileges the conceptualisation of Hollywood in terms of an industry with its origins in film. As will be clear with Chapters 1 and 3 on copyright and piracy, however, the legal history of Hollywood demands that even this narrow focus on film must inevitably bring in attention to the media of television, home video and online media such as video-on-demand (VoD). As Chapter 4 shows, the conglomeration of Hollywood continues to raise questions regarding ownership and control of the media industries, and Hollywood has featured among some of the most high-profile cases of antitrust action in the USA. Widespread trans-border flows of finance, products and people might suggest globalisation disembeds cultural production from any firm grounding in national or local specificity. This abstract notion is somewhat out of keeping, however, with the practical realities of legal jurisdiction and the operational management of Hollywood. Despite their global extensity, the major entertainment corporations of Hollywood are still centrally managed from headquarters in New York or Southern California and, with the exception of the Sony Corporation (parent company of Sony Pictures Entertainment), are registered for business purposes in the USA. In the globalised universe, it therefore remains the case that there is good cause for seeing Hollywood's management as principally an American enterprise. For this reason, the studies that follow are largely embedded in the context of US jurisdiction. Even so, as the discussions in Chapters 3, 6 and 7 of unauthorised sales of film prints in South Africa, the expansion of Warner Bros.' exhibition operations into Cuba and China, or tax write-offs for film production in Australia indicate, the legal lives of Hollywood must constantly negotiate positions in relation to the specificities of international contexts.

Hollywood and the Law therefore argues for the necessity of critically examining how legal frameworks mould the culture and commerce of popular cinema. In Chapters 1 and 2, the discussions of copyright and trademark encourage attention to Hollywood as a system based on the ownership and exploitation of intellectual property rights. Chapter 3 sees the endemic presence of piracy in film history as forming an alternative sphere of production and distribution, creating a 'shadow history' of Hollywood. Each of these contributions necessitates moving beyond understanding films as aesthetic and semiotic texts and towards thinking of moving images as property. What emerge from this perspective are issues regarding how Hollywood has used intellectual property law as an instrument for the 'ownership and control of content'.[7] Interrogating the legal conditions of Hollywood's existence also demonstrates the need for understanding the conduct of the industry in relation to external institutions, most obviously the interventions of the legislature and the judiciary through their making, interpreting and administrating of laws. More specifically, with the history of censorship outlined in Chapter 5, those external influences can be seen to have also extended to the moral disciplining of Hollywood by the Catholic Church.

As Richard Caves has suggested, Hollywood is a creative business built on contracts between art and commerce. In contract theory, the firm is 'regarded as a *nexus of contracts*'.[8] This is a viewpoint that might be extended beyond the firm and to Hollywood more generally, for, as the study of talent contracts in Chapter 8 suggests, Hollywood continually operates through the micro exchanges of deal-making. Chapter 9 also offers an important reminder that Hollywood cannot be adequately understood through the operations of 'big media' alone but must also be grasped from how labour conflicts and struggles have defined the status and welfare of those who work in the industry.

When considered overall, these various interventions do not simply extend the intellectual scope of existing studies; they also invite a reconceptualisation of the field's object of study. By bringing the law into film/cinema/media studies, our purpose is precisely not to provoke any new sub-division of scholarship – 'legal studies of the moving image' – but rather to encourage the more general integration of legal perspectives across all areas of research. To this end, *Hollywood and the Law* provides readers working across film/cinema/media studies with a foundation from which to explore the implications of legal frameworks and doctrine for historical and contemporary studies of film.

Historical Overview

Legal struggles have played a key role in Hollywood history, becoming the contexts in which matters of aesthetic content, creative independence, technological change, or economic power have been opened up to debate and scrutiny. This collection provides a foundation for understanding these tensions. To set the scene and situate the studies that follow, it is therefore useful to take a brief historical overview of engagements between Hollywood and the law.

Aspects of intellectual property law, particularly copyright and trademark, have become the terrain over which the most bitter legal battles around Hollywood film have been fought (see Chapters 1 and 2). Since the earliest films, piracy has plagued the industry (see Chapter 3). With the Townsend Amendment of 1912 to the 1909 Copyright Act, for the first time film received protected status in the very period when the American film business began to migrate to California. It could be argued, therefore, that Hollywood was built on copyrighted works. Subsequently, fights to protect copyright have formed an arena of legal contestation deeply embedded in the making of Hollywood history. This has been particularly true in moments of technological innovation, for, as the arrival of the videocassette recorder or the popularisation of the internet both show, new media constantly present Hollywood with fresh legal challenges. Understanding the ways in which intellectual property issues apply to cinema is, therefore, crucial to grasping how film is a business based less on the making or circulation of things, but rather more on the *rights* to sell, show or reproduce those things.

Questions of censorship are at the forefront of issues over film and content regulation (see Chapter 5). With the establishment of the Production Code Administration (PCA) in the 1930s, then the ratings system now operated by the Motion Picture Association of America (MPAA), Hollywood has preferred to maintain systems of self-regulation rather than allow its output to be subject to the imposition of any external censorial agency. In this respect, Hollywood has policed film content by producing its own internal 'law'. Hollywood's global business requires the studios to engage with the standards of other nations as well. Today, as the major Hollywood corporations attempt to increase their market share at the Chinese box office, they must contend with that nation's censorship policies, linked to quotas and other trade protectionist measures. Issues of censorship therefore remain fertile ground for debating what forms of representation are available to the public and what is constrained by law.

Talent contracts have a similar history of struggle, in this instance between studios and the talent (often represented by agents and lawyers). Disputes over employment – especially long-term personal service contracts – have represented not only conflicts between the respective parties, but also wider issues of creative independence and the status of labour within Hollywood's mode of production. When actress Olivia de Havilland famously opposed the extension of her contract beyond the seven-year limit, the case had far-reaching ramifications as it contributed to the breakdown of the studios' use of suspension policies for stars. As a result, Section 2855 of the California Labor Code is still known as the 'De Havilland Law' (see Chapter 8). With the growth of a freelance labour market, performers and other personnel are no longer employed on the same restrictive terms, yet contracting continues to define how creative talent is employed and remunerated. Contract law has also played an important role in protecting ideas, which are not covered under copyright law. When bit-part actor Victor Desny sued Billy Wilder, claiming the director's film *Ace in the Hole* (1951) stole the premise of a story which Desny had related by phone to Wilder's secretary, the California Supreme Court took the view that the communication could be regarded as an 'implied-in-fact' contract and decided that Desny's case could go to trial. Subsequently, the case has provided a valuable precedent for protecting authors when offering their ideas in the marketplace.[9]

Hollywood is a business based on inequality. For over a century, the American film industry has been controlled by small clusters of firms dominating the film markets in North America and many overseas territories. While, in principle, the major studios have always been competitors, suspicions of collusion have seen Hollywood frequently facing allegations of anti-competitive behaviour. Applying the Sherman Antitrust Act, the Department of Justice brought actions against the studios in the 1930s and 40s, culminating in their structural transformation as exhibition was divorced from production and distribution (see Chapter 4). Although this outcome brought about massive changes in how the business operated, a core of studios has continued to dominate in Hollywood. Since the mid-1960s, as successive waves of acquisitions have seen the growth of conglomerate Hollywood, so concerns have persisted over the impact of the Hollywood oligopoly on the domestic and international film markets. These anxieties have become particularly acute with the emergence of new exhibition outlets such as cable, video/DVD rental and VoD. Furthermore, as the recent, unsuccessful, countersuit brought by RealNetworks against the MPAA shows, charges of collusion now follow Hollywood into the online sphere. Moreover, since the 1980s, Hollywood's media industries have been dramatically restructured due to historic changes in antitrust and regulatory policy. This 'deregulation' began during the Reagan era and continued into the Clinton presidency. At the beginning of Reagan's presidency, the businesses of film, broadcast and cable television were primarily distinct and separate from one another. By 1996, the passage of the Telecommunications Act sanctioned the mergers of film, cable, telecommunications and broadcast interests and made legal the global media conglomerates that continue to dominate the entertainment industry today. Antitrust law therefore provides important ground for questioning the economic power of Hollywood (see Chapter 4).

Tax regulation has also impacted on the industry in various ways (see Chapter 7). For example, the high earnings of Hollywood stars and directors have often been subject to the highest income tax brackets. Consequently, Hollywood history has seen talent seeking to exploit loopholes in the tax system through deductions for business expenses or working less in order to move between tax rates. It has been widely noted that the 1940s led to an increase in production among newly formed independent companies. In part, this trend was motivated by strategies to reduce tax payments, as stars, directors and producers formed 'collapsible corporations' as a means of receiving modestly taxed capital gains rather than heavily taxed earned income. Prior to taking up presidential office, Ronald Reagan reflected on his experience as a contract player for Warner Bros. to repeatedly voice his opposition to what he saw as the injustices of an income tax system which required the highest earners (including Hollywood stars) to surrender as much as 90 per cent of their earnings to the government. When he became President, Reagan oversaw the passage of the Tax Reform Act of 1986, which drastically reduced individual and corporate tax rates.[10] Hollywood has not only found ways of responding to and manipulating tax law but, as the case of Reagan shows, has also played its part in the making of such legislation. The current cycle of film production tax shelters and subsidies – which started with the UK's 'sale and leaseback' scheme in the 1980s and has proliferated to the point where numerous states in the USA and many countries overseas now offer tax subsidies to film productions – demonstrates the continuing significance of tax law to Hollywood.

Frameworks for Studying Hollywood and the Law

Hollywood and the Law can be understood as part of a broader movement of contemporary scholars seeking to bring humanities disciplines into dialogue with the law. In 2005, the Association for the Study of Law, Culture and Humanities launched the journal, *Law, Culture and the Humanities*, which, along with the Association's annual conference, provides a home for interdisciplinary research that 'highlights an understanding of law as a complex interpretive and cultural phenomenon, rooted in distinctive historical and social circumstances'.[11] We share the Association's objective to bring together researchers 'from inside and outside of law schools'.[12] Three of the authors featured in this collection – Catherine L. Fisk, Mark Bartholomew and John Tehranian – hold law degrees and faculty appointments in law schools. Their books and articles sit at the juncture between law, culture and the humanities.[13] We are grateful for their willingness to share their legal expertise and interdisciplinary research interests with a group of editors working in departments of film studies and media studies.

Expanding the field of film and cinema studies to more fully consider the law requires adjustments to research practice. Just as the law demands evidence, so film historiography requires substantiation and verification. Researching how the legal lives of Hollywood have changed over time necessitates that film and media scholars work with an enlarged body of primary materials, including briefs, transcripts, contracts and statutes. One can trace the consultation and incorporation of legal documents into the writing of film and media historiography to what has been described as the 'historical turn' in film scholarship, which began in the 1970s and 80s and was galvanised in the early 90s.[14] In 1975, Edward Buscombe called for a new type of film study and historiography, one that was grounded in industrial history but simultaneously limited by 'very real practical problems' – put simply, the few archival sources available with pertinent primary materials, particularly studio archives (a situation that has somewhat improved since his writing, yet still remains a challenge for film historians).[15] As Eric Smoodin notes, Buscombe's 'call for a different emphasis in film studies was part of a movement in a number of scholarly fields … against the literariness of so many humanities disciplines that began in the early to mid 1970s'.[16]

Robert C. Allen and Douglas Gomery echoed this call. In addition to noting various approaches to studying film history (aesthetic, economic, technological, social), Allen and Gomery espoused a film history approach grounded in primary materials.[17] Working with these forms of evidence produced what Smoodin describes as 'film scholarship without films … using primary materials other than films themselves for examining the history of the cinema'.[18] Following in this tradition, key studies in film historiography turned to using non-filmic primary documents to highlight the complex relationship between Hollywood, its regulation and its institutional and labour practices. Lea Jacobs examined how Hollywood self-enforced censorship regulated a particular cycle of films, while Danae Clark investigated actors' labour in the studio system during the 1930s *vis-à-vis* the formation of the Screen Actors Guild (SAG).[19] Although these studies did not tend to work with court case files or legal documents, Jacobs made use of the Motion Picture Producers and Distributors of America's (MPPDA) PCA files, while Clark utilised the trade periodical *Variety*, newspapers and guild magazines as her evidence.

The studies from Jacobs and Clark are illustrative of how working with non-filmic sources not only influences the forms of evidence historians draw upon, but also the types of history produced. Along with histories of representation, which traditionally have studied film texts for matters of meaning, narrative, genre or authorial style, Eric Smoodin sees the historical turn in film and cinema studies as inspiring histories of industry, regulation and audiences.[20] Producing the historiography of Hollywood's legal lives cuts across all these categories. Charting the history of film censorship alone, for example, deals with a form of regulation that not only circumscribes permissible forms of representation, but also, in turn, affects industrial practices of production while defining what forms of film content are available to audiences. Similarly, copyright imposes rights of ownership across the whole chain of industry, text and audience.

Within this milieu, Jane Gaines's *Contested Culture: The Image, the Voice and the Law* (1991) represented a landmark intervention in the exploration of legal influences on visual and aural culture. Drawing on historical primary sources, Gaines synthesised American entertainment law history, critical legal studies, cultural studies and post-structuralist film studies to examine how image ownership rights and intellectual property law are objects of culture. Through the analysis of star contracts and key court cases of image use, Gaines resituated 'legal doctrine back into the context of US history, literature and mass culture, from which it has been divorced by the very methodology of legal studies'.[21] Although Hollywood film and media remain continually framed within legal contexts, over two decades after Gaines brought together film and critical legal studies much of the complex relationship between cinema and the law remains uncharted. Contributions to the 2004 collection *Law's Moving Image* provided a rare exception. Although *Law's Moving Image* largely followed in the tradition of analysing filmic representations of the law, contributions to the third section headed 'Regulation: Histories, Cultures, Legalities' dealt with historical contexts where 'the fashioning and refashioning of ideas of cinema … are produced in and through … legal encounters not only limited but also forming the very idea of film and cinema'.[22] *Hollywood and the Law* shares something of this purpose, although we examine the implications of such encounters through a broader range of areas of law.

By enriching our understanding of Hollywood's history, this book contributes to a rapidly growing body of scholarly literature on the global media industries. What has been termed by some 'media industry studies' is a highly heterogeneous sub-field – ranging from political economy analyses of conglomeration, to ethnographic studies of trade shows and television productions.[23] Especially relevant to this collection are those works that address the relationships across business institutions, policy and culture. Peter Decherney, for instance, has highlighted how the history of intellectual property law in the USA has impacted Hollywood significant ways.[24] Similarly, Jennifer Holt analyses key federal court cases to examine the politics of deregulation and the reinterpretation of antitrust law as film, broadcast and cable television became interconnected, synergistic components in the global media conglomerates of the 1980s and 90s.[25] Correspondingly, *Hollywood and the Law* represents a recent example of media industry studies and echoes Gaines's hybrid methodology to understand how Hollywood and the law have, and continue to, mutually influence each other through their practices and policies. As the chapters in this book emphasise, the stakes in these institutional and cultural interactions are as high today as they have ever been.

American Law and International Law: The Basics

Hollywood and the Law is designed to be accessible to readers without any formal legal training. Every chapter attempts to communicate, as clearly as possible, the essential aspects of its area of the law. However, there are some foundations of the American legal system that structure all the areas of law discussed in this book. Additionally, the structures of international trade laws and the role of Hollywood trade organisations are discussed in multiple chapters. Before proceeding, then, we would like to introduce readers to the basics of the American legal system and international trade law. In particular, it is important to understand the American common law system, the distribution of legal authority across the state and federal governments and the hierarchical structure of courts.

US law is grounded in a common law tradition. In a common law system, laws are based on judicial decisions; judges make laws and they look to the precedent of other judicial decisions when evaluating a case. The USA inherited its common law system from England, which also continues to operate in this model (it is worth noting that fellow former British colonies Canada and Australia also possess common law systems). In contrast, France, Germany and most other western European nations adhere to a civil law system. In a civil law system, laws are written by governments and codified as statutes; judges interpret and administer laws, but they do not create laws and precedents.[26]

These are generalisations, to be sure. In practice, the US legal system contains aspects of civil law. The US federal government and state governments pass statutes that become laws. To provide just one example, the Federal Copyright Act is composed of a series of statutes passed by Congress concerning the topic of copyright. Yet, even in this example, the common law continues to matter. Although Congress passes the statutes, US judges must interpret the statutes and, in making their interpretations, judges look to the precedents of other judicial decisions. This is one reason why the US Supreme Court's copyright-related decisions, which Peter Decherney and Paul McDonald discuss in their chapters, are so important. In cases ranging from *Kalem Co. v. Harper Brothers* (1911) to *MGM v. Grokster* (2005), the US Supreme Court made decisions that changed both the theory and practice of copyright law.

Every chapter in this anthology profiles at least two legal cases in depth. Most of the cases are civil actions (not to be confused with the European tradition of civil law discussed above and also as differentiated from criminal actions). In a civil action, a plaintiff files a complaint against a defendant, demanding remedy for some harm caused by the defendant. These cases are frequently dramatic – consisting of high-stakes confrontations between conflicting parties. Yet the significance of these case studies goes beyond their compelling narratives. Indeed, their significance goes beyond providing an in-depth description and analysis of a particular event in order to make broader generalisations – the reason why case studies are included in many history, anthropology and business books. The case studies in *Hollywood and the Law* contain both drama and rich analysis, but they also represent *situations in which law is produced*. The case studies in this book generally begin with a plaintiff suing a defendant (actress Olivia de Havilland suing Warner Bros., for example, to become a free agent and change the terms of her contract). However, some of the case studies end with some change in the law itself, often with implications that extend beyond the entertainment industry (de Havilland's case changed California labour law, though the losing party, Warner Bros., may have got some consolation from the fact that the California Appeals Court misspelled her name with only one 'l', inspiring countless law review articles to do the same).

Why did *Kalem Co. v. Harper Brothers* create a copyright precedent for the entire USA when *De Haviland v. Warner Bros.* only created a contract precedent for the state of California? The answer has to do with the second important foundation of the American legal system to understand: the distribution of legal authority between federal and state laws. The fifty American states all have their own laws, legislatures and courts. Each state has laws pertaining to crime, marriage, real estate and, importantly for the entertainment industry, business contracts. So when de Havilland sued Warner Bros. in a contract dispute, the state of her employment, California, was the governing legal authority. Whereas contract law is a matter for the states, copyright law is federal in nature. The US Constitution authorises Congress to pass statutes for certain purposes, such as the regulation of interstate trade, patents and copyrights. When there is a conflict between a valid federal statute and state law, federal law is considered the 'supreme law of the land' and it pre-empts state law.[27] So when Harper Brothers sued the Kalem Company for infringing its copyright to General Lew Wallace's bestselling book *Ben-Hur*, the case first went to a federal trial court. This trial court, one of the US District Courts, sided with Harper Brothers and granted an injunction against further exhibitions of the film.[28]

At this point, we can use the Kalem lawsuit to understand the three-tiered hierarchical structure of US federal courts. The first tier is a trial court; the dozens of US District Courts are trial courts. Most cases begin and end at the trial court level. In fact, most lawsuits are settled or dismissed before they reach anything resembling the dramatic trials we are accustomed to watching in Hollywood movies. In some cases, though, the lawsuit will go to trial and the judge or a jury will reach a decision in favour of the plaintiff or defendant. The losing party may then decide to appeal the trial court's decision. If an appellate court agrees to hear a case, then it progresses to the second tier – a US Regional Circuit Court of Appeals. The USA currently has twelve Regional Circuit Courts (three more than it had in 1909) that hear appeals from the trial courts in their territories.[29] New York is part of the Second Circuit's territory and California is part of the Ninth Circuit's territory, making those two appellate courts the most important for the entertainment industry. When Kalem appealed the trial court's decision, the Second Circuit heard the case and affirmed the District Court's decision, finding in favour of Harper Brothers. In response, the Kalem Company appealed to the US Supreme Court – the nation's highest court and the third tier of its federal court structure. The US Supreme Court accepts very few of the thousands of petitions it receives, but it took Kalem's case based on the legal theories at dispute in the case. As Decherney describes in Chapter 1, the US Supreme Court, with Justice Oliver Wendell Holmes Jr writing for the majority of the nine Justices, affirmed the Second Circuit's decision and expanded the protection of copyright law to include motion picture adaptations of novels and plays.[30] Through this example, we can see the foundations of the American legal system at play – judges creating new law, jurisdictional distinctions between state and federal laws and the way cases, on appeal, can move up the hierarchical three-tier court system.

It is worth noting that most US states also have similar hierarchical tiered court structures. However, states generally distinguish between two different types of trial courts: courts of 'limited jurisdiction' that handle common, routine matters (such as a municipal court that handles traffic tickets) and superior courts that handle more serious civil and criminal cases. Additionally, some states have intermediate appellate courts, which are roughly equivalent in structure, if not in stature, to the US Regional Circuit Courts. However, in other states, appeals go straight to the state's highest appeals court, frequently a state supreme court.[31] One final note about US and state laws: although most of the areas of law discussed in this book are rooted in civil procedure, we should remember that there is a wide body of criminal law and criminal procedure not discussed here.

Even more varied and complex than the American legal system are the numerous customs, treaties and laws that we can categorise under the broad heading of international trade law. International trade law is itself a branch of international law, which concerns itself with the relationships between sovereign nation states and, in some cases, the rights of humans living within nation states. The Berne Convention for the Protection of Literary and Artistic Works is one example of a multilateral treaty that functions as international trade law. In 1886, ten nations signed the Berne Convention, establishing basic standards for the protection of intellectual property within and across the borders of member states. Writing in 1967, copyright expert (and former Paramount and Writers Guild of America counsel) Melville B. Nimmer called the Berne Convention 'one of the earliest and in some ways most successful ventures into world law' and noted the 'controversy and irritation' among authors and copyright specialists that the USA had still not signed (Nimmer would have to wait another two decades before the USA finally became signatory to Berne).[32]

As an international trade law, the Berne Convention is notable for another reason: it is fundamentally about restricting the circulation of goods and protecting intellectual property, rather than opening up markets for supposedly more liberalised trade – the goal that has driven most international commercial treaties over the last century. When the MPPDA was established in 1922, the organisation's member companies confronted a global marketplace with numerous *quotas* (restricting the quantity of films imported or exhibited) and *tariffs* (duties paid by distributors to import films).[33] Although numerous American industries grappled with tariffs, Hollywood faced some trade protections that were specific to the movies, such as quotas guaranteeing screen time to domestic productions. Numerous national governments realised, in the words of film historian Ruth Vasey, that 'Hollywood movies acted as extended advertisements for the product-oriented lifestyle that was the hallmark of twentieth-century America – and, more directly, for American products.'[34] For some, including the declining British Empire, this represented a threat, both economically and culturally.[34] For the US Department of Commerce, this represented an opportunity. 'Trade follows the motion pictures,' the slogan went and, in 1926, the Department of Commerce created a special Motion Picture Section.[36] Over the next several decades, the Department of Commerce and MPPDA tracked what they called 'restrictive trade' policies on a territory-by-territory basis and lobbied for more favourable policies for Hollywood.

The year 1947 proved to be momentous, both in Hollywood's fight against policies that limited the profitability of its export business and, more broadly, the liberalisation of global trade. As Eric Hoyt describes in his chapter on tax law (Chapter 7), Hollywood's most important foreign market, the UK, imposed a 75 per cent duty on imported films, which prompted the studios to boycott the British market in retaliation. Meanwhile, that same year, in Geneva, eight nations signed a landmark multinational treaty to reduce tariffs, arbitrate disputes and ease the constraints on global trade. The General Agreement on Tariffs and Trade (GATT) was borne, in part, from a belief among postwar economists and legislators that protectionist trade policies had worsened the economic depressions of the 1920s and 30s.[37] Among the GATT's many provisions were two important non-discrimination clauses. First, Article I's 'most-favoured nation' clause meant that any trade advantage, such as lower tariffs, that a state extended to one GATT state must be extended to all GATT states. Second, Article III's national treatment obligation clause meant that once imported goods cleared customs, governments were required to treat them no less favourably than domestically produced goods.[38] The GATT stood as the key treaty governing international trade until the formation of the World Trade Organization (WTO) in 1994, which took over this role.

However, in the same round of talks in Uruguay that formally established the WTO, the interests of the US film, television, music and publishing industries came close to upsetting the whole set of negotiations. France, with the backing of the European Union (EU), argued for a 'cultural exception' – the idea that Hollywood and other cultural industries should be treated differently in trade agreements than other industries. The USA voiced strong opposition to any cultural exceptions, but, ultimately, caved in to the EU's demands. Audiovisual products were excluded from the 1994 GATT agreement, to the fury of the MPAA's chief, Jack Valenti, who was heavily involved in the lobbying and negotiations.[39] This disagreement is indicative of the different understandings of cultural goods and markets in international trade, yet also of the self-serving nature of Hollywood's international lobbying. Hollywood consistently lobbies, on the one hand, for its products to receive the free trade benefits of any other exported US goods and, on the other hand, for its products to enjoy protections that are quite different from leading US exports like oil, plastics and metal (which, unlike movies and television, are not copy-rightable). In 1994, the EU reminded Hollywood that the studios cannot have it both ways, insisting that it was domestic cultural producers who needed protection from Hollywood. The 1994 dispute was indicative of different understandings of international trade and cultural goods. Although the EU succeeded in gaining this 'cultural exception' concession, the MPAA ensured that the exception was not permanent. The Trade-related Aspects of Intellectual Property Rights (TRIPS), implemented by the WTO in 1995, further extended the reach of Hollywood power into international territories through a globally agreed intellectual property right agreement.

Conflicts in global trade policy-making, such as the GATT cultural exception debate, tend to receive considerable attention from journalists and legal scholars and there is no question they are important.[40] However, if we only focus on the policies and high-profile disputes, we risk ignoring how a wider range of global exchanges and investments play out in practice and in different territories. Whereas scholars have tended to examine Hollywood and international trade laws in terms of distribution and production, Ross Melnick's chapter in this book sheds new light on the activities of the Hollywood studios in global cinema exhibition. As Melnick discusses in Chapter 6, the Hollywood studios owned movie theatres in Cuba, China and other foreign countries and they had to contend with changes in the legal and political structures of those nations. Melnick's analysis aligns with legal scholar Mark W. Janis's observation that 'states have long been in the business of using their legal systems to promote, protect and facilitate and at times to frustrate international trade'.[41] In other words, studying the global interactions between Hollywood and law often leads us to the legal systems of sovereign nations, not just international treaties between nations.

Such a brief summary as this cannot fully account for the rich, complex and frequently baffling systems that are American law and international law. Readers who want a more complete understanding of the process of how de Havilland's or Kalem's lawsuits – or any litigation – move through the court(s) may want to read one of the numerous books on state and federal civil procedure.[42] Similarly, there are good sources that offer fuller accounts of international law.[43] Hopefully, though, this primer helps clarify why lawsuits play out in particular venues and why the stakes of those cases can be so high (the setting of far-reaching precedents). For researchers of the film and media industries, a basic understanding of the legal system can also be a treasure map. Documents and exhibits from federal court cases are archived in the regional repositories of the National Archives; the papers from most Hollywood contract lawsuits reside either in the Los Angeles Superior Court Record Center or the New York County Clerk Records Office. In these archives, it is possible to find testimonies from historically significant figures who did not donate their papers to any library or institution. They also contain disclosures from contemporary Hollywood studios that would otherwise never have entered the public record. The history of Hollywood and the law is, among other things, the history of an archive.

Book Structure and Chapter Descriptions

Hollywood and the Law is structured across three parts, each containing three chapters. The first part, 'Ownership and Infringement', examines two areas of intellectual property law that are foundational for the entertainment industry – copyright and trademark – and the industry's attempts to prosecute alleged infringements. In Chapter 1, 'One Law to Rule Them All: Copyright Goes Hollywood', Peter Decherney introduces readers to the major concepts of US copyright law and explains how Hollywood has been shaped through its encounters with copyright and sought to shape the law. Exploring a wide range of historical and contemporary cases, Decherney analyses how Hollywood studios and US courts have grappled with new technologies, conceptions of authorship and genre and what constitutes a 'fair use' (those instances in which a copyrighted work can be used without permission). Decherney also calls our attention to the shrinking public domain – the result of copyright legislation and Supreme Court decisions, such as *Golan v. Holder* (2012). Decherney points out that these developments hamstring contemporary creators, arguing that 'a public domain that does not grow does not support innovation at any level'.

With Chapter 2, 'The Changing Landscape of Trademark Law in Tinseltown', Mark Bartholomew and John Tehranian explore how US courts have sought to balance the competing interests at stake when film-makers employ brand names and images in their work and brand owners threaten liability for trademark infringement. Specifically, they discuss *Rogers v. Grimaldi* (1989) as a primary pivot point to trace the remarkable change in approaches that courts have taken to First Amendment defences in trademark cases over the past few decades. Case studies of two opinions – *Dallas Cowboys Cheerleaders, Inc. v. Pussycat Cinema, Ltd.* (decided a decade before *Rogers*) and *Louis Vuitton Malletier S.A. v. Warner Bros. Entertainment Inc.* (decided two decades after *Rogers*) – illustrate the increasing recognition of free speech defences to trademark infringement claims against film-makers.

In its struggles to both allow and restrict public access to a mass reproduced and mass disseminated product, the movie business has continually taken legal action aimed at preventing acts of copyright infringement, colloquially known as 'piracy'. In the third chapter, 'Piracy and the Shadow History of Hollywood', Paul McDonald considers how these legal battles provide the substance for charting an alternative history of film. Exploring Hollywood's efforts to combat piracy across different technological phases, McDonald looks at how the move from film prints to videocassettes, DVD and digital networks differently configured the legal terrain of the fight against piracy. To illustrate these changes, case studies explore the first major crackdown on piracy by federal authorities in the USA with the trial of Budget Films in 1975 and how failed attempts to press for legislative change to control online piracy have exposed larger divisions between Hollywood and the digital media economy.

The book's second part, 'Competition and Circulation', explores how the law has influenced the industry's structure and the production, distribution and exhibition of media content. From the Motion Picture Patents Company (MPPC) in the early twentieth century, to the modern diversified media conglomerates, various formations of corporate collusion, combination and concentration have dominated the American film business. Hollywood has therefore repeatedly conflicted with the statutory restrictions of antitrust or competition law, the form of legislation designed to protect against anti-competitive business practices. In Chapter 4, 'The Preservation of Competition: Hollywood and Antitrust Law', Jennifer Porst traces the history of how market regulation and deregulation has transformed the structural organisation of Hollywood. Porst explores Hollywood's relationship to antitrust law in connection with issues concerning restraint of trade, vertical integration and market concentration. Case studies of the antitrust actions brought against the MPPC, Paramount and the other major Hollywood corporations, and the 2011 merger between General Electric and Comcast, illustrate how Hollywood has been continually shaped by antitrust enforcement.

In Chapter 5, 'Controlling Content: Governmental Censorship, the Production Code and the Ratings System', Laura Wittern-Keller introduces three contexts necessary to understanding the regulation of movie content in the USA during the twentieth century. First, she examines the manner in which legislatively empowered bureaucrats dictated what could not be seen on movie screens, starting in 1907, spreading widely in the 1910s and solidified by the *Mutual* US Supreme Court opinion in 1915 and continuing through 1965. Second, she considers the response of the Hollywood studios to this legal censorship and to pressure groups by creating their own internal control mechanism, the Motion Picture Production Code. Finally, Wittern-Keller looks at how, even when legal challenges to governmental censorship succeeded in curbing most restrictions after 1965, Hollywood responded to real and perceived pressure group activity by creating today's ratings system.

In Chapter 6, 'Hollywood Embassies, Labour and Investment Laws and Global Cinema Exhibition', Ross Melnick provides a rich account of Hollywood's operations overseas and, in particular, presents two detailed case studies of international exhibition in Cuba and China. When Hollywood was forced to divest its exhibition chains in the USA in the 1940s, it was able instead to turn towards exhibition overseas, which was not restricted by the antitrust ruling in the USA. Both Cuba and China represent the intensive struggles and negotiations required to operate exhibition chains in territories markedly different to the USA and the frequent collision between local industrial practices and those adopted by the studios. Melnick reminds us that US-run cinemas overseas were not simply 'outposts for the exhibition of Hollywood films; but also "cultural embassies", designed to attract local audiences to American films and moviegoing practices'. The entangled political and economic context in which such cinemas and their managers found themselves shows the importance of the laws pertaining to the country in which Hollywood's international cinemas were located and how US practices had to accommodate and negotiate these.

The third part, 'Negotiation and Labour', extends the previous part's interest in how law influences the industry's structure, but it looks especially closely at how the industry's workers have responded to legal challenges and opportunities and, in some cases, prompted changes in the law itself. In Chapter 7, 'Asset or Liability?', Eric Hoyt explores the fraught and generative relationship between Hollywood and tax law. Historically, a range of taxes have been levied on Hollywood, including taxes on movie theatre admissions, foreign distribution and film prints as property. Additionally, high US income tax rates in the 1930s, 40s and 50s changed the behaviour of highly paid directors and actors, such as Charles Laughton, who went to tax court to defend his personal corporation. In the contemporary era, tax shelters and incentives have played key roles in the areas of film finance and runaway production. Hoyt explores the Australian Tax Office's controversial decision involving *Moulin Rouge* (2001) and the rise and fall of numerous US state tax incentives over the last decade. Hoyt argues that these decisions and debates hold creative, social and economic stakes. Tax incentives, while great for film producers, can have adverse consequences for Hollywood labour and tax payers, who may find there is less revenue available to pay for schools, law enforcement and other government services.

For Chapter 8, 'Doing the Deal', Emily Carman and Philip Drake focus on the industry contract that has attracted the most visibility in Hollywood: the above-the-line talent contract. Initially, the chapter traces the evolution of the standard seven-year long-term option contract for actors in the studio system in the 1930s–40s through to Olivia de Havilland's lawsuit against Warner Bros. in 1944 that culminated in a landmark California Supreme Court decision that legally declared actors the right to be free agents. The chapter also examines the talent contract in the post-studio system, considering the development of complex and intricate contracts that include detailed net profit and break-even definitions, extensive credit demands and – in comparison to union and guild minimum contracts – inflated up-front salaries and deferred payments. The complexity of such contracts has been matched by the labyrinthine accounting processes adopted by Hollywood – exposed in Art Buchwald's 1990 lawsuit against Paramount – and negotiated through agents and lawyers, representing an ongoing battle for economic power between major talent and the studios. The 'Buchwald decision' caused alarm not just for Paramount Pictures but right across Hollywood, as it revealed that the contracting process had the potential to be legally flawed.

Employment in Hollywood extends from the wealth and influence of above-the-line talent at one end, to a large low-pay or no-pay workforce at the other. In the final chapter, 'Will Work for Screen Credit', Catherine L. Fisk explores how labour law has regulated overall employment in Hollywood. Fisk outlines how employment contracts, statutory wage and hour regulation and collective bargaining agreements govern labour conditions in Hollywood. She looks at the formation of the Writers Guild and its role in securing for writers contractual rights to screen credit and the payment of residuals for the reuse of films or television programmes they worked on. Shifting attention to the lowest tier of the labour hierarchy, Fisk explores how the oversupply of eager aspirants attracted to working in the film and television industries creates conditions in which labour law violations become prevalent, illustrated by a case study of the class action lawsuit arising from the use of unpaid interns during the production of the films *Black Swan* (2010) and *(500) Days of Summer* (2009).

Although each chapter focuses on a different area of Hollywood's relationship with the law, the nine chapters of this book, taken together, can be understood as speaking to one another about an interlocking set of conflicts and issues. For example, copyright law offers creators a limited monopoly over their work and these monopolies have been leveraged to build valuable brands, fight disruptive technologies and block competitors from entering the industry. State censorship laws, in effect, placed a tax on film distributors, while the enactment of official tax policies have prompted Hollywood talent to reformulate contracts and LA production crews to confront periods of high unemployment. The chapters of this book, like the laws and developments they describe, are best understood as connected rather than isolated.

The authors featured in this anthology are critical in their analyses of industry and legal changes and developments. However, they are not cynical. In editing this book, we were pleased to see common values emerge across chapters – particularly, the desire for more equitable media and social landscapes and the recognition that this requires some balance of the needs of artists, companies, labour and the public at large. How that balance might be best achieved remains open for debate.

The authors featured in this book also share a belief in the importance of studying history. The following nine chapters ask us to reflect on our present moment in relation to the past. Doing so enables us to see how the law is produced, reproduced and transformed. We gain valuable context for understanding the significant shifts in copyright, trademark, antitrust, censorship and tax laws since the formation of the major Hollywood studios. And we better understand the stakes of the policy and legal decisions that lay ahead. Indeed, the stakes are high. They include the ability of creators to produce and share expressive works; the opportunity for the public to access those works; the possibility of new companies to enter the marketplace; and the needs of media workers to earn a living. The legal lives of Hollywood remain very much alive.

Notes

1. Leslie J. Moran, Emma Sandon, Elena Loizidou and Ian Christie, 'Introduction', in Leslie J. Moran, Emma Sandon, Elena Loizidou and Ian Christie (eds), *Law's Moving Image* (London: GlassHouse, 2004), p. xi.

2. These include: Steve Greenfield, Guy Osborn and Peter Robson, *Film and the Law*, 2nd edn (Oxford: Hart, 2010); David A. Black, *Law in Film: Resonance and Representation* (Urbana: University of Illinois Press, 1999); Anthony Chase, *Movies on Trial: The Legal System on Screen* (New York: New Press, 2002); Paul Bergman and Michael Asimow, *Reel Justice: The Courtroom Goes to the Movies* (Kansas City, MO: Andrews McMeel, 2006); Michael Asimow and Shannon Mader, *Law and Popular*

Culture: A Course Book, 2nd edn (New York: Peter Lang, 2004); and Orit Kamir, *Framed: Women in Law and Film* (Durham, NC: Duke University Press, 2006), and the contributions to Rennard Strickland, Teree E. Foster and Taunya Lovell Banks (eds), *Screening Justice: The Cinema of Law* (Buffalo, NY: William S. Hein, 2006); John Denvir (ed.), *Legal Reelism: Movies as Legal Texts* (Champaign: University of Illinois Press, 1996); and Stefan Machura and Peter Robson (eds), *Law and Film* (Oxford: Blackwell, 2001).

3. Rosemary J. Coombe, 'Contingent Articulations: A Critical Cultural Studies of the Law', in Austin Sarat and Thomas R. Kearns (eds), *Law in the Domains of Culture* (Ann Arbor: University of Michigan Press, 2000), pp. 21–64.

4. Coombe discusses what she calls 'the legal life of cultural forms', ibid., p. 59. See also Rosemary J. Coombe, *The Cultural Life of Intellectual Properties: Authorship, Appropriation and the Law* (Durham, NC: Duke University Press, 1998).

5. The conglomeration of Hollywood followed a general pattern. Broadly speaking, film and entertainment assets were first acquired by parent companies widely diversified across multiple and disconnected areas of business. There then followed a second phase as those companies then sold or spun off some of their holdings to focus their operations more tightly around a portfolio of media and communication businesses. In this way, the major Hollywood corporations became elements of diversified media and communication conglomerates.

6. Allen J. Scott, *On Hollywood: The Place, The Industry* (Princeton, NJ: Princeton University Press, 2005), p. 138.

7. Ronald Bettig, *Copyrighting Culture: The Political Economy of Intellectual Property* (Boulder, CO: Westview, 1996), p. 4.

8. Richard E. Caves, *Creative Industries: Contracts Between Art and Commerce* (Cambridge, MA: Harvard University Press, 2000), p. 15, emphasis original.

9. Eric Hoyt, 'Writer in the Hole: *Desny v. Wilder*, Copyright Law and the Battle Over Ideas', *Cinema Journal* vol. 50 no. 2 (Winter 2011): 21–40.

10. Eric Hoyt, 'Hollywood and the Income Tax, 1929–1955', *Film History* vol. 22 no. 1 (2010): 16–18.

11. Austin Sarat, 'Editorial', *Law, Culture and the Humanities* vol. 1 no. 1 (2005): 1. For information about the Association for the Study of Law, Culture and the Humanities and its annual conference, see the Association's website, accessed 16 December 2014, http://law2.syr.edu/academics/centers/lch/journal.html

12. Sarat, 'Editorial': 1.

13. Mark Bartholomew, 'A Right is Born: Celebrity, Property and Postmodern Lawmaking', *Connecticut Law Review* vol. 44 no. 2 (2011): 301–68; Catherine L. Fisk, *Working Knowledge: Employee Innovation and the Rise of Corporate Intellectual Property, 1800–1930* (Chapel Hill: University of North Carolina Press, 2009); John Tehranian, *Infringement Nation: Copyright 2.0 and You* (New York: Oxford University Press, 2011).

14. Sumiko Higashi, 'In Focus: Film History, or a Baedeker Guide to the Historical Turn', *Cinema Journal* vol. 44 no. 1 (1995): 94–100.

15. Edward Buscombe, 'Notes on Columbia Pictures Corporation, 1926–1941', *Screen* vol. 16 no. 3 (1975): 68. In addition to the Production Code Administration files (held at the Academy of Motion Picture Arts and Sciences' Margaret Herrick Library), the most significant Hollywood manuscript collections available to scholars for research access are the Warner Bros. Archive at the University

of Southern California, the David O. Selznick Collection at the Harry Ransom Center at the University of Texas at Austin and the United Artists Collection at the University of Wisconsin-Madison. For more information on using studio archives, see Emily Carman, 'That's Not All, Folks: Excavating the Warner Bros. Archive', *The Moving Image: The Journal of the Association of Moving Image Archivists* vol. 14 no. 1 (2014): 30–48; and Eric Smoodin, 'The History of Film History', in Eric Smoodin and Jon Lewis (eds), *Looking Past the Screen: Case Studies in American Film History* (Durham, NC: Duke University Press, 2007), pp. 15–19.

16. Smoodin, 'The History of Film History', p. 9.

17. Robert C. Allen and Douglas Gomery, *Film History: Theory and Practice* (New York: Knopf, 1985), pp. 38–42.

18. Smoodin, 'The History of Film History', p. 2.

19. Lea Jacobs, *The Wages of Sin: Censorship and the Fallen Woman Film, 1928–1942* (Berkeley: University of California Press, 1995); Danae Clark, *Negotiating Hollywood: The Cultural Politics of Actors' Labor* (Minneapolis: University of Minnesota Press, 1995).

20. Smoodin, 'The History of Film History', pp. 3–4.

21. Jane Gaines, *Contested Culture: The Image, the Voice and the Law* (Chapel Hill: University of North Carolina Press, 1991), p. 5.

22. Moran *et al.*, 'Introduction', p. xvii.

23. For an excellent overview of media industry studies approaches, see Jennifer Holt and Alisa Perren (eds), *Media Industries: History, Theory and Method* (Malden, MA: Wiley-Blackwell, 2009).

24. Peter Decherney, *Hollywood's Copyright Wars: From Edison to the Internet* (New York: Columbia University Press, 2012).

25. Jennifer Holt, *Empires of Entertainment: Media Industries and the Politics of Deregulation, 1980–1996* (New Brunswick, NJ: Rutgers University Press, 2011).

26. Joseph Dainow, 'The Civil Law and the Common Law: Some Points of Comparison', *The American Journal of Comparative Law* vol. 15 no. 3 (1966–7): 419–35; Lawrence M. Friedman, *American Law: An Introduction*, 2nd edn (New York: W. W. Norton & Co., 1998), pp. 30–1.

27. Henry Paul Monaghan, 'Supremacy Law Textualism', *Columbia Law Review* vol. 110 no. 3 (2010): 731–96; *Edgar v. MITE Corp.*, 457 US 624 (1982).

28. For a much more detailed description and analysis of *Kalem Co. v. Harper Brothers*, see Decherney, *Hollywood's Copyright Wars*, pp. 48–53.

29. US Courts, 'Federal Courts' Structure', accessed 16 December 2014, http://www.uscourts.gov/FederalCourts/UnderstandingtheFederalCourts/FederalCourtsStructure.aspx

30. Decherney, *Hollywood's Copyright Wars*, pp. 48–53.

31. Friedman, *American Law*, pp. 75–82.

32. Melville B. Nimmer, 'Implications of the Prospective Revision of the Berne Convention and the United States Copyright Law', *Stanford Law Review* vol. 19 no. 3 (1967): 499–554.

33. Ibid., p. 499.

34. Mark W. Janis, *An Introduction to International Law*, 4th edn (New York: Aspen, 2003), p. 293.

35. Ruth Vasey, *The World According to Hollywood, 1918–1939* (Madison: University of Wisconsin Press, 1997), p. 42.

36. For more on Britain and India specifically, see Priya Jaikumar, *Cinema at the End of Empire: A Politics of Transition in Britain and India* (Durham, NC: Duke University Press, 2006).

37. Vasey, *The World According to Hollywood*, pp. 42–3.

38. Jeffrey L. Dunoff, Steven R. Ratner and David Wippman, *International Law: Norms, Actors, Process: A Problem-Oriented Approach*, 2nd edn (New York: Aspen, 2006), pp. 828–9.

39. Ibid.

40. Patricia M. Goff, 'Invisible Borders: Economic Liberalization and National Identity', *International Studies Quarterly* vol. 44 no. 4 (December 2000): 534; Kevin Lee, '"The Little State Department": Hollywood and the MPAA's Influence on US Trade Relations', *Northwestern Journal of International Law and Business* vol. 28 (2007–8): 384.

41. Mary E. Footer and Christoph Beat Graber, 'Trade Liberalization and Cultural Policy', *Journal of International Economic Law* vol. 3 no. 1 (2000): 115–44; Goff, 'Invisible Borders': 533–62.

42. Janis, *An Introduction to International Law*, p. 293.

43. The West 'Nutshell' series of books are especially helpful for those seeking an overview of civil procedure. See, especially: Mary Kane, *Civil Procedure in a Nutshell*, 7th edn (St Paul, MN: West Academic, 2013); William R. Slomanson, *California Civil Procedure in a Nutshell*, 5th edn (St Paul, MN: West Academic, 2014).

44. Dunoff, *International Law*; Janis, *An Introduction to International Law*.

References

Allen, Robert C. And Douglas Gomery, *Film History: Theory and Practice* (New York: Knopf, 1985).

Asimow, Michael and Shannon Mader, *Law and Popular Culture: A Course Book*, 2nd edn (New York: Peter Lang, 2004).

Bartholomew, Mark, 'A Right is Born: Celebrity, Property and Postmodern Lawmaking', *Connecticut Law Review* vol. 44 no. 2 (2011): 301–8.

Bergman, Paul and Michael Asimow, *Reel Justice: The Courtroom Goes to the Movies* (Kansas City, MO: Andrews McMeel, 2006).

Bettig, Ronald, *Copyrighting Culture: The Political Economy of Intellectual Property* (Boulder, CO: Westview, 1996).

Black, David A., *Law in Film: Resonance and Representation* (Urbana: University of Illinois Press, 1999).

Buscombe, Edward, 'Notes on Columbia Pictures Corporation, 1926–1941', *Screen* vol. 16 no. 3 (1975): 65–82.

Carman, Emily, 'That's Not All, Folks: Excavating the Warner Bros. Archive', *The Moving Image: The Journal of the Association of Moving Image Archivists* vol. 14 no. 1 (2014): 30–48.

Caves, Richard E., *Creative Industries: Contracts Between Art and Commerce* (Cambridge, MA: Harvard University Press, 2000).

Chase, Anthony, *Movies on Trial: The Legal System on Screen* (New York: New Press, 2002).

Clark, Danae, *Negotiating Hollywood: The Cultural Politics of Actors' Labor* (Minneapolis: University of Minnesota Press, 1995).

Coombe, Rosemary J., 'Contingent Articulations: A Critical Cultural Studies of the Law', in Austin Sarat and Thomas R. Kearns (eds), *Law in the Domains of Culture* (Ann Arbor: University of Michigan Press, 2000), pp. 21–64.

Coombe, Rosemary J., *The Cultural Life of Intellectual Properties: Authorship, Appropriation and the Law* (Durham, NC: Duke University Press, 1998).

Dainow, Joseph, 'The Civil Law and the Common Law: Some Points of Comparison', *American Journal of Comparative Law* vol. 15 no. 3 (1966–7): 419–35.

Decherney, Peter, *Hollywood's Copyright Wars: From Edison to the Internet* (New York: Columbia University Press, 2012).

Denvir, John (ed.), *Legal Reelism: Movies as Legal Texts* (Champaign: University of Illinois Press, 1996).

Dunoff, Jeffrey L., Steven R. Ratner and David Wippman, *International Law: Norms, Actors, Process: A Problem-Oriented Approach*, 2nd edn (New York: Aspen, 2006).

Edgar v. MITE Corp., 457 US 624 (1982).

Fisk, Catherine L., *Working Knowledge: Employee Innovation and the Rise of Corporate Intellectual Property, 1800–1930* (Chapel Hill: University of North Carolina Press, 2009).

Footer, Mary E. And Christoph Beat Graber, 'Trade Liberalization and Cultural Policy', *Journal of International Economic Law* vol. 3 no. 1 (2000): 115–44.

Friedman, Lawrence M., *American Law: An Introduction*, 2nd edn (New York: W. W. Norton & Co., 1998).

Gaines, Jane, *Contested Culture: The Image, the Voice and the Law* (Chapel Hill: University of North Carolina Press, 1991).

Goff, Patricia M., 'Invisible Borders: Economic Liberalization and National Identity', *International Studies Quarterly* vol. 44 no. 4 (December 2000): 533–62.

Greenfield, Steve, Guy Osborn and Peter Robson, *Film and the Law*, 2nd edn (Oxford: Hart, 2010).

Higashi, Sumiko, 'In Focus: Film History, or a Baedeker Guide to the Historical Turn', *Cinema Journal* vol. 44 no. 1 (1995): 94–100.

Holt, Jennifer, *Empires of Entertainment: Media Industries and the Politics of Deregulation, 1980–1996* (New Brunswick, NJ: Rutgers University Press, 2011).

Holt, Jennifer and Alisa Perren (eds), *Media Industries: History, Theory and Method* (Malden, MA: Wiley-Blackwell, 2009).

Hoyt, Eric, 'Hollywood and the Income Tax, 1929–1955', *Film History* vol. 22 no. 1 (2010): 16–18.

Hoyt, Eric, *Hollywood Vault: Film Libraries before Home Video* (Berkeley: University of California Press, 2014).

Hoyt, Eric, 'Writer in the Hole: *Desny v. Wilder*, Copyright Law and the Battle Over Ideas', *Cinema Journal* vol. 50 no. 2 (Winter 2011): 21–40.

Jacobs, Lea, *The Wages of Sin: Censorship and the Fallen Woman Film, 1928–1942* (Berkeley: University of California Press, 1995).

Jaikumar, Priya, *Cinema at the End of Empire: A Politics of Transition in Britain and India* (Durham, NC: Duke University Press, 2006).

Janis, Mark W., *An Introduction to International Law*, 4th edn (New York: Aspen, 2003), p. 293.

Kamir, Orit, *Framed: Women in Law and Film* (Durham, NC: Duke University Press, 2006).

Kane, Mary, *Civil Procedure in a Nutshell*, 7th edn (St Paul, MN: West Academic, 2013).

Kemper, Tom, *Hidden Talent: The Emergence of Hollywood Agents* (Berkeley: University of California Press, 2010).

Lee, Kevin, '"The Little State Department": Hollywood and the MPAA's Influence on US Trade Relations', *Northwestern Journal of International Law and Business* vol. 28 (2007–8): 371–98.

Machura, Stefan and Peter Robson (eds), *Law and Film* (Oxford: Blackwell, 2001).

Monaghan, Henry Paul, 'Supremacy Law Textualism', *Columbia Law Review* vol. 110 no. 3 (2010): 731–96.

Moran, Leslie J., Emma Sandon, Elena Loizidou and Ian Christie (eds), *Law's Moving Image* (London: GlassHouse, 2004).

Nimmer, Melville B., 'Implications of the Prospective Revision of the Berne Convention and the United States Copyright Law', *Stanford Law Review* vol. 19 no. 3 (1967): 499–554.

Sarat, Austin, 'Editorial', *Law, Culture and the Humanities* vol. 1 no. 1 (2005): 1.

Scott, Allen J., *On Hollywood: The Place, The Industry* (Princeton, NJ: Princeton University Press, 2005).

Slomanson, William R., *California Civil Procedure in a Nutshell*, 5th edn (St Paul, MN: West Academic, 2014).

Smoodin, Eric, 'The History of Film History', in Eric Smoodin and Jon Lewis (eds), *Looking Past the Screen: Case Studies in American Film History* (Durham, NC: Duke University Press, 2007), pp. 1–32.

Strickland, Rennard, Teree E. Foster and Taunya Lovell Banks (eds), *Screening Justice: The Cinema of Law* (Buffalo, NY: William S. Hein, 2006).

Tehranian, John, *Infringement Nation: Copyright 2.0 and You* (New York: Oxford University Press, 2011).

Vasey, Ruth, *The World According to Hollywood, 1918–1939* (Madison: University of Wisconsin Press, 1997).

PART I
OWNERSHIP AND
INFRINGEMENT

❚ ONE LAW TO RULE THEM ALL
COPYRIGHT GOES HOLLYWOOD

PETER DECHERNEY

In the USA, copyright began as a limited monopoly given to creators as an incentive to produce new works. In exchange for providing society with books, maps and, later, movies and YouTube videos, creators were given the exclusive, though limited, right to exploit their work. Copyright has since grown into much more. It has become a de facto means of regulating new media technologies. It has become a major bargaining chip in international trade negotiations, and it is often used as a form of backdoor censorship.[1] With the rise of home video and the internet, the class of potential copyright holders has grown to encompass anyone with a video camera, blog, or mobile phone. We are all now potential copyright plaintiffs as well as consumers of copyrighted media. This chapter is a brief historical account of the expansion of film, television and digital media copyright. How did we get into our current copyright situation, and what are some possible ways forward?

What is Copyright?

Many of the framers of the US Constitution were themselves authors. They knew first hand the value of incentives in the creative economy, but they only reluctantly included an intellectual property clause. As the framers considered checks on the abuse of power in the new state, they worried about granting any monopoly privileges such as those conveyed by copyrights and patents. In a famous letter, Thomas Jefferson set out many of the problems that legislators continue to struggle with. Ideas, he opined, are not the natural property of their creators. On the contrary, nature seems to resist the very notion of owning intellectual property. Ideas are what economists refer to as public goods. Like fire and air (Jefferson's examples), but not like private real estate or physical objects, ideas can be held by many people at the same time without losing their potency. Moreover, there is a social benefit to the unfettered circulation of knowledge. 'That ideas should freely spread from one to another over the globe, for the moral and mutual instruction of man, and improvement of his condition,' Jefferson wrote, 'seems to have been peculiarly and benevolently designed by nature . . . incapable of confinement or exclusive appropriation.'[2] And thus Jefferson laid out the balancing act that is copyright law: how to create incentives for the creation of new art and ideas without overly hindering their proper diffusion.

In the end, of course, the framers decided that copyright is a necessary monopoly, and the Constitution empowers Congress to fashion rights in creative work. Contemporary copyright protection comes with what lawyers refer to as a bundle of rights (see also Chapter 3). Copyright holders have the exclusive right to authorise copies, performances, adaptations and translations of their work. These rights adhere automatically, as soon as a work is created. It is no longer necessary to register a work with the US Copyright Office, pay a fee, or place a copyright symbol (©) on the work. A mobile phone video, for example, is protected by copyright immediately after it has been captured. In the USA, where copyright is seen as a statutory invention rather than a natural right, some or all rights to a work may be sold or given away. And if the work is created in the normal course of employment, as most Hollywood films are, then the company becomes not only the owner of the copyright but the legal author as well (this is known as a 'work-for-hire' and it is discussed in greater depth in Chapter 9). Once a work has been created, all rights are reserved for the next three-quarters of a century or more.

But just as the Copyright Act delineates all of these protections for creators, it also places limits on the copyright monopoly. One limit is what the Constitution calls *limited times*. Copyright may not be perpetual, and the current term is seventy years after the death of the creator or ninety-five years for corporate works (works-for-hire). The copyright term has been extended many times since the first US Copyright Act of 1790 gave authors a fourteen-year copyright with the option of renewing for another fourteen years. How long should copyright last? The Constitutional goal of copyright is to 'promote the progress of science', where science retains its eighteenth-century meaning of learning or knowledge.[3] The proper calculus for evaluating the term of copyright, then, entails determining when knowledge and learning continue to be furthered by copyright. One way that knowledge is furthered is through the incentive that copyright gives to creators as a reward for their productivity. But knowledge is also furthered when creations enter the public domain and can freely be used by society. To balance these competing goals, one would need to ask: at what point does the grant to the individual creator start to weigh against society's ability to prosper from easy access to the new work? As a point of comparison, think about drug patents. Drug companies invest significant resources in developing new medications. Their incentive and reward is the exclusive right to sell those medications for twenty years (the patent term). But after that point, other companies are free to produce generic versions of the drug, allowing it to be deployed more widely. Is twenty years the right length to reward drug companies? Is ninety-five years the ideal length for Hollywood studios? Calculating copyright (or patent) terms is not an easy task, to be sure. Setting terms is also complicated by the fact that copyright is a one-size-fits-all doctrine. Copyright expert William Patry has suggested the adoption of variable term limits, adjusting the length of copyrights to fit their respective media. Does an email, for example, require the same incentive as a movie score?[4] Several times, Congress has considered (though they have not adopted) a one-of-a-kind, three-year term for fashion designers who are not currently able to protect their creations. For now, however, all works get the same term of copyright.

Providing another important limit, copyright protects expression but not ideas. It protects the specific language that Laura Mulvey used to describe 'Visual Pleasure and Narrative Cinema', but the ideas themselves are free to be restated by other theorists and put into practice by film-makers. Similarly, the idea of a 'fast forward' or 'record' button on a digital video recorder (DVR) cannot be protected by copyright, although perhaps the specific design of an interface could be. Giving Mulvey or Tivo a monopoly on their ideas, in addition to the way that they expressed them, would inevitably lead to limits on debate, discourse and innovation. The US Copyright Act also contains exemptions for educational and library uses. Government works fall completely outside of the scope of copyright. Since they are created by public servants, they are a sort of people's work-for-hire; we all own them equally. Many areas of artistic creation like cuisine and fashion design, as I've already mentioned, are also excluded from the scope of copyright, although both are thriving commercial and artistic industries.[5]

When a work does fall within the scope of copyright, only certain aspects of that work are protected. Copyright, for example, protects the artistic but not useful properties of a work. A furniture designer may not claim the exclusive right to the four legs and back of a chair she has designed. But the designer may claim rights in a specific seat pattern or a flourish on the foot of the chair's legs. In one surprising example, the UK's Supreme Court found that Storm Trooper helmets were useful objects that could be sold by their original manufacturer without the permission of Lucasfilm.[6] Copyright protection is also limited to a work's original contributions. In John Ford's *The Searchers* (1956), the generic elements of the plot (the kidnapping and revenge narrative, the wedding interrupted by a fistfight, etc.) remain in the public domain, free to be used by all. But the original dialogue, visual compositions and even the characters fall under the scope of copyright law. Originality, it is important to remember, is about the spark of innovation and not the labour that goes into producing new works, or what is often called 'sweat of the brow' or 'sweat equity'.[7] In one landmark US Supreme Court case, the Court found that the list of names and numbers in a phonebook were facts that could not be protected by copyright. No matter how much legwork it took to compile the data, there is no originality in presenting factual information in alphabetical order.[8] At least this is true in the USA. In Europe, databases of facts are protected and, in one English case, the BBC successfully prevented *Time Out* listings magazine from reprinting its television schedule without permission.[9]

An exception that has grown increasingly important in the digital age is *fair use*, instances when copyrighted work can be reused without permission. Despite a common myth, fair use is not measured by the percentage of a work used or by the number of words or minutes taken. Instead, work may be reused and reproduced without permission when the context has been significantly transformed and the amount of the work used is appropriate. Authors, filmmakers and educators are free to quote from works in order to provide comment and criticism. Political campaigns rely on fair use regularly when they use clips from their opponent's advertisements in rebuttal ads. Fans exercise fair use somewhat differently when they create mash-up videos exploring the emotional lives of minor characters in *Firefly* (2002–3) or another television show.[10] Moreover, the work of political candidates and fans remains fair use even when they are shared publicly on the web and commercialised through ads served on the side. Neither public display nor commercial use necessarily disqualifies a work from being fair use. Fair use is always about context and, in some cases, fair use permits an entire work to be repurposed. A television show may be recorded for later viewing and whole movie posters may be used as part of a collage that visually narrates the history of a studio.[11] These uses, like many others, foster debate, criticism and education, which the fair use doctrine was designed to protect and nurture.

Fair use, as we will see below, is not limited to authors' reuse of media. It also extends to home video technologies, and fair use has become essential to the development of new technologies for storing and consuming every kind of media. In part as a result of the explosion of digital technologies made possible by fair use, Israel and South Korea have adopted US-style fair use statutes over the past decade and many other countries from the Netherlands to Australia have considered adopting fair use doctrines.

For more than a century, copyright law has been in the process of being globally har-monised through international copyright treaties and organisations such as the World Trade Organization and the United Nations' World Intellectual Property Organization. But different national cultures still have very different attitudes towards intellectual property, and they often have different legal regimes. What are often referred to as *author's rights* countries, like France, give creators an additional bundle of rights called *moral rights*. Moral rights can give a creator a right to attribution and to protect the integrity of his or her work. On the other side of the spectrum, Communist Yugoslavia and Maoist China experimented with rewarding authors for the labour they put into creating work rather than the success of individual creations.[12] Copyright is far from a one-size-fits-all system.

There are so many misconceptions about copyright that it is impossible to dispel them all. Copyright does not protect the *life rights* that Steven Spielberg will purchase when he makes your biopic; life rights are a nebulous entity that includes privacy, publicity and defamation, but there is no copyright in your life story. Similarly, copyright does not protect your ingenious movie idea, even if you mail yourself a copy of a plot outline to demonstrate that you had it first. Story ideas can be protected through contracts, but there is no copyright in ideas. Copyright is, as Jefferson would have it, the distinctly unnatural creation of statute. It is a limited monopoly devised with the goal of bringing more creative works to society. Moreover, it is a doctrine in constant flux as it adjusts to the possibilities of new media, new conceptions of authorship and new definitions of progress.

Film as a New Medium

New media have always driven changes in copyright law, and moving image technologies are no exception. From the very beginning, judges were not sure what to make of the new medium. Was film a new form of photography? Drama? Or was it something entirely novel? Photography itself was a relatively recent addition to the copyright statute when the earliest film copyright cases began to be decided in 1903. At the time, industry leaders including the Edison, Lubin and Biograph companies engaged each other in disputes over when and how they could copy their competitors' films. Building on the work of others is essential to the cre-ation of art and culture, and new rules needed to be established for the new medium. Since moving pictures were not included in the list of copyrightable material, it was not clear that copyright applied to film at all.[13]

The early film moguls initiated a series of lawsuits, asking judges to consider the common practices of 'duping' and remaking films (see also Chapter 3). Duping entailed striking a new negative from a competitor's film and then printing and selling it as part of the duper's own cat-alogue. It was a widespread practice in the first decade and a half of the film industry, and indeed duping in some form has never disappeared. Virtually every early film company duped works by both US and overseas competitors. The supply of films could not keep up with the growing audience demand, and preventing duping was extremely difficult. Similarly, the remakes of the time were, for the most part, not interpretive adaptations but shot-for-shot copies of rival companies' films. Remaking films in this manner allowed film-makers to meet the broad demand for a particular story, but it also served as a form of education. According to the pioneering scholar of early film Jay Leyda, the rapid global circulation of film facilitated by duping and remakes allowed the art of film to develop at breakneck speed.[14] Film-makers learned from each other by viewing the latest editing innovations and by remaking the films the way art students copy great masters in the Louvre.

At first, film companies adopted several methods of self-regulation. They devised technical standards of copy protection that prevented the Lumière Company's films, for example, from being played on Edison projectors. The primary technical barrier was the inclusion of proprietary sprocket hole designs. Some companies used round sprocket holes, while some were rectangular. Others had no sprocket holes at all and worked purely by friction. In general, the lack of format interoperability led companies to make dupes that could be displayed using their own technology. Much as copy protection does today, early film copy protection had the opposite of its intended effect: it increased the amount of duping. Some companies also blocked known dupers like Edison and Lubin from purchasing their new releases, which often led the frustrated dupers to make shot-for-shot remakes. By 1903, however, the landscape had become too chaotic, and the companies brought a number of copyright lawsuits, hoping to impose a legal regime on the previously self-regulated market.[15]

In the case of *Edison v. Lubin* (1903), the Third Circuit Court of Appeals examined the issue of duping. For close to a decade the Edison Company had been printing films on long strips of photographic paper, known as paper prints, and registering them with the Copyright Office of the Library of Congress. At the time, copyright was still an opt-in system: works had to be deposited and registered in order to receive a copyright. The court's difficult task was to decide if films could be registered and protected as photographs. A lower court had already ruled that film was a new medium and could not be covered by the existing statute; Congress would have to intervene if film copyright was to be created. But the Third Circuit reversed that decision, reasoning that viewers experienced film as moving photographs, and the existing law could be used to regulate film as well. 'To require each of numerous undistinguishable pictures to be individually copyrighted, as suggested by the court,' the decision read, 'would, in effect, be to require the copyright of many pictures to protect a single one.'[16] And so it became illegal to dupe a film that had been registered as a paper print.

The *Edison v. Lubin* decision proved difficult to enforce in the decentralised film business. Edison himself was back in court a year later, having been discovered duping European films registered in the USA by the Biograph Company.[17] And duping remained a standard practice of film companies until the formation of the Motion Picture Patents Company (MPPC) in 1908 created a centralised, heavily monitored and repressive network of film manufacturers.

Regulating new media can be difficult and the *Edison v. Lubin* decision turned out to be limited in another way as well. Film is not only the offspring of photography; it is derived from drama and, of course, many other media as well. In 1905 Edison was in court again: this time as the defendant in a case involving remakes. Biograph made a film about a French nobleman who places an ad in a New York personal column asking for a potential spouse to meet him at Grant's Tomb. More than one woman arrives, and the throng chases the nobleman until they finally catch him. Biograph refused to sell the film to its competitors, and the Lubin, Pathé and

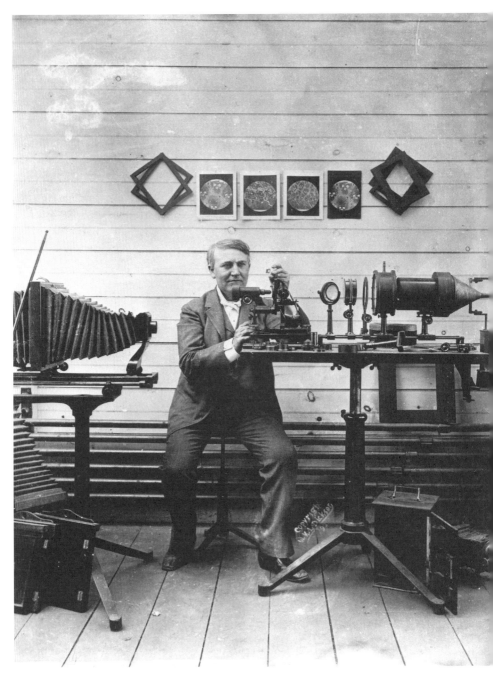

Before US copyright law protected motion pictures, Thomas Edison and the Edison Company printed films on strips of paper and registered them as photographs with the Copyright Office of the Library of Congress (BFI)

Edison companies all remade the film with some slight differences. Biograph sued Edison for copyright infringement, and both Thomas Edison and his director Edwin S. Porter defended their right to take the idea but not the expression of the Biograph film (though they did not use those copyright terms of art). The New Jersey Circuit Court agreed with Edison and Porter. The Edison and Biograph films shared the same general plot and location, and they both mixed the comedy and chase genres. But a film-maker cannot own a genre, location, or even the outline of a plot. Both films dressed those ideas in significantly different creative expression and, as a result, film-makers were free to experiment with and improve upon the same formulas.[18] Two decades later, Buster Keaton used a similar plot device in *Seven Chances* (1925), the Three Stooges used it in several films and the newspaper ad-for-a-bride plot was still going strong in 1999 when it was employed in the Chris O'Donnell–Renée Zellweger vehicle *The Bachelor*.

Kalem Co. v. Harper Brothers

The relationship between film and existing media was further elaborated in the influential 1911 US Supreme Court case *Kalem Co. v. Harper Brothers*. In addition to duping and remakes, the early film industry was built on another kind of copying. A staple of early film production was the unauthorised adaptation of novels and plays. Film-makers would take great moments from a bestseller or sold-out Broadway play and illustrate them on film, without asking permission from the copyright holders or compensating them. Frequently, more than one company adapted a well-known title. In this case, the Kalem Company, a member of the MPPC, made a film version of the popular novel and play *Ben-Hur*. In response, *Ben-Hur*'s publishers teamed up with the author's estate and the Broadway producers who had adapted the novel to the stage to sue Kalem. The MPPC agreed to pay the defence's legal fees, tacitly acknowledging that the film industry was built on the practice of unauthorised adaptations.[19]

There were two legal issues in the *Kalem* case. First, the Kalem Company's lawyers argued that film was a visual medium, and when translating work from the page to the screen it is only possible to take ideas, not expression. US Supreme Court Justice Oliver Wendell Holmes Jr dismissed this argument quickly. There is both a language of words and a language of images, he reasoned, and the language of images could be analogous to and infringe upon the language of words. Media scholars might quibble with the notion that images have a language, but, for the first time in close to two decades of film production, film-makers needed permission before adapting works in other media.

The second and more complicated issue in the case was who to hold responsible for the infringement. Copyright protects against unauthorised public performances and displays, but it was not clear who was displaying a film. Film is a virtual technology. The producers, director and actors are not present when a film is shown. Technically, the projectionist seemed to be most directly responsible for showing the film, but it seemed ludicrous to place the blame on the projectionist. Holmes solved the problem by borrowing the doctrine of contributory infringement from patent law. If a company makes a product that can only be used for an illegal purpose – a counterfeit currency press, for example – then the manufacturer can be held liable when the device is put to use. Similarly, Holmes decided, Kalem had made a product, an unauthorised film adaptation, that could only be used for an illegal purpose, to be shown before an audience. As a result, the Kalem Company was held liable when the film was shown.[20]

Holmes's decision had major long- and short-term consequences. In the short term, the MPPC lost its control of the film industry. Its members had built businesses on the practice of unauthorised adaptations and they could not adjust to the new legal standard. The independents forged exclusive relationships with publishers and theatre companies, which proved to be an important step in their eventual takeover of the US film industry.[21] In the long term, the decision established a legal doctrine that has driven the business of media distribution and consumption from the VCR to file sharing (see Chapter 3). When new technologies are created, investors (and sometimes courts) have to decide whether the inventors have designed a tool for the sole purpose of facilitating piracy or if they are fostering a new media revolution.

As we can see from the early history of film, the problems faced by courts were not upstart companies using new technologies to challenge incumbents. In fact, the big companies of the day, Edison and Biograph, were consistently on both sides of cases, as defendants and plaintiffs, and they were on both sides of decisions, as winners and losers. Courts and film companies were not leading a crusade to stop piracy but wrestling with the ontology of the medium. How is film like photography or theatre? Is there a language of film? How are real people implicated in the virtual art of movies? These are questions that still haunt us today, and when we peel back the veneer of piracy cases, we continue to find investigations into the meanings of media.

Authorship and the Genre System

All creative industries have a paradoxical relationship to copyright. On the one hand, they seek protection for their original creations. On the other hand, they need the latitude to rework and build upon the cultural traditions that came before. One explanation for Hollywood's copyright ambivalence is historical; studios spent the golden years of the studio system (roughly the 1920s–60s) fighting for the right to reuse storytelling devices that had been developed by artists in other media. As the studio system was remade into what media historians call the New Hollywood in the 1960s and 70s, film-makers began to claim for themselves the very genre tropes that studios had for years fought to borrow from novelists and playwrights.

The Grant's Tomb and *Ben-Hur* decisions were the beginning and not the end of court intervention in disputes over what film-makers could borrow from novelists, playwrights and each other. Before the 1960s, film and television artists, including Charlie Chaplin, Harold Lloyd, the Marx Brothers, James M. Cain, Billy Wilder, Jack Benny and Sid Caesar, were involved in copyright cases that centred on questions of authorship and genre.[22] The cases were different, but they all attempted to separate the building blocks of storytelling from the original contributions of individual film-makers and authors. Hollywood fought for the right to reuse narratives and characters that artists had already used in existing media, and courts began to devise methods for determining originality in films. In one court decision, the judge developed the *scènes à faire* doctrine, which suggests that many plot elements derive inevitably from certain dramatic circumstances. When two characters take shelter from the rain in an empty church, for example, eventually they are likely to start playing the organ.[23] Judges also modelled the practice of drawing a line between generic plot structures (ideas) and novel chains of events (expression). And they began to develop a language for determining sufficiently original characters from their stock counterparts. The history of film copyright decisions offers a parallel development of film analysis that only occasionally looks over the disciplinary fence to the work of film and media theorists.

It may be difficult to remember that Hollywood studios spent the first half-century of their existence defending the right to use the storytelling methods that had been developed for literature and the theatre. If it is difficult to remember, it is because, since the 1970s, Hollywood has vigorously claimed ownership over its intellectual property. The major shift occurred during the emergence of the New Hollywood when, among other changes to the studio system, a generation of auteurs that included George Lucas, Steven Spielberg and William Friedkin tried to possess the very genres that the studios had spent decades claiming were in the public domain.

Lucas, Spielberg and Friedkin all made blockbusters by taking drive-in genre fare and turning it into special effects-driven extravaganzas. Friedkin made a horror film, *The Exorcist* (1973), Spielberg made a shark-attack film, *Jaws* (1975), and Lucas made a science-fiction film, *Star Wars* (1977). By their very definition, genre films follow formulas and the low-budget independent producers had always followed up on one successful film with a cycle of similar films; but the New Hollywood auteurs all attempted to use copyright law to prevent independent film companies and television producers from using the genres they had reinvented (an oxymoronic term if ever there was one). Friedkin's and Spielberg's studios both sued low-budget film-maker Edward Montoro, who released exorcism and shark-attack films on the heels of the studio releases. Lucas's studio, Fox, went after the producers of the television series *Battlestar Galactica* (1978–9), despite the fact that the *Star Wars* special effects designer and crew were working on the show. In the Friedkin and Lucas cases, judges recognised the danger of one company having too much control over a narrative template, and the decision in the *Star Wars* case even said explicitly that 'no one owns the genre of space fantasy and of warfare in space'.[24]

In the *Jaws* case, however, the same California court that heard the *Exorcist* case found in favour of the studio. The decision declared that a film released as *Great White* (aka, *The Last Shark*, 1981) bore too many similarities to *Jaws*, that the two films shared what the Ninth Circuit Court of Appeals has termed the same 'look and feel'. I wrote about this case in my book, *Hollywood's Copyright Wars* (2012).[25] When writing the book, I had not seen *Great White*, which had been enjoined from distribution. At the time I was unconvinced by the court's listing of stock characters and predictable plot points shared by the two films. After all, the originality of *Jaws* does not lay in its use of an anxious mayor or a seasoned shark hunter. Indeed, it would be unrecognisable as a genre film without those characters. It is *Jaws*'s treatment of the genre clichés that is original. Just reading the court's decision without seeing the second film, I was persuaded, however, that *Great White* might have gone too far in using deep base tones on the soundtrack to signal the presence of the shark. John Williams' score for *Jaws* is clearly a signature of the film, and one of the most iconic narrative devices in film history. Luckily, *Great White* is now easily viewable on YouTube, and we can decide for ourselves. After watching the film, I am even less convinced that the two films share more than well-worn genre conventions. The musical motif used for the shark in *Great White* is formally very different from the one used in *Jaws*; it uses a few electronic instruments rather than a symphony orchestra; and, perhaps most significantly, it connotes a late-night television film, not a summer blockbuster. The leitmotif is a convention that long predates film history, and in no way, in my opinion, do the two films seem 'substantially similar' or share the same 'look and feel', the standards the court applied. What the *Jaws* decision points to, I think, is the changing perception of film directors by the 1970s, who popularly came to be thought of as visionary artists or auteurs, often at the mercy of a commercial system of production. As a result, the court over-determined Steven Spielberg's influence on the shark-attack genre.

As the names on all of these new Hollywood auteur cases remind us, 20th Century-Fox, Warner Bros. and Universal hold the copyright to the films, not the directors or writers or producers. In most cases, copyright regulates the studios that are the legal authors of Hollywood films and not the many artists who labour to produce them. Since the 1930s, studios and talent guilds have used contracts and collective bargaining agreements to manage a system of self-regulation in Hollywood (see also Chapter 8 for more on talent contracts in Hollywood). Copyright regulated the revenue streams for the industry, but agreements and unions manage credit disputes, compensation and other authorial matters.

Is Spike Lee the Author of *Malcolm X*?

Is Spike Lee the author of *Malcolm X* (1992) is, of course, the wrong question. Films do not have authors. They have directors. They have writers. They have key grips and best boys. Film is a collaborative medium, and, despite the best efforts of Alexandre Astruc and Andrew Sarris, we cannot speak of a film author in the same way that we can (generally) identify the author of a book or a painting.[26] And the particular collaborative nature of film has always posed a problem for courts trying to apply copyright law to motion pictures. For the most part, as I suggest above, talent guilds and contracts have pre-empted copyright cases about film or TV authorship. But in one important case,[27] an authorial claim arose without a contract, and a court was asked to decide whether Jefri Aalmuhammed is a co-author of the 1992 film *Malcolm X*, directed by Spike Lee.

The very notion of authorship in copyright case law is fraught, and the clearest definition of authorship goes back to an 1884 case involving a photograph of Oscar Wilde. In that case, *Burrow-Giles v. Sarony*, the US Supreme Court did not find that releasing the shutter on a camera took enough creativity to make the great nineteenth-century photographer Napoleon Sarony an author. Nevertheless, they did find him to be an author because he posed Wilde and arranged the background. And in the closest we have come to a legal definition of authorship, the Court defined Sarony as the 'master mind' behind the work, 'the person who gives effect to the idea, fancy, or imagination'.[28]

So, is Aalmuhammed a co-author of *Malcom X*? Aalmuhammed is an expert on the Nation of Islam, and he served as an advisor on the film. He helped write dialogue, and he also worked with actors on the set, coaching performers during the sections of the film shot in Egypt. After the film was completed, Aalmuhammed helped secure important endorsements for the film from Islamic groups. He was clearly a substantive contributor to the film, and after the film was completed Spike Lee sent him a cheque for $25,000, which he cashed. The film's star, Denzel Washington, sent him a cheque for $100,000, which he did not cash. Both Lee and Washington clearly thought that Aalmuhammed had made a valuable contribution, but there was never a contract or formal agreement about his compensation or title in the credits, where he is listed as 'Islamic technical consultant'.

In *Aalmuhammed v. Lee*, the Ninth Circuit Court of Appeals evaluated who deserved credit as the 'author' of the biopic *Malcolm X* (1992) (BFI)

When deciding whether Aalmuhammed was a co-author, the Ninth Circuit Court of Appeals invoked theories of film authorship by Sergei Eisenstein, auteur critics and others. The panel of judges also reviewed the definition of authorship in the Sarony case, and they acknowledged that the vision of a writer at a desk conjured by the word author was insufficient when considering the question of film authorship. They also noted that Spike Lee had signed a work-for-hire contract with Warner Bros. This, in effect, made Warner Bros. the legal author of the film and it also gave the studio 'final cut' (the right to approve the final version of the film).[29]

After weighing the theories and facts, the court decided that Lee is the sole author of *Malcolm X*, dismissing Aalmuhammed's claims to co-authorship (he should have cashed Denzel Washington's cheque!). Lee, the decision went on to explain, is the person who is generally thought of as the 'mastermind' behind the film. He is credited as the director, while Aalmuhammed's name came far down in the credits. Many people in addition to Aalmuhammed had contributed to the film, including the actors, the cinematographer and the clothing designer. However, in most cases we still consider the director to be the author because he or she makes the decisions about which contributions to include and which to reject. The decision implicitly endorses a kind of Foucauldian view of the author effect: Lee is the author because of the placement of his name on the credits. Cultural norms give him credit for the aesthetic contributions and political positions of the film, but the court overlooked its own finding that Warner Bros. and not Lee had final cut. Lee too worked within a commercial and collaborative system. He needed to deliver a film that the studio would approve and release. The studio's logo also features prominently in the opening credits, and *Malcolm X* is truly a corporate work as much as it represents the vision of one or more individuals. Lee could not fund and distribute the film on his own and his film was both supported and limited by the demands of the studio system.

Like the Sarony decision, the *Malcolm X* decision feels slightly compromised. In 1884, the Supreme Court was not ready to acknowledge that pushing a button constituted an act of authorship. One hundred and sixteen years later, the Ninth Circuit refused to acknowledge the collaborative industrial model of production that characterises Hollywood film-making. Despite their careful consideration of differing theories of film authorship, the panel of judges down-played the role of Warner Bros. in order to identify Lee as the sole film author.

Fair Use and Authorship

Copyright protects the work of original authors, but in many circumstances it also protects authors' right to reuse copyrighted work without permission. Many countries contain specific exceptions for research, teaching, or news reporting, often known as fair dealing. In addition to specific exemptions, US copyright law contains a flexible fair use standard, which has proved to be a nimble tool able to adapt to changes in technology and culture. Fair use has become so important in recent years that, as I've mentioned above, there is a global movement to adopt fair use, mimicking the conditions that allowed for the success of companies like YouTube and Amazon. Israel adopted a fair use doctrine in 2007, South Korea adopted one in 2011 and many other countries, including the UK, Canada, the Netherlands and Australia, have investigated a move to US-style fair use. British Prime Minister David Cameron went so far as to call on the UK to adopt fair use in order to create a 'Silicon Roundabout' that might rival California's Silicon Valley.[30]

If there has been a fair use revolution in recent decades, then it began with a 1990 *Harvard Law Review* essay by Second Circuit Judge Pierre Leval.[31] In the essay, Leval changed the way that we think about fair use when he introduced the term 'transformative use'. Before Leval's essay, fair use regularly hinged on the commercial impact of works that reused copyrighted material. But Leval, who has decided many important copyright cases, shifted the emphasis onto the purpose for reusing work. Leval explained that when the context has been changed and value added, the reuse of a work is likely to be a fair use. In the 2005 documentary film *Enron: The Smartest Guys in the Room*, for example, Academy Award winner Alex Gibney uses a clip from *The Simpsons* (1989–) to demonstrate cultural responses to the collapse of the corporate behemoth. The clip is clearly transformed in the film from a work of comic social analysis to an indicator of popular opinion. Moreover, Gibney uses an appropriate amount for his purpose. He does not use a long clip just for laughs, although the *Simpsons* clip is very funny. He uses just enough to set up and present the references to Enron. The clip serves the film perfectly, but without fair use it is unlikely that this piece of the story could have been included. Indeed, Fox initially refused to license the clip.[32]

The doctrine of transformative use has been developed over a number of landmark cases since the publication of Leval's essay. Significantly, in 1994, the US Supreme Court employed the concept to explain that the hip-hop group 2 Live Crew's parody of Roy Orbison's 'Oh, Pretty Woman' functioned as social criticism, revealing the naiveté of Orbison's 'white-bread' 1960s pop classic.[33] But the case that really clarified transformative use is *Bill Graham Archives v. Dorling Kindersley Publishing* (2006). Dorling Kindersley (DK) is a big com-

mercial publisher that produces the popular Eyewitness series of travel guides and glossy reference books. When the press wanted to publish a coffee table book about the 1960s jam
band the Grateful Dead, DK's lawyers initiated negotiations to use images from the collection
of legendary concert promoter Bill Graham. After negotiations broke down, however, DK
went ahead and used the material anyway. Not only did the publishers use the images, they
used entire posters and concert tickets. They used entire works, their purpose was clearly
commercial and they had asked permission and were denied. Could it really be fair use? In a
clearly reasoned decision, the court saw that the archival material had indeed been transformed. DK's book, *Grateful Dead: The Illustrated Trip* (2003), used entire works, but it placed
them in collages along with other memorabilia and contextual information. The collages
added up to an interpretation of a moment in the history of the band and the Haight-
Ashbury music scene of the period. The posters were originally used to promote concerts
and the Bill Graham Archives might display them as aesthetic objects and historical memorabilia. But, reduced in size and juxtaposed with other information, the posters became a
visual historical narrative, functioning the way a well-placed textual quotation might be used
in a book.[34]

Many cases have since refined the idea of transformative use, and it has helped to clarify
the work of media fans, experimental artists, documentary film-makers and, on occasion, even
Hollywood studios. Fan work, in particular, has taken on new prominence with the widespread
availability of video editing software and the distribution platform of YouTube. As past aesthetic
movements like Dada and the French New Wave moved from modes of film reception to new
styles of film production, fan video artists have created new genres for expressing their engagement with commercial media, on the one hand, and expressing something about themselves
through the reuse of commercial media, on the other.

Hollywood studios too have been actively engaged with fair use, usually displaying mixed
feelings about the doctrine. Warner Bros., for example, became enmeshed in the fertile world
of Harry Potter fandom when it began producing that franchise's films. Warner Bros. quickly
clamped down on the very active Harry Potter fan communities.[35] But at the same time author
J. K. Rowling gave out awards to the best fan websites. One winner of a Rowling award was The
Harry Potter Lexicon, an online Potter encyclopedia started by school librarian Steve Vander
Ark. When Vander Ark decided to publish a print edition of the encyclopedia (at the same time
that Rowling planned a similar book), however, Warner Bros. and Rowling sued. Warner
Bros. argued that, although the encyclopedic reorganisation of details from the Harry Potter
universe may have been transformative, many of the encyclopedia's entries used excessive
amounts of text from Rowling's writings. The judge who decided the case agreed, and many
fair use advocates applauded what they considered the enforcement of a just limit on fair use.[36]
Even when the use is transformative, the amount of material used must be still appropriate for
the use to qualify as fair use.

In other instances studios have defended the fair use of quotation in Hollywood films. Sony
successfully championed Woody Allen's right to paraphrase a famous phrase from William
Faulkner's 1950 novel *Requiem for a Nun* in his film *Midnight in Paris* (2011).[37] Just a few weeks
later, the Weinstein Company prevented the copyright holders of 1970s porn sensation *Deep
Throat* (1972) from blocking the opening of *Lovelace* (2013), the company's biopic of the original

film's star Linda Lovelace, by claiming that use of over five minutes of footage from *Deep Throat* qualifies as fair use.[38] Film companies, it is easy to forget, can be on both sides of fair use disputes. Hollywood lobbyists at the Motion Picture Association of America (MPAA) are often outspoken in their policing of artist's and media conglomerate's rights. But the Hollywood studios, on the whole, have by necessity learned to walk a middle path. Not only do they benefit directly from fair use in instances like *Midnight in Paris* and *Lovelace* or when a studio makes a parodic film or television show, but increasingly Hollywood studios look to online fan communities for marketing, new talent and, occasionally, creative input.[39]

Home Video in the Digital Age

Fair use and its related doctrine of personal use have not only been important for content creation, they have also allowed for the proliferation of media technology. Fair use and home video, in particular, have been closely intertwined since the 1980s. In *Sony v. Universal* (1984), also known as the Betamax decision, the US Supreme Court revisited the doctrine of contributory infringement that it had introduced more than seventy years earlier in the *Ben-Hur* case (see also Chapter 3). The Court found timeshifting – recording television shows for later viewing – to be fair use, and the Court established the legal footing for decades of inventions from the iPod to the DVR.[40] In addition, courts and Congress have handed down decisions and legislation dealing with a wide variety of home video and mobile technology, including cable television, file-sharing services and remotely programmed DVD players. These precedents have consistently upheld consumers' rights to manipulate media for personal use, though they have often drawn a line when new technologies facilitated sharing of media files with others.

Today, consumers want the unlimited access to media that new technologies promise. But the complex licensing infrastructure created by content companies has continued to make that a very difficult fantasy to realise. Case law may begin to hold a key, and a case in the Second Circuit Court of Appeals has set the tone for personal use in the age of digital networks. *Cartoon Network v. CSC Holdings* revolved around Cablevision's introduction of a *remote storage* or *cloud-based* DVR. Since the 1990s, consumers have been replacing VCRs with their digital successors: DVRs. Cablevision sought to take the DVR to the next level, housing them virtually on servers at corporate data centres rather than in customers' homes. This new design allows the cable company to service the machines without sending technicians to homes, saving both the company and customers time and money. The viewer at home still pushes buttons on a remote control in order to record television shows, but the hard drive that contains the show sits on Cablevision's premises. While it might be logical to have one recording of a show that many customers can access, Cablevision's copyright analysis suggested that every viewer still needs to record his or her own copy. If a hundred people in a Manhattan apartment building want to record the State of the Union speech for later viewing, Cablevision's system makes a hundred copies. This new technology was premised on the idea of personal use clarified by the Betamax decision, but it was also made possible by higher bandwidth speeds and lower hard drive storage costs.[41]

The Hollywood studios and cable channels lined up to complain that since the copies were not being made in homes, Cablevision was, in effect, making copies and streaming them to customers – a service that resembled their traditional cable business and required a licence. But the Second Circuit sided with Cablevision, reasoning that this was, in effect, no different from using a VCR or DVR. 'We do not believe,' the decision read, 'that an RS[remote storage]-DVR customer is sufficiently distinguishable from a VCR user.'[42] The customer still pushes the buttons and controls the copies and each customer only accesses his or her personal copy. It does not matter that the machine that does the copying and playback is located somewhere else. The court had expanded the idea of personal use to encompass server-based or cloud-based technology.

With the Cablevision decision, technology and the law seemed to reach a new symbiosis, and a host of companies jumped in with new services. The Cablevision case gave Amazon and Google the confidence to release virtual storage lockers for consumers to hold all of their personal media files in the cloud.[43] Dish Network developed a DVR called the 'Hopper', capable of recording an evening's worth of prime-time shows with the push of a single button. In addition, the Hopper allows its users to watch live television over the internet. Most creatively, Aereo, a company backed by media mogul Barry Diller, began to store thousands of tiny digital video antennas, which could stream digital broadcast video to phones, tablets and other media. Each Aereo customer had his or her own individually controlled remote antenna, just like each Cablevision customer had his or her own remote DVR. Courts have found that Dish's Hopper is not guilty of copyright infringement.[44] But the Supreme Court decided that Aereo had gone too far; their streaming of broadcast television was too close to the traditional cable television model.[45] Clearly, the future of home video is still up in the air as the internet and mobile media expand the definition of home video.[46]

The Digital Millennium Copyright Act

While courts have addressed new technology and fair use, the major copyright legislation regulating the internet dates to 1998. That year's Digital Millennium Copyright Act (DMCA) introduced two policy innovations that have profoundly affected the development of media technology and the web.

The first policy innovation is the *anti-circumvention* provisions of the DMCA. In short, when digital media comes with encryption (software locks), it is illegal to bypass the encryption without a licensed decryption key. These locks on digital media are commonly referred to as digital rights management (DRM). iTunes videos, for example, all have Apple's Fairplay DRM, although Apple removed encryption from its music in 2007. In order to play iTunes videos, users must use a device with an Apple-licensed key, such as a computer or mobile device running an Apple or Microsoft operating system. If you have a Android phone or Linux computer, you cannot play iTunes videos without breaking the law, even if you legally purchased the video, or your use is clearly a fair use, or you are covered by the classroom teaching exemption. DRM trumps both fair use and statutory exceptions.[47]

We are back to the days of Edison and Lumière, with their competing sprocket hole designs. The anti-circumvention provisions, however, make the digital media world very different from the analogue world. They legally enforce the kinds of monopolies that come with tight controls over interoperability. They frustrate consumers, who can't understand why their media will play on some devices and not others. And they stifle research and other activities built on fair use.

Luckily, the DMCA also created an exemption process, empowering the US Copyright Office to create exemptions in a triennial rule-making. The exemptions have all been narrow and hard won, going to organisations that represent handicapped readers, media archivists, documentary and non-commercial film-makers and educators. The one consumer exemption, a 2006 exemption that allowed mobile phone owners to unlock their phones from one carrier's network and connect them to another (as they can in Europe), was withdrawn in 2010. The exemptions have helped to restore some elements of fair use, but, on the whole, they have revealed the dramatic shift that anti-circumvention laws have brought to users of copyrighted material.[48]

The DMCA's second innovation is its equally significant *safe harbour provision*. The safe harbour provision has made YouTube, eBay and many other so-called Web 2.0 sites possible. Basically, the safe harbour provision protects internet service providers (e.g., Comcast and Verizon) and web hosting companies (e.g., YouTube and Pinterest) when their customers upload infringing material. The hosting companies are able to stand aside when Paramount, for example, complains that (fictional) user TrekFan11 has used its content in a mash-up video. After the video is posted, Paramount might send a take-down notice to YouTube. YouTube will remove the video. If TrekFan11 thinks that her video has been unfairly taken down, she can inform YouTube that the video is protected by fair use. YouTube would then restore the video and Paramount can decide whether or not to take action against TrekFan11. As a result of this process, YouTube retreats to its safe harbour, free to let copyright owners and users work out disputes on their own.

Without the DMCA, YouTube and many other websites could not exist in their present form. If YouTube had to evaluate every video uploaded for potential copyright infringement, it could never sustain the staggering volume of videos that are uploaded and viewed daily. Nevertheless, while the safe harbour has allowed for myriad websites to be created, it has also opened a legal can of worms. It will clearly be a long time before media conglomerates, websites and artists discover the best practices for monitoring the media explosion unleashed by the DMCA safe harbours.

Downsizing the Public Domain

Not every twentieth-century copyright decision involves high technology. In fact, the first copyright cases heard by the US Supreme Court under the leadership of Chief Justice John Roberts, who assumed the office of Chief Justice in 2005, have dealt with foundational copyright doctrines, including the public domain and first sale (the right to resell, give and lend books and other physical copies of copyrighted material).[49]

In the 2012 case of *Golan v. Holder*, the US Supreme Court reviewed a 1994 law in which Congress took millions of works out of the public domain and either restored their lapsed copyrights or gave them copyrights for the first time. The history of the case begins in 1988, when the USA ratified the Berne Convention – the largest international copyright treaty. The Berne Convention had originally been signed in 1886, but it took the USA more than a century to join the other member states, largely because US copyright law was out of step with the demands of Berne and the conventions of other nations. The USA required creators to register their work, where Berne insisted that work be protected automatically with no fees, registrations, or other formalities. In addition, Berne requires member states to protect moral rights (discussed briefly above), which give creators an additional control over the dissemination and use of their work. In order to fall into line with Berne requirements, the USA eventually eliminated its registration requirements. And the Visual Artists Rights Act of 1990[50] gives limited moral rights to some visual artists (though not film-makers); the USA successfully argued that other areas of US law protect creators from misrepresentation and other harms protected by moral rights legislation.[51]

Since the USA became a member of the Berne Convention, works created in other counties are automatically protected in the USA when they are protected in their home country. In 1994, six years after joining Berne, Congress extended this reciprocity, and it retroactively restored the copyrights of foreign works that had fallen into the public domain or had never had US copyrights at all. Many works, for example, had never been registered or they had not had their registrations renewed when the USA required a formal registration process. Among the millions of works affected by the 1994 law, called the Uruguay Round Agreements Act (URAA), are *Metropolis* (1927), *The Third Man* (1949), Hitchcock's British films and other landmarks of film history.

Opponents of the URAA claimed that the law was unconstitutional for two reasons. The first reason is that retroactively rewarding copyright cannot 'promote the progress of science'. Copyright provides an incentive for creators to bring new works of art and culture to society. Once a work exists, it is logically impossible to create an incentive for its creation. The second argument against the URAA came from language the US Supreme Court used in an earlier copyright decision. In *Eldred v. Ashcroft* (2003), the Court stated that Congress could not pass legislation that altered the 'traditional contours' of copyright law.[52] Taking works out of the public domain and giving them copyrights seems like an unprecedented and contour-altering action.

On the other side, the government argued that the URAA provided an indirect incentive to creators. The URAA showed a respect for non-US copyrights, and by giving non-US works new protection now, other countries might, in the future, be more predisposed to revise their own copyright laws to increase protection of US works.

The MPAA and other representatives of media conglomerates supported the government's defence of the URAA, hoping that it would help to strengthen their international anti-piracy campaigns. The petitioners in the case, the groups opposed to the law, were a conductor whose orchestra could no longer afford the work of Soviet composers and film distributors who specialised in public domain films. Many others worried about the unprecedented expansion of Congress's power to make copyright law. If Congress could take foreign works out of the public domain, what was to stop them from restoring the copyrights of US works? In a lively exchange during the oral arguments, Chief Justice Roberts asked if Congress had the power to extend copyright protection to government works (which are now in the public domain), and if they did what might happen to works like Jimi Hendrix's rendition of the national anthem? Donald Verrilli, the solicitor general, fumbled for a few minutes after hearing the question. He admitted that the URAA might indicate that Congress had this extreme power to alter copyright law, but eventually he hit on a very good answer to the Chief Justice's specific example. Perhaps, he suggested, Hendrix could claim fair use.[53]

In a decision written by Justice Ruth Bader Ginsburg, the court upheld the URAA. The Justices decided that the law did not change the contours of copyright law, because Congress had taken works out of the public domain once before – with the first US Copyright Act of 1790. Moreover, the Justices in the majority endorsed the indirect incentive theory put forth by the MPAA and others.[54]

Did the 1790 Act take works out of the public domain? This is a deeply philosophical question. One view holds that copyright law itself created the public domain. Once works reach the end of their copyright term, they enter the public domain. But what is the state of works that existed before a federal copyright law in the USA or before any copyright law at all? Were they in the public domain or not? What is the natural (or pre-legal) state of a work? This question did not seem to bother the Justices in the majority, although Justice Anthony Kennedy did bring it up during the oral arguments.[55] The Justices were also not in complete agreement over the indirect incentive theory, and Justice Stephen Breyer wrote a forceful dissenting opinion, joined by Justice Samuel Alito, showing that throughout history copyright law has always sought to create direct incentives, making the indirect incentive a true change in the contours of the law.

The Golan decision was only one in a series of moves to downsize the public domain. In 1998, Congress passed the Copyright Term Extension Act, extending the length of copyright by twenty years, bringing it to the current term of the life of the author plus seventy years or ninety-five years for corporate works. In the 2003 Eldred decision, the Supreme Court upheld that extension, ensuring that it would be a long time before any new published works enter the public domain. With the Golan decision, it became clear that, in addition to the millions of works that would not be entering the public domain, the millions of works Congress had taken out of the public domain would stay that way.

The shrinking public domain has had a significant impact on Hollywood. The Copyright Term Extension Act is sometimes known by the nickname the 'Mickey Mouse Protection Act', because the Walt Disney Company led the lobbying effort to have copyright extended in order to protect early Mickey Mouse films before they entered the public domain.[56] Disney gets another twenty years on its exclusive monopoly to exploit the Mickey Mouse character, assuring the studio continued revenue. Taxes will continue to flow to the government and intellectual property exports can remain strong. But another view holds that the copyright extension goes against the very nature of copyright law if intellectual property exists to create incentives for creators. What is Disney's incentive to take a chance on new works when it can continue to exploit its existing works? We know that long copyright terms have turned the descendants of great authors like A. A. Milne, James Joyce and Theodor Geisel (Dr Seuss) into full-time defenders of their inherited estates.[57] Overlong copyright terms keep valuable cultural products out of circulation, but they can also hurt the very creators they were intended to encourage.

The Eldred and Golan decisions have created an additional problem for Hollywood. The downsized public domain has expanded the number of *orphan works* – works whose copyright term has not yet ended but whose owners cannot be located. It is very risky to adapt orphan novels, restore deteriorating orphan prints and distribute orphan films for fear that a copyright owner might appear after the fact, demanding compensation or objecting to the use of the work.[58] Studios and archivists are in a bind when they want to use orphan works. Moreover,

Hollywood studios have relied on adaptations of public domain classics to fill their vaults from Disney's *Snow White* (1937) to the many popular adaptations of *Little Women* (1917, 1933, 1949, 1978, 1994). Without a vibrant public domain, we are not only seeing the studios' lifeblood congeal, but also new media companies do not have access to the same intellectual resources that created the great American film and television industries. A public domain that does not grow does not support innovation at any level.

The Future of Copyright

Copyright law is constantly changing and big shifts are always in progress. In the first decade and a half of the twenty-first century, the UK has undertaken several studies aimed at revamping its intellectual property laws, while the US Register of Copyrights, Maria Pallante, has called on the US Congress to consider revising its copyright statute.[59] It is clear from some of the examples discussed above that the growing fair use doctrine has met many of the demands of a rapidly changing technological and creative environment. But fair use cannot do everything. The last few decades have seen many bold policy suggestions and experiments. Both the recording and motion picture industries have unsuccessfully tried intimidating and suing customers. The French government has attempted to kick alleged copyright infringers off the internet. Scholars have suggested turning back the clock, restoring the US copyright registration system and making copyright an opt-in system again. The small Isle of Man attempted to legalise file sharing in a fashion, allowing its citizens to download what they wanted and pay for it through a tax. Beginning in Sweden, the Pirate Party has spread quickly on a copyright reform platform, and its leaders have gained more than one seat in the European Parliament. And its religious counterpart, the Missionary Church of Kopimism, is gaining converts.[60]

Among other copyright success stories, the Free Software Foundation (FSF) and Creative Commons (CC) have sought to find solutions without reforming the law. Where copyright automatically claims the entire bundle of rights for creators, the FSF and CC collectively give out millions of free licences every year that creators can attach to their work, promoting distribution, modification and collaboration – not every work or creator needs to reserve all of the rights given by US copyright. Open source software, made possible by FSF licences, now underlies crucial video production software and it powers servers that carry videos efficiently across the internet. CC-licensed films play in movie theatres and online, and they have even won Oscars.[61]

As Thomas Jefferson knew well, copyright is a legal doctrine built on an exchange: it gives something to individuals in order to get something for society. And this exchange is in constant need of rebalancing. Official government policies have broadened the copyright monopoly over the last century, expanding the rights of copyright holders as well as extending the length of copyright terms. But, at the same time, courts and organisations like Creative Commons have added more subtlety to the copyright system and given some power back to creators and users who rely on the reuse of copyrighted work. At some level, after all, every work of art, culture and technology is built on past creations and innovations. Copyright is inevitably a fraught negotiation between these two groups – the creators and companies who hold copyrights, on one hand, and the creators and companies that need to build on the existing storehouse of culture, on the other. As we have already seen, in many if not all cases, the same creators sit on both sides of the equation, and even Hollywood studios sometimes fight for fair use. Like any good negotiation, however, both sides have lost and gained something in the bargain, and, if all goes smoothly, no one will ever be entirely happy with the copyright system for long.

Notes

1. Lyman Ray Patterson, *Copyright in Historical Perspective* (Nashville, TN: Vanderbilt University Press, 1968). Patterson explains copyright's origin as a form of censorship.

2. 'Thomas Jefferson Letter to Isaac McPherson', in Andrew A. Lipscomb and Albert Ellery Bergh (eds), *The Writings of Thomas Jefferson*, vol. 13 (Washington, DC: Thomas Jefferson Memorial Association, 1905), pp. 333–5.

3. Copyright Act of 1790, 1 USC § 124 (1790).

4. William Patry, *How to Fix Copyright* (New York: Oxford, 2011), pp. 189–202. Congress's most recent attempt to pass fashion copyright legislation was in the Innovative Design Protection Act of 2012. The Innovative Design Protection Act of 2012, S. 3523, 112th Cong. (2012).

5. Kal Raustiala and Christopher Sprigman, *The Knockoff Economy: How Imitation Sparks Innovation* (New York: Oxford University Press, 2012). Raustiala and Sprigman explain how the fashion industry and others function without copyright.

6. *Lucasfilm Limited v. Ainsworth*, UKSC 39 UK (2011).

7. See *Feist Publications, Inc., v. Rural Telephone Service Co.*, 499 US 340 (1991) for a discussion of 'sweat of the brow'.

8. Ibid.

9. *BBC v. Time Out* (1984) FSR 64.

10. On copyright and fan art, see Rebecca Tushnet, 'User-Generated Discontent: Transformation in Practice', *Columbia Journal of Law and Arts* vol. 31 (2008): 100–20. See also the website of the Organization for Transformative Works: http://transformativeworks.org

11. *Sony Corp. v. Universal Studios, Inc.*, 464 US 417 (1984). The example of a studio history montage is extrapolated from *Bill Graham Archives v. Dorling Kindersley Ltd.*, 448 F.3d 605 (2d Cir. 2006).

12. William P. Alford, *To Steal a Book is an Elegant Offense: Intellectual Property Law in Chinese Civilization* (Stanford, CA: Stanford University Press, 1995).

13. Peter Decherney, *Hollywood's Copyright Wars: From Edison to the Internet* (New York: Columbia University Press, 2012), pp. 11–58.

14. Jay Leyda, 'A Note on Progress', *Film Quarterly* vol. 21 no. 4 (1968): 28–33.

15. Decherney, *Hollywood's Copyright Wars*, pp. 19–21.

16. *Edison v. Lubin*, 122 F. 240 (3d Cir. 1903).

17. *American Mutoscope & Biograph Co. v. Edison Manufacturing Co.*, 137 F. 262 (D. N. J. 1905).

18. Ibid.

19. *Kalem Co. v. Harper Brothers*, 222 US 55 (1911). For more on the case, see Decherney, *Hollywood's Copyright Wars*; Paul Goldstein, *Copyright's Highway: From Guttenberg to the Celestial Jukebox*, rev. edn (Stanford, CA: Stanford University Press, 2003); and Siva Vaidhyanathan, *Copyrights and Copywrongs: The Rise of Intellectual Property and How It Threatens Creativity* (New York: New York University Press, 2001).

20. *Kalem Co. v. Harper Brothers*, 222 US.

21. Other well-known factors in the independents' takeover of the US film industry are the promotion of movie stars and the development of feature-length films.

22. All of these cases are discussed in Decherney, *Hollywood's Copyright Wars*.

23. *James M. Cain v. Universal Pictures Co.*, 47 F. Supp. 1013 (S. D. Cal. 1942).

24. *Twentieth-Century Fox Film Corp. v. MCA, Inc.*, 209 USPQ (BNA) 200, 201 (C.D. Cal. 1980); *Warner Bros. Inc. v. Film Venture International*, 403 F. Supp. 522 (C.D. Cal. 1975); *Universal v. Film Venture International*, 543 F. Supp. 1134 (C.D. Cal. 1982). For more on the three cases, see Decherney, *Hollywood's Copyright Wars*, pp. 108–54.

25. Decherney, *Hollywood's Copyright Wars*, pp. 134–6.

26. Alexandre Astruc, 'Du stylo à la caméra et de la caméra au stylo', *L'Ecran française*, 30 March 1948; Andrew Sarris, *The American Cinema: Directors and Directions 1929–1968*, 1st Da Capo Press edn (New York: Da Capo Press, 1996).

27. *Aalmuhammed v. Lee*, 202 F.3d 1227 (9th Cir. 2000).

28. *Burrow-Giles Lithographic Co. v. Sarony*, 111 US 53 (1884).

29. *Aalmuhammed v. Lee*, 202 F.3d.

30. Duncan Geere, 'Transcript: David Cameron Sets Out Britain's High-Tech Future', *Wired*, 4 November 2010, accessed 5 October 2013, http://www.wired.co.uk/news/archive/2010-11/04/david-cameron-silicon-roundabout. For more, see Peter Decherney, 'Fair Use Goes Global', *Critical Studies in Media Communication* vol. 31 no. 2 (2014): 146–52.

31. Pierre N. Leval, 'Toward a Fair Use Standard', *Harvard Law Review* vol. 103 (1990): 1105–36.

32. Alex Gibney, conversation with the author, 7 November 2005.

33. *Luther R. Campbell v. Acuff-Rose Music*, 510 US 569 (1994).

34. *Bill Graham Archives v. Dorling Kindersley Ltd.*, 448 F.3d.

35. Lawrence Lessig, *Remix: Making Art and Commerce Thrive in the Hybrid Economy* (New York: Penguin, 2008), pp. 205–13.

36. *Warner Bros. Entertainment, Inc. v. RDR Books*, 575 F. Supp. 2d 513 (SDNY 2008). For one positive assessment of the case, see Jonathan Band, 'How Fair Use Prevailed in the Harry Potter Case', American Library Association and Association of Research Libraries, 29 September 2008, accessed 27 April 2015, http://old.arl.org/bm~doc/harrypotterrev2.pdf

37. *Faulkner Literary Rights v. Sony Pictures Classics, Inc.*, 953 F. Supp. 2d 701 (N.D. Miss. 25 October 2012).

38. Matthew Belloni, 'Judge: "Deep Throat" Owners Can't Stop *Lovelace* Release', *Hollywood Reporter*, 7 August 2013, accessed 27 April 2015, http://www.hollywoodreporter.com/thr-esq/judge-deep-throat-owners-cant-602020

39. For a bemused take on the MPAA's ambivalent relationship to fair use, see this blog post by an MPAA lawyer: Ben Sheffner, 'MPAA and Fair Use: A Quick History', *Policy Focus: An In Depth Look at Policies and Positions*, 22 October 2013, accessed 27 April 2015, http://www.mpaa.org/mpaa-and-fair-use-a-quick-history/#.U3UHUI6yjwI

40. *Sony Corp. v. Universal Studios, Inc.*, 464 US.

41. *Cartoon Network v. CSC Holdings*, 536 F.3d 121 (2d Cir. 2008).

42. Ibid.

43. Timothy B. Lee, 'Unlicensed: Are Google Music and Amazon Cloud Player Illegal?', *Ars Technica*, 4 July 2011, accessed 27 April 2015, http://arstechnica.com/tech-policy/2011/07/are-google-music-and-amazon-cloud-player-illegal/

44. *Fox Broadcasting v. Dish Network*, 12-04529 (C.D. Cal. 2015).

45. *ABC v. Aereo*, 573 US _____ (2014), slip opinion.

46. See Peter Decherney, 'Aereo and the Supreme Court Could Redefine the Digital Home', *Forbes.com*, 22 April 2014, accessed 27 April 2015, http://www.forbes.com/sites/belt-way/2014/04/22/aereo-and-the-supreme-court-redefine-the-digital-home/

47. Jessica Litman, *Digital Copyright: Protecting Intellectual Property on the Internet* (Amherst: Prometheus, 2000). Litman provides a detailed account of the drafting and impact of the Digital Millennium Copyright Act.

48. All documents relating to the exemption hearings are archived at: www.copyright.gov/1201

49. *Golan v. Holder*, 132 S. Ct. 873 (2012) and *Kirtsaeng v. John Wiley & Sons, Inc.*, 133 S. Ct. 1351 (2013).

50. 17 USC § 106A (1990).

51. Although the USA was a late addition to the Berne Convention, it did join the other major international copyright convention, UNESCO's Universal Copyright Convention, which was developed in 1952 as an alternative to the Berne Convention.

52. *Eldred v. Ashcroft*, 537 US 186 (2003).

53. *Golan v. Holder*, 132 S. Ct., oral arguments at 40–2.

54. *Golan v. Holder*, 132 S. Ct.

55. *Golan v. Holder*, 132 S. Ct., oral arguments at 16–17.

56. Steve Schlackman, 'How Mickey Mouse Keeps Changing Copyright Law', *Art Law Journal*, 15 February 2014, accessed 27 April 2015, http://artlawjournal.com/mickey-mouse-keeps-changing-copyright-law/; Daniel Tencer, '"Mickey Mouse Protection Act" Headed for Canada After Feds "Cave" in Trade Talks: Reports', *Huffington Post Canada*, 7 February 2015, accessed 27 April 2015, http://www.huffingtonpost.ca/2015/02/07/mickey-mouse-protection-act_n_6633502.html

57. On *Schloss v. Estate of James Joyce*, see Gordon Bowker, 'An End to Bad Heir Days: The Posthumous Power of the Literary Estate', *The Independent*, 6 January 2012, accessed 27 April 2015, http://www.independent.co.uk/arts-entertainment/books/features/an-end-to-bad-heir-days-the-posthumous-power-of-the-literary-estate-6285277.html; Andrew Clark, 'Disney Wins Winnie the Pooh Copyright Case', *Guardian*, 30 September 2009, accessed 27 April 2015, http://www.the-guardian.com/business/2009/sep/30/winnie-the-pooh-disney-law-suit. On the Dr Seuss estate's lobbying for the Copyright Term Extension Act, see Lawrence Lessig, *Free Culture: The Nature and Future of Creativity* (New York: Penguin, 2004), pp. 233–4.

58. For more on orphan works, see Dan Streible, 'The Role of Orphan Films in the 21st Century Archive', *Cinema Journal* vol. 46 no. 3 (Spring 2007): 124–8.

59. Ian Hargreaves, 'Digital Opportunity: A Review of Intellectual Property and Growth' (May 2011). Statement of Maria Pallante to the Subcommittee on Courts, Intellectual Property and the Internet Committee on the Judiciary, United States House of Representatives, 113th Congress, 1st Session (20 March 2013).

60. Associated Press, 'Record Industry Sues Hundreds of Internet Music Swappers,' *The New York Times*, 8 September 2003, accessed 27 April 2015, http://www.nytimes.com/2003/09/08/technology/08WIRE-MUSI.html. Information about the French anti-piracy HADOPI law is available at: http://www.hadopi.fr/en; Christopher Jon Sprigman, 'Reform(aliz)ing Copyright', *Stanford Law Review* vol. 57 no. 2 (2004): 485–68; John Timmer, 'Inside the Isle of Man's', *Ars Technica*, 26 February 2009, accessed 27 April 2015,

http://arstechnica.com/business/2009/02/inside-the-isle-of-mans-1month-unlimited-music-plan/;
Nicholas Kulish, 'Pirates' Strong Showing in Berlin Surprises Even Them', *The New York Times*,
19 September 2011, accessed 27 April 2015, http://www.nytimes.com/2011/09/20/world/
europe/in-berlin-pirates-win-8-9-percent-of-vote-in-regional-races.html; John Tagliabue, 'In Sweden,
Taking File Sharing to Heart. And to Church', *The New York Times*, 25 July 2012, accessed 27 April
2015, http://www.nytimes.com/2012/07/26/world/europe/in-sweden-taking-file-sharing-to-heart-
and-to-church.html

61. The 1997 documentary *A Story of Healing* was the first CC-licensed film to win an Oscar.

References

Aalmuhammed v. Lee, 202 F.3d 1227 (9th Cir. 2000).

ABC v. Aereo, 573 US _____ (2014), slip opinion.

Alford, William, *To Steal a Book is an Elegant Offense: Intellectual Property Law in Chinese Civilization*
    (Stanford, CA: Stanford University Press, 1995).

American Mutoscope & Biograph Co. v. Edison Manufacturing. Co., 137 F. 262 (D. N. J. 1905).

Astruc, Alexandre, 'Du stylo à la caméra et de la caméra au stylo', *L'Ecran française*, 30 March 1948.

BBC v. Time Out (1984) FSR 64.

Bill Graham Archives v. Dorling Kindersley Ltd., 448 F.3d 605 (2d Cir. 2006).

Burrow-Giles Lithographic Co. v. Sarony, 111 US 53 (1884).

Cartoon Network v. CSC Holdings, 536 F.3d 121 (2d Cir. 2008)

Decherney, Peter, 'Fair Use Goes Global', *Critical Studies in Media Communication* vol. 31 no. 2 (2014):
    146–52.

Decherney, Peter, *Hollywood's Copyright Wars: From Edison to the Internet* (New York: Columbia University
    Press, 2012).

Edison v. Lubin, 122 F. 240 (3d Cir. 1903).

Eldred v. Ashcroft, 537 US 186 (2003).

Faulkner Literary Rights v. Sony Pictures Classics, Inc., 953 F. Supp. 2d 701 (N.D. Miss. 25 October 2012).

Feist Publications, Inc., v. Rural Telephone Service Co., 499 US 340 (1991).

Fox Broadcasting Co., Inc. v. Dish Network LLC, 723 F.3d 1067 (9th Cir. 2013).

Fox Broadcasting v. Dish Network, 12-04529 (C.D. Cal. 2015).

Golan v. Holder, 132 S. Ct. 873 (2012).

Goldstein, Paul, *Copyright's Highway: From Guttenberg to the Celestial Jukebox*, rev. edn (Stanford, CA:
    Stanford University Press, 2003).

James M. Cain v. Universal Pictures Co., 47 F. Supp. 1013 (S. D. Cal. 1942).

Jefferson, Thomas, 'Thomas Jefferson Letter to Isaac McPherson', in Andrew A. Lipscomb and Albert
    Ellery Bergh (eds), *The Writings of Thomas Jefferson*, vol. 13 (Washington, DC: Thomas Jefferson
    Memorial Association, 1905), pp. 333–5.

Kalem Co. v. Harper Brothers, 222 US 55 (1911).

Kirtsaeng v. John Wiley & Sons, Inc., 133 S. Ct. 1351 (2013).

Lessig, Lawrence, *Free Culture: The Nature and Future of Creativity* (New York: Penguin, 2004),
    pp. 233–4.

Lessig, Lawrence, *Remix: Making Art and Commerce Thrive in the Hybrid Economy* (New York: Penguin,
    2008).

Leval, Pierre N., 'Toward a Fair Use Standard', *Harvard Law Review* vol. 103 (1990): 1105–36.

Leyda, Jay, 'A Note on Progress', *Film Quarterly* vol. 21 no. 4 (Summer 1968): 28–33.

Litman, Jessica, *Digital Copyright: Protecting Intellectual Property on the Internet* (Amherst: Prometheus, 2000).

Lucasfilm Limited v. Ainsworth, UKSC 39 UK (2011).

Luther R. Campbell v. Acuff-Rose Music, 510 US 569 (1994).

Patry, William, *How to Fix Copyright* (New York: Oxford, 2011).

Patterson, Lyman Ray, *Copyright in Historical Perspective* (Nashville, TN: Vanderbilt University Press, 1968).

Raustiala, Kal and Christopher Sprigman, *The Knockoff Economy: How Imitation Sparks Innovation* (Oxford: Oxford University Press, 2012).

Sarris, Andrew, *The American Cinema: Directors and Directions 1929–1968*, 1st Da Capo Press edn (New York: Da Capo Press, 1996).

Sony Corp. v. Universal Studios, Inc., 464 US 417 (1984).

Sprigman, Christopher Jon, 'Reform(aliz)ing Copyright', *Stanford Law Review* vol. 57 no. 2 (2004): 485–568.

Streible, Dan, 'The Role of Orphan Films in the 21st Century Archive', *Cinema Journal* vol. 46 no. 3 (Spring 2007): 124–8.

Tushnet, Rebecca, 'User-Generated Discontent: Transformation in Practice', *Columbia Journal of Law and Arts* vol. 31 (Summer 2008): 100–20.

Twentieth Century-Fox Film Corp. v. MCA, Inc., 209 USPQ (BNA) 200 (C.D. Cal. 1980).

Universal v. Film Venture International, 543 F. Supp. 1134 (C.D. Cal. 1982).

Vaidhyanathan, Siva, *Copyrights and Copywrongs: The Rise of Intellectual Property and How It Threatens Creativity* (New York: New York University Press, 2001).

Warner Bros. Inc. v. Film Venture International, 403 F. Supp. 522 (C.D. Cal. 1975).

Warner Bros. Entertainment Inc. v. RDR Books, 575 F. Supp. 2d 513 (SDNY 2008).

WNET v. Aereo, 712 F.3d 676 (2d Cir. 2013).

2 THE CHANGING LANDSCAPE OF TRADEMARK LAW IN TINSELTOWN

FROM *DEBBIE DOES DALLAS* TO *THE HANGOVER*

MARK BARTHOLOMEW AND JOHN TEHRANIAN

Hollywood both creates and borrows. This duality simultaneously implicates intellectual property law and the First Amendment. While movies, television shows, sound recordings and video games constitute valuable pieces of intellectual property in and of themselves, they frequently make use of the intellectual property of others, often without authorisation or payment. Trademarks – legally protectable symbols used to indicate the source of goods and distinguish those goods from those sold or made by others – constitute one such of type of intellectual property. Film-makers often employ trademarks for expressive purposes to contextualise their work in the cultural and commercial milieu in which we live. But in the process of exercising creative judgment by employing the use of trademarks in their works, they may find themselves subject to legal liability for infringement.

Brand owners have grown increasingly sensitive to the (mis)use of their trademarks in entertainment content. In 2012, the venerable *Hollywood Reporter* went so far as to muse about whether all the Mayan talk of the coming Armageddon was actually referring to (what it billed as) a Hollywood 'trademarklawpocalypse'.[1] In the span of a few weeks, a series of significant trademark disputes erupted, putting the entire industry on notice. On the eve of the release of *The Hobbit: An Unexpected Journey* (2012), Warner Bros., New Line Cinema and MGM successfully enjoined the distributor Global Asylum from releasing its own new film about hobbits under the name *Age of the Hobbits* (the film was later released as *Clash of the Empires* [2013]). Anheuser-Busch took umbrage at the fact that Denzel's Washington's alcoholic pilot in *Flight* (2012) used Budweiser as his choice inebriant while drinking and driving. Rizzoli Publications objected to NBC's use of 'Rizzoli' as the name of comedian Ray Romano's character on the series *Parenthood* (2010–). And when one of the characters in Woody Allen's *Midnight in Paris* (2011) (mis)quoted author William Faulkner, the Faulkner Estate sued the film's distributor Sony Pictures Classics for improperly associating the author with the movie.[2]

Feuds between trademark holders and film-makers are nothing new. For example, in 1979, the Dallas Cowboys Cheerleaders sued a New York cinema for showing the pornographic film *Debbie Does Dallas* (1978). They alleged that the film was confusing to moviegoers because it contained a scene where a character wore a cheerleading uniform strikingly similar to the blue and white boots, blouses and vests adorning the sideline representatives of 'America's Team'.[3] The court hearing the case held in favour of the Dallas Cowboys Cheerleaders, rejecting the cinema's First Amendment defence on the ground that there were other ways to discuss sexuality and athletics without appropriating the Cheerleaders' famous trade dress.[4]

Just a decade later, a decision by the same court regarding the balance between trademark rights and free speech produced a strikingly different result. When famed Italian director

Federico Fellini produced a movie about two fictional Italian cabaret performers who imitated Ginger Rogers and Fred Astaire, he titled his movie *Ginger and Fred* (1986). Screen legend Ginger Rogers sued for trademark infringement. Just as the Dallas Cowboys Cheerleaders alleged unlawful use of their trademarked uniforms, Rogers contended that Fellini had improperly used her name without permission, thereby creating consumer confusion over her endorsement of the film.[5] Yet, in sharp contrast to the Cheerleaders' case, the court rejected Rogers' arguments, instead vindicating the film-maker's right to free expression in a crucial, precedent-setting victory.[6] The court announced a new free speech safeguard (subsequently styled by other courts as 'the *Rogers* defence') for those using trademarks in an artistic fashion.[7]

Fellini's fortune forever changed the way courts have approached the balancing of trademark and free speech rights. In the past two decades, courts have used the *Rogers* defence to protect numerous content creators and distributors from liability for unauthorised use of trademarks in artistic works. In a recent suit, for example, a federal court drew on the *Rogers* defence to quickly dismiss claims of trademark infringement and unfair competition brought by Louis Vuitton against the makers of the blockbuster *The Hangover II* (2011) for a misleading reference to its name and famous Toile Monogram in a scene in the film.[8]

This chapter explores how courts have sought to balance the competing interests at stake when film-makers employ brand names and images in their work and brand owners threaten liability for trademark infringement. Specifically, we use *Rogers v. Grimaldi* as a primary pivot point to trace the remarkable change in approaches that courts have taken to First Amendment defences in trademark cases over the past few decades. To this end, we conduct case studies of two opinions – *Dallas Cowboys Cheerleaders, Inc. v. Pussycat Cinema, Ltd.*[9] (decided a decade before *Rogers v. Grimaldi*) and *Louis Vuitton Malletier S.A. v. Warner Bros. Entertainment Inc.*[10] (decided two decades after *Rogers v. Grimaldi*) – to illustrate the increasing recognition of free speech defences to trademark infringement claims against film-makers. We also examine what may have precipitated this change and its potential impact on Hollywood's future. As we shall also see, the growing First Amendment defences to trademark liability are not without limits and the case law has not always favoured the First Amendment rights of content creators over the intellectual property rights of trademark holders. Even as courts have come to recognise greater protections for creators over the years, the increased presence of brands in everyday life means that Hollywood's attempts at verisimilitude will continue to cause conflicts with the claims of brand owners.

The Legal Landscape Before *Rogers v. Grimaldi*

In the USA, trademark law is primarily the preserve of federal law, not the law of the individual states. In the main, one federal statute – the Lanham Act of 1946 – governs the use of trademarks.[11] Aggrieved trademark holders turn to the statute to seek legal recourse. Over time, trademark law has expanded well beyond just the protection of words; images, colours, sounds and even distinctive packaging or the design of the product itself (known by the legal term of art 'trade dress') can enjoy protection.

When the owner of one of these protectable symbols objects to another's use of it, the Lanham Act provides one central ground for legal suit: likelihood of consumer confusion. Initially, actionable consumer confusion referred to situations where a defendant successfully passed off its goods as the goods of the mark holder. Over time, however, courts have grown increasingly generous in recognising confusion, even countenancing scenarios where consumers only think that the authorised mark holder has somehow sponsored the defendant's activities or where any initial consumer confusion is dispelled prior to purchase. Once the mark holder demonstrates a likelihood of consumer confusion, a court will often issue a legal order halting the objectionable use. One key exception comes when the defendant invokes a recognised defence to a claim of trademark infringement. This is where the First Amendment can sometimes find a starring role within the world of trademark law. There are times when, despite a likelihood of consumer confusion, the free speech interests of an unauthorised mark user can trump the intellectual property rights of the mark holder.

In the decades prior to the Second Circuit's influential 1989 decision in *Rogers v. Grimaldi*, the way in which courts evaluated the trade-off between trademark rights and free expression in film was inconsistent. Perhaps most prevalent was a legal test that asked whether 'alternative avenues' existed for a film-maker making unauthorised use of someone else's brand. Under the test, if no alternative avenues to the mark's use exist, then the use must be permitted under the First Amendment. On the other hand, if the film-maker can make her expressive point without using the plaintiff's trademark, then the film-maker has no free speech defence and can be held liable for trademark infringement. The test is based on *Lloyd Corp. v. Tanner*,[12] a US Supreme Court decision outside of trademark law upholding a shopping mall owner's decision to prohibit the distribution of handbills opposing the Vietnam War.[13] The prohibition did not violate the First Amendment, the Court reasoned, because the protestors had other avenues for making their views heard, including distribution of their handbills on the public streets and sidewalks surrounding the shopping centre.[14]

Lower courts evaluating free speech defences in trademark infringement cases ran with the unrelated *Lloyd Corp. v. Tanner* decision, declaring that the First Amendment only safeguards the unauthorised use of trademarks in movies (and other creative endeavours) when the use is so closely connected to the subject matter of an artistic work that the author has no alternative way of expressing what the work is about.[15] In other words, if the film-maker has another viable way to communicate her message, then she must forgo use of the complaining party's trademark.

Applying the 'Alternative Avenues' Test in the Case of *Dallas Cowboys Cheerleaders, Inc. v. Pussycat Cinema, Ltd.*

As its heading implies, *Dallas Cowboys Cheerleaders, Inc. v. Pussycat Cinema, Ltd.* involved a combustible combination of two mainstays of modern American popular culture – pornography and professional athletics. By the late 1970s, the Dallas Cowboys Cheerleaders were a nationally known brand. They sold over three-quarters of a million posters through 1977–8 and 70 million viewers watched them perform at the 1978 Super Bowl.[16] The Cheerleaders vigorously policed unauthorised uses of their brand, particularly when the use came in the context of adult entertainment. When a group of former cheerleaders appeared in *Playboy* magazine in a faux Dallas Cowboys Cheerleaders ensemble, and then attempted to resell a photo from the *Playboy* shoot as a commercial poster, the Cheerleaders successfully sued for trademark infringement.[17] As Suzanne Mitchell, coordinator for the Cowboys Cheerleaders stated, 'They can walk down Main Street, just don't do it in our uniform.'[18]

The Cheerleaders' legal strategy also targeted the pornographic film industry. In 1978, adult cinemas began to screen the popular pornographic film, *Debbie Does Dallas*.[19] The plot of the film, which the court in review described as 'a gross and revolting sex film', features a group of high school cheerleaders trying to travel to Texas for try-outs for the fictional 'Texas Cowgirls' cheerleading squad. To raise the necessary travel funds, the cheerleaders turn to prostitution. In the film's final scene, the movie's eponymous star engages in a variety of sexual acts with the owner of a sporting goods store. She performs these acts in various states of dress (and undress) while wearing her 'Texas Cowgirls' uniform. Debbie's uniform, with its particular striping, studding, buckle and colour schemes, bears a striking resemblance to the regalia of the Dallas Cowboys Cheerleaders.

Objecting to the use of their uniform in this undignified manner, the Dallas Cowboys Cheerleaders sued several entities associated with *Debbie Does Dallas* for trademark infringement, contending the filmgoing public would find such use 'confusing'. They sought injunctions to prevent distribution or exhibition of the film. One of the targets of the Cheerleaders' litigation was the Pussycat Cinema, an adult theatre located just off Times Square in New York City. The Pussycat Cinema operated at a time when adult theatres flourished in New York. 42nd Street, dubbed by *Rolling Stone* 'the sleaziest block in America', housed 121 adult establishments at the time of the lawsuit.[20] In the past, New York theatres like the Pussycat Cinema had welcomed lawsuits as the increased publicity only served to fuel, rather than depress, ticket sales.[21] But, by the late 1970s, politicians were beginning to crack down on Times Square's adult establishments. In response to petitions from Times Square businesses, New York Mayor Abraham Beame created the Midtown Enforcement Project, which began targeting the theatres, and others trading in adult-themed merchandise, for city inspections and possible legal action.[22] In 1978, when *Debbie Does Dallas* was released, Mayor Ed Koch continued this process, pushing existing adult theatres to close their doors or switch over to more 'legitimate' fare.[23] In addition to initiating legal proceedings, Koch mobilised New York's elite arts community, including performing arts and architectural preservation groups, to pressure the theatres and place Times Square on a more culturally and economically desirable footing.[24] Hence, the Cheerleaders' lawsuit coincided with a government crackdown on theatres like the Pussycat Cinema and films like *Debbie Does Dallas*, thereby providing a painful one-two punch to Times Square's besieged adult industry.

It was in this context that a federal court in New York heard the Cheerleaders' case against the Pussycat Cinema. The court wasted little time in finding that *Debbie Does Dallas* violated the Cheerleaders' trademark rights. It determined the Cheerleaders' uniform to be protectable trade dress. It also agreed with the Cheerleaders that viewers of the pornographic film would find the similarities between it and the fictional 'Texas Cowgirls' uniform worn in the film to be 'confusing'. As a result, the court held the Pussycat Cinema liable for trademark infringement.

Finding themselves legally naked under trademark law, the defendants unsuccessfully attempted to shroud their case under the banner of the First Amendment by claiming that they were making a commentary on the nature of 'sexuality in athletics' in US society. A successful appeal to the First Amendment meant that, even if *Debbie Does Dallas* did violate the

Cheerleaders' trademark rights, the interests of free speech should still allow its screening. Applying the alternative avenues test, the court rejected this defence. Barely able to contain its revulsion towards the theatre owner and the film at issue, the court grudgingly acknowledged that the film represented 'speech', potentially protected under the First Amendment. Nevertheless, it found that an injunction barring the movie theatre from showing the film posed no First Amendment concerns. Although failing to specify actual alternatives to the white boots, white shorts, blue blouse and white star-studded vest and belt employed by both Debbie and the Dallas Cowboys Cheerleaders, the court maintained that the film could convey its message in another fashion. It explained that 'there are numerous ways in which defendants may comment on sexuality in athletics without infringing plaintiff's trademark'.[25]

The court also brushed aside concerns that a judicial bar on the film's screening constituted a forbidden 'prior restraint' on speech. The judicial doctrine of prior restraint, first crystallised in the Supreme Court's 1931 decision in *Near v. Minnesota*, is a longstanding guidepost in First Amendment law that requires courts to strongly disfavour any kind of judicial or administrative order that prohibits speech being made in advance of its publication. Normally, the doctrine presumes that any attempt to block use of a communicative forum before actual expression has taken place is unconstitutional; instead, to further society's interest in free communication, courts typically allow the expression to occur and leave potential plaintiffs to seek relief, through monetary damages, after the fact.[26] Yet the court contended that because trademark law is 'content-neutral' and enforced by private parties, not the government itself, the prior restraint doctrine was not at issue.[27]

The *Dallas Cowboys Cheerleaders* case illustrates just how narrow free speech protection for creative actors accused of trademark infringement was before 1989.[28] The court's willingness to discard typical First Amendment concerns over prior restraints on speech stands in marked contrast to other free speech analyses where attempts to pre-emptively enjoin expression have been denied even when those expressions have been deemed libellous, obscene, or threatening to national security.[29] Moreover, under the alternative avenues test, the First Amendment only comes into play when the mark at issue is so intimately related to the work's subject matter that the author has no other possible means of explaining what their work is about. It is almost always possible to conceptualise the author's creative interest in some way such that other means of expressing that interest are available. In the *Dallas Cowboys Cheerleaders* case, the court broadly characterised the film-maker's expressive point as a commentary on sexuality in athletics. Yet an equally apt characterisation of the film-maker's project might have been as a commentary on the sexuality of the Dallas Cowboys Cheerleaders themselves. Even in 1979, the Dallas Cowboys Cheerleaders were known for being far different from other cheerleading units. With their signature low-cut vests and provocative dance routines akin to Las Vegas burlesque, they were the first professional squad to make the connection between cheerleading and sexuality so explicit.[30] Under such a characterisation, the film-maker might have had little alternative to using the Cheerleaders' protected trade dress and been inoculated from suit under the First Amendment. The court's decision to describe *Debbie Does Dallas* in the particular manner it chose demonstrates the tremendous potential for judicial censorship under the alternative avenues test. In other cases, courts used the same test to reject the First Amendment claims of film-makers and block their chosen means of expression. For example, the Edgar Rice Burroughs estate filed a trademark infringement suit to stop exhibition of an X-rated film titled *Tarz & Jane & Boy & Cheeta* (1975)[31] and American Dairy Queen Corporation used trademark law to force a studio to abandon the title 'Dairy Queens' for its film about a Minnesota beauty pageant.[32]

By limiting protectable speech interests to only those situations in which use of the trademark is absolutely necessary to the author's expressive project, the 'alternative avenues' test stands in marked contrast to other areas of First Amendment law. In other contexts, American law rejects such a cramped view of free speech, preferring not to second-guess a speaker's chosen vernacular and to allow greater breathing space for expressive activities. For example, in *Cohen v. California*, the Supreme Court recognised that the use of certain words, rather than their synonyms, is fundamental to the exercise of First Amendment rights. The Court overturned the conviction of Paul Robert Cohen for disturbing the peace when he walked into a California courtroom wearing a jacket emblazoned with the words 'Fuck the Draft'.[33] Responding to the government's argument that Cohen should have expressed his anti-draft sentiments in more polite terms, the Court explained: '[W]e cannot indulge in the facile assumption that one can forbid particular words without also running a substantial risk of suppressing ideas in the process.'[34] Yet, prior to 1989, under the 'alternative avenues' test, courts did forbid the use of particular words and images by moviemakers and associated entities when those words and images symbolised a particular business or product.

Not every court of the time embraced the 'alternative avenues' test. Some assessed the claims of trademark owners against film-makers under what can best be described as an ad hoc balancing approach. This method involves determining whether consumer confusion is likely – as noted earlier, the *sine qua non* for any successful trademark infringement claim – but with a simultaneous eye towards the defendant's interest in free speech. For example, once a court identifies the defendant's work as a successful parody, an important means of expressing criticism and commentary, it may discount evidence traditionally offered to show consumer confusion, like the degree of similarity between the plaintiff's trademark and the mark used by the defendant. The problem with the ad hoc balancing approach is that it offers little predictive comfort to content creators accused of infringement. Just because a court determined that, on balance, there is little likelihood of confusion from an expressive work in one case, it is hard to know how such a context-specific analysis should translate to the next case. For example, when a lower court determined that consumers were unlikely to confuse Walt Disney Productions' use of the name *Tron* for a 1982 science-fiction film with the electric fuses trademarked under the same name, a higher court reversed, contending that the lower court had been overly charitable to Disney in how it interpreted the evidence of consumer confusion.[35] Whether ad hoc balancing or the alternative avenues test was used, Hollywood studios and other content producers faced an uncertain and often restrictive legal landscape when it came to using brand names and images in their works.

Rogers v. Grimaldi and the Artistic-relevance Standard

If film-makers utilising brand imagery had to tread on hostile and uncertain ground in the 1970s and 80s, the legal terrain dramatically shifted in their favour at the decade's end. As we have seen, up until then courts charged with balancing the rights of film-makers with those of trademark holders often chose the latter, and jettisoned some time-honoured First Amendment protections in the process. This trend began to change, however, in 1989 with the decision in the case of *Rogers v. Grimaldi*. Even though the Second Circuit for the US Court of Appeals – the same court that decided the *Dallas Cowboys Cheerleaders* case – issued the ruling, the results were diametrically different. In fact, the *Rogers v. Grimaldi* decision expressly repudiated the alternative avenues test and ushered in a new, more film-maker-friendly approach towards the balancing of free speech and trademark rights.

The case started when famed Italian director Federico Fellini made a movie about two fictional Italian cabaret performers who imitated Ginger Rogers and Fred Astaire. Fellini titled his movie, his third to last film, *Ginger e Fred* (*Ginger and Fred*). Reviewers praised Fellini's work, which premiered in Rome in 1986.[36] *Ginger and Fred* has been described as a 'hyperfilm', as the film serves as both a fictional narrative and an autobiographical exploration of the great director and his filmography. Frequent Fellini collaborator Marcello Mastroianni played the role of 'Fred', who serves as Fellini's surrogate in the film. Meanwhile, Giulietta Masina, Fellini's real-life wife, played the role of 'Ginger'.[37] Although not all critics were so kind, Vincent Canby of *The New York Times* placed the film favourably within the Fellini canon, remarking that the film looked and sounded 'like the work of no other director'.[38]

Actress and dancer Rogers did not view *Ginger and Fred* so positively, however. After months of silence, Rogers issued a statement following the release of Fellini's film. She proclaimed the film 'offensive to her reputation and personality', and presumably to her former co-star's as well.[39] She also initiated an $8 million lawsuit against Alberto Grimaldi and MGM, the motion picture's producer and distributor, for false endorsement under trademark law. Shortly thereafter, when asked by the press about Rogers' lawsuit, Fellini wryly commented 'perhaps she has not seen the film . . . or has been misinformed'.[40] But the lawsuit was more than a

minor irritant for the director. Originally scheduled to present the Oscar for Best Picture, alongside famed directors Akira Kurosawa and Billy Wilder, at the 1986 Academy Awards, Fellini declined to travel to Hollywood after the lawsuit was filed, instead allowing John Huston to take his place.[41]

In her lawsuit, Rogers contended that Fellini had improperly used her name without permission, thereby creating consumer confusion over her endorsement of the work. Rogers' permission would definitely have added symbolic and economic capital to the film. Rogers is listed at Number 14 on the American Film Institute's list of the greatest female screen legends in film history and

Hyperfilm: Masina and Mastroianni in *Ginger and Fred* (1986) (BFI)

previously lent her name to a line of lingerie sold by J. C. Penney. The court remarked that she is 'among that small elite of the entertainment world whose identities are readily called to mind by just their first names'. Nevertheless, Grimaldi and MGM countered that enforcement of Rogers' alleged trademark interest in her name would trample their First Amendment rights by restricting freedom of expression in the production of a creative work.

In the end, Grimaldi and MGM won a seminal victory, reducing the scope of trademark law and strengthening First Amendment protections for artists. The court announced that it was discarding the alternative avenues test – a test that the Fellini film would have clearly failed.[42] It explained that, while the test might have been appropriate in its original application involving claims against landowners, it was not a good match for trademark law. Unlike a landowner's decision to prevent certain speech in a physical location, a trademark owner's infringement suit not only influences the speech's location but also its actual content.[43] The typical result in a trademark case is an injunction completely stopping the defendant from using the mark at issue. Given the ability of a successful trademark infringement lawsuit to remove particular speech from the marketplace of ideas entirely, the court concluded that the alternative avenues test was too restrictive and had to be replaced with another mechanism better suited to balancing free expression with trademark rights.[44]

The court's solution was a new test – one that was more solicitous of artistic choice and, hence, more friendly to Hollywood film-makers. Instead of simply asking whether the film-maker could have made her point in an alternative fashion, the court announced a new sort of enquiry: whether 'the title has no artistic relevance to the underlying work whatsoever, or, if it has some artistic relevance, [whether] the title explicitly misleads as to the source or the content of the work'.[45] A title satisfying both the 'some artistic relevance' and not explicitly misleading criteria receives First Amendment immunity from a trademark infringement action.

The court easily concluded that Fellini's film met both of the newly announced criteria. First, the title was artistically relevant to the underlying film. The court described this requirement as merely requiring a 'minimum threshold of artistic relevance to the film's content'.[46] The film's main characters were named 'Ginger' and 'Fred'. Moreover, these names were not arbitrarily chosen to capitalise on the fame of Ginger Rogers and Fred Astaire. Rather, they were selected because the two main characters made their living imitating the famous Rogers and Astaire duo. As a result, the names had the requisite amount of artistic relevance.

The court spent more time on the second criterion. Rogers maintained that the film's title was explicitly misleading. She offered a survey of likely moviegoers, 14 per cent of which, when presented with an advertisement featuring the film's title, seemed to believe that Rogers was involved with the making of the *Ginger and Fred* film.[47] She also made the argument that the film's title misled consumers not just as to her involvement, but also as to its subject, by causing them to believe that the film was about her and Fred Astaire in a direct, biographical sense.[48]

The court, however, concluded that the risk of some consumer confusion was tolerable in order to protect interests in artistic expression.[49] As a result, it was willing to ignore the survey data showing a small segment of the consuming public would be confused as to Rogers' involvement with Fellini's project.[50] In addition, the court emphasised that the 'Ginger and Fred' title was susceptible to multiple interpretations and, as a result, it could not be described as explicitly misleading.[51] It was true, the court admitted, that those who thought the title referred to a true biography of the real-life singing duo were being fooled. But the court also noted that the title has 'an ironic meaning' that was equally valid.[52] It credited an affidavit from Fellini himself, which explained that he selected Rogers and Astaire as 'a glamorous and care-free symbol of what American cinema represented during the harsh times which Italy experienced in the 1930s and 1940s'.[53] Rather than being misleading, the title, argued the court, 'is an integral element of the film and the filmmaker's artistic expressions'.[54] Because the title was artistically relevant to the film and not explicitly misleading, Grimaldi and MGM's First Amendment defence succeeded and Rogers' complaint was dismissed.

The *Rogers v. Grimaldi* decision has proved influential and expansive. Over the past two decades, several other federal courts have adopted the *Rogers* test. The test soon grew to encompass not just movie titles, but trademark claims against works of artistic expression, including claims where the challenged trademark use occurs in the body of the work. For example, when the video game *Grand Theft Auto* borrowed from the trademark and trade dress of a Los Angeles strip club to depict a Los Angeles-like city, the Court of Appeals for the Ninth Circuit held that the uses were immunised under the *Rogers* test.[55]

Courts have also construed *Rogers'* two prongs broadly. One might worry that an open-ended judicial enquiry into 'artistic relevance' could short-change the expressive interests of content creators. It would seem that the judges deciding the *Dallas Cowboys Cheerleaders* case would be loath to credit any artistic design to the creators of *Debbie Does Dallas*. A similar response might result when asked to apply *Rogers* to other seemingly unsavoury or transgressive works. Giving the benefit of the doubt to Fellini's artistic vision is one thing; giving this benefit to film-makers not legitimated by the cultural elite is another.

Yet, in deciphering artistic relevance, courts have generally given great deference to the vision of defendants. As the court in the *Grand Theft Auto* case characterised it, 'the level of relevance merely must be above zero'.[56] Even if the connection between the trademark use and underlying work's communicative goal is 'tenuous', the artistic relevance standard is still satisfied.[57] Hence, it is extremely rare for this criterion not to be satisfied. In fact, after *Rogers v. Grimaldi*, courts have recognised the First Amendment interests of pornographic film-makers as well as the makers of notoriously violent video games and dismissed the trademark lawsuits against them – a far cry from the approach of the *Dallas Cowboys Cheerleaders, Inc. v. Pussycat Cinema, Ltd.* court, which appeared to factor the supposedly 'gross and revolting' nature of the allegedly infringing work against the defendants when weighing the merits of the plaintiff's claims.[58] It may have taken the artistic patina of someone like Fellini to dislodge the 'alternative avenues' test, but, once dislodged, courts have looked favourably upon the expressive rights of a host of creative entities, not just those of highbrow directors.

Under *Rogers*, once it has ascertained the mark's artistic relevance, a court proceeds to consideration of whether the defendant's use was explicitly misleading. Again, the courts have construed this criterion in a speech-friendly fashion. In any trademark infringement lawsuit, the trademark holder bears the burden of demonstrating a likelihood of consumer confusion from the defendant's use. Courts have been careful to require something over and above this proof of likely consumer confusion when the *Rogers* test is called into play. The Second Circuit and other courts mandate the evidence of confusion be 'particularly compelling' to invalidate a *Rogers* defence.[59] Other courts replace the likelihood of confusion analysis entirely, trading it for one more tilted in the defendant's favour. In fact, it seems that once courts determine that the trademark is being used in an artistic manner, they are more than willing to jettison the notoriously unpredictable likelihood of confusion analysis for their own 'common sense' analysis, which is geared towards allowing the challenged uses.[60]

Of course, the broad protections granted by *Rogers* raise the question as to why, when it comes to unauthorised use of trademarks, courts have moved in the direction of greater artistic latitude for film-makers and other content creators over the past two decades. Part of the reason might have to do with simply getting used to the notion of movies as speech. Works of entertainment did not qualify as speech under the First Amendment until 1952 (see Chapter 5). Not unrelatedly, until recently, defendants in trademark disputes rarely asserted a First Amendment defence.[61] It has taken some time for courts and litigants to explicitly wrestle with the balancing of expressive interests in film with the perhaps more established rights of trademark holders.

Notably, during the same period, not every legal regime has moved in the direction of greater creative authority for content creators. Copyright law can often be invoked to restrict the activities of film-makers, even when the film-maker's activities touch on expression most would deem at the core of the First Amendment. For example, when conservative politician Charles 'Chuck' DeVore produced two music videos, 'The Hope of November' and 'All She Wants to Do is Tax', for campaign advertisements that meant to skewer Barbara Boxer – his liberal opponent for California's seat in the US Senate – and to riff on musician Don Henley's 1980s megahits 'The Boys of Summer' and 'All She Wants to Do is Dance', Henley invoked copyright law to force the videos' removal from YouTube. Notably, the court held in DeVore's favour on a related trademark infringement claim, but granted judgment for Henley on the copyright claims. DeVore attempted to make a First Amendment argument to justify his unauthorised use of Henley's songs under copyright's 'fair use' defence, but to no avail, even though his allegedly infringing songs constituted core political speech made during the heat of an electoral campaign.[62]

This points to another possible reason for the courts' increasing reluctance to stifle film-makers' use of trademarked materials. Unlike copyright law, which is principally guided by the language of a comprehensive federal statutory regime, trademark law relies heavily on judge-made tests and standards. Although a federal statute does provide some grounding for trademark law, legislatures have encouraged courts to develop the 'common law' of trademarks on their own initiative. This gives judges deciding trademark cases more freedom to manoeuvre than if they were simply applying statutory language. With courts operating under the assumption that copyright's statutory provisions effectively address free speech concerns and foreclose additional judicial innovations in this area, copyright cases rarely invoke the First Amendment; by contrast, trademark cases do, at times, expressly weigh free speech interests. Trademark law's common law tradition permits judges to conceptualise the law at a high level of abstraction, allowing for more judicial discretion when it comes to balancing trademark holder property rights with the free speech interests of those accused of infringement. The *Rogers* test elucidates this common law innovation, as it was a test that not only rejected a prior test deemed insufficiently solicitous of speech interests, but it also was created by a group of judges completely on their own initiative with no applicable statutory language to restrict their innovation.

Balancing Trademark Protection and First Amendment Rights in the Post-*Rogers v. Grimaldi* World and the Case of *Louis Vuitton Malletier S.A. v. Warner Bros. Entertainment Inc.*

Over time, the *Rogers* test has expanded to provide potential cover for all uses of trademarks in artistic works, not just uses in titles. In addition, courts have generally interpreted its two prongs in an increasingly speech-protective fashion. As a result, the legal system has given film-makers greater expressive latitude in their unauthorised use of household brands. But this discretion is not without bounds. Trademark holders are still, at times, able to flex their legal muscles in a way that has consequences for Hollywood content. Judicial interpretation of the *Rogers* test continues to evolve, leading to exploitable legal grey areas for owners of famous brand names.

The results of the Louis Vuitton suit against the makers of *The Hangover II* illustrate the strong protection that film-makers have typically enjoyed under the *Rogers* test. As one of Hollywood's most successful comedy franchises, *The Hangover* trilogy grossed more than a billion dollars for Warner Bros. and its partners. But the wild profit party thrown by the movie franchise was not without its own litigation hangover, as the trilogy spawned its own cottage industry of intellectual property suits. Perhaps most famously, the artist who created Mike Tyson's Maori-inspired facial tattoo took Warner Bros. to court for its failure to license rights to the marking when one of the characters in the movie ended up, after a night of debauchery, with a look-alike rendition emblazoned on his visage.[63] The case settled shortly thereafter on confidential terms.[64] By contrast, the other intellectual property dispute related to the movie touched directly on claims of trademark infringement and unfair competition for the unauthorised use of a famous mark in the course of the movie.

In the suit,[65] luxury handbag manufacturer Louis Vuitton sued Warner Bros. for misidentifying a knock-off item featuring their most celebrated and iconic design, the so-called Toile Monogram, in the movie. In an early scene, *The Hangover*'s fearless protagonists make their way through Los Angeles International Airport en route to Thailand, where, of course, hilarity and hijinks ensue. Alan, played by Zach Galifianakis, carries what appears to be an over-the-shoulder Louis Vuitton 'Keepall'. When the group arrives at the gate, Alan sets the bag on a chair. As Stu, played by Ed Helms, moves the bag to make room for one of their pals to sit, Alan vociferously objects: 'Careful that is … that is a Lewis Vuitton,' he exhorts. In fact, the bag in question was neither a Louis Vuitton nor a 'Lewis Vuitton', but, rather, a notorious Louis Vuitton knock-off made by copycat manufacturer Diophy, a company that had sold its less expensive versions of faux Louis Vuitton merchandise throughout the USA. Consequently, the real Louis Vuitton was thoroughly unamused and a civil action resulted.

Interestingly, in the course of litigation, Louis Vuitton strategically limited its claims. It did not assert that Warner Bros.' use deceived the public into thinking that Louis Vuitton sponsored or was affiliated with the movie. Rather, Louis Vuitton believed that the scene in question infringed its marks by mischaracterising the Diophy bag as an authentic Louis Vuitton bag. According to Louis Vuitton, Warner Bros.' misrepresentation created a likelihood of confusion in the minds of the consuming public and thereby injured the Louis Vuitton brand by conflating it with an inferior product. In response to the allegations, Warner Bros. moved to dismiss the suit on the basis of the *Rogers* defence.

The court hearing the case took a broad and favourable view of the defence. On the first element of the *Rogers* test, the decision provided a generous reading of artistic relevance, noting that the standard is 'purposely low' and satisfied unless the use has no artistic relevance '*whatsoever*'.[66] This threshold was clearly met with Alan's ironic use of the Diophy bag and mispronunciation of 'Louis' while grousing at the mistreatment of his purported luxury good. On the second element of the *Rogers* test, the court found that the use did not 'explicitly mislead … as to the source or the content of the work'. As such, the *Rogers* defence immunised the film-makers from liability. Importantly, the court rejected Louis Vuitton's argument that the 'explicitly misleading' test should include consumer confusion about the source or content of a third party's goods (here, the Diophy bag). Prior cases limited the 'explicitly misleading' test to confusion as to whether the defendant's work was sponsored by the plaintiff-rights holder. To support its argument for a more expansive view of 'explicitly misleading', Louis Vuitton drew on the object of this chapter's first case study – the *Dallas Cowboys Cheerleaders, Inc. v. Pussycat Cinema, Ltd.* case.[67]

Significantly, the court expressly contrasted that case to *Rogers v. Grimaldi* and rejected the viability of the former in favour of the latter. First, the court noted that the former case's approach to First Amendment defences to trademark claims had been properly criticised by a number of courts and observers and had been effectively replaced with the latter case's approach in matters involving artistic works.[68] Second, the court noted that even the *Dallas Cowboys Cheerleaders, Inc. v. Pussycat Cinema, Ltd.* case did not allow the type of broad application of the Lanham Act being advocated by Louis Vuitton in its suit against Warner Bros. Specifically, Louis Vuitton claimed liability based on consumer confusion that 'the Diophy bag is really a genuine Louis Vuitton bag; and … that Louis Vuitton approved the use of the Diophy bag in the [f]ilm'.[69] However, neither type of confusion described by Louis Vuitton spoke to the actionable theory approved by *Dallas Cowboys Cheerleaders, Inc. v. Pussycat Cinema, Ltd.* – that the film itself (rather than a product within it) was sponsored or approved by the trademark holder. In so doing, the court furthered the emerging *Rogers*-inspired view disfavouring Lanham Act claims that attack content within artistic works. As the court held, any such claims must be read narrowly and must demonstrate forms of consumer confusion that are '*particularly compelling*'.[70]

It is also worth noting that the *Louis Vuitton Malletier S.A. v. Warner Bros. Entertainment Inc.* court even decided the issue on a motion to dismiss, prior to the initiation of discovery and despite Vuitton's insistence that it should have the right to determine, among other things, whether Warner Bros. meant to use a Diophy bag or not. The early adjudication of trademark claims involving artistic works bodes well for the expressive rights of film-makers, especially those who may not be well-financed or supported by the major studios. The threat of litigation can have a chilling effect on expressive uses of trademarks, even when the claims advanced by a rights holder have little or no merit. Given the high costs of litigation, especially for infringement suits in federal court, many creators have eschewed uses of anyone else's intellectual property for fear of the hassle and expense of defence. Furthermore, claims of infringement can attach liability to downstream distributors and exhibitors, thereby creating a cloud on the title and making release of a film difficult. *Louis Vuitton Malletier S.A. v. Warner Bros. Entertainment Inc.* adds to an emerging body of case law that expressly affirms courts' option to quickly dispense with claims stemming from the unauthorised use of trademarks in artistic works.

Finally, the latter court immunised the defendants from additional unfair competition and New York state law dilution claims. It reasoned that the same First Amendment considerations (i.e., those embodied in the *Rogers* test) that immunised Warner Bros. from liability under the Lanham Act provided a safe harbour for Warner Bros. from these common law and state law claims as well.[71] Thus, the *Rogers* test's First Amendment moorings allow it to grant broad protection for liability flowing from unauthorised trademark uses in artistic content.

The Limits of *Rogers*

Despite the *Louis Vuitton* case and other recent successes for content creators warding off legal claims pertaining to unauthorised use of trademarks in artistic works, *Rogers*' influence should not be overstated. Although implemented by most courts that have considered it, at least one federal circuit court (the Third Circuit) has repeatedly expressed scepticism, contending that *Rogers* immunises too many unauthorised trademark uses.[72] Moreover, even in jurisdictions that have adopted the *Rogers* test, there continue to be restrictions on film-makers' activities. The Ninth Circuit has expressly adopted *Rogers*, for example,[73] yet that fact did not stop a court in the Central District of California from issuing an injunction in 2012 against the release of the aforementioned 'mockbuster' *Clash of the Empires* in advance of the summer release of the New Line Cinema blockbuster *The Hobbit: An Unexpected Journey*.[74]

In the case, *Warner Bros. Ent. v. The Global Asylum, Inc.*,[75] the court found that the defendants ran badly afoul of the *Rogers* safe harbour due to several factors. Specifically, based on its reading of the language of relevant Ninth Circuit precedent, the court divined and identified two implicit limitations on the *Rogers* defence that applied in the case.[76] First, the court supplanted the previously lax standard for meeting artistic relevance by holding that a usage is, per se, not artistically relevant if the defendant 'merely borrow[s] another's property to get attention'.[77] The imposition of this additional requirement fundamentally narrows the defence and moves it far from the deferential version applied by the actual *Rogers v. Grimaldi* court and such decisions as *Louis Vuitton Malletier S.A. v. Warner Bros. Entertainment Inc.* – cases where courts held that the threshold for artistic relevance was 'purposefully low' and was met unless a use of a mark had no artistic relevance 'whatsoever'.[78]

Second, the *Warner Bros. Ent. v. The Global Asylum, Inc.* court held that any excusable artistic use must be related to the original mark itself.[79] As the court reasoned, every case in the *Rogers* universe to date had involved use of a mark that was related to the original mark itself, whether it was Fellini referring to Ginger to evoke the spirit of Ginger Rogers, or Rockstar Games drawing on the name of a real Los Angeles strip club in order to heighten the realism of their *Grand Theft Auto* game, which is set in the fictional, but LA-influenced, city of San Andreas.[80] Since the defendants in *Warner Bros. Ent. v. The Global Asylum, Inc.* had expressly disclaimed any link between their use of the term 'Hobbit' and author J. R. R. Tolkien's Hobbits, the court held that the defendants had effectively waived their claim of artistic relevance.[81]

Of course, with such an analysis, the latter court threatens to put defendants in a troubling 'Catch-22'. After all, a defendant will frequently claim that their use of an allegedly infringing term had an unrelated genesis and was not drawn from the allegedly infringed term. Such a tactic is used to avoid a finding of bad faith in the likelihood of confusion analysis that courts must conduct when determining if the plaintiff has made a *prima facie* case under the Lanham

Act and if the use is explicitly misleading and therefore ineligible for the *Rogers* safe harbour. Moreover, contrary to its holding on the artistic relevance issue, the court actually found that the defendants were trying to refer to Tolkien's Hobbits in several other parts of the decision in areas where such an attempt would factor *against* the defendants, rather than *for* them. Indeed, the court made much ado about the fact that, rather than just using the word 'Hobbit' in their title, the defendants also mimicked the distinctive gold, stylised and capitalised font of the plaintiff when they made use of the term 'Hobbit', thereby making the association with the plaintiff even more explicit. The court also noted that media coverage of *Age of the Hobbits* described the work as a 'reimagined version of J. R. R. Tolkien's mythical universe' and 'a fantasy tale inspired by J. R. R. Tolkien's *The Lord of the Rings*'.[82] With these facts in mind, the court held that the defendants' use was explicitly misleading and therefore not subject to the *Rogers* defence, even if it had been artistically relevant in the first place. All told, the *Warner Bros. Ent. v. The Global Asylum, Inc.* decision exemplifies the types of restrictions that courts may place on the *Rogers* defence – limitations that can effectively neutralise the defence despite its *de jure* availability.

At the same time, the *Rogers* test continues to evolve and, over time, could change in a manner that is not as protective of artistic expression. One court tried to limit *Rogers*' application by requiring a defendant asserting the defence to prove that the mark at issue is 'of such cultural significance that it has become an integral part of the public's vocabulary'.[83] Although other courts have declined this invitation to effectively limit the protections of *Rogers* to only uses of truly iconic brand names,[84] this example reveals the flexible nature of common law decision-making in this area and raises the concern that the free speech protections now available to film-makers may disappear in the future.

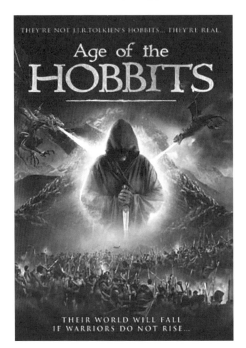

A more significant limitation on *Rogers* is that it only applies to non-commercial speech. According to some courts, once a work is deemed 'commercial', a court is no longer obligated to address a *Rogers* defence or any other First Amendment appeal.[85] Such a rule has profound consequences on the availability of the *Rogers* defence. Determining where the boundary between commercial and non-commercial speech falls is a task riddled with uncertainty. Those making movies can take comfort in various decisions holding that films, music videos, video games and books all constitute forms of non-commercial speech, even when they are obviously produced and sold to realise a profit. That said, this position is

Tolkien 'reimagined': *Age of the Hobbits* (2012) (Source: http://s0.discshop.se/img/front_large/110645/ age_of_the_hobbits_video_on_demand.jpg)

not black letter law – at least not yet. Several cases have contributed to the uncertain legal landscape by labelling the entertainment industry's unauthorised use of third-party intellectual property
in titles or content as 'commercial' in certain contexts from which it is difficult to divine a coherent
rule.[86] For example, use of the 'Dairy Queen' trademark in the title of the film *Dairy Queens* about
fictional beauty pageants in the Midwest was deemed 'commercial' by the court review and, therefore, ineligible for any First Amendment solicitude. As a result, New Line Cinema was forced to
change the film's title to *Drop Dead Gorgeous* prior to its release in 1999. Similarly, the use of Dr
Seuss's trademarks and copyrights in a book about the O. J. Simpson trial written in the style of
The Cat in the Hat was deemed 'commercial', thereby strengthening infringement claims that
resulted in the issuance of an injunction against the book's publication and distribution.[87]

Furthermore, the distinction between commercial and non-commercial speech as applied to
film may become more difficult to make as studios increasingly turn to product placement and
merchandising tie-ins to maximise revenue. At some point, a motion picture crosses the line from
'film' to 'advertisement'. At that point, courts appear willing to let First Amendment interests
recede. On this front, the decision *Facenda v. NFL. Films, Inc.*[88] is instructive in that it expressly denied
a *Rogers* defence for the National Football League when it used, without authorisation, the voice
of legendary sports announcer John Facenda in its twenty-two-minute film *The Making of Madden
NFL 06*.[89] Facenda is, of course, the legendary 'Voice of God' from NFL Films fame. Shortly before
his death, Facenda had provided the NFL with a broad release allowing them to exploit his audio
recordings in any way, so long as the use does not 'constitute an endorsement or sponsorship of
any product or service'.[90] Facenda's estate raised a trademark claim for false endorsement, contending that fans hearing his voice on the film would assume that he had lent his approval to the
film and the video game it was describing, *Madden NFL* (1988–). The NFL maintained that its periodic use of Facenda's voice represented an artistic choice for a documentary film, not an effort to
confuse consumers as to endorsement or sponsorship.[91] The court rejected this argument,
explaining that the NFL's 'economic motivation' rendered the film commercial speech.[92] Because
no one in the film had anything negative to say about the video game (i.e., in the style of a hagiog-
raphy, it served as an unabashed celebration of the work and its making), the court did not believe
the film had a 'documentary purpose'[93] and, in the end, concluded it was only meant to serve as
an advertisement for the Madden video game.[94] As a result, the promotional use was commercial
and the NFL could not take advantage of the *Rogers* defence.[95]

The *Facenda* case also flags two other potentially noteworthy limitations to the *Rogers*
defence. First, *Facenda* casts some doubt about the extension of *Rogers* to protect trademark
uses in artistic *content*, rather than just artistic *titling*. Although the *Facenda v. NFL. Films, Inc.*
court admitted that the *Rogers* test had been expressly adopted by four circuits,[96] it took pains
to point out that only two circuit court decisions had actually applied the test to immunise anything more than the title of an artistic work.[97] And, in one of those decisions, a dissenting opinion refused to apply *Rogers* precisely because it was being extended from its original scope
(titles) to a broader application (content).[98] Admittedly, since *Facenda v. NFL. Films, Inc.*, that
number has increased.[99] Yet it is correct that the vast majority of *Rogers*-related cases – like the
Rogers case itself – have involved the use of trademarks in titles rather than in the underlying
content itself.[100] The continued expansion of *Rogers* to cover underlying content therefore
remains probable but nevertheless uncertain.

Second, and more broadly, *Facenda v. NFL. Films, Inc.* demonstrates that the *Rogers* test itself has not (yet?) earned acceptance across all US courts. The *Facenda* decision acknowledged that the defence had been adopted, at the time, by four federal circuit courts (including the influential Second and Ninth Circuits).[101] Yet that fact did not prevent the Third Circuit from expressing scepticism about the defence and declining to adopt it in the case presented.[102] Given the reality of national (if not international) distribution of entertainment content and the risks of favourable forum shopping by trademark-holding plaintiffs, the absence of universal adoption of the *Rogers* defence can create the spectre of liability in less protective jurisdictions and can implicate content decisions by creators and distributors of film.

Conclusion

Over the past quarter-century, the legal approach to balancing trademark rights with freedom of artistic expression has undergone a seismic shift. Films are now considered forms of art fully within the scope of First Amendment protection and courts have adopted a mechanism for reconciling the property interests of trademark holders with the expressive interests of film-makers (and other creative actors) in a way that often tilts in the latter's favour. Fellini's film enjoyed only a middling critical reception, but it ushered in a new legal paradigm for those who use trademarks to create new expression. It is important to recognise, however, that not everyone whom this film-maker-friendly trend in the law is meant to protect can effectively harness it. Major studios with significant resources can take advantage of the *Rogers* test and subsequent generous judicial glosses on its 'artistically relevant' and 'explicitly misleading' terms. But smaller film-makers may feel the need to capitulate to the claims of trademark holders rather than investing in expensive and uncertain legal proceedings. In addition, changes to the film industry, including greater use of product placement and an increased focus on building and monetising 'brands' spawned by successful movie franchises, threaten the vitality of the current balance between film-making and trademark law. As the line between cinematic artistry and advertising continues to dissolve, and business models and incentives continue to change, the law in this area will not stand still. Just like future film-makers, future courts will need to innovate.

Notes

1. Eriq Gardner, 'Hollywood's IP Wars: Inside the Fight Over Trademarks', *Hollywood Reporter*, 21 November 2012, http://www.hollywoodreporter.com/thr-esq/denzel-washingtons-flight-parent-hood-inside-393168. In an emblematic sign of the times, intellectual property attorney Charles Colman has actually sought trademark protection for the term 'trademarklawpocalypse'. See TRADEMARKLAWPOCALPYSE Application, United States Patent and Trademark Office, Serial No. 85765482, 28 October 2012 (pending intent-to-use trademark application).

2. See *Faulkner Literary Rights, LLC v. Sony Classic Pictures, Inc.*, 12CV100-M-A (N.D. Miss., 25 October 2012). The suit also included claims for copyright infringement.

3. *Dallas Cowboys Cheerleaders, Inc. v. Pussycat Cinema, Ltd.*, 604 F.2d 200, 203 (2d Cir. 1979).

4. Ibid., 206.

5. *Rogers v. Grimaldi*, 875 F.2d 994, 997 (2d Cir. 1989).

6. Ibid., 1005.

7. Ibid., 1000.

8. *Louis Vuitton Malletier S.A. v. Warner Bros. Entertainment Inc.*, 868 F. Supp. 2d 172 (SDNY 2012).

9. *Dallas Cowboys Cheerleaders, Inc. v. Pussycat Cinema, Ltd.*, 604 F.2d 200.

10. *Louis Vuitton Malletier S.A. v. Warner Bros. Entertainment Inc.*, 868 F. Supp. 2d 172.

11. 5 USC § 1125.

12. *Lloyd Corp. v. Tanner*, 407 US 551 (1972).

13. Ibid.

14. Ibid., 566–7.

15. *Mut. of Omaha Ins. Co. v. Novak*, 836 F.2d 397, 398 (8th Cir. 1987); *Dallas Cowboys Cheerleaders, Inc. v. Pussycat Cinema, Ltd.*, 604 F.2d 200, 206.

16. *Dallas Cowboys Cheerleaders, Inc. v. Scoreboard Posters, Inc.*, 600 F.2d 1184, 1186 (5th Cir. 1979); Bill Curry, 'Something Else to Cheer About in Dallas: The Big Business of Being a Sidelines Star', *Washington Post*, 17 January 1979, E1.

17. James Ward Lee, 'Legends in Their Own Time: The Dallas Cowboy Cheerleaders', in Francis Edwards Abernethy (ed.), *Legendary Ladies of Texas* (Austin: University of Texas Press, 1994), p. 198.

18. Curry, 'Something Else to Cheer About in Dallas', E1.

19. Linda Williams, *Hard Core: Power, Pleasure, and the 'Frenzy of the Visible'* (Berkeley: University of California Press, 1999), p. 170.

20. Gretchen Dykstra, 'The Times Square Business Improvement District and Its Role in Changing the Face of Times Square', in Robert P. McNamara (ed.), *Sex, Scams, and Street Life: The Sociology of New York City's Time Square* (Westport, CT: Praeger, 1995), p. 78.

21. Peter Bart, *Infamous Players: A Tale of Movies, the Mob (and Sex)* (New York: Weinstein Books, 2011), p. 91.

22. William H. Daly, 'Law Enforcement in Times Square, 1970s–1990s', in McNamara, *Sex, Scams, and Street Life*, p. 98.

23. Ibid., p. 99.

24. Lynne B. Sagalyn, *Times Square Roulette: Remaking The City Icon* (Cambridge, MA: MIT Press, 2001), p. 172.

25. *Dallas Cowboys Cheerleaders, Inc. v. Pussycat Cinema, Ltd.*, 604 F.2d 206.

26. See *Near v. Minnesota*, 283 US 697, 706 (1931) (deeming that prior restraints are presumptively invalid and heavily disfavoured under First Amendment analysis).

27. *Dallas Cowboys Cheerleaders, Inc. v. Pussycat Cinema, Ltd.*, 604 F.2d 206.

28. It is worth noting that 1989 is not a bright-line date. There were philosophically similar decisions prior to *Rogers v. Grimaldi*, such as the *L.L. Bean* case decided two years earlier. In *L.L. Bean, Inc. v. Drake Publishers, Inc.*, the court rejected trademark dilution claims brought by the outdoor catalogue giant against an adult magazine for its unauthorised use of the L.L. Bean mark in a ribald mock-catalogue. See *L.L. Bean, Inc. v. Drake Publishers, Inc.*, 811 F.2d 26, 32 (1st Cir. 1987) ('It offends the Constitution . . . to invoke the [Maine] anti-dilution statute as a basis for enjoining the noncommercial use of a trademark by a defendant engaged in a protected form of expression'). That said, no case providing First Amendment defences for content creators facing claims of trademark infringement has had the widespread impact of *Rogers v. Grimaldi*.

29. Mark A. Lemley and Eugene Volokh, 'Freedom of Speech and Injunctions in Intellectual Property Cases', *Duke Law Journal* vol. 48 no. 2 (1998): 210.

30. For this view, see Pamela J. Bettis and Natalie Guice Adams, 'Short Skirts and Breast Juts: Cheerleading, Eroticism, and Schools', *Sex Education: Sexuality, Society, and Learning* vol. 6 no. 2 (2006): 123.

31. *Edgar Rice Burroughs, Inc. v. Manns Theatres*, 195 USPQ 159 (C.D. Cal. 1976).

32. *Am. Dairy Queen Corp. v. New Line Prods., Inc.*, 35 F. Supp. 2d 727, 734 (D. Minn. 1998).

33. *Cohen v. California*, 403 US 15, 16–17 (1971).

34. Ibid., 26.

35. *McGraw-Edison Co. v. Walter Disney Prods.*, 787 F.2d 1163 (7th Cir. 1986).

36. Hollis Alpert, *Fellini: A Life* (New York: Atheneum, 1986), p. 298.

37. Millicent Marcus, *After Fellini: National Cinema in the Postmodern Age* (Baltimore, MD: Johns Hopkins University Press, 2002), p. 184.

38. Vincent Canby, 'Fellini's "Ginger and Fred"', *The New York Times*, 28 March 1986, C8.

39. John Baxter, *Fellini* (London: Fourth Estate, 1993), p. 346; Ginger Rogers, *Ginger: My Story* (New York: HarperCollins, 1991), p. 414.

40. Alpert, *Fellini*, p. 300.

41. Baxter, *Fellini*, p. 346.

42. *Rogers v. Grimaldi*, 875 F.3d 999.

43. Ibid.

44. Ibid., 997–1001.

45. Ibid., 999.

46. Ibid., 1001.

47. Ibid., 1001n8.

48. Ibid., 1001.

49. Ibid.

50. Ibid.

51. Ibid.

52. Ibid.

53. Ibid.

54. Ibid.

55. *E.S.S. Entm't 2000, Inc. v. Rock Star Videos, Inc.*, 547 F.3d 1095 (9th Cir. 2008).

56. Ibid., 1099.

57. *Roxbury Entm't v. Penthouse Media Grp., Inc.*, 669 F. Supp. 2d 1170, 1176 (C.D. Cal. 2009). See also *Parks v. LaFace Records*, 329 F.3d 437, 454 (6th Cir. 2003), adopting the *Rogers* defence but reversing and remanding to the District Court on the question of whether the use of Rosa Parks's name had any artistic relevance to the song 'Rosa Parks' from hip-hop group OutKast, which was at issue in the suit.

58. See, for example, *E.S.S. Entm't 2000, Inc. v. Rock Star Videos, Inc.*, 547 F.3d 1095, 1099; *Roxbury Entm't v. Penthouse Media Grp., Inc.*, 669 F. Supp. 2d 1170, 1175–6; *Lucasfilm Ltd. v. Media Mkt. Group, Ltd.*, 182 F. Supp. 2d 897, 900–1 (N.D. Cal. 2002).

59. For example, *Westchester Media v. PRL USA Holdings, Inc.*, 214 F.3d 658, 664–5 (5th Cir. 2011); *Twin Peaks Prods., Inc. v. Publ'ns Int'l, Ltd.*, 996 F.2d 1366, 1379 (2d Cir. 1993).

60. See, for example, *Mattel, Inc. v. MCA Records, Inc.*, 296 F.3d 894, 899–902 (9th Cir. 2002); *Club Mediterranee, S.A. v. Fox Searchlight Pictures, Inc.*, No. 04-20273-CIV-MARTINEZ, 2004 US Dist.

LEXIS 3543, 9–11; *Volkswagen AG v. Dorling Kindersley Publ'g, Inc.*, 614 F. Supp. 2d 793, 801–2, 810 (E.D. Mich. 2009).

61. Lisa P. Ramsey, 'Increasing First Amendment Scrutiny of Trademark Law', *Southern Methodist University Law Review* vol. 61 (2008): 385.

62. *Henley v. DeVore*, 733 F. Supp. 2d 1144 (C.D. Cal. 2010).

63. See *Writmill v. Warner Bros. Ent. Inc.*, 4:11-cv-00752 (E.D. Mo. 2001).

64. Matthew Belloni, 'Warner Bros. Settles "Hangover II" Tattoo Lawsuit (Exclusive)', *The Hollywood Reporter*, 20 June 2011, accessed 14 November 2014, http://www.hollywoodreporter.com/thr-esq/warner-bros-settles-hangover-ii-203377

65. *Louis Vuitton Malletier S.A. v. Warner Bros. Entertainment Inc.*, 868 F. Supp. 2d 172.

66. Ibid., 178 (citing *Rogers v. Grimaldi*, 875 F.2d 999) (original emphasis).

67. In *Dallas Cowboys Cheerleaders, Inc. v. Pussycat Cinema, Ltd.*, the Second Circuit recognised that the plaintiff's claim did not necessarily require a finding of consumer confusion as to the origin of the film; confusion as to the plaintiff's sponsorship or approval of the trademark use alone sufficed for a cognisable Lanham Act violation.

68. *Louis Vuitton Malletier S.A. v. Warner Bros. Entertainment Inc.*, 868 F. Supp. 2d 172, 180 (describing *Dallas Cowboys Cheerleaders, Inc. v. Pussycat Cinema, Ltd.* as 'a decision whose First Amendment approach *Rogers* expressly declined to follow and which has been criticised by other courts').

69. Ibid., 181.

70. Ibid. 182 (citing *Twin Peaks Prods., Inc. v. Publ'ns Int'l, Ltd.*, 996 F.2d 1366, 1379), emphasis added by court.

71. Ibid., 184.

72. *Hart v. Elec. Arts, Inc.*, No. 3-09-cv-05990, 22–3 (3d Cir., 21 May 2013). See also *Facenda v. N.F.L. Films, Inc.*, 542 F.3d 1007, 1018 (3d Cir. 2008).

73. *Mattel, Inc. v. MCA Records, Inc.*, 296 F.3d 894, 902.

74. Eriq Gardner, 'Judge Blocks Release of "Age of the Hobbits" Movie'. *The Hollywood Reporter*, 10 December 2012, accessed 14 November 2014, http://www.hollywoodreporter.com/thr-esq/judge-blocks-release-age-hobbits-400062

75. *Warner Bros. Ent. v. The Global Asylum, Inc.*, No. CV 12-9574 PSG (CWx), 2012 WL 6951315 (C. D. Cal., Dec. 10, 2012).

76. The court also stated that, besides showing that the allegedly infringing use had artistic relevance and was explicitly misleading, a defendant also needed to demonstrate that the mark in question had obtained a widespread meaning beyond its source-identifying function. Ibid., 17 [asterisk in original]. Otherwise, reasoned the court, access to the verbiage making up the mark did not impact a legitimate First Amendment right. Ibid. Here, the court found that the defendants had barely demonstrated that the word 'Hobbit' had a non-source-identifying function among some consumers. Ibid. Although the use of this factor as part of the *Rogers v. Grimaldi* test did not hurt the defendants in this particular case, ibid., it established another hurdle for reliance on the defence going forward – at least in the Ninth Circuit. Ibid.

77. Ibid., *16.

78. Ibid., *15.

79. Ibid., *16.

80. Ibid.

81. Ibid., *17.

82. Ibid., *13. Though the court admits that 'there is no evidence on the record that Asylum itself was responsible for disseminating these statements, Asylum has also presented no evidence that it made any effort to correct the misrepresentations about the film or disassociate itself from Plaintiffs' works – at least not until Plaintiffs threatened legal action against it if it failed to take such steps'.

83. *Rebelution, LLC v. Perez*, 732 F. Supp. 2d 883, 887–8 (N.D. Cal. 2010).

84. *Winchester Mystery House, LLC v. Global Asylum, Inc.*, 210 Cal. App. 4th 579 (2012).

85. *Facenda v. N.F.L. Films, Inc.*, 542 F.3d 1007, 1016–18.

86. Ramsey, 'Increasing First Amendment Scrutiny of Trademark Law': 397–8.

87. *Dr. Seuss Enters., L.P. v. Penguin Books USA, Inc.*, 109 F.3d 1394, 1402–6 (9th Cir. 1997); *Am. Dairy Queen Corp. v. New Line Prods., Inc.*, 35 F. Supp. 2d 727, 735.

88. *Facenda v. N.F.L. Films, Inc.*, 542 F.3d 1007.

89 Ibid., 1018.

90. Ibid., 1019, quoting release language.

91. Ibid., 1016.

92. Ibid., 1017.

93. Ibid., 1018.

94. Ibid., 1017.

95. Ibid., 1016, 1018. See also *Dillinger, LLC v. Elec. Arts, Inc.*, 2011 WL 2457678, *4 n.1 (S.D. Ind. 16 June 2011) (describing the *Rogers v. Grimaldi* test as interrogating 'intentional use of another's intellectual property for commercial profit'); *Louis Vuitton Malletier, S.A. v. Hyundai Motor America*, 2012 WL 1022247 (SDNY 22 March 2012) (failing to even consider a *Rogers* defence in granting summary judgment to Louis Vuitton on claims of trademark dilution for car manufacturer Hyundai's one-second shot of a basketball with a pattern suggestive of Louis Vuitton's monogram in a Super Bowl advertisement).

96. Ibid., 1015. This number has increased since the ruling. See, for example, *Univ. of Alabama Bd. of Trustees v. New Life Art, Inc.*, 683 F.3d 1266, 1276–7 (11th Cir. 2012) (adopting the *Rogers* defence in the Eleventh Circuit).

97. Ibid., 1016 (citing *Cliffs Notes, Inc. v. Bantam Doubleday Dell Publ'g Group*, 886 F.2d 490, 495 (2d Cir. 1989)); *ETW Corp. v. Jireh Publ'g, Inc.*, 332 F.3d 915, 936–7 (6th Cir. 2003). As the *Cliffs Notes, Inc. v. Bantam Doubleday Dell Publ'g Group* court held, '[T]he *Rogers* balancing approach is generally applicable to Lanham claims against works of artistic expression.'

98. *ETW Corp. v. Jireh Publ'g, Inc.*, 332 F.3d 943–9 (Clay, J., dissenting).

99. See, for example, *E.S.S. Entm't 2000, Inc. v. Rock Star Videos, Inc.*, 547 F.3d 1099.

100. See, for example, *Rogers v. Grimaldi*, 875 F.2d 994 (movie title); *Mattel, Inc. v. Walking Mountain Prods.*, 353 F.3d 792 (9th Cir. 2003) (photograph name and the body of the work), *Parks v. LaFace Records*, 329 F.3d 437, 453 (song title); *Westchester Media v. PRL USA Holdings, Inc.*, 214 F.3d 658, 668 (magazine name).

101. *Facenda v. N.F.L. Films, Inc.*, 542 F.3d 1015.

103. Ibid., 1018 ('Because we hold that "The Making of Madden NFL 06" is commercial speech rather than artistic expression, we need not reach the issue whether our Court will adopt the *Rogers* test. We acknowledge that commercial speech does receive some First Amendment protection… Yet the Lanham Act customarily avoids violating the First Amendment, in part by enforcing a

trademark only when consumers are likely to be misled or confused by the alleged infringer's use') (internal citations omitted).

References

15 USC § 1125.

Alpert, Hollis, *Fellini: A Life* (New York: Atheneum, 1986).

Am. Dairy Queen Corp. v. New Line Prods., Inc., 35 F. Supp. 2d 727 (D. Minn. 1998).

Bart, Peter, *Infamous Players: A Tale of Movies, the Mob (and Sex)* (New York: Weinstein Books, 2011).

Baxter, John, *Fellini* (London: Fourth Estate, 1993).

Bettis, Pamela J. and Natalie Guice Adams, 'Short Skirts and Breast Juts: Cheerleading, Eroticism, and Schools', *Sex Education: Sexuality, Society, and Learning* vol. 6 no. 2 (2006): 121–33.

Cliffs Notes, Inc. v. Bantam Doubleday Dell Publ'g Group, 886 F.2d 490 (2d Cir. 1989).

Club Mediterranee, S.A. v. Fox Searchlight Pictures, Inc., No. 04-20273-CIV-MARTINEZ, 2004 US Dist. LEXIS 3543, 9–11.

Cohen v. California, 403 US 15 (1971).

Dallas Cowboys Cheerleaders, Inc. v. Pussycat Cinema, Ltd., 604 F.2d 200 (2d Cir. 1979).

Daly, William H., 'Law Enforcement in Times Square, 1970s–1990', in Robert P. McNamara (ed.), *Sex, Scams, and Street Life: The Sociology of New York City's Time Square* (Westport, CT: Praeger, 1995), pp. 97–106.

Dillinger, LLC v. Elec. Arts, Inc., 2011 WL 2457678, *4 n.1 (S.D. Ind. 16 June 2011).

Dr. Seuss Enters., L.P. v. Penguin Books USA, Inc., 109 F.3d 1394 (9th Cir. 1997).

Dykstra, Gretchen, 'The Times Square Business Improvement District and Its Role in Changing the Face of Times Square', in Robert P. McNamara (ed.), *Sex, Scams, and Street Life: The Sociology of New York City's Time Square* (Westport, CT: Praeger, 1995), pp. 75–82.

Edgar Rice Burroughs, Inc. v. Manns Theatres, 195 USPQ 159 (C.D. Cal. 1976).

E.S.S. Entm't 2000, Inc. v. Rock Star Videos, Inc., 547 F.3d 1095 (9th Cir. 2008).

ETW Corp. v. Jireh Publ'g, Inc., 332 F.3d 915, 936-37 (6th Cir. 2003).

Facenda v. NFL Films, Inc., 542 F.3d 1007 (3d Cir. 2008).

Faulkner Literary Rights, LLC v. Sony Classic Pictures, Inc., 12CV100-M-A (N.D. Miss., 25 October 2012).

Hart v. Elec. Arts, Inc., No. 3-09-cv-05990, 22–3 (3d Cir., 21 May 2013).

Henley v. DeVore, 733 F. Supp. 2d 1144 (C.D. Cal. 2010).

Lee, James Ward, 'Legends in Their Own Time: The Dallas Cowboy Cheerleaders', in Francis Edwards Abernethy (ed.), *Legendary Ladies of Texas* (Austin: University of Texas Press, 1994), pp. 195–202.

Lemley, Mark A. and Eugene Volokh, 'Freedom of Speech and Injunctions in Intellectual Property Cases', *Duke Law Journal* vol. 48 no. 2 (1998): 147–242.

L.L. Bean, Inc. v. Drake Publishers, Inc., 811 F.2d 26 (1st Cir. 1987).

Louis Vuitton Malletier, S.A. v. Hyundai Motor America, 2012 WL 1022247 (SDNY 22 March 2012).

Louis Vuitton Malletier S.A. v. Warner Bros. Entertainment Inc., 868 F. Supp. 2d 172 (SDNY 2012).

Lucasfilm Ltd. v. Media Mkt. Group, Ltd., 182 F. Supp. 2d 897 (N.D. Cal. 2002).

Marcus, Millicent, *After Fellini: National Cinema in the Postmodern Age* (Baltimore, MD: Johns Hopkins University Press, 2002).

Mattel, Inc. v. MCA Records, Inc., 296 F.3d 894 (9th Cir. 2002).

Mattel, Inc. v. Walking Mountain Prods., 353 F.3d 792 (9th Cir. 2003).

McGraw-Edison Co. v. Walter Disney Prods., 787 F.2d 1163 (7th Cir. 1986).

Mut. of Omaha Ins. Co. v. Novak, 836 F.2d 397 (8th Cir. 1987).

Near v. Minnesota, 283 US 697 (1931).

Parks v. LaFace Records, 329 F.3d 437 (6th Cir. 2003).

Ramsey, Lisa P., 'Increasing First Amendment Scrutiny of Trademark Law', *Southern Methodist University Law Review* vol. 61 (2008): 381–458.

Rebelution, LLC v. Perez, 732 F. Supp. 2d 883 (N.D. Cal. 2010).

Rogers, Ginger, *Ginger: My Story* (New York: HarperCollins, 1991).

Rogers v. Grimaldi, 875 F.2d 994 (2d Cir. 1989).

Roxbury Entm't v. Penthouse Media Grp., Inc., 669 F. Supp. 2d 1170 (C.D. Cal. 2009).

Sagalyn, Lynne B., *Times Square Roulette: Remaking The City Icon* (Cambridge, MA: MIT Press, 2001).

Twin Peaks Prods., Inc. v. Publ'ns Int'l, Ltd., 996 F.2d 1366 (2d Cir. 1993).

Univ. of Alabama Bd. of Trustees v. New Life Art, Inc., 683 F.3d 1266 (11th Cir. 2012).

Volkswagen AG v. Dorling Kindersley Publ'g, Inc., 614 F. Supp. 2d 793 (E.D. Mich. 2009).

Warner Bros. Ent. v. The Global Asylum, Inc., No. CV 12-9574 PSG (CWx), 2012 WL 6951315 (C. D. Cal., 10 December 2012).

Westchester Media v. PRL USA Holdings, Inc., 214 F.3d 658 (5th Cir. 2011).

Williams, Linda, *Hard Core: Power, Pleasure, and the 'Frenzy of the Visible'* (Berkeley: University of California Press, 1999).

Winchester Mystery House, LLC v. Global Asylum, Inc., 210 Cal. App. 4th 579 (2012).

Writmill v. Warner Bros. Ent. Inc., 4:11-cv-00752 (E.D. Mo. 2001).

3 PIRACY AND THE SHADOW HISTORY OF HOLLYWOOD

PAUL McDONALD

With the consumer videocassette market still in its infancy, on Sunday, 25 February 1979 CBS-TV's newsmagazine show *60 Minutes* broadcast a feature on video piracy titled 'Who Stole Superman?' Speaking to presenter Harry Reasoner, Jack Valenti, president (1966–2004) of the Motion Picture Association of America (MPAA) – the industry trade association representing the collective interests of the Hollywood entertainment corporations – proclaimed:

> Piracy, as it is now and as it could be in the future, is a cancer in the belly of the film business. … it is there, it is rampant, and unless we can get a hold of it, alongside the police forces of the world, it can cause serious injury to the body and soul of the movie business.[1]

It would not be the last time that Valenti, described by William Patry as the 'master of moral panics',[2] resorted to such emotive language to communicate his vehement objection to video piracy. In the early 1980s, as voices in Hollywood raised fears over the reproductive function of the consumer videocassette recorder (VCR), Valenti testified to the House of Representatives, famously saying 'the VCR is to the American film producer and the American public as the Boston strangler is to the woman home alone'.[3]

Comparing the impact of piracy on the movie business to cancer or a convicted serial killer, Valenti struck choice corporeal, somatic metaphors, anthropomorphising the movie industry as a living and vulnerable being – the body Hollywood – an organism attacked both internally and externally by malignant or malevolent forces. Combating piracy has been, and will continue to be, high on Hollywood's agenda, for behind the show of show business, fundamentally, Hollywood is a business based on monetising the exclusive rights to use, reproduce, disseminate, adapt and present symbolic products. Although over time Hollywood has transformed from a film industry to a multiple media business, throughout it has always remained an intellectual property (IP) industry. Piracy is therefore regarded by the industry as a serious threat, for it strikes at the very foundations of what Hollywood is.

To justify the fight against piracy, Hollywood has broadly adopted two lines of argument: one moral, the other economic. Appealing to the conscience of the media-consuming public, anti-piracy advertising represents piracy as theft and therefore a crime.[4] Making the case to policy-makers for the necessity of strong copyright protection, Hollywood emphasises piracy has economic impacts reaching beyond the film and television industries to the US economy more generally. The core economic complaint is that piracy substitutes for legitimate sales, resulting in loss of jobs, earnings and tax income.[5] Further lines of argument allege connections between film piracy and organised crime or terrorism.[6]

It is for these reasons that piracy has consistently proved to be one issue where Hollywood corporations have repeatedly spoken with a joint voice through the trade associations representing their collective interests – the Motion Picture Producers and Distributors of America (MPPDA) (1922–45), the MPAA (1945–) and their international subsidiary divisions, the Motion Picture Export Association (MPEA) (1945–94) and Motion Picture Association (MPA) (1994–). Alongside rating films for public exhibition, today the modern MPAA identifies 'content protection' as its other major function, 'work[ing] with governments around the world to pursue commonsense solutions that advance innovative consumer choices, while protecting the rights of all who make something of value with their minds, their passion and their unique creative vision'.[7] Consequently, the MPAA has assiduously lobbied Washington and overseas governments to ensure current standards of legislation and enforcement create a trading environment favourable to protecting Hollywood's properties across international markets.

In the context of intellectual property, 'piracy' operates as a highly suggestive synonym for the far more prosaic legal language of 'infringement', a catch-all term for '[r]eproducing, distributing, publicly displaying, publicly performing, or producing a derivative version of a copyrighted work without the copyright holder's permission'.[8] For the entertainment industries, deploying the evocative language of 'pirates' and 'piracy' serves rhetorical and strategic purposes, making the rather obtuse workings of copyright infringement immediately intelligible to the lay public by setting off a chain of associations dating back to antiquity when sea-faring pirates represented 'irritants to the civilized order itself' and were 'enemies to humankind in general'.[9]

This uncivilised otherness is also reflected in film historiography, which has consistently focused on the legitimate, 'overground' industry and cultural sphere of moving images. Piracy is invisible or at least marginal to film history, yet, since the very earliest years, the American film industry has been littered with incidents of producers or distributors alleging the works in which they claim ownership have been infringed. Although consigned to the historiographic margins, acts of infringement have endured as an endemic force in the commerce and culture of Hollywood. This is, perhaps, understandable as the commodity form of film rests on a fundamental paradox. As vehicles for commercial public entertainment, films can only reap economic rewards if they are publicly accessible. At the same time, it is only possible to place economic value against that availability if mechanisms of exclusion are used to create artificial scarcity. Consequently the business of moving images is forever locked into the dialectic of access and exclusion.

Matters of copyright were covered earlier, in Chapter 1, but dedicating additional space to piracy is necessary for a series of reasons. Media piracy is more than a matter of copyright, for, as the following discussion shows, frequently Hollywood's struggle against the unauthorised uses of moving images has involved legal actions outside the domain of intellectual property, including indictments for incidents of larceny, fraud, conspiracy, or violating restrictions on the interstate transportation of stolen property. Second, through exploring piracy, the various practical measures taken by Hollywood to actively police and control copyright become evident. On a related point, examining how Hollywood has attempted to prevent infringement demonstrates how piracy is more than a legal issue, for the protection of rights extends beyond the enactment of legislation, judicial proceedings and enforcement actions, to bring the law into interactions and clashes with technological innovation, industrial organisation, the operations of media markets, entrepreneurial opportunism and the practices of media consumers. Finally, engaging with this sphere of illegal commerce and culture necessitates uncovering a history beyond the legally authorised realm of moving image production, circulation and consumption that has traditionally preoccupied film historiography. Piracy provides the prism through which to chart an alternative history of Hollywood, a 'shadow history' of Hollywood.[10]

While in a sense hidden, this is a history that has always asserted its presence by its collisions with the 'legitimate' sphere of film culture. Focusing on print piracy, this chapter initially looks at how pirate entrepreneurship fulfilled booming demand in the emergent film industry, and established numerous practices for the unauthorised acquisition, use, copying and presentation of moving images. It outlines how illegal trade dispersed the geographic extensity of film piracy and how, in response, the US film business organised to combat piracy. These dynamics are brought together in a case study examining the 1975 trial of Budget Films, when criminal charges were brought for the first time in the USA against individuals for film and television piracy. A third section is concerned with the ways in which the introduction of the videocassette recorder in the late 1970s, and its popularisation in the 1980s, transformed the market and scale of commercial piracy. Video CD and DVD marked the transition from analogue to digital media piracy, but the rise of networked communications and cultures intensified challenges to copyright protection. Hollywood found new pirate enemies in the online universe, targeting legal actions against hackers of video encryption technologies, providers and users of file-sharing networks and file-hosting services. Situated in this context, a second case study focuses on how support for legislative change with the Protect IP Act and Stop Online Piracy Act positioned the 'old' media of Hollywood entertainment in conflict with the 'new' networked media economy represented by key players from the internet and technology community of Silicon Valley. Tracing these encounters between Hollywood and piracy, the chapter tracks the industry's efforts to control the access/exclusion dialectic. To close, the chapter offers some concluding reflections on the implications and challenges which piracy brings to writing not only the historiography of Hollywood, but also that of media more generally.

Proto-piracy and the Formation of the American Film Industry

From its earliest years, the growth of the American film business was accompanied by multiple practices for the unauthorised sale, copying, remaking or display of moving images. With the emergent industry operating a business based on direct sales of prints to exhibitors, opportunities for the theft and illicit sale of prints were possible throughout the supply chain.[11] As the industry moved from sales to a rental distribution system, the availability of prints in the market receded, but this did little to halt print theft or other forms of unsanctioned use. Regardless of whether a print was stolen or legitimately purchased, it could be used as a positive master for *duping*, the practice of reproducing prints without the permission of, and remuneration to, the copyright owner. For a business based on mass reproduction, duping was probably inevitable, but for the growing industry, it was also a necessity. As nickelodeons fed the booming public appetite for moving image entertainment, in the period 1908–13 the practice of 'daily change' dominated, with exhibitors needing fresh films and prints in sufficient volume to present a new show every day.[12] To operate this system, some exhibitors were prepared to turn to both authorised and unauthorised sources to obtain the prints they needed.

Exhibitor and consumer demand not only strained the supply of prints but also the supply of original ideas. Consequently, unauthorised copying was also practised in a second way, with producers remaking the films of their competitors without authorisation. In the emergent American film industry, unauthorised duping and remaking was not confined to an aberrant bunch of pirate 'outsiders'. Alongside producing their own original films, companies such as Edison and Lubin – firms who ostensibly represented the legitimate industry – duped and remade the products of their competitors (see Chapter 1). When reflecting on the importance of unauthorised reproduction for the industry in this period, Jane Gaines suggests 'copying was as much an industry practice as an industry problem',[13] and Peter Decherney argues 'the film industry had been built on duping'.[14] The industry wanted bigger audiences, those audiences wanted more films and illegal entrepreneurs were prepared to fill any gap between demand and supply. Acts of unauthorised duplication, circulation, adaptation and presentation therefore played a formative role in the overall making of the film business in the USA.

Other unauthorised deeds included *holdovers* and *bicycling*, practices that broke the obligations of exhibition contracts. Holdovers occurred where an exhibitor deceptively took advantage of the time taken for transporting prints in order to make additional presentations of a film beyond what had been agreed in the contract. Bicycling involved booking a print for one movie theatre but then ferrying it for presentation at other outlets not included in the rental agreement.[15] Together, print theft, duping, unauthorised adaptations, holdovers and bicycling variously represented forms of proto-piracy, foundational practices in the history of film infringement.

Illegal entrepreneurialism only partially explains the emergence of these practices. Proto-piracy thrived in a context where film did not enjoy secure copyright protection. For nearly two decades, the US legal system struggled to conceptualise the new medium of moving images under existing intellectual property legislation. In this context, the only copyright protection afforded films in the USA came through makeshift arrangements whereby moving images were registered as photographs with the Copyright Office of the Library of Congress. This arrangement did not, however, bring secure protection to films for two key reasons: uncertainties still remained over the status of photographs as protected works; and disputes arose concerning whether moving images should be considered an extension of photography – and therefore entitled to protection – or otherwise a whole new medium as yet not covered by copyright. This latter issue was resolved in 1903 when the decision in *Edison v. Lubin* granted the same protection to moving images as to other types of photography.[16] By regarding films as animated photographs, the decision offered some clarification over the protected status of film, but this did not halt duping; the practice was too widespread to prosecute every case and the embryonic industry remained dependent on the practice to meet the demands of exhibitors and audiences. Consequently, Decherney suggests the 'decision was the beginning and not the end of the process of defining and controlling film piracy'.[17]

Moving images continued to be a focus for legal dispute surrounding the unauthorised adaptation of books and stage plays as material for films. This matter reached a head in 1911 when the decision in the case of *Kalem Co. v. Harper Brothers* ruled film producers could be held liable for unauthorised adaptations (for a study of this case, see Chapter 1).[18] The following year, congressman Edward Townsend drove through an amendment to the Copyright Act of 1909 adding two categories of subject matter: photoplays of dramatic subject matters; and other forms of moving images based on factual material – for example, newsreels.[19] Only with the passing of the Townsend amendment did moving images finally become formally recognised as a distinct medium under US copyright legislation.

It is notable that the Townsend amendment came into effect during the very earliest years when the production centre of the American film business migrated westwards. Consequently, the formation of 'Hollywood' coincided with the accommodation of film into the culture of copyright and, as the industry matured, so copyright and Hollywood were intertwined. Proto-piracy thrived in a climate of necessity and, rather than impeding industrial development, acts of infringement helped supply the reels necessary for exhibitors to meet booming audience demand, playing a part in establishing the commerce and culture of film on which Hollywood came to be built.

Internationalising Illegal Trade and Anti-Piracy Organisation

For the American film industry, the protections afforded by the Townsend amendment could only reach so far. National statutes offer merely a partial barrier to infringement, for piracy practices never respect territorial borders. Rather, the extension of international markets for cultural goods is forever shadowed by the expansion of illegal trade. Formalising the status of film under US copyright law not only failed to halt the piracy of domestically produced films, but also had no authority to prevent the duping, remaking or theft of American films overseas.

In the years following World War I, growth in the international market for American-produced films amplified pressure on the access/exclusion dialectic for two reasons. First, the market dominance achieved by US suppliers in many overseas territories sustained and was sustained by the desire of audiences to see American movies. As that desire could be met by either legal or illegal supply, so the internationalisation of the film trade had the concomitant effect of stimulating the international piracy of Hollywood movies. Hollywood's supremacy certainly asserted control over legal markets, but, ironically, that dominance also ensured American movies became the most popular currency circulated through international film piracy. Britain, Germany, Italy, Turkey, Japan, India, Mexico, Palestine, Poland and Cuba were just a few of the territories alleged to be destinations or distribution points for the international traffic in illegal prints of American films.[20] Fundamental to international film piracy was the formation of transnational networks for receiving, duping and shipping illegal prints. One report from 1926 detailed how an investigation by a representative for the Pathé exchange in New York uncovered how prints legitimately rented in Vienna were then 'borrowed' by individuals in Warsaw to make copies for Poland and for exporting to the Baltic States, Bulgaria, Egypt, Greece, Iran, Romania, Russia and Turkey.[21] As this example indicates, illicit flows have been endemic to the history of media globalisation, creating the shifting terrain of what can be described as the geography of film piracy, the spatial dispersal of markets and networks for the unauthorised exchange of moving images.

A second challenge facing American films in the world market came from gaps and inconsistencies in copyright protection across international territories. Echoing the situation in the USA, among the leading film-producing nations in the emergent international industry, commercial exploitation of moving images was already into a second decade before copyright modernisation came to formally recognise films as a distinct category of protected work. In western European nations, for example, during the first decade of the twentieth century the protection of films had to draw analogies with photographs or dramatic works, although, even then, differences existed between nations as to whether photographs were afforded full, limited, or uncertain protection. Not until the 1910s and 20s did amendments to national statutes in Europe take the first steps towards granting protection for films as a distinct category of work.[22]

Efforts to internationally harmonise copyright protection had commenced in 1886 with the enactment of the Berne Convention for the Protection of Literary and Artistic Works, the multilateral treaty aimed at establishing minimum standards of copyright protection between signatory nations. According to Berne, contracting countries agreed to automatically grant the same terms and levels of copyright protection to works originating from other signatory countries as they would to works created by their own nationals. At the Berlin Conference in 1908, amendments to Articles 14(2) and 14(3) accorded protection to 'cinematographic productions' where treatment of the subject matter (i.e., 'the arrangement of the acting form or the combination of the incidents represented') gave the work a 'personal and original character', and to cinematographic reproductions of pre-existing 'literary, scientific and artistic' works. As these protections treated film as a form of dramatic work or a medium for adapting other categories of work, films were not added to the list of protected works under Article 2. This situation persisted through the amendments made at the Rome Conference in 1928 until the 1948 Brussels Conference approved the inclusion of cinematographic works in Article 2(1) without qualification.[23]

Initial membership of the Berne Union was almost entirely confined to western European nations, although by the mid-twentieth century over forty members had signed. The USA, however, abstained from Berne, for implementation of the Convention would have required significant change to US copyright law in the areas of moral rights and formal procedures of copyright registration and deposit. Copyright protection for American works in Latin American countries was covered under the Buenos Aires Convention in 1911, but by refusing to sign up to Berne, the USA otherwise opted out of the international intellectual property regime. In the case of films, this had the effect that any films imported to the USA from nations belonging to the Berne Union were not afforded copyright protection, while in return exports of American film to Berne nations were similarly treated. Just one example of the implications arising from this legislative gap was illustrated when the case against the aforementioned Warsaw pirates collapsed; the defence attorney argued the actions of his clients were entirely justified because of the failure by the USA to sign up to Berne.[24] Rather than join Berne, in 1955 the USA signed the Universal Copyright Convention (UCC), the rival multilateral IP treaty adopted by nations abstaining from Berne. Many parties to Berne also signed the UCC simply to secure protection in those other territories. Not until the Berne Implementation Act of 1988 did the USA join the Berne Union. By withholding for so long, the US government actually contributed to creating a leaky environment for copyright protection favourable to international film piracy, including the infringement of American movies abroad.

Faced by multiple infringing practices, it did not take long for the nascent American film industry to make its first moves towards collectively organising to combat piracy. Formed initially in 1916 to self-regulate the industry and avoid state censorship, the National Association of the Motion Picture Industry (NAMPI) three years later founded its Film Theft Committee, working with law enforcement authorities to stop domestic piracy and the international traffic in stolen prints. For example, a 1921 campaign aimed at halting shipments of prints to Asia recovered copies of Charlie Chaplin's *The Kid* (1921) and the Mary Pickford feature *Suds* (1920) stolen in New York and destined for shipping to Japan.[25] NAMPI was superseded in 1922 by the MPPDA, and in 1927 the new organisation established the Copyright Protection Bureau (CPB), appointing Jack H. Levin, who'd previously led the investigative unit of the New York Film Club, to head the Bureau.

By 1931, the CPB was operating nationally to detect and prevent piracy and fraudulent practices, including investigating incidents of duping, smuggling, bicycling and holdovers.[26] In 1940, it was reported the eight leading corporations in Hollywood were each spending $200,000 per annum to fund the CPB. From the central office in New York, the CPB ran a nationwide network of branches with a staff of between 1,500 and 3,000 investigators checking on fraudulent practices across a distribution system that, at the time, daily supplied 50,000 prints to 18,000 movie theatres. When tackling duping and smuggling, the CPB worked in collaboration with government agencies, including the FBI, Coast Guard and Customs officials. Levin saw the CPB as:

> necessary to a far-flung copyright industry such as the movies with its only source of income derived from its millions of license transaction annually. There will always be some small fringe of exhibitors tempted to chisel and the Copyright Bureau will not lack for work as long as the human race needs policing.[27]

For example, a 1936 investigation by the CPB uncovered a ring of exhibitors in San Diego booking films for their houses to then smuggle over the border and beat release dates in Mexico by four to eight months.[28]

After the MPPDA became the MPAA in 1945, the Bureau continued its work, and in 1975 the MPAA established the Film Security Office (FSO), staffed by former FBI agents William J. Nolan and Ewing G. Layhew.[29] Through the Federal Trade Commission (FTC), CBP and FSO, the American film industry mounted an organised response to piracy and, as such, these efforts should be seen as participants in what Adrian Johns has called the 'intellectual property defence industry'.[30]

Print Piracy and the Case of Budget Films

A single case from 1975 serves to illustrate how illegal entrepreneurism, the extended geography of film piracy and countervailing measures by the IP defence industry met in the print piracy era. In what was regarded as the first major crackdown on piracy by federal authorities in the USA, in September 1974 it was revealed a grand jury had been meeting in secret to lead a widespread international investigation into film and television piracy concentrating on film laboratories and other businesses in the Los Angeles area.[31] For nearly a year the FBI had been gathering evidence and agents were issued with search warrants to enter businesses and seize films. Among those targeted was the distributor Budget Films, whose business premises were raided in January 1975, leading to charges being brought against the company and its principal executives. *Budget* became a landmark case for it was the first time that criminal charges were brought against individuals for film and television piracy. Furthermore, the case became a show(biz) trial, as high-ranking studio executives and famous actors were called to give testimony for both the prosecution and defence.

Central to the case was the practical workings of the film print distribution system. Distribution contracts define the *who*, *where* and *when* of film releasing by specifying the parties authorised to handle releasing, in which territory and over what period of time. Producers strike distribution agreements with distributors to conduct the releasing of a film on their behalf and the distributor then pays for the reproduction of print copies. Distributors may self-distribute through their own operations or otherwise delegate that function to a sub-distributor for certain international markets. Prints are then made available to exhibitors for screening. Although each of these transactions may sometimes be termed 'sales', the fact remains that the print is only ever licensed and never sold outright to the sub-distributor or exhibitor. Sales is therefore a misnomer for what is actually a print *rental* business, for the print always remains the property of the main distributor, and is leased out on the expectation that it should be returned once the term of the rental agreement expires.

Budget was a legitimately licensed sub-distributor for some of the major Hollywood corporations, and, following the raid, the company's president Albert C. Drebin protested that 90 per cent of the films seized were legally handled through leasing contracts, with the remainder acquired over several years.[32] In the month following, the grand jury indicted Drebin and Budget for violating copyright on three Warner Bros. films, *Bonnie and Clyde* (1967), *Cool Hand Luke* (1967) and *The Great Race* (1965), plus Columbia's *On the Waterfront* (1954). The indictment said Budget did 'wilfully and for profit, vend, to wit, lease for profit, prints of said motion pictures, without authorization' of the rights holders.[33] These original charges were superseded in April when a new ten-count indictment was issued, additionally naming the company's vice president Lawrence S. Fine and salesman Bruce M. Venezia as assisting Drebin.

The new indictment set out in greater detail the grounds for alleging Budget was involved in infringing activity. Although Budget was in the legitimate film rental business, it was not authorised to sell prints. Evidence showed, though, that, from January 1971, Drebin had begun to operate a system whereby Budget became a 'front' for 'illegal activities' as he sold stolen original prints and illegal 16mm copies. Copies of *Paper Moon* (1973) were exchanged for $275 each and *The Take* (1974) went for $400.[34] Charges were made on ten counts: the first for conspiracy, the second to fourth for violating laws restricting interstate transportation of stolen property and the remainder for criminal copyright infringement.[35] When the grand jury concluded its investigation in May 1975, Drebin, Fine, Venezia and Budget represented just one of sixteen indictments returned against laboratories and distributors on charges of copyright violation, interstate transportation and foreign commerce in stolen property.

South Africa was identified as a crucial destination for Budget's unauthorised trade and the country was widely regarded as a trouble spot for piracy.[36] As part of the same FBI anti-piracy operation, Harry David Katz of Johannesburg was arrested after travelling from South Africa to the USA to buy films from Woodrow Wise, owner of the Hollywood Film Exchange. Katz was charged with conspiracy to 'knowingly transport into interstate and foreign commerce goods, wares and merchandise, i.e. pirated motion pictures, which are stolen, converted or taken by fraud, which have a value in excess of $5,000'.[37] Affidavits filed by the FBI claimed Katz was a primary source of pirated films to South Africa, where it was claimed as much as 90 per cent of the US films and programmes shown were illegal.

From the start of the decade, South Africa had been identified as a prime market for piracy, with an estimated forty individuals or organisations supplying exhibitors with illegal copies of films obtained from print overruns duplicated in US labs. Robert Howey, general manager for African Consolidated Films, the distribution division of the major South African distributor-exhibitor Kinekor, identified a cluster of reasons encouraging this illegal trade.

> Firstly, the removal of import duty on cinematograph films in the early '60s, facilitating imports; secondly, the ease with which infringing copies of films can be obtained; thirdly, the ease with which copies of films can be made in South Africa itself; and fourthly, the flaw in South African censorship laws which permits the screening of uncensored versions of films in certain circumstances.[38]

As South Africa was a signatory to the Berne Convention but not the UCC, the perception held that imported American films did not enjoy copyright protection in the territory, although US distributors took strategic steps to obtain protection in all Berne nations by releasing their films in at least one country covered by Berne simultaneously with a domestic opening. Furthermore, with the white minority government of the National Party delaying the introduction of television from fear the medium would undermine their control of broadcasting, a market was created for illegal 16mm prints to fill this vacuum in home entertainment.[39] As William J. Nolan, director of the MPAA's Film Security Office, noted, 'South Africa, until recently, has had no TV – films are a big thing, and the biggest supplier is the United States.'[40]

At the end of August 1975, when the *Budget* case went to trial in the US District Court in Los Angeles, Assistant US Attorney Chester Brown argued the defendants had not abided by the principle that prints are licensed and not sold, and so dealt in films which they knew were stolen or fraudulently obtained. Among the first witnesses to appear for the prosecution were Frank Wells, co-chairman of Warner Bros., Dennis C. Stanfill, president and board chairman of 20th Century-Fox, and Sam Arkoff, president of American International Pictures. All emphasised distributors leased but did not sell prints for theatrical exhibition.[41] Granted immunity from prosecution, a number of South African distributors, including Katz, were also called to testify they had obtained films or television programmes from Budget.[42]

Seeking to refute the government's case, defence attorney Gerald M. Singer tried to establish how prints were indeed sold to individuals for private film libraries. Ownership of private film libraries was an issue that had gained some public exposure earlier in the year, when, as part of the FBI's operation, agents had seized over 500 print or videocassette copies of films and television shows from the home of actor Roddy McDowall, including films in which he'd appeared, such as the *Planet of the Apes* series (1968, 1971, 1972 and 1973) and *Lassie Come Home* (1943). Evidence was found linking McDowall to buying from and selling to Raymond Joseph Atherton and his associate Roy Henry Wagner, both of whom were later named among the sixteen indictments returned by the grand jury. No criminal action was ever brought against

Con artists: Budget sold copies of *Paper Moon* (1973) when Paramount wouldn't (BFI)

McDowall but the issue of private collecting returned in the *Budget* trial. Singer questioned prosecution witness David Begelman, president of Columbia Pictures, asking if he knew of anyone who kept a large film library – with large defined as six films or more – in their home: Begelman denied any knowledge of anyone who did.[43] Leading actors Robert Young (who at the time was taking the lead in the television series *Marcus Welby, MD*) and Ryan O'Neal were also called by the prosecution to explain how, despite their status within the industry, they were unable to buy copies of the works they appeared in. O'Neal told how he'd legitimately asked Paramount for a private copy of *Paper Moon* to give to his daughter Tatum, winner of the Academy Award for Best Actress in a Support Role for her performance in the film. He told the court how although he owned 10 per cent of the film's gross revenues, he was still unable to get his hands on a copy.[44] When high-profile actors Rock Hudson and Gene Hackman were called as defence witnesses, however, Hudson talked about his private collection and Hackman described obtaining films on loan. Also testifying for the defence, Paul Frizler, an academic at Chapman College and the University of California at Irvine, explained how prints were donated to educational institutions.[45]

When the four-week trial concluded, a guilty verdict was passed on all ten counts.[46] Judge E. Avery Crary sentenced Drebin to three months in prison and a fine of $20,000, plus three years' probation, making him the first individual to be sentenced to serve time for piracy. Fine and Venezia were respectively fined $10,000 and $1,000 and placed on probation, while the company was fined $18,000.[47] At news of the convictions, Jack Valenti hailed the decision as a precedent-setting verdict: 'The film pirates may have had a run in the industry, but they are now on the run and will be until behind bars and put out of the filthy business of stealing and selling motion pictures.'[48] But Valenti spoke too soon. Print piracy simply moved further underground. More significantly, the convictions came just as new consumer technology was about to open up a fresh outlet for illegally reproduced copies that would see infringing activity grow exponentially.[49]

VCRs, Cassettes and Bringing Piracy Home

A moment of historical irony: two days before sentences were passed down in the *Budget* trial, celebrated as a landmark in Hollywood's fight against piracy, on 1 November 1975 Sony began marketing the LV-1901 in the USA, the first model of its Betamax videocassette recorder. Betamax was not the first home video system but it became the first to grow a large consumer base. At the press demonstration for the launch of Betamax in the USA, Harvey Schein, president of the Sony Corporation of America, dismissed any concerns over uses of the VCR as an instrument for copyright infringement, saying such uses were merely a 'minor problem … no more significant than with an audio cassette recorder'. Schein, however, seemingly unwittingly augured the future use of the VCR as a tool for infringement when he promoted the product by claiming 'We're selling a Xerox for television.'[50]

Reconfiguring the time and spaces of film consumption, the VCR was in every way a 'disruptive technology'. For rights holders, VCRs took films into new spaces, creating additional revenue streams through which to exploit their properties by opening secondary 'release windows' for the renting and retailing of copyrighted works. For consumers, videocassettes drew film consumption away from the public space of cinemas and into the privacy of the home, while the 'timeshift' facility liberated television viewing from the broadcast schedules. These access opportunities came, however, at the expense of weakening the control of legitimate suppliers over the public circulation of their product. Before home video, film prints ensured piracy remained a specialised matter, practised by only the few – distributors, laboratories and exhibitors – who owned the technologies and resources for illegally reproducing or exhibiting prints. Introduction of 16mm film in the 1920s had made available a medium which was easily transportable and simple to use, testing the efforts of rights holders to control the circulation of prints, for over the following decades private collectors built personal libraries and hotels held unauthorised screenings.[51] Still, the majority of the consuming public had no access to actual copies of films. From the late 1970s onwards, therefore, consumer-priced video recording technology effectively democratised and deprofessionalised the means of film reproduction and exhibition. Home video fundamentally transformed both the time and space of moving image commerce and culture in ways that impacted not only on legitimate film and television markets, but also the piracy business.

Hollywood responded to the VCR in two ways – through the courts and the market. For some in Hollywood, the VCR could only spell a bleak future in which rights holders lost control over their properties. One year after Betamax went on sale, Universal Studios and the Walt Disney Company sued Sony.[52] In the view of the plaintiffs, the capacity of VCRs to record television programmes was an open invitation for infringement. While Sony was not regarded as directly infringing copyright, by manufacturing and marketing a technology that others could use for infringing purposes, the plaintiffs argued Sony must be held liable according to the doctrine of contributory infringement, for the company was enabling and inducing others to contravene copyright. Contributory liability applies when a party does not directly commit an act of infringement but can be seen to contribute to, enable and possibly benefit from infringement by another party (see Chapter 1). After two years, the District Court found in Sony's favour, deciding private home video recording was a non-commercial practice and so represented fair use, and that the company was unable to directly supervise how VCR owners used their machines.[53] When the outcome was appealed, however, the Ninth Circuit Court in part reversed that decision.[54]

When the case went in front of the Supreme Court, opinion was narrowly divided five to four in favour of Sony. The majority opinion sought to protect the interests of rights holders while preventing the erection of barriers to impede technological and commercial innovation. It took the view that there was the need to 'strike a balance between a copyright holder's legitimate demand for effective – not merely symbolic – protection of the statutory monopoly, and the rights of others freely to engage in substantially unrelated areas of commerce', reaching the conclusion that 'the sale of copying equipment, like the sale of other articles of commerce, does not constitute contributory infringement if the product is widely used for legitimate, unobjectionable purposes. Indeed, it need merely be capable of substantial noninfringing uses.'[55] It was the view of the Court that timeshift viewing for private and non-commercial purposes legitimately represented fair use and that the supply of a new reproductive technology should not be stifled simply because some owners may use it for infringing purposes. *Sony Corporation of America v. Universal City Studios, Inc.* set a precedent regarding contributory infringement, with an impact reaching beyond the VCR, as the decision was invoked over twenty years later when media piracy moved into a new phase once the copyright industries went to war against online file sharing (see following discussion).

By accepting home video recording into the realm of fair use, *Sony Corp. of America v. Universal City Studios, Inc.* cleared away any potential legal obstacle to VCRs becoming a mass-market consumer technology. While Universal and Disney sought to combat the VCR, other elements in the American film business were committed to fully exploiting the market opportunities afforded by home video. Although many independent distributors moved quickly to immediately embrace the video market, it was not until July 1977 that 20th Century-Fox became the first of the Hollywood majors to release its films on cassette, initially licensing titles to Magnetic Video before acquiring that company in March 1979 to form its own video distribution subsidiary.[56] By 1981, all the major entertainment corporations of Hollywood were self-distributing or sub-contracting distribution.[57] Legitimate outlets for Hollywood films were therefore established in the early 1980s, and from the mid-1980s onwards, video revenues came to surpass the theatrical box office. In many respects, this switch from initial hostility to all-out acceptance, replayed the pattern seen at earlier moments of technological change in Hollywood history witnessed with the coming of synchronised sound and broadcast television.

Hollywood may have taken time to grasp the commercial opportunities of home video but illegal entrepreneurs immediately saw the market potential of the VCR. Prefiguring by several years the direction in which the legal market would eventually go, by the end of the 1970s it was already clear videocassettes had become the preferred medium of film and television piracy. MPAA figures showed annual numbers of confiscated cassettes rapidly outstripping film prints: in 1975, 2,010 prints and 638 cassettes of films were confiscated; by 1978 that balance had shifted to 1,083 prints and 7,466 cassettes.[58] One opinion held the reason why the illegal market in cassettes was able to grow so quickly was precisely because the Hollywood majors delayed their entry into the video business. Noting how illegal copies of Hollywood films catered for unfulfilled demand, in 1982 market analyst Allan Raphael remarked, 'In that sense, the studios were already in the business … They just weren't getting any of the revenue for it. All the money was going underground.'[59]

Even without Hollywood's delay in entering the video market, it was, perhaps, inevitable that videocassettes would come to be used in unauthorised ways. Just as print piracy had taken many forms, so the VCR could equally be applied in a plurality of ways as a medium of infringement. When the Hollywood corporations embraced video, they quickly established the practice of creating artificial scarcity: a video release was delayed for several months while a film played out its theatrical run, after which the video release was staggered between rental and retail windows, and across different international territories. Ironically, this delay actually opened up windows for illegal commerce; while films were still showing in cinemas or had yet to appear on theatrical release, stolen prints could be scanned to create high-quality master tapes. Film-to-tape piracy still demanded high-end technology but a major part of the appeal of the video-cassette came from how the VCR deprofessionalised the means of media reproduction. With prices pitched at consumer levels, and operation of the technology requiring no specialised skill, VCRs offered pirate entrepreneurs a non-professional tool for illegal duplication. Growth of the legitimate video business also brought pre-recorded videocassette copies onto the market as an alternative source of high-quality masters for use in tape-to-tape copying. Equally, recordings taken off-air from network television broadcasts or cable provided master copies to set off a chain of illegal reproduction and distribution. Just as the legitimate business bifurcated into retail and rental markets, so illegal copies circulated for sale or hire. Rather in the manner that early exhibitors had fulfilled demand during the nickelodeon boom by acquiring unauthorised prints, so some video rental storeowners answered the video boom by supplementing their stock with illegal dupes. Meanwhile, pirated copies could be purchased through the channels of mail order or market stalls. Until the early 1980s, the video camera was strictly a professional media technology, but once cameras reached the consumer market and became progressively miniaturised, they could be used as a clandestine tool for 'camcording' films off cinema screens.[60] VCRs similarly deprofessionalised the means of exhibition, with a number of store-front operations in the USA running businesses by using cassettes for the unauthorised presentation of films to paying customers.[61]

This sheer flexibility made the videocassette the ideal medium for infringing the rights to reproduce, distribute and exhibit films or television programmes. Something of that flexibility can be grasped by looking at just one incident of video piracy from the late 1970s. When FBI agents raided the business premises of Television Systems Co. in September 1977, they found a large quantity of video recording equipment and seized around 400 illegally copied films on cassette, which were claimed to have a value of $4 million.[62] Following the raid, a group of seven men were indicted on multiple counts of conspiracy, criminal copyright infringement, mail fraud and the making of false statements to a bank in order to secure a loan. Members of the group were charged with:

> knowingly and wilfully conspir[ing] to infringe for profit the copyrights of various copyrighted
> motion pictures … by illegally reproducing and causing the reproduction of copyrighted motion
> pictures in the form of video cassettes and by distributing the video cassettes by rental to
> various consumers for profit.[63]

The charges alleged the defendants operated several lines of business. One scheme involved inducing apartment owners to rent cassettes to their tenants, while the charge of committing mail fraud related to the receipt of cheques for sending rental cassettes through the postal service; customers paid a $50 per-title non-refundable deposit, plus a $7.25 rental charge. The operations of the defendants first came to light when – while staying at the Sam Houston Inn at Huntsville, Texas – an employee of 20th Century-Fox viewed a presentation of the studio's *Star Wars* (1977) through a closed circuit television system installed by the group to exhibit films to guests without the authority of the copyright holders.[64] As this case illustrates, consumer video facilitated innovative opportunities for illegal enterprise.

Furthermore, the compact portability of the cassette made it an ideal medium for illegal trade. Placing additional strains on the access/exclusion dialectic, cassettes disrupted the regulation of national media markets by representing what Tom O'Regan calls a 'porous' medium, 'facilitat[ing] trans-frontier circulation and piracy'.[65] As noted earlier, Hollywood staggered release windows to maximise revenues from different distribution outlets and territories. However, the majors were very aware that creating artificial scarcity in this way actually produced gaps in the world market for illegal supply to fill. As Vice President of the MPAA and leader of the Association's worldwide anti-piracy team, James Bouras remarked in 1982 that 'given the fact that we don't service simultaneously all the markets in which a demand for our product exists, there are always going to be vacuum areas … It's those gaps that the pirates run into – that's where the money is.'[66] Although aware of the effects of the market vacuum they created, by sticking hard to their established distribution practices, the Hollywood corporations were actually foremost in creating and preserving market opportunities for illegal entrepreneurs. This situation is representative of a far more general dynamic at work in the formation of pirate markets, whereby artificially delaying or denying legitimate access to copyrighted works has frequently proven to create an opportunity space for illegal enterprise to occupy, or for consumer acquisitiveness to find ways and means to bypass the restrictions imposed by suppliers.

In the geography of film piracy, at the start of the 1980s the MPAA was identifying South Africa, Venezuela and the West Indies as territories where illegal duplication was widely practised. Seizures of illegally reproduced cassettes were reported in the major film markets of western Europe, with London identified as 'unquestionably the pirate capital of the world in the video market'.[67] High levels of VCR ownership made the Gulf States a hot market for illegal cassettes. According to one source, it was estimated that at least 80 per cent of the videos available in the region were illegal copies. It was also reported that, on the back of the cassette market, pirate entrepreneurs were finding a secondary revenue stream by selling advertising time on pirated copies of first-run films.[68]

Moves to combat video piracy combined anti-copying technologies, Hollywood's formation of an international network of national anti-piracy organisations and legislative revision. Video Duplication, Inc. worked with the FBI and the MPAA's FSO to develop Copy Guard, a technological system designed to scramble and make the picture roll on any illegal copy. This met with little success, however, after Japanese VCR manufacturers installed a correcting device in their products.[69] With the boom in consumer video, in late April 1985, Embassy Home Entertainment began issuing pre-recorded cassettes of *The Cotton Club* (1984) with Macrovision, a further Copy Protection System (CPS). With any attempt to make unauthorised copies, Macrovision confused the VCR's automatic gain control, the mechanism used to regulate the signal on a tape, thereby creating dim pictures with video 'noise'. For professional pirates, though, Macrovision presented few obstacles. John Ryan, the product's inventor, admitted the device was aimed at 'the casual copier, not the professional', although Embassy's CEO Andre Blay claimed 'professional piracy isn't the major problem inside the United States'.[70] Anti-anti-copying technology appeared on the market very quickly, with image stablisers selling for as little as $300.[71]

Video also produced changes in Hollywood's contribution to the intellectual property defence industry. As the work of the FSO became predominantly taken up with tackling video piracy, the MPAA spread its anti-piracy operations overseas, so that, by the early 1980s, the FSO was operating beyond its central base in Los Angeles, with branch offices in London, Johannesburg, New York, Paris and Hong Kong.[72] This would eventually lead to the creation of an international network of MPAA-sponsored national anti-piracy partner organisations. For example, in the UK, the Federation Against Copyright Theft (FACT) was formed in 1983, while the following year the Gesellschaft zur Verfolgung von Urheberrechtsverletzungen e.V. (GVU, Society for the Prosecution of Copyright Infringement) and Federación para la Protección de la Propiedad Intelectual (FAP) were established in Germany and Spain, and in 1988 the Federazione Anti-Pirateria Audiovisiva (FAPAV) was launched in Italy.[73]

Hollywood's embrace of home video coincided with the start of a period when successive revisions to US copyright law granted greater protections to rights holders. The Copyright Act of 1976, the first major revision since 1909, extended the duration of copyright; previously, protection lasted for twenty-eight years with the option for a twenty-eight-year extension, but the 1976 Act expanded this to the life of the author plus fifty years, or seventy-five years from date of publication for anonymous works and works-for-hire. In a move expressly targeted at deterring the pirating and counterfeiting of records, tapes and films, in May 1982 President Ronald Reagan signed the Piracy and Counterfeiting Amendments Act, amending Titles 17 and 18 of the United States Code by increasing maximum fines and terms of imprisonment from $25,000 and two years, to $250,000 and five years. This move was justified on the grounds that many illegal entrepreneurs regarded the penalties imposed as a relatively insignificant cost for conducting their business. The thinking here was that these revisions brought 'penalties for record and film piracy and counterfeiting into line with the enormous profits which are being reaped from such activities'.[74]

When reflecting on these developments, the history of video piracy in the USA can be seen as passing through at least three phases. Like any other consumer product, the market for illegal videocassettes was subject to basic economic constraints. When first launched on the US market, VCR units retailed for prices in the region of $2,300 and $1,300.[75] As the median income among households in the USA in 1980 stood at $16,354[76] few homes could afford a VCR. By Christmas 1982, US stores were selling VCRs at prices between $400 and $700; four years later, they sold for around $200 to $300 each.[77] The VCR therefore became a common-place item of domestic technology: estimates for 1980 indicated only 2.4 per cent of television households (TVHHs) in the USA owned a VCR; a decade later, it was estimated 70.2 per cent of TVHHs owned the technology.[78] As the video software market was initially based on rental rather than retail, cassettes sold in the region of $79.95 or higher, priced for the rental outlets that recovered the relatively high cost through repeated rental turns. This pattern was reflected in the cost of illegal copies, with the MPAA and FBI in the late 1970s reporting pirated cassettes retailing for $75 to $150.[79] It didn't matter, therefore, whether the source of cassettes was legal or not – until the mid-1980s home video was a luxury, affordable by relatively few. Legitimate and illegal markets for video entered a second phase as VCR sales boomed from the mid-1980s onwards, creating a mass market for home video. This growth continued into the 1990s, so that, by 1997, it was estimated 82 per cent of TVHHs owned a VCR. Pirated cassettes of camcorded movies were reported that year to be selling in New York for as little as $5 each.[80]

During the 1980s and into the 90s, then, the expansion of the home video business created the space for video piracy to transition from niche to mass market. This change marked the first step in resetting the terrain of Hollywood's battles against moving image piracy. Illegal entrepreneurs remained the target of legal action, but, with the VCR, the space of potential infringement became more dispersed, moving from the relatively restricted public realm of theatrical exhibition to the far more scattered private domain of home media. The significance of this transition would become even more apparent in future decades as moving image piracy moved from physical to virtual space, with access to authorised material dispersed across millions of internet users.

Digital Infringements and Hollywood's Battle Against Online Piracy

Video piracy entered its third phase as the introduction to the market of Video CDs (VCDs) in 1993 and Digital Video Disc (DVD) in 1996 brought home video into the digital age. DVD became the more widely adopted digital format, although a large VCD market emerged in many East Asian territories.[81] In the legitimate market, low pricing of 'sell-through' retail DVDs stimulated sales so that the format rapidly replaced cassettes as the preferred medium of home entertainment, and the pattern was mirrored in the illegal market. Once DVD was rolled out across international markets, rights holders witnessed a second video boom as DVD sales and rentals grew exponentially. Ironically, the technological innovations of DVD serviced unauthorised reproduction and exchange extremely well. Unlike the loss in 'generations' produced by successive instances of tape-to-tape transfer, DVD reproduction could create copies with little or no degradations in quality. Differences in analogue broadcast television system standards (NTSC, PAL, SECAM) around the world impeded international flows of illegally reproduced videocassettes and, while those limitations persisted with the digital medium of DVD, the easy availability of multi-standard televisions and DVD players bypassed these restrictions. Designed to segment the global DVD market, regional coding of DVDs installed a form of digital rights management technology into discs, yet the coding could be circumvented to create all-region discs, or consumers could buy or otherwise hack for themselves modified DVD players to dodge the restrictions of regioning. Beyond these technological hurdles, DVD also unlocked some of the cultural barriers to illegal flows, for, with some commercial releases using the expanded data storage capacity of discs to include multiple subtitle options or audio tracks, illegally reproduced copies could easily pass between language markets.[82] Aware of how high-quality reproduction could be exploited for infringing purposes, the consortium of media, computing and consumer electronics firms behind the development of DVD integrated copy protection technology into the format from the very start. DVD hardware and software manufacturers were required to install the Content Scrambling System (CSS) in their products, an encryption and authentication system licensed by the DVD Copy Control Association (DVD-CCA) that was designed to prevent illegal access and copying. But, like Macrovision before it, CSS presented no real obstacle to unlicensed copying, with software programs for circumventing the encryption technology to 'rip' the video and audio data from DVDs available over the internet. Widespread inclusion of writeable DVD drives in home computers also made it easy to 'burn' that data to disc, thereby extending the means of illegal reproduction. Just as the legitimate market for home video entered a new phase with DVD, the unauthorised copying and exchange of DVDs created a boom for video piracy.

DVD piracy should be regarded as a bridging period, representing the final phase of physical video piracy and the first phase of digital piracy. With celluloid prints and videocassettes, film piracy always dealt in physical, tangible forms. Digitisation, however, turned films, television programmes, music, or games into dematerialised 'content' that could be reproduced, stored, moved, or modified with relative ease, posing questions over what constitutes a copy or adaptation of a copyrighted work. Popularisation of the internet from the 1990s onwards formed a virtual mediascape, creating brand new channels for one-to-one, many-to-one and one-to-many communication. In this context, online networks added to the array of piracy practices by introducing new means for circulating and accessing moving image content without the approval of rights holders. Peer-to-peer (P2P) file sharing innovated online channels of distribution, with files held on the computers of individual users ('peers') made available for exchange with other users. As certain forms of P2P allowed files to be exchanged without passing through any centralised server, then P2P presented copyright industries with significant challenges to governing and controlling networks. File-hosting services, or 'cyberlockers', allowed paying subscribers to both upload and download files from centralised hosting servers. While both could be used as legitimate means for transferring files, equally cyberlockers and P2P represented the movement of media piracy into virtual space.

These developments presented two key challenges for copyright legislation. First, as digital media innovates the means and social practices of infringement, so copyright needed *modernisation* to keep pace with technological change and provide effective tools for rights protection. Second, as networks greatly facilitate trans-border flows of media content as data, further dissolving the borders of the nation state, then revisions to statutes are required to *harmonise* minimum standards for protection. These tasks were addressed in 1996 when member states of the World Intellectual Property Organization (WIPO) adopted the WIPO Copyright Treaty (WCT) and WIPO Performances and Phonograms Treaty (WPPT), setting standards for the addition of new protections to existing legislation.[83] With regard to media piracy in the digital age, of particular note were the articles contained in both treaties obligating contracting parties to provide adequate legal protection and remedies prohibiting circumvention of any technical measures used by rights holders to protect their works, and also the unauthorised removal or alteration of electronic rights management information.[84] Subsequently, both treaties were implemented through the enactment of Title I in the Digital Millennium Copyright Act (DMCA) in 1998 in the USA and the European Union's Copyright Directive in 2001. With the DMCA, Subsection 1201(a)(1)(A), the 'anti-circumvention provision', prohibits bypassing any techno-logical measure designed to control access to copyrighted works, while Subsections 1201(a)(2) and 1201(b)(1), the 'anti-trafficking provisions', forbid anyone from making, importing or offering to the public the means to circumvent technologies preventing unauthorised access to, or copying of, protected works.

In addition to complying with the WIPO treaties, the DMCA further innovated US copy-right with Title II, the Online Copyright Infringement Liability Limitation Act. Section 512, or what became known as the 'safe harbour' provisions, limits the liability of certain categories of online service provider for any acts of direct infringement performed by the users of their serv-ices providing they meet certain conditions. These include: having no knowledge of the infring-ing activity on their service; closing the subscriber accounts of repeat infringers; receiving no financial benefit from such activity; and acting quickly to take down or block access to infringing material once notified by the rights holder of the availability of that material (see Chapter 1 for further discussion of the DMCA).[85]

A first test for the DMCA's anti-circumvention provision came in 1999 when the MPAA successfully brought a lawsuit against Eric Corley for posting the program DeCSS on his web-site, 2600.org. DeCSS could rip data from commercial DVDs without the authorisation of the rights holder, and then that data could be either burned to disc or freely distributed over the internet. On 2600.org, Corley had covered the release of DeCSS, including the object and source code of DeCSS in his report and posting links to the program. After the MPAA won an initial injunction, however, 2600 removed the code but, in an act of 'electronic civil disobe-dience', continued posting hundred of links to foreign sites outside US jurisdiction where the code and program remained available. While 2600.org was no longer directly posting DeCSS, the MPAA claimed the situation still represented trafficking in circumvention technologies, and the case concluded with the plaintiffs winning a permanent injunction.[86]

Beyond the immediate circumstances of the case, what is interesting here is how the DeCSS trial became a rallying point for broader controversies disputing the DMCA's privileging of property rights over consumer interests, and questions regarding whether the Act violated constitutional protection of free speech. Academic, educational and civil liberties organisations complained the DMCA's comprehensive prohibition on circumvention prohibited legitimate fair uses. Libraries or museums, for example, would be forbidden from making back-up copies of DVDs, while creating video clips for the purposes of criticism, teaching or news reporting would be illegal. A further complaint was that by restricting access to older films where the copyright term had already expired and which had passed into the public domain, DVD encryption gave 'copyright holders, in effect, an extralegal, indefinite extension of their copyright term'.[87]

Constitutional issues arose over whether computer code, such as DeCSS, could be classed as a form of speech and therefore entitled to protection under the First Amendment. When Corley argued this defence, it was rejected by the Second Circuit Court of Appeals. In a concurrent and related trial, however, where the DVD-CCA sued Andrew Bunner for posting DeCSS, the California Court of Appeal accepted this defence. With the *Bunner* case, the DVD-CCA had adopted a different line of complaint, alleging that, by publishing DeCCS, Bunner violated California's strict trade secret laws. When the case was heard by the California Supreme Court, the seven-judge panel overturned the Court of Appeal's decision, unanimously agreeing that computer code is 'speech' and as such is entitled to protection in principle, but ruling that trade secret law should still be applied to prevent publication so long as application of the law was primarily undertaken to protect intellectual property and not to prohibit speech based on its content. The state Supreme Court referred the case back to the Court of Appeal with instructions to assess whether DeCSS was legitimately a secret when Bunner posted the program. Deciding in Bunner's favour, in February 2004 the Court of Appeal found the DVD-CAA had not presented adequate evidence that CSS remained a trade secret when Bunner posted DeCSS, and, in fact, knowledge of how CSS had been hacked had become so widely known at that point that the protection system could no longer be counted as a trade secret. Consequently, the injunction was deemed to be an unlawful prior restraint on Bunner's right to free speech.[88]

Efforts to combat online media piracy in the USA were initially led by the recorded music industry. In 2000, the leading music companies collectively organised to file a lawsuit against the P2P network Napster. Although it was not the first P2P network, Napster's ease of use made it the most popular network for exchanging music files: inevitably numbers were uncertain, but at its peak, in February 2001, Napster claimed over 80 million registered users and 2.79 billion downloads.[89] *A&M Records, Inc. v. Napster, Inc.* returned to the same ground as *Sony Corp. of America v. Universal City Studios, Inc.*, with the central issue resting on whether the providers of products or services were liable for infringements committed by others.[90] Plaintiffs in the *Napster* case alleged the network held secondary liability for infringing behaviour by its users. Courts have developed two doctrines for secondary infringement: *contributory liability* applies when a party is proven to knowingly induce, cause, or materially contribute to acts of direct infringement committed by others; *vicarious liability* arises when a party has the right and ability to supervise or control the infringing conduct of others and may also have an obvious and direct financial interest in the infringement.[91] Rejecting the defendant's recourse to the DMCA's safe harbour provisions and First Amendment defences, the District Court for the Northern District of California found grounds for contributory and vicarious liability and granted a preliminary injunction. In February 2001 the Court of Appeals for the Ninth Circuit affirmed the lower court's decision, passing some burden of responsibility onto rights holders by revising the terms of the injunction to require record companies to provide Napster with the track title, artist name and file name in the Napster directory of works they alleged were being infringed.[92] Still unable to fully comply with the zero tolerance order imposed by the Court, in 2002 Napster shut down and filed for bankruptcy.

A&M Records, Inc. v. Napster, Inc. set the precedent for assessing the liability of P2P networks in the digital age. Hollywood film and television corporations entered this arena in October 2001 when members of the MPAA and the Record Industry Association of America (RIAA), the trade association for the sound and music recordings business, joined forces to file complaints with the Central California District Court against three P2P networks: Kazaa, Grokster and Morpheus.[93] Operated by an Amsterdam company, Kazaa was sued in early 2002 by Buma/Stemra, the Dutch collecting society for music composers and publishers. This action was avoided, however, when the company was sold to the Australian firm Sharman Networks, incorporated in the South Pacific island of Vanutala. Meanwhile, Grokster continued operating from the island of Nevis in the West Indies, while the Tennessee company MusicCity – later renamed StreamCast Networks – distributed the Morpheus software.[94] Unlike Napster's central server, this second generation of P2P networks used the FastTrack P2P protocol, licensed by Kazaa, to create a decentralised structure in which users with high-speed internet connections acted as 'SuperNodes' – situated between the company and the network – to route traffic. In another departure from Napster, the companies didn't keep directories of users; instead, SuperNodes held addresses. This decentralised model of distribution therefore raised questions over the extent to which P2P networks could be held responsible, and therefore liable, for infringements by users.

Like the *Napster* case before it, *Metro-Goldwyn-Mayer Studios Inc., et al., v. Grokster, Ltd, et al.* turned on questions of secondary liability. On 25 April 2003 the District Court decided in favour of the defendants. Judge Stephen Wilson cited the *Betamax* case, stating, 'Grokster and StreamCast are not significantly different from companies that sell homevideo recorders or copy machines, both of which can be and are used to infringe copyrights.'[95] Guided by its interpretation of *Sony v. Universal*, four months later the Ninth Circuit Court upheld the District Court's decision on the grounds that Grokster and StreamCast could have no actual knowledge of specific instances of infringement due to the decentralised architecture of their networks. Furthermore, the Circuit Court took the view that it was the users who retrieved and stored infringing files and the defendants had no other involvement beyond providing the software they used.

Appealing this outcome, the plaintiffs asked for the case to be referred to the Supreme Court, arguing the appellate court misread the protection offered by 'substantial non-infringing uses' in *Sony v. Universal*. According to the plaintiffs, Grokster and StreamCast occupied the status of gatekeepers and so were liable for contributory and vicarious infringement. Regarding contributory infringement, the plaintiffs claimed Grokster and StreamCast had knowledge of infringing activity because they'd received notices identifying over 8 million unauthorised copies of 80,000 separate copyrighted works. It was also argued the defendants induced, caused and materially contributed to infringement by providing services which operated as 'engines of infringement' and 'actively encouraged and assisted' infringement by users through promoting their services as alternatives to Napster.[96] A series of arguments were presented for why the protections of the Sony decision could not be applied to the defendants' services: the *Betamax* decision held that Sony had not intended the VCR to be used for infringing purposes, whereas the defendants intentionally facilitated, encouraged and assisted infringement; analysis failed to provide evidence of 'commercially significant noninfringing uses'; whereas it was impossible to eliminate infringing use while preserving the non-infringing uses of the Betamax, the defendants had decided not to separate these uses and block infringement despite having the technological means to do so; and it was argued Grokster and StreamCast could only remain commercially viable and sustainable by allowing infringement.[97] Finally, the plaintiffs argued that the Ninth Circuit's ruling created perverse incentives that rewarded infringement while undermining legitimate online commerce.[98]

The plaintiffs contended Grokster and StreamCast were vicariously liable because they had a direct financial interest in allowing infringement on their services, profiting from sales of advertising to their users and operating as 'vast on-line bazaars for the distribution of music, movies, and other works subject to copyright'.[99] Although the decentralised network system delegated the indexing function to the computers of users, it was argued the defendants could still supervise and control infringement, for they retained the legal right to terminate the access of infringing users, together with the practical ability to restrict the access of such users through the log-in and registration functions of the networks. Consequently, the DMCA safe harbour protection could not apply because the defendants had not adopted and implemented measures to terminate the access of repeat infringers.[100]

In June 2005 the Supreme Court unanimously reached judgment in favour of the plaintiffs, satisfied that sufficient evidence had been presented of Grokster and StreamCast having knowledge of the infringements committed by their users, openly promoting their services as alternatives to Napster, reaping direct financial benefits from advertising and failing to filter or otherwise impede the sharing of copyrighted works. Consequently, the Court concluded the Ninth Circuit had erroneously interpreted the *Sony* decision, upsetting the 'balance between the interests of protection and innovation' that the earlier case achieved.[101] A few months later, on 7 November 2005, Grokster agreed to a financial settlement, paying $50 million in damages and closing down its service to leave just a warning notice for any visitors.[102]

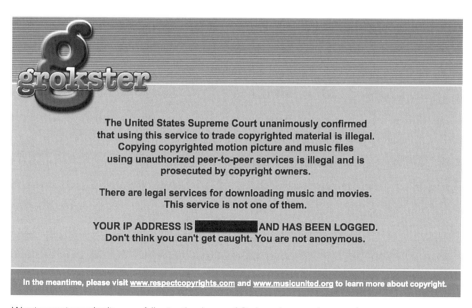

Warning: cautionary landing page following the closure of Grokster (www.grokster.com)

The wrangles around DeCSS, Napster and Grokster are just specific instances of a more general change, as Hollywood's battles over infringement shifted from the reproduction and dissemination of physical things, to the virtual sphere of code or networks. Digital technologies dematerialise the legal, technical and political terrain of media piracy. Among the most significant developments in this context has been how anti-piracy campaigning by the media industries has unintentionally led to the legal authority and legitimacy of copyright becoming opened up to interrogation and contestation. As litigation in the digital age repeatedly throws up questions and anxieties concerned with how copyright violates fair use, freedom of speech and consumer rights, or impedes technological innovation, so voices from many quarters have lined up to either defend or challenge the principles and protections of intellectual property. The consumer electronics industry, the information technology business, advocates of consumer rights, free speech activists, retailers and public users of media have all variously adopted oppositional stances to contend the defences of copyright promoted by the media industries. A sign that the protections of copyright are now open to contestation has been the establishment of numerous groups, non-governmental bodies or political parties organising to advocate for either the abolition or reform of copyright. This problematising of copyright and infringement is set within a new climate of consumption, for with the online universe making so much 'content' available for free, arguably the age of 'digital natives' produces a generation of media consumers unaware, uncertain or unaccepting of the financial compensations that copyright is designed to protect. Cumulatively, these developments have posed questions over what should or should not be defined as infringement, problematising the very meaning of 'piracy'. This has the effect of exposing Hollywood's control of the access/exclusion dialectic to scrutiny and dispute. For decades Hollywood occupied the moral high ground, proclaiming piracy as a problem to be urgently combated and that its perpetrators should be chased down. But, in this new climate, such claims are now equally met by voices countering how the powers of the copyright industries must be resisted, and persuasively portraying Hollywood and big media more generally as the real villains.

PIPA, SOPA and the Battle Against Hollywood

After *MGM v. Grokster*, the copyright industries achieved other notable successes, including shutting down the P2P network LimeWire (2010) and cyberlocker Megaupload (2012). While the MPAA and RIAA always rushed to celebrate these outcomes as important steps in winning their battle against online piracy, at best they were short-term victories, for widespread file sharing continued to defeat legal and technical controls. Prosecuting offending networks through the courts could only provide temporary solutions, and so Hollywood turned to backing statutory revisions aimed at giving rights holders increased powers to enforce controls over the online universe. When broad-based opposition mounted against the proposals, however, Hollywood found itself losing the legal, political and moral battle over piracy.

Moves for statutory revision commenced with the introduction in September 2010 of the Combating Online Infringement and Counterfeits Act (COICA), a US Senate bill aimed at empowering the Attorney General to bring a lawsuit against any domain name used by an internet site primarily involved in offering goods or services violating copyrights, or which sold or distributed counterfeit products.[103] Although passed by the Senate Judiciary Committee,

COICA never went to a full vote on the Senate floor and, instead, appeared in revised form as the Preventing Real Online Threats to Economic Creativity and Theft of Intellectual Property Act, otherwise known as the PROTECT IP Act or PIPA. PIPA aimed to strengthen enforcement measures against 'rogue websites' operated and registered overseas.[104] A companion bill, the Stop Online Piracy Act (SOPA), was submitted in October 2011 to the House of Representatives, targeting any foreign sites directed at (i.e., providing goods or services to) users in the USA, which could be proven to 'enable' or 'facilitate' violations of copyright, or the sale, distribution or promotion of counterfeit goods and services.[105] SOPA and PIPA sought to empower the Attorney General to issue owners, operators and domain name registrants of infringing sites with court orders demanding they cease and desist from further infringing activities. Sweeping measures were proposed to cut off infringing sites from user traffic and financial support facilitated by sources under US jurisdiction. After receiving a copy of a court order, internet service providers (ISPs) were required to take measures preventing their US subscribers from accessing infringing sites, while search engines had to stop serving links to those sites, payment services should cease processing transactions from US residents for the sites and internet advertising services were expected to discontinue business with sites subject to the order.[106]

In Congress, SOPA and PIPA received bipartisan support, with industry backing coming from the MPAA, RIAA and other trade organisations and guilds representing the interests of content creators in the entertainment business, including the Entertainment Software Association, Directors Guild of America and Screen Actors Guild. Supporters had not anticipated, however, the strength and scale of opposition directed against SOPA and PIPA. Internet services, independent businesspeople and venture capitalists, cybersecurity experts, library associations, digital rights groups, journalists and individual artists and creators all declared their opposition.[107] A key problem was how the language of 'enabling' and 'facilitating' infringement, as employed in the bills, was so broad that potentially all sites on the internet might be found to be involved in infringements, risking the shut-down of legitimate companies. Also, as sites could potentially be made responsible for all content and links posted by their users, there were fears that SOPA and PIPA rolled back the DMCA's safe harbour provisions. Other concerns were that the bills created a climate of uncertainty impeding investment in start-ups, while endangering online security, and that blocking Americans from seeing sites visible to the rest of the world represented censorship of the internet.[108] Among the most high-profile opponents were leading names in the network economy. In November 2011, AOL, eBay, Facebook, Google, LinkedIn, Mozilla, Twitter, Yahoo! and Zynga posted an open letter in *The New York Times* supporting the goals of the bills but protesting how they:

> would expose law-abiding US internet and technology companies to new and uncertain
> liabilities, private rights of action, and technology mandates that would require monitoring of
> websites. We are concerned that these measures pose a serious risk to our industry's
> continued track record of innovation and job creation, as well as to our nation's
> cybersecurity.[109]

Of particular concern was how 'the bills as written would seriously undermine the effective mechanism Congress enacted in the Digital Millennium Copyright Act … to provide a safe harbor for Internet companies that act in good faith to remove infringing content from their sites'.[110] Grass-roots opposition was mobilised as millions signed online petitions and sent emails to Congress.[111] Awkwardly positioned between deciding whether to shun the support which the Democrat Party received from wealthy members of Hollywood or the tech community, while equally wanting to avoid alienating young internet users in an election year, on 14 January 2012 the administration of President Barrack Obama declared it would not support legislation 'that reduces freedom of expression, increases cybersecurity risk, or undermines the dynamic, innovative global internet'.[112] A series of organised online protests brought the processes of law-making to the attention of millions of internet users worldwide, peaking on 18 January 2012 when the English-language online encyclopaedia Wikipedia and over 115,000 other sites voluntarily shut down for the day. Supporters of the bills countered saying the opposition was spreading misinformation, but, feeling the weight of protest, law-makers began withdrawing their support and, two days later, it was announced that Senate and the House were postponing progress on the bills until a point where greater consensus could be reached.

For Hollywood and the other supporters, this was more than a legal setback. In lobbying for statutory change, Hollywood put itself in a corner where it could easily be portrayed as advocating reforms threatening free speech and technological innovation. Battle lines were drawn, pitching old media against new media, Hollywood against Silicon Valley and restricted content against open networks. Stewart Baker, a former official in the government of President George W. Bush, effectively summed up the public relations fallout from Hollywood's defeat when he said:

> From the start, studios saw the fight over SOPA as a struggle with a bunch of other companies – Google and Internet service providers among them – that were hoping to profit from the Internet travails of the entertainment industry.
>
> That turned out to be wrong. In fact, the industry is fighting what amounts to a new popular culture.
>
> Unlike the old pop culture Hollywood dominated, this one is largely independent of the music, movie and broadcast industries. …
>
> The content industry has made itself into the villain. Increasingly, it looks like an occupying power, obeyed at gunpoint, despised for its ham-handed excesses and resisted from every dark corner. Unfortunately for Hollywood, as its customers migrate to the Internet, it is losing not just their money but their hearts and minds as well.[113]

Legislative squabbling over SOPA and PIPA exposed Hollywood's larger failings in trying to control, while not fully comprehending, a new media universe. As efforts to combat piracy moved into the online sphere, Hollywood needed to build bridges with the internet and technology community, and yet, by seeking to implement draconian measures, Hollywood alienated the very parties it should have been forming partnerships with. At the same time, blundering efforts in prosecuting online infringement significantly tarnished Hollywood's public reputation, as purveyors of popular entertainment found themselves occupying positions in open conflict with the protection of civil liberties and consumer rights. Although the Wikipedia blackout and the opposition voiced by leading names in the online economy grabbed headlines, the defeat of PIPA and SOPA was the result of a far broader coalition of interests including advocacy and litigation-directed non-governmental organisations, technology writers, legal scholars, public intellectuals and users of the internet. Bill Herman traces how the stopping of PIPA and SOPA became a defining moment for a radical transformation in the politics of copyright, marking the 'rise of a potent group of political actors who seek to defend [new digital] technologies against encroachment by copyright law'.[114] Although lacking the organisational focus and financial or lobbying power of the copyright industries, these parties variously succeeded in foregrounding the defence of digital rights as a key political battleground for the contemporary media economy. For the purposes of the discussion here, the significance of this development has been that continuing attempts made by Hollywood and its allies in the copyright business to expand the realm of what constitutes infringement, and therefore 'piracy', will be openly challenged, not only in the courts, but also the wider public sphere.

Piracy and Hollywood History

At the opening of this chapter it was proposed that piracy provides the prism through which to trace the shadow history of Hollywood. In part, this is a history of technologies, with the preferred media of infringement changing from celluloid prints, to magnetic tape, optical discs and online networks. Those changes have been accompanied by the multiplication of infringing practices, from duping and bicycling, to decryption and file sharing. These practices have marked transformations in the business of piracy, for the specialised and professionalised realm of commercial piracy that characterised the print and video eras has been at least partially displaced by a 'post-commercial' era typified by unauthorised free online exchanges of media content between 'amateurs'. Along the way, the spatial and temporal contexts of consuming unauthorised material have relocated, as the public spaces of nickelodeons, movie theatres, or hotels, have given way to the privacy of home entertainment or personal computing, and now the privacy-in-public afforded by connected media devices. In addition, the configuring of space has seen illegal trade and unauthorised flows remapping the geography of piracy. This is also a history of legislative change, with moves to extend the scope and duration of protection afforded by copyright producing the accompanying effect of enlarging the sphere of what constitutes acts of infringement. A key component of the shadow history of piracy is, therefore, how legal revision has constructed and revised the very definition of what constitutes 'piracy'.

Recognising piracy as endemic to media history enhances critical knowledge of Hollywood, the global markets in which Hollywood operates and the complex relationship the industry has with its audiences. Reading Hollywood history through piracy requires uncovering and interrogating how the American entertainment industry has been locked into long-term fights over controlling the access/exclusion dialectic. This project does not simply involve viewing the business from an alternative perspective, but also fundamentally changing the very object of historiographic enquiry. Charting this transmuting realm of unauthorised media production and consumption takes Hollywood history in new directions, thinking beyond the sphere of legitimate creation, circulation and exploitation to examine an expanded arena of legal, technical and commercial contestation. Certainly, the major entertainment corporations of Hollywood all feature in this shadow history, but they are only players in a space where illegal entrepreneurs, law-makers, enforcement agencies, technology firms and cultural consumers all participate and variously jostle to exert influence over the ownership, use and value of moving images.

This all suggests piracy must feature as a necessary part of Hollywood history. But how can we recover and know the history of a realm of cultural production that is essentially undocumented and covert? Here this chapter has drawn on a range of source materials: national intellectual property statutes, multilateral copyright treaties, legal case papers, newspaper and trade paper articles, research reports commissioned by the copyright industries for the purposes of lobbying for stricter enforcement, archival video clips, websites for a UN agency and an industry trade body, and selected contributions from the existing bodies of scholarship concerned with intellectual property, media piracy, American film history and historical developments in the diffusion of moving image technologies. When trying to uncover this hidden history, these all provide the media historian with something to hold onto. But how possible is it to take that history beyond this institutionally authored realm of discourse? If this is the most that is available, then rather than claim to write a history of piracy, in truth it must be acknowledged that what is actually being written is only a history of efforts to *combat* piracy. Furthermore, as the US copyright industries have overwhelmingly applied the greatest force in combating piracy in both their domestic and overseas territories, then what documentation is available largely tells a story from the perspective of only one set of interests. Cumulatively, these questions, and the gaps and asymmetries in knowledge they reveal, have implications for the entire project of media historiography. For if piracy is ever present and widely practised, it must occupy a central and not a marginal position in the writing of media history, and yet if piracy is a realm of cultural production that is largely undocumented and unknowable, or at least is only known through certain institutionalised sources, this remains a necessary but ultimately fragmented and partial history.

Notes

1. See "'60 Minutes" on Video Piracy – 1979 – part 1 of 2!', YouTube video, from a story about video piracy called 'Who Stole Superman?' from *60 Minutes* in 1979, posted by 'videoholic50s60s70s', 12 October 2011, http://www.youtube.com/watch?v=7Uln6HUXAmg

2. William Patry, *Moral Panics and Copyright Wars* (Oxford University Press, 2009), p. 139.

3. *Home Recording of Copyrighted Works: Hearings Before the Subcommittee on Courts, Civil Liberties, and the Administration of Justice of the Committee on the Judiciary of the US House of Representatives*, 97th Cong., 2 (1982).

4. For example, see 'MPAA Anti-Piracy Commercial', YouTube video, posted by 'Rohan-Ron Live', 23 March 2014, https://www.youtube.com/watch?v=KV1GDIQbk_w. This MPAA-sponsored ad was translated into different languages for multiple territories.

5. See Stephen E. Siwek, *The True Cost of Motion Picture Piracy to the US Economy* (Lewisville: Institute for Policy Innovation, 2006). Often aligning with other intellectual property industries, particularly the music business, Hollywood regularly commissions research to evidence the value added by intellectual property to US GDP – for example, Stephen E. Siwek, *Copyright Industries in the US Economy: The 2013 Report* (Washington, DC: International Intellectual Property Alliance, 2013).

6. See, for example, the MPA commissioned report, Gregory F. Treverton, Carl Matthies, Karla J. Cunningham, Jeremiah Goulka, Greg Ridgeway and Anny Wong, *Film Piracy, Organized Crime, and Terrorism* (Santa Monica, CA: RAND Corporation, 2009).

7. 'Why We Care About Copyright', MPAA, accessed 4 August 2013, http://www.mpaa.org/content-protection/copyright-info (website no longer live).

8. Ashley Packard, *Digital Media Law*, 2nd edn (Chichester: Wiley-Blackwell, 2013), p. 175.

9. Adrian Johns, *Piracy: The Intellectual Property Wars from Gutenberg to Gates* (Chicago: University of Chicago Press, 2009), p. 35.

10. 'Shadow' is used in this context to evoke an alternative historiography charting the trajectory of what have been described as 'shadow economies' of media. See Paul McDonald, *Video and DVD Industries* (London: BFI, 2007), p. 179, and Ramon Lobato, *Shadow Economies of Cinema: Mapping Informal Film Distribution* (London: BFI, 2012).

11. 'Arrest in Theft Case', *Variety*, 21 March 1919, p. 56.

12. Eileen Bowser, *The Transformation of Cinema 1907–1915* (Berkeley: University of California Press, 1990), p. 18.

13. Jane Gaines, 'Early Cinema's Heyday of Copying: Too Many Copies of *L'Arroseur arrosé* (*The Waterer Watered*)', *Cultural Studies* vol. 20 no. 2–3 (2006): 227.

14. Peter Decherney, *Hollywood's Copyright Wars: From Edison to the Internet* (New York: Columbia University Press, 2012), p. 34.

15. Ezra Goodman, 'Hollywood's Private Gumshoes', *The New York Times*, 1 December 1940, p. 4.

16. Although his own company openly copied imported films from overseas producers, Thomas Edison filed a complaint against his domestic competitor Siegmund Lubin over the duping of original Edison productions. When the Third Circuit Court of Appeals reached a decision in favour of Edison, it did so by recognising moving images as an extension of photography and that any film produced a unified experience which should be registered for copyright as a single photograph and not a series of separate images.

17. Decherney, *Hollywood's Copyright Wars*, p. 32.

18. See ibid., pp. 45–55.

19. Library of Congress, *Report of the Register of Copyrights for the Fiscal Year 1911–1912* (Washington, DC: Government Printing Office, 1912), pp. 136–8.

20. Kerry Segrave, *Piracy in the Motion Picture Industry* (Jefferson, NC: McFarland, 2003), pp. 35–40.

21. 'Gigantic Film Plot Exposed in Warsaw', *The New York Times*, 10 June 1926, p. 29.

22. Pascal Karmina, *Film Copyright in the European Union* (Cambridge: Cambridge University Press, 2002), pp. 11–52.

23. A further notable development from the Brussels revisions was the addition to Article 2(1) of 'works produced by a process analogous to cinematography'. While this category potentially established protection for future forms of work combining moving image and sound, the growth of television raised questions whether broadcast production could be regarded as analogous to the making of cinematographic works. The issue was finally resolved at the 1967 Stockholm Conference, where Article 2(1) was amended to include the additional category of 'cinematographic works to which are assimilated those expressed by a process analogous to cinematography', which is accepted to also cover video recordings. For a fuller discussion of how cinematographic works were accommodated and treated by Berne, see Sam Ricketson, *The Berne*

Convention for the Protection of Literary and Artistic Works: 1886–1986 (London: Centre for
Commercial Law Studies, 1987), pp. 549–89. The full text of the Convention is available at
www.wipo.int/treaties/en/text.jsp?file_id=283693

24. 'Gigantic Film Plot Exposed', p. 29.
25. 'To Check Piracy of American Films', *The New York Times*, 17 August 1921, p. 19.
26. 'Fine Bicycling Exhib $11,500 in Cincinnati', *Variety*, 12 December 1928, p. 27.
27. Goodman, 'Hollywood's Private Gumshoes'.
28. 'Bare Mex Border's Smuggling of Pix', *Daily Variety*, 3 September 1936, p. 1.
29. Frank Segers, 'Print Pirates, News Leaks to Variety: Targets of New MPAA Security Force', *Daily Variety*, 12 March 1975, pp. 1, 18.
30. Johns, *Piracy*, p. 498.
31. Steve Toy, 'US Pic-TV Piracy Inquiry', *Daily Variety*, 12 December 1974, pp. 1, 14.
32. Robert Rawitch and John Kendell, 'LA Film Piracy', *Los Angeles Times* pt 1, 11 January 1975, pp. 1, 26.
33. 'US Grand Jury Indicts Budget on Piracy Charges', *Daily Variety*, 19 February 1975, pp. 1, 7.
34. Other films named in the indictment included *Portnoy's Complaint* (1972), *Dusty and Sweets McGee* (1971), *The Way We Were* (1973), *New Centurions* (1972), *Dillinger* (1973), *Forty Carats* (1973), *The Hot Rock* (1972) and *Shamus* (1973), while television programmes included *Marcus Welby, MD* (1969–76), *Hawaii Five-O* (1968–80), *Ironside* (1967–75), *Mission: Impossible* (1966–73), *The Big Valley* (1965–9), *Judd for the Defense* (1967–9) and *The Doris Day Show* (1968–73).
35. 'FBI Arrests 3 Indicted on Pic-TV Piracy Charges', *Daily Variety*, 7 April 1975, pp. 1, 19.
36. Steve Toy, '16 Indictments Handed Down by Federal Grand Jury Probing Piracy of Films and TV Shows', *Daily Variety*, 30 May 1975, pp. 1, 6, 27; 'Gov't, Industry Film Pirate Probes Zero in on South Africa', *Daily Variety*, 14 May 1975, p. 1.
37. Toy, 'US Pic-TV Piracy Inquiry'.
38. Quoted in 'Major South Africa Distribs Press Fight Vs. Widespread Print Piracy', *Variety*, 26 May 1971, p. 24.
39. 'Film Piracy Hits Record Level In So. Africa Market', *Variety*, 24 March 1971, p. 31. South Africa launched an experimental television service in 1975 and a national service the year after.
40. 'Gov't, Industry Film Pirate'.
41. 'Film Theft Trial Jury Hears Testimony from Wells, Stanfill', *Daily Variety*, 28 August 1975, pp. 1, 4; 'Arkoff On Stand at Pic-theft Trial', *Daily Variety*, 2 September 1975, p. 24.
42. 'Bought Series, Pix from Budget, Ex-Distrib Says', *Daily Variety*, 5 September 1975, p. 17; 'Budget Films Jury Hears From SA Distrib', *Daily Variety*, 8 September 1975, p. 11.
43. 'Begelman on the Stand at Budget Film Theft Trial', *Daily Variety*, 29 August, p. 3.
44. 'Defense Opens Its Case This Week in Budget Films Trial', *Daily Variety*, 15 September, p. 2.
45. 'Gene Hackman Takes Stand in Pic Piracy Trial', *Daily Variety*, 19 September 1975, pp. 1, 6.
46. Steve Toy, 'Three Convicted in Budget Films Piracy Trial', *Daily Variety*, 24 September 1975, pp. 1, 15.
47. 'Budget Films Figures Sentenced for Piracy', *Daily Variety*, 4 November 1975, p. 4.
48. 'Valenti Hails Film Piracy Convictions', *Daily Variety*, 25 September 1975, p. 2.
49. 'Film Pirates Are Less Bold, But Still Active, Prosecutor Says', *Daily Variety*, 13 September 1976, pp. 1, 12.
50. Quoted in 'Something for the TV Viewer Who Has Everything', *Broadcasting*, 3 November 1975, p. 49.

51. Eric Hoyt, *Hollywood Vault: Film Libraries Before Home Video* (Oakland: University of California Press, 2014), pp. 97, 136.

52. *Universal City Studios, Inc. v. Sony Corporation of America*, 480 F. Supp. 429 (C.D. Cal. 1979), accessed 5 May 2014, https://w2.eff.org/legal/cases/betamax/betamax_dist_ct.pdf

53. Ronald Bettig succinctly summarises fair use as the doctrine which 'limits the monopolistic privileges of copyright by permitting uses of works for non-commercial and educative purposes – e.g., research, teaching, parody, and news gathering – without the authorization of, or compensation to, the rights holder'. *Copyrighting Culture: The Political Economy of Intellectual Property* (Boulder, CO: Westview, 1996), p. 160.

54. *Universal City Studios, Inc. v. Sony Corporation of America*, 659 F.2d 963 (9th Cir. 1981), accessed 5 May 2014, https://w2.eff.org/legal/cases/betamax/betamax_9th_cir.pdf

55. *Sony Corp. v. Universal City Studios, Inc.*, 464 US 417 (1984), accessed 5 May 2014, https://w2.eff.org/legal/cases/betamax/betamax_supreme_ct.pdf

56. A. D. Murphy, 'Fox Pix Into Home Tape Market', *Daily Variety*, 8 August 1977, pp. 1, 8; *Daily Variety*, '20th-Fox Wraps Purchase of Magnetic Video Corp.', 8 March, p. 4.

57. Frederick Wasser, *Veni, Vidi, Video: The Hollywood Empire and the VCR* (Austin: University of Texas Press, 2001), pp. 96, 98.

58. Mats Mullern, 'Primer on Combating Int'l Piracy', *Variety*, 1 October 1980, p. 100.

59. Quoted in 'Video Bootleggers: Bane of Film Studios', *The New York Times* (*Business Day*), 23 October 1982, p. 43.

60. Linda Lee, 'Bootleg Videos: Piracy With a Camcorder', *The New York Times* (*Business Day*), 7 July 1997, pp. 1, 6.

61. Unlicensed exhibition of cassettes by storefront exhibitors was seen to be a particular problem by the adult entertainment business. See Will Tusher, 'Assault on Storefront Exhibs', *Daily Variety*, 24 March 1981, pp. 1, 34.

62. 'Grab Pirated Cassettes in Motels on "Star Wars," "Jaws" & "Rocky"', *Variety*, 28 September 1977, p. 32.

63. Quoted in 'Federal Grand Jury in Houston, Tex. Indicts 7 in Film Piracy Operation', *BoxOffice*, 8 January 1979, p. 8.

64. 'Seven Indicated for Alleged Pic Piracy in Houston Area', *Daily Variety*, 19 December 1978, pp. 1, 23.

65. Tom O'Regan, 'From Piracy to Sovereignty: International Video Cassette Recorder Trends', *Continuum* vol. 4 no.2 (1991): 120.

66. Quoted in 'Video Bootleggers: Bane of Film Studios'.

67. Mullern, 'Combating Int'l Piracy', p. 100.

68. Douglas Boyd and Nawaf Adwan, 'The Gulf States, Jordan and Egypt', in Manuel Alvarado (ed.), *Video World-wide: An International Study* (London: UNESCO/John Libbey, 1988), pp. 168–9.

69. 'Video Duplication Refines Its Copy Guard Anti-Piracy System', *Daily Variety*, 12 March 1979, p. 10; Tom Bierbaum, 'Homevid "Club" Has Surprise for Pirates', *Daily Variety*, 24 April 1985, pp. 1, 14. Copy Guard was originally developed by Trans-American Video.

70. Both quoted in Aljean Harmetz, '"Cotton Club" Cassettes Coded to Foil Pirates', *The New York Times* (Living Section), 24 April 1985, C15.

71. Hans Fantel, 'Tangles in the Anti-copying Thicket', *The New York Times* (Arts and Leisure), 30 August 1987, H22.

72. Miles Beller, 'Film Studios Hoping to Force Video Pirates to Walk the Plank', *Los Angeles Herald Examiner*, 10 October 1982, A-1.

73. McDonald, *Video and DVD Industries*, p. 191.

74. US Copyright Office, 'The Piracy and Counterfeiting Amendments Act of 1982', accessed 7 June 2014, http://www.copyright.gov/history/mls/ML-285.pdf

75. Bruce C. Klopfenstein, 'The Diffusion of the VCR in the United States', in Mark R. Levy (ed.), *The VCR Age: Home Video and Mass Communications* (Newbury Park, CA: Sage, 1989), p. 23.

76. 'Median Household Income in the United States', *David Manuel.com*, accessed 29 June 2014, http://www.davemanuel.com/median-household-income.php

77. Daniel Herbert, *Videoland: Movie Culture at the American Video Store* (Berkeley, CA: University of California Press, 2014), p. 26.

78. '1997 US Economic Review', MPAA, accessed 11 February 1999, http://www.mpaa.org/useconomicreview/1997/vcr97.htm (website no longer live).

79. '"Pirated" Films Taken in Raid in Witchita', *BoxOffice*, 19 June 1978, C-4; Maurice H. Orodenker, 'Two Philadelphia Men Arrested for Piracy', *BoxOffice*, 22 January 1979, E-1.

80. Linda Lee, 'The Good, the Bad and the Soundless', *The New York Times* (*Business Day*), 7 July 1997, p. 6.

81. On VCD in Asia, see McDonald, *Video and DVD Industries*, pp. 54–5, 101–5; Shujen Wang, *Framing Piracy: Globalization and Film Distribution in Greater China* (Lanham, MD: Rowman & Littlefield, 2003), pp. 50–6.

82. Language never presented an absolute block to illegal trade, however, for during the video-cassette and print piracy eras, illegal entrepreneurs aided exchange with language adaptations produced using their own subtitle translations. This practice continued into the DVD and online eras.

83. Established in 1967, the WIPO assumed responsibility from the Bureaux Internationaux Réunis pour la Protection de la Propriété Intellectuelle (BIRPI) (United International Bureaux for the Protection of Intellectual Property) for administering both the Berne Convention and the Paris Convention for the Protection of Industrial Property. Seven years later, the WIPO became a specialised agency of the UN, mandated to administer IP matters recognised by UN member states. 'WIPO – A Brief History', WIPO, accessed 12 September 2014, http://www.wipo.int/about-wipo/en/history.html

84. See Articles 11 and 12, 'WIPO Copyright Treaty', WIPO, accessed 12 September 2014, http://www.wipo.int/treaties/en/text.jsp?file_id=295166#P89_12682, and Articles 18 and 19, 'WIPO Performances and Phonograms Treaty', WIPO, accessed 12 September 2014, http://www.wipo.int/treaties/en/text.jsp?file_id=295578

85. *Digital Millennium Copyright Act*, US Copyright Office, accessed 12 September 2014, http://www.copyright.gov/legislation/hr2281.pdf

86. *Universal City Studios, Inc. v. Corley*, 273 F.3d 429 (2d Cir. 2001), accessed 12 September 2014, http://cyber.law.harvard.edu/people/tfisher/IP/2001%20Corley%20Abridged.pdf

87. Paul Sweeting, 'DVD Protection Faces "Fair-Use" Challenge', *Variety*, 3 April 2000, p. 20.

88. *DVD Copy Control Association Inc., v. Andrew Bunner*, 116 Cal. App. 4th 241, 10 Cal. Rptr. 3d 185, 69 USPQ 2d 1907 (Cal. Ct. App. 2004), accessed 24 April 2015, https://w2.eff.org/IP/Video/DVDCCA_case/20040227_Decision.pdf

89. Parliamentary Office of Science and Technology, *Postnote: Copyright and the Internet* (London: Parliamentary Office of Science and Technology, 2002), p. 1.

90. *A&M Records, Inc. v. Napster, Inc.*, 239 F.3d 1004 (2001), accessed 12 September 2014, http://www.cs.virginia.edu/~evans/cs588-fall2001/manifests/napster.pdf

91. Packard, *Digital Media Law*, p. 176.

92. John Alderman, *Sonic Boom: Napster, MP3, and the New Pioneers of Music* (Cambridge, MA: Perseus, 2001).

93. Justin Oppelaar, 'Music, Film Industries Sue File-sharing Nets', *Daily Variety*, 4 October 2001, p. 8. As well as entering litigation, Hollywood and the music industry also sought to combat P2P through the market with their own authorised online services. Major music companies backed the MusicNet and PressPlay services launched in December 2001. Meanwhile, from 2002 onwards, the Hollywood corporations began licensing films for VoD through the Movielink, MovieBeam, or CinemaNow services. See McDonald, *Video and DVD Industries*, pp. 172–4.

94. Justin Oppelaar, 'Kazaa Suspends Software Downloads', *Daily Variety*, 21 January 2002, p. 8; Justin Oppelaar, 'A Software Switch', *Daily Variety*, 22 January 2002, p. 7.

95. Quoted in Justin Oppelaar, 'Geeks Tweak Hollywood', *Daily Variety*, 28 April 2003, p. 26.

96. 'Brief for Motion Picture Company', *MGM Studios v. Grokster*, US, 25.

97. Ibid., 26–38.

98. Ibid., 38–42.

99. Ibid., 44.

100. Ibid., 44–9.

101. Ibid., 23–4.

102. William Triplett, 'Grokster Sings Swan Song', *Daily Variety*, 8 November 2005, pp. 4, 14.

103. Combating Online Infringement and Counterfeits Act, accessed 21 September 2014, http://www.gpo.gov/fdsys/pkg/BILLS-111s3804rs/pdf/BILLS-111s3804rs.pdf

104. Protect IP Act, accessed 23 September 2014, http://www.gpo.gov/fdsys/pkg/BILLS-112s968rs/pdf/BILLS-112s968rs.pdf

105. Stop Online Piracy Act, accessed 23 September 2014, http://www.gpo.gov/fdsys/pkg/BILLS-112hr3261ih/pdf/BILLS-112hr3261ih.pdf

106. Ibid., pp. 10–18.

107. Centre for Democracy and Technology, 'Google Friends Facebook Against Hollywood-Backed Piracy Bill', 16 November 2011, accessed 23 September 2014, https://cdt.org/press/google-friends-facebook-against-hollywood-backed-piracy-bill/

108. Mike Masnick, 'The Definitive Post on Why SOPA and Protect IP Are Bad, Bad Ideas', *Techdirt*, 22 November 2011, access 24 September 2014, https://www.techdirt.com/articles/20111122/04254316872/definitive-post-why-sopa-protect-ip-are-bad-bad-ideas.shtml

109. AOL, eBay, Facebook, Google, LinkedIn, Mozilla, Twitter, Yahoo! and Zynga, 'We Stand Together to Protect Innovation', 15 November 2011, accessed 23 September 2014, http://boingboing.net/2011/11/16/internet-giants-place-full-pag.html

110. Ibid.

111. Jenna Wortham, 'Many Voices on the Web, Amplified by Social Media', *The New York Times*, 20 January 2012, B1, p. 6.

112. Quoted in Kim Masters, 'How Hollywood Lost the SOPA War', *The Hollywood Reporter*, 3 February 2012, p. 32.

113. Stewart Baker, 'Why the GOP Turned on Piracy', *The Hollywood Reporter*, 10 February 2012, p. 32.

114. Bill D. Herman, *The Fight Over Digital Rights: The Politics of Copyright and Technology* (Cambridge: Cambridge University Press, 2013), p. 206.

References

Alderman, John, *Sonic Boom: Napster, MP3, and the New Pioneers of Music* (Cambridge, MA: Perseus, 2001).

Bettig, Ronald V., *Copyrighting Culture: The Political Economy of Intellectual Property* (Boulder, CO: Westview, 1996).

Bowser, Eileen, *The Transformation of Cinema 1907–1915* (Berkeley: University of California Press, 1990).

Boyd, Douglas and Nawaf Adwan, 'The Gulf States, Jordan and Egypt', in Manuel Alvarado (ed.), *Video World-wide: An International Study* (London: UNESCO/John Libbey, 1988), pp. 158–79.

Decherny, Peter, *Hollywood's Copyright Wars: From Edison to the Internet* (New York: Columbia University Press, 2012).

Gaines, Jane, 'Early Cinema's Heyday of Copying: Too Many Copies of *L'Arroseur arrosé* (*The Waterer Watered*)', *Cultural Studies* vol. 20 no. 2–3 (2006): 227–44.

Herbert, Daniel, *Videoland: Movie Culture at the American Video Store* (Berkeley: University of California Press, 2014).

Herman, Bill D., *The Fight Over Digital Rights: The Politics of Copyright and Technology* (Cambridge: Cambridge University Press, 2013).

Hoyt, Eric, *Hollywood Vault: Film Libraries Before Home Video* (Oakland: University of California Press, 2014).

Johns, Adrian, *Piracy: The Intellectual Property Wars from Gutenberg to Gates* (Chicago, IL: University of Chicago Press, 2009).

Karmina, Pascal, *Film Copyright in the European Union* (Cambridge: Cambridge University Press, 2002).

Klopfenstein, Bruce C., 'The Diffusion of the VCR in the United States', in Mark R. Levy (ed.), *The VCR Age: Home Video and Mass Communications* (Newbury Park, CA: Sage, 1989), pp. 21–39.

Lobato, Ramon, *Shadow Economies of Cinema: Mapping Informal Film Distribution* (London: BFI, 2012).

McDonald, Paul, *Video and DVD Industries* (London: BFI, 2007).

O'Regan, Tom, 'From Piracy to Sovereignty: International Video Cassette Recorder Trends', *Continuum* vol. 4 no.2 (1991): 120.

Packard, Ashley, *Digital Media Law*, 2nd edn (Chichester: Wiley-Blackwell, 2013).

Parliamentary Office of Science and Technology, *Postnote: Copyright and the Internet* (London: Parliamentary Office of Science and Technology, 2002).

Patry, William, *Moral Panics and Copyright Wars* (New York: Oxford University Press, 2009).

Ricketson, Sam, *The Berne Convention for the Protection of Literary and Artistic Works: 1886–1986* (London: Centre for Commercial Law Studies, 1987).

Segrave, Kerry, *Piracy in the Motion Picture Industry* (Jefferson, NJ: McFarland, 2003).

Siwek, Stephen E., *Copyright Industries in the US Economy: The 2013 Report* (Washington, DC: International Intellectual Property Alliance, 2013).

Cases Cited

PART 2
COMPETITION AND CIRCULATION

4 THE PRESERVATION OF COMPETITION
HOLLYWOOD AND ANTITRUST LAW

JENNIFER PORST

When Thomas Edison filed a patent application in 1891 for his motion picture camera and film, it coincided almost exactly with Congress's approval of the Sherman Antitrust Act in 1890. The Sherman Act prohibits anti-competitive business behaviours and requires the federal government to investigate and prosecute corporate trusts. Since that time, the Act has influenced and shaped the film industry in fundamental ways. While the film industry has innovated and grown, the interpretation and enforcement of the Act and subsequent regulation has also evolved to meet the demands of changing political and economic conditions.

This chapter examines Hollywood's relationship with antitrust law and, consequently, issues related to monopoly, restraint of trade, vertical integration and market concentration. Antitrust law is meant to enjoin those practices that allow corporations to dominate their industry through abusive practices that exclude competition. Although the law might have successfully, if temporarily, derailed the anti-competitive behaviours of the Hollywood majors in the early and mid-twentieth century, shifts in the political climate and the rapid innovation and expansion of global Hollywood allowed for those same practices to flourish just a few decades later. Legislation enacted in the 1970s and the embrace of neoliberal economic policies during the Reagan administration ushered in a period of renewed conglomeration and consolidation, and shifted antitrust enforcement away from the prosecution of antitrust violations after the fact, to an emphasis on merger and acquisition review intended to prevent future antitrust violations. Those changes played an important role in allowing contemporary Hollywood studios to return to the market dominance they had enjoyed as a vertically integrated oligopoly prior to the Supreme Court's decision in the Paramount antitrust case in 1948. Analyses of the antitrust cases against the Motion Picture Patents Company (MPPC), Paramount Pictures *et al.* and the merger between General Electric (GE) and Comcast to form the joint venture NBCUniversal in 2011 provides a clear roadmap of the role of antitrust in the evolution of Hollywood, and illustrates how the flexibility inherent in the Sherman Act has allowed for its enforcement to shift over time. Although these cases occurred in very different industrial, social and political environments, they provide clear lessons about the nature of competition and the invisibility and influence of antitrust enforcement in the contemporary film industry.

The Sherman Antitrust Act

In the 1800s, courts and legislatures in the USA expanded property law, and a number of informal and formal methods of corporate combination and collusion developed. They included gentlemen's agreements, trade associations, alliances, holding companies, patent pools, trusts and interlocking directorates.[1] The opponents of those forms of combination, typically smaller and medium-sized competitors, complained about the problems of restraints of trade, such as accumulated capital and the higher costs that resulted from price fixing.[2] At the time, common law, or law that develops out of judicial decisions on a case-by-case basis, largely ruled any disputes that arose regarding restraints of trade. The common law was ineffectual, however, in prosecuting certain types of anti-competitive behaviour, and rising public concern about the abuses of corporate giants such as the Standard Oil Company and others that dominated major markets led to calls for legislation to curb corporate abuses of power. During the campaigns for the 1888 presidential election, both major parties' platforms contained strongly worded condemnations of monopolies.[3]

In 1890, Senator John Sherman introduced an 'An Act to Protect Trade and Commerce Against Unlawful Restraints and Monopolies', which became known as the Sherman Antitrust Act. The Act was motivated largely out of concerns about collusion in markets for homogeneous, industrial products such as steel.[4] The Act got its name from its original target: trusts, which 'placed the stock of many previously competing companies in the hands of a single group of owners'.[5] The terminology in the Act drew largely from the language in common law, and, as Senator Sherman explained to his colleagues, the law 'does not announce a new principle of law, but applies old and well recognized principles of the common law'.[6] Congress passed the law with relatively little debate on 2 July 1890, and the Act has been the cornerstone of antitrust policy in the USA ever since.[7] Although there are eight sections in the Act, the first and second sections are the ones under which the majority of alleged violations take place. The first section declares combinations in restraint of trade to be illegal. The second section condemns monopoly. Section 1 of the Sherman Act outlaws all contracts, combinations and conspiracies that unreasonably restrain interstate trade. Since this applies to unlawful agreements among competitors in a market, it does not cover single-firm, or unilateral, conduct, such as might occur within a vertically integrated company. The agreements can take the form of anything from a formal written contract to an informal, tacit understanding.[8] Agreements that are clearly anti-competitive such as price fixing are per se, or inherently, illegal, and violate Section 1 regardless of the reasonableness of the restraint or its effect on competition. Agreements that do not fall within the per se category are tested under the 'rule of reason' standard.[9] Under the rule of reason, the court must consider the circumstances in which the alleged violations took place, and then they can determine whether the behaviours were reasonable. Although the rule of reason standard was first used in common law in 1711, it was only applied to federal antitrust law in the court's decision in the antitrust action against the Standard Oil Company in 1911.[10] As Chief Justice Edward Douglas White wrote in the decision, 'In every case where it is claimed that an act or acts were in violation of the statute the rule of reason, in the light of the principles of law and the public policy which the act embodies, must be applied.'[11] Although the meaning of 'reasonable' can be very subjective and has changed over time, the rule of reason remains the basic standard for deciding antitrust cases. Section 2 of the Sherman Act differs from Section 1 in that Section 2 it makes it illegal to monopolise any part of interstate commerce. 'Monopoly power' means the power to control prices or exclude competitors. Such power can be exerted in a number of ways – for example, through creating barriers to competitors entering markets, artificially increasing prices, reducing market supply and so on. However, the fact that a firm holds monopoly power does not in itself violate Section 2. That firm has to have obtained its monopoly not because its product or service is superior, but by suppressing competition through unreasonably exclusionary conduct. So, in order to violate Section 2, there needs to be both a monopoly, or an attempt to monopolise, and exclusionary conduct.[12]

As part of its duties as the federal department responsible for enforcing the laws of the USA, the Department of Justice (DOJ) is required to investigate and pursue companies suspected of violating the Sherman Antitrust Act. From 1890 to 1903, the Attorney General handled antitrust matters. Then, in 1903, under President Theodore 'trust buster' Roosevelt, the office of the Assistant to the Attorney General was established and took over antitrust enforcement. It was not until 1933, under the administration of President Franklin D. Roosevelt, that the Antitrust Division of the DOJ was created, and that Division has had enforcement responsibility ever since. The Assistant Attorney General heads the Antitrust Division, and he or she is nominated by the president and confirmed by the Senate. All of the Division's lawsuits are brought in federal courts. According to Makan Delrahaim, former Deputy Assistant Attorney General of the DOJ's Antitrust Division, the primary function of the Department of Justice's Antitrust Division 'is criminal and civil enforcement of the federal antitrust laws and other laws relating to the protection of competition and the prohibition of restraints of trade and monopolisation'.[13] By providing a federal law that established conduct standards, and giving a federal agency the power to intervene when the monopolisation of trade or commerce was suspected, the Sherman Antitrust Act went far beyond the common law's case-by-case adjudication of restrictive agreements. At the same time, the flexibility inherent in the law as a result of malleable concepts such as the rule of reason, or the specificities of market conditions in different industries, would lead to a constant evolution and reinterpretation of the law and its enforcement.

Regulating the Early Movie Business: *United States v. Motion Picture Patents Company, et al.*

The first significant antitrust action brought against the Hollywood film industry was filed on 15 August 1912 in the District Court of the USA for the Eastern District of Pennsylvania. The defendants included the Motion Picture Patents Company, General Film Company, Biograph Company, Thomas A. Edison (Inc.), Essanay Film Manufacturing Company, the Kalem Company (Inc.), George Kleine, Lubin Manufacturing Company, Méliès Manufacturing Company,[14] Pathé Frères, the Selig Polyscope Company, the Vitagraph Company of America, Armat Moving Picture Company, Frank L. Dyer, Henry N. Marvin, J. J. Kennedy, William Pelzer, Samuel Long, J. A. Berst, Siegmund Lubin, Gaston Méliès, Albert E. Smith, George K. Spoor and W. N. Selig.[15] Each of the individual defendants was an officer and director of one or more of the corporate defendants.

The roots of the case go back to the earliest years of motion pictures when the industry was beset by lawsuits over patent infringement, which drained producers', distributors' and exhibitors' time and resources.[16] Then, in November 1907, some of the major film manufacturers and renters held the first in a series of meetings wherein they formed the Edison Licensees and the Film Service Association, respectively, with the goal of putting an end to the patent wars.[17] They agreed that the members of the Film Service Association would purchase film only from the Edison Licensees who included: Edison Manufacturing Co., Pathé Cinematograph Co., American Vitagraph Co., Kalem Co., Selig Polyscope Co., S. Lubin, Méliès Co. and Essanay

Members of the Motion Picture Patents Company
(lightsfilmschool.com/blog/what-is-an-independent-
film/12256)

Co. Biograph and Kleine refused to join the
association, and the film business divided into
two camps that immediately launched patent
infringement suits against each other. Edison
tackled this situation when, in July 1908, he
told Biograph and Kleine that if they agreed
to join the other manufacturers, the many
lawsuits then pending against them would
disappear.[18] With the division now resolved,
the ground was clear for the formation, on
18 December 1908, of the Motion Picture
Patents Company. The MPPC acquired all of
the patents owned by its member compa-
nies. The Edison Co. owned the patent for the camera and negative film, and Biograph owned
patents for the Latham loop, the Pross shutter and the Biograph friction-feed camera. Vitagraph
owned six patents related to projectors and the Armat Co. owned five patents related to cameras and projectors.[19] In return, each member company took an identical licence from the
MPPC to produce and lease motion pictures, and earned a share of the profits made by the
MPPC.[20] The Film Service Association continued operating until January 1909, when the
exchanges were asked to enter licence agreements with the MPPC. Since there was no adequate supply of films available outside the MPPC companies, the exchanges could essentially
either accept the agreements or go out of business.[21] Manufacturers maintained a list of
approved exchanges and theatres, and only distributed and presented their films through those
outlets. No exchange could distribute films other than those made by the combined manufacturers, or distribute films to any cinemas except those named on the list. No cinemas could display a film not made by one of the manufacturers in the MPPC and distributed through an
exchange on the list. Uniform prices were explicitly agreed upon by the manufacturers, and
penalties for violating any of those rules were imposed and enforced. The MPPC also made an
agreement with Eastman Kodak Co., the only manufacturer of film for motion picture cameras
at that time, not to furnish film to any manufacturer outside of the MPPC.[22] The MPPC entered
licence agreements with the manufacturers of projectors stipulating their technology could only
be sold to MPPC approved exhibitors, and the agreements fixed the prices at which the projectors could be sold. The manufacturers were also to pay the MPPC a $5 royalty payment
called 'machine royalties' for each projector sold. Even exhibitors who had purchased their projectors long before the formation of the MPPC had to pay a $2-a-week 'royalty' payment for
each of their projectors. If the exhibitors refused to pay the royalty, they could no longer obtain
films from the MPPC. The MPPC's threats were not empty: between 18 August 1909 and 30
December 1912, the MPPC cancelled the licences of over 500 movie theatres (referred to as
'theatres' hereafter) in the USA after they exhibited unlicensed pictures.[23] In April 1910, the
MPPC took control of distribution as well as production by forming the General Film Company

(GFC). By 1 January 1912, the GFC had purchased, driven out of business, or cancelled the MPPC licences of every rental exchange in the country except for the Greater New York Film Company,[24] which was owned and run by William Fox in defiance of the GFC.[25]

When the DOJ, therefore, filed its complaint against the MPPC, it alleged the defendants had combined to restrain trade and obstruct the free flow of commerce in interstate transactions in the sale of positive motion pictures and other necessary accessories of the motion picture art.[26] The DOJ wanted the court to dissolve both the Motion Picture Patents Company and the GFC. The DOJ also asked that the licence agreements made by and between the MPPC and GFC be declared illegal and cancelled.[27] In their defence, the MPPC members argued that motion pictures were an art, and they were therefore charged with controlling an art, which, unlike commerce, was not subject to prosecution under the antitrust laws.[28] They also argued that prior to the formation of the MPPC, the defendants were infringing on each other's patents, and it was only after the MPPC was formed that there was a lawful trade and commerce in motion pictures. They claimed: 'We transferred the patents to one company not in an effort to dominate and monopolize the motion-picture art but in a repentant spirit and with a desire to use the patents without infringement.'[29] The defendants further argued that the GFC corrected the abuses of the earlier exchanges and exhibitors by regulating the distribution and improving the quality of the supply of films.[30] The MPPC claimed that the GFC's well-organised system made it easier for theatres to rely on a consistent supply of quality films and properly advertise for those films. For example, the GFC's policy of leasing films to exchanges rather than selling the films outright made it possible for the GFC to take damaged prints out of circulation. Previously, when exchanges purchased the prints, they had the right to re-run them until they were literally falling apart, which many of them did, and theatres often complained about the poor quality of the films they received. The MPPC argued that the profits they made from their business were a fair return for the good they had done the industry.[31] The most compelling argument made by the MPPC, however, was that they were simply asserting the legal rights they held through their ownership of a number of overlapping patents.[32] Patents provide their owners with the right to make, use, or vend their patented articles, as well as a legal remedy if another person or corporation uses the patented article without the owner's consent or in a manner in which the patent owner has not approved. By its nature, a patent owner has a monopoly over the right to sell or license his patented article, but the difficulty this posed for the courts then was the need to distinguish between the monopoly rights of a patent owner and a monopoly as outlawed by the Sherman Act. Although patent rights allow patent holders a certain kind of monopoly, the terms under which they use their patented articles have to be legal. Patent holders cannot use their patents to seek 'an unlawful end' or employ 'unlawful means'. For example, as noted by the judge in this case, if someone used their patented device 'as a weapon to disable a rival contestant, or to drive him from the field, he cannot justify such use, because of his patent right'. So while the owner of the patent for a plough handle might join with the owners of the patents for other parts of a plough in order to control the trade in ploughs, they may not also combine with patent owners and other dealers in order to control the entire field of agriculture.[33]

On 1 October 1915, District Judge Oliver B. Dickinson rendered his decision. He wrote, 'Certain it is that the end and purpose of the plan was to dominate and control the trade in all

the accessories of the art, and, in order to assure this, to control the entire motion picture business.'[34] He dismissed the MPPC's defence that they had good intentions and had improved the
art of motion pictures. Even if that was the case, Dickinson said, it would not excuse their illegal
conduct. As Judge Dickinson found the MPPC did monopolise, the question turned to whether
it was a lawful monopoly under their patent rights or an unlawful restraint of trade. The Judge
found that the MPPC's restraint of trade went far beyond the fair and normal possible scope
of any efforts to protect patent rights, and that the direct and intentional result of those undue
and unreasonable restrictions was that the defendants monopolised 'a large part of the interstate trade and commerce in films, cameras, projecting machines, and other articles of commerce accessory to the motion picture business'.[35] The Judge concluded:

> The contracts enumerated in the petition, and the combination there described, were a
> conspiracy in restraint of trade or commerce among several states and with foreign nations,
> and were and are illegal, and that the defendants and each of them (with the exception next
> noted) have attempted to monopolize, and have monopolized, and have combined and
> conspired, among themselves and with each other, to monopolize, a part of the trade or
> commerce among the several states and with foreign nations, consisting of the trade in films,
> cameras, projecting machines, and other accessories of the motion picture business, as charged
> in the petition of complaint filed.[36]

The exception was that the defendant Méliès Manufacturing Company was excluded from the
decision. French brothers George and Gaston Méliès claimed they had been duped into becoming involved with the MPPC, and had never participated in its activities, and the Judge had been
unable to find proof to the contrary.[37] A decree dated 24 January 1916 ordered the dissolution
of the MPPC and on 3 June 1918 the MPPC's appeal to the Supreme Court was dismissed.[38]
By 1918, however, the MPPC's power had been waning for years. They lost their dominance in
part because of the District Court's earlier decision, but also because of the rise of the multi-
reel feature film and independents such as Universal, Triangle Film Corporation and World Film
Company, and because of the success of a variety of other lawsuits brought against the MPPC
by film exchanges and independents over issues such as residual payments and the patent rights
of the Latham Loop. So the Supreme Court's dismissal of the case was merely the final nail in
the coffin.[39] The lawsuit was a significant one, however, for both the film industry and for antitrust
law. Not only did it spur the fundamental reorganisation of the motion picture industry, it clarified
the relationship between the Sherman Act and patent laws for businesses and the courts.

The Clayton Act, the Federal Trade Commission and Antitrust in the 1920s and 30s

While the antitrust case against the MPPC made its way through the courts, a number of significant changes in antitrust law were underway. Woodrow Wilson won the 1912 presidential
election, and he believed that effective antitrust enforcement required a clearer definition of
unlawful business practices than was available in the Sherman Antitrust Act. He argued that the
'rule of reason' denied businesses adequate guidance and gave courts too much discretion to
distort the law through interpretation. He therefore proposed supplementing the Sherman Act

and, as a result, Congress passed the Clayton Act of 1914.[40] The Clayton Act outlined four illegal practices: (1) price discrimination, wherein a product is sold at different prices to similar buyers; (2) exclusive dealing contracts that require a buyer stop dealing with the seller's competitors; (3) corporate mergers, or the acquisition of competing companies; and (4) interlocking directorates where competing companies have common board members. The Act clarified, however, that the first three of those practices were only illegal where the effect was to create a monopoly or lessen competition.[41] Section 7 of the Clayton Act would become more significant, particularly in the film industry, in the late twentieth and early twenty-first century, as it is designed to prohibit mergers or acquisitions that are likely to substantially lessen competition. The Act required all corporations considering a merger or acquisition above a certain size to notify both the Antitrust Division and the Federal Trade Commission. Under the Act, the government can challenge mergers that an economic analysis shows are likely to increase prices to consumers.[42] Further, the Clayton Act provided for consent judgments in antitrust cases.[43] A consent decree is a settlement between parties to a criminal case or lawsuit in which the company or companies that have been accused of antitrust violations agree to take specific actions without admitting fault or guilt for the situation that led to the lawsuit. Companies often agree to consent decrees instead of continuing the case through a trial or hearing, or in return for the government not pursuing criminal penalties.[44] It is part contract and part judicial settlement, and they are as enforceable as any other court order. The Clayton Act required that proposed consent judgments in antitrust cases be subject to a sixty-day comment period, after which the court shall determine whether entry of the proposed Final Judgment is in the public interest.[45]

The Federal Trade Commission Act, also passed in 1914, worked in tandem with the Clayton Act to shore up perceived weaknesses in the Sherman Act. The Federal Trade Commission Act established the Federal Trade Commission (FTC), which shares enforcement responsibilities for the Clayton Act with the DOJ's Antitrust Division. The FTC is composed of five commissioners who are appointed by the president with the approval of the Senate. With the introduction of the FTC, there were now three ways in which federal antitrust laws were enforced: criminal and civil actions brought by the Antitrust Division of the DOJ; civil enforcement actions brought by the FTC; and through lawsuits brought by private parties asserting damage claims. The Act provides that 'unfair methods of competition in or affecting commerce, and unfair or deceptive acts or practices in or affecting commerce are hereby declared unlawful'.[46] Despite the strengthening of antitrust law and regulation in the 1910s, antitrust enforcement diminished somewhat from the end of World War I through the 1930s. In the 1920s, the DOJ and the FTC concentrated more on promoting 'fair' competition than on eliminating restrictive practices and attacking monopoly power. Responding to the Great Depression and the New Deal's National Recovery Administration (NRA), in the early 1930s US economic policy emphasised industry-wide coordination of output and pricing. Only by the decade's end, after the collapse of the NRA and the appointment of Thurman Arnold – another 'trust buster' – to head the DOJ's Antitrust Division, did antitrust emerge from what has been called the 'era of neglect'.[47] Although, broadly speaking, this time was a relatively idle one for antitrust, there were a number of antitrust actions taken against the film industry in the late 1920s through the 30s. For example, in 1925, West Coast Theatres, Inc., an operator of more than a hundred cinemas in the largest cities in California, was charged with violating the Sherman Act through their systems of pricing, runs, clearances and zoning. Those charges resulted in consent decrees meant to eliminate those practices. Then in 1932, the DOJ charged Balaban and Katz, a Paramount subsidiary that controlled exhibition in Chicago, with violating the Sherman Act by monopolising first- and second-run exhibition in the Chicago area through the exclusion of independent exhibitors and the use of excessive clearances. This case also resulted in a consent decree that was meant to curb those illegal behaviours. However, in both decrees the industry was given the responsibility of policing themselves, which simply led to further violations and contributed to the development of an oligopolistic industry that was about to be served with what would become the most infamous antitrust lawsuit in Hollywood history, the *United States v. Paramount Pictures, Inc., et al.*[48]

By 1916, when the MPPC was dissolved by order of the court, future studio moguls like William Fox, Carl Laemmle and Louis B. Mayer were working as smaller, independent producers, distributors and exhibitors. However, Adolph Zukor and Jesse Lasky's Famous Players-Lasky Corporation (which later became known as Paramount Pictures, Inc.) had already become an important production company in the film industry. In 1917, twelve producing companies merged with Famous Players-Lasky Corporation, and they acquired a national distribution system through a merger with Artcraft Pictures Corporation and Paramount Pictures Corporation, which had been originally organised by San Francisco exhibitor and distributor William W. Hodkinson.[49] Also in 1917, the First National Exhibitors Circuit, an association of exhibitors, noticed that the costs they were paying to exhibit the films made by companies like Famous Players kept increasing at an alarming rate. In order to ensure their access to a supply of reasonably priced films, the exhibitors began financing the production of their own films. By 1919, Famous Players felt that the market for the exhibition of their films was being threatened by the films produced by the First National Exhibitors Circuit, so Famous Players began acquiring theatres of their own in order to ensure their films had adequate exhibition. Famous Players' corporate name was changed, on 1 April 1927, to Paramount Famous Lasky Corporation and, on 24 April 1930, was changed again to Paramount Publix Corporation. Also by 1930, the other majors (Loew's, Warners Bros., Fox and RKO) had expanded their businesses to vertically integrate control of production, distribution and exhibition. Those mergers, particularly deals between Fox and Loews, and Warner Bros. and First National, prompted the DOJ to open investigations into the legality of the newly expanded corporations. Although Fox and Warner Bros. had, under the terms of the Clayton Act, sought and received approval from the Justice Department prior to their mergers, the inauguration of Herbert Hoover and the appointment of a new attorney general in 1929 changed the landscape for businesses and antitrust. Although Hoover championed a 'hands off' attitude towards antitrust, particularly in the wake of the stock market crash, his attorney general took a different tack, and said that their earlier approval of the mergers had only been verbal and, therefore, left open the possibility of future action.[50] Those actions led to consent decrees that attempted to enforce competition, and eventually the Fox–Loew's merger was not approved; but the studios continued working to ensure their dominance as vertically integrated powerhouses. As a result, independent cinema owners continued to complain to the DOJ about the unfair business practices of the majors.[51] Even though these complaints kept the DOJ's attention focused on the film industry, by the mid- to late 1930s, the vertically integrated studios were releasing the vast majority of the features produced in the USA with budgets over $250,000, and were the only companies with national distribution systems and established first-run outlets to finance such high budgets.[52] Their global dominance also meant that they could use overseas revenues to reinforce domestic market power.

United States v. Paramount Pictures, Inc., et al.

All of the consolidation of the 1920s and 30s finally led, in July 1938, to the chief of the DOJ's Antitrust Division, Thurman Arnold, filing a lawsuit against the major Hollywood studios accusing them of violating Sections 1 and 2 of the Sherman Act. Subsequently the DOJ filed an amended and supplemental complaint on 14 November 1940.[53] The defendants included: Paramount Pictures, Inc.; Paramount Film Distributing Corporation; Loew's, Incorporated; Radio-Keith-Orpheum Corporation; RKO Radio Pictures, Inc.; Keith-Albee-Orpheum Corporation; RKO Proctor Corporation; RKO Midwest Corporation; Warner Bros. Pictures, Inc.; Vitagraph, Inc.; Warner Bros. Circuit Management Corporation; 20th Century-Fox Film Corporation; National Theatres Corporation; Columbia Pictures Corporation; Screen Gems, Inc.; Columbia Pictures of Louisiana, Inc.; Universal Corporation; Universal Pictures Company, Inc.; Universal Film Exchanges, Inc.; Big U Film Exchange, Inc.; and United Artists Corporation.

From among these, Paramount, Loew's, RKO, Warner Bros., 20th Century-Fox and their subsidiaries were the major defendants, charged with combining and conspiring unreasonably to restrain trade and commerce in the distribution and exhibition of motion pictures and to monopolise such trade and commerce in violation of the Sherman Act. The minor defendants, Columbia, Universal and their subsidiaries, were producers and distributors but not exhibitors, while United Artists was a distributor only. These were likewise charged with combining and conspiring with the five major defendants and with each other to unreasonably restrain and

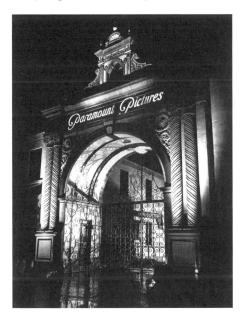

monopolise trade and commerce in motion pictures. The DOJ alleged that, as a result of the defendants' actions, independent exhibitors were systematically excluded from the opportunity to procure preferred runs of pictures distributed by the defendants in the localities in which defendants' theatres operated, and at times refused any run at all in order to protect defendants' theatres from competition.[54] The DOJ asked the court to: declare illegal the contracts, combinations and conspiracies in restraint of trade, together with attempts to monopolise the same; enjoin the defendants from continuing to carry out attempts at monopolisation and

Bronson Gate, Paramount Studios (BFI)

all restraints of trade in distribution and exhibition of motion pictures; establish a nationwide system of impartial arbitration tribunals to enforce the prohibitions of illegal practices that may be contained in the decree; and require the five major defendants and their subsidiaries to divest themselves of all interest and ownership, both direct and indirect, in any theatres which the court shall find to have been used by one or more of them unreasonably to restrain trade and commerce in motion pictures.[55] Before the case went to trial, the major defendants nego-tiated a consent decree, which was entered 20 November 1940.[56] The decree enjoined the defendants from blind selling and block booking, and stipulated that any disputes or complaints that arose would be handled in arbitration. The defendants agreed not to expand their theatre holdings and the DOJ agreed that during the life of the decree there would be no request for the divorcement of the production studios from their theatres. The decree was to last three years, and at any time after the three years, any of the parties could apply to the court for modifications to the decree.[57]Although the major defendants agreed to the decree, the three minor defendants – Columbia, Universal and United Artists – and their subsidiaries did not. The DOJ later found that the system of arbitration introduced by the decree was not effectual enough at remedying the restraints of trade practised by the defendants. After the end of the decree's three-year period, the DOJ therefore moved for trial against all defendants.[58]

During the trial that began on 8 October 1945, the DOJ echoed the concerns of its orig-inal complaint, alleging the defendants violated the Sherman Act through their practices of price fixing, clearances and runs, discrimination among licensees, pooling agreements, block booking and blind selling, formula deals, master agreements and franchises (see also Chapter 6). Those practices, the DOJ argued, resulted in discrimination against small independent exhibitors and in favour of the large affiliated and unaffiliated circuits.[59] The defendants were accused of main-taining a price-fixing system and conspiring with each other to maintain minimum prices. Those actions were per se violations of the Sherman Act. Additionally, the distributors were accused of illegally combining with exhibitors in agreeing to and maintaining minimum admission prices. The DOJ argued that the resulting price structure limited exhibitors' ability to compete against each other in admission prices. In 1933–4, the eight defendants distributed 77.6 per cent of all features nationally, which essentially meant that they controlled the prices to be charged for most of the motion pictures exhibited either by the defendants, or by independents, within the USA. The defendants had argued that the Copyright Act permitted them to exhibit films to which they owned the rights in their own theatres upon such terms as they saw fit. But the court found that while that may be true, the Copyright Act did not sanction a conspiracy among licensors and licensees to artificially maintain prices.[60]

The DOJ argued that the defendants' clearance practices operated to produce unreason-able restrictions of competition between theatres. Clearances determined the amount of time or physical space that had to be 'cleared' before a film could move from one group of theatres to another. Those clearance practices included any or all of the following: a given period between designated runs, admission prices charged by competing exhibitors, a given period of clearance over specifically named theatres, a fixed number of days' clearance over specified areas or towns, and clearances as fixed by other distributors, or a combination of those formu-las.[61] The DOJ asserted that those clearance practices favoured the defendants' affiliated exhi-bition chains and allowed the defendants to control the admissions prices of the theatres involved. Defendants were also accused of restraining competition through formula deals, master agreements and franchises. Formula deals were agreements wherein an exhibitor circuit negotiated the terms of their licence agreements with the defendants based upon the collective earning power of the circuit's theatres, rather than on a theatre to theatre basis. Master agreements determined the terms of exhibition in two or more theatres of a particular circuit. Franchises involved agreements between distributors and exhibitors that covered more than one season and included all of the films released by the distributor.[62] In all of those cases, the DOJ alleged that the practices seriously disadvantaged independent theatre owners who could not, on their own, match or outbid the offers of entire exhibition circuits. Distributor defendants were also accused of block booking and blind selling, which meant they licensed their films in blocks before the films had actually been produced. In many cases, licences for all of the films in a block had to be accepted in order to obtain any films. The DOJ argued that the Sherman Act prohibited such behaviour because it was illegal to condition the licensing of one film upon the acceptance of another. Both block booking and blind selling prevented competitors from bidding for single films on their individual merits.[63] The theatre-owning defendants were also accused of 'pooling their theatres' through operating agreements, leases, joint stock ownership of theatre-operating corporations, or through joint ownership of what were called theatres 'in fee'. If a theatre was owned 'in fee' that meant that while the defendant corporations may not have technically owned the theatre, the fee payments made by the theatre to the defendants were such that the defendants effectively, even if not literally, owned the theatre. These pools allowed the defendants to operate theatres collectively, rather than competitively.[64]

In June 1946, Judge Augustus Hand found the defendants guilty of antitrust violations. He wrote that, in spite of the defence's argument that business convenience and long-term use ought to sanction their behaviours, 'In various ways the system stifles competition and violates the law[,] and that business convenience and loyalty to former customers afford a lame excuse for depriving others of rights to compete and for perpetuating unreasonable restrictions.'[65] Judge Hand found that the clearance practices were not in and of themselves restrictive of competition, but that they were illegal so far as the distributors acted in concert to form a uniform system of clearances. Consequently, defendants were enjoined from agreeing to maintain a system of clearances. Excessive clearances were also declared invalid. The Judge did not agree, however, with the DOJ's request that producers and distributors should be forced to divest themselves of their theatres. The court argued that the existing system provided a quality of exhibition that a sudden shift to completely new and inexperienced theatre owners could not provide for the public. The court also concluded that ownership of exhibition by producers/distributors was not in itself a problem, rather the problem lay in their price fixing, non-competitive granting of runs and clearances, unreasonable clearances, formula deals, master agreements, franchises, block booking, pooling agreements and the discriminatory granting of licences in favour of affiliates and old customers. As an alternative remedy to complete divorcement, the court introduced a bidding system for films and runs that Judge Hand believed would be as effective at remedying the defendant's antitrust violations as would complete divorcement. The system would require the defendants to license their films for reasonable clearances and runs to the highest bidder as long as the bidder was 'responsible' and could exhibit the films in 'a theatre of a size, location, and [with] equipment to present the picture to advantage'. The Judge believed that such a system would benefit the entire industry as well as the public, but admitted that the administrative details of managing and overseeing such a system would 'require further consideration'.[66]

In December 1946, a consent decree was granted that dismissed all claims asserted by the plaintiff, and enjoined the defendants from continuing the practices that had been found illegal by the court. Defendants and their subsidiaries were required to offer the licence for their films to all operators of theatres within any given area, and the licence should be granted to the highest responsible bidder. The studios were no longer allowed to discriminate in favour of any theatres, including affiliates or longstanding customers. Each licence had to be 'offered and taken theatre by theatre and picture by picture'.[67] Theatres that were 'pooled' or co-owned by defendants were also forbidden. Pooling agreements involved the theatres of two or more exhibitors, which would normally compete, operating as a single unit, with profits divided between the theatre owners. Defendants were also ordered to 'cease and desist from ownership of an interest in any theatre, whether in fee or in stock or otherwise, in conjunction with another defendant-exhibitor'.[68] The defendants appealed the case and it was argued before the Supreme Court between the 9 and 11 February 1948. Justice William O. Douglas wrote the opinion for the majority, published on 3 May 1948, which was supported by seven of the eight Justices hearing the case. They affirmed most of the lower court's decision but reversed their remedy. The Court disagreed with the DOJ's contention that vertical integration of production, distribution and exhibition was illegal per se. Instead, the Court stated that the legality of vertical integration depended upon the purpose of intent with which it was conceived, and whether or not it used its power to exclude competition. The most significant area where the Supreme Court disagreed with the lower court was over the finding that the only way to reintroduce competition was through a bidding system. The Court found that such a system would require an enormous amount of judicial supervision, and did not go far enough in dissolving the unlawful restraints and combination. The Supreme Court asked the lower court to reconsider their findings and develop a more effective decree. Although not directing the lower court to require the divorcement of production and distribution from exhibition, the Supreme Court suggested this might be the best remedy.[69]

Once the case was sent back to the District Court, Judge Hand again wrote the opinion. This time the court directed that a divorcement or separation of the business of the motion picture distributors as exhibitors of films from their business as producers and distributors was necessary as a remedy for the violations established in the case. Judge Hand found that, although vertical integration was not illegal per se, the practices engaged in by the defendants were 'powerfully aided by the system of vertical integration'. He continued,

> We do not suggest that every vertically integrated company which engages in restraints of trade or conspiracies will thereby render its vertical integration illegal. The test is whether there is a close relationship between the vertical integration and the illegal practices. Here, the vertical integrations [sic] were a definite means of carrying out the restraints and conspiracies we have described.[70]

Since the Supreme Court had found Judge Hand's previous remedy of competitive bidding insufficient, and since the chief arguments were about the monopoly of and restraints on exhibition, Judge Hand concluded that the divorcement of exhibitors from producers and distributors was the best remedy. The defendants and plaintiffs were to submit amended decrees and findings on or before 20 September 1949.[71] RKO was the first studio to agree to divest itself of its theatres, in part because, with only 109 movie theatres, it had the least to lose of all of the studios. In February 1949, Paramount followed, divesting the company of its theatre holdings. After unsuccessfully attempting to negotiate new consent decrees with the DOJ, by the mid-1950s the remaining defendant studios had sold their theatres.

Shifts in Hollywood and Antitrust from the 1950s to the Twenty-first Century

The effect of the decrees was to dismantle the vertical integration of production, distribution and exhibition that the Hollywood studio system had used to dominate the film industry for decades. In the 1950s, the fallout from the studios' mandated divorcement from their theatres, in combination with the disruption of television and the social and cultural changes in American society post-World War II, forced Hollywood into a period of significant change. Hollywood evolved into an industry where the studios were primarily financiers and distributors of films, with above-the-line talent (i.e., actors, writers and directors) hired on short-term contracts to work on single-film projects. The decrees opened nationwide distribution to independent producers, and resulted in a dramatic increase in independent film-making and distribution. Although the studios remained, and still remain, dominant forces in the industry, the locus of power was reconfigured as a new trend shaped Hollywood's industrial landscape – as well as antitrust regulation and enforcement – into the twenty-first century: conglomeration. Conglomeration is a practice wherein two or more corporations that engage in different businesses are owned by one parent company. For example, in 1969, Warner Bros. was purchased by the conglomerate Kinney National Company which also owned National Periodical Publications (later DC Comics) and Panavision as well as companies like wood flooring manufacturer Circle Floor. When a conglomerate's interests engage in different businesses in a similar industry, such as Warner Bros. and DC Comics, they can engage in synergy through practices like cross-promotion and economies of scale. As Hollywood studios moved into the 1960s and were purchased by, or merged with, larger conglomerates, antitrust laws and enforcement were also undergoing profound changes. As the USA transitioned out of the industrial age and into the information age, the Sherman Act and its enforcement had to evolve as well. Since the original motivation for the Sherman Act had been the elimination of monopoly in industrial markets with homogeneous products such as steel, now that the products and markets were becoming increasingly heterogeneous and complex, the interpretation and enforcement of the Act had to change to meet those new market conditions.

One of the most significant changes in antitrust policy and enforcement occurred in the 1970s when Congress passed the Hart–Scott–Rodino Antitrust Improvements Act of 1976 (HSR). The primary function of the Act was to give antitrust agencies the opportunity to review mergers and acquisitions for potential antitrust violations before they occur. The Act provided those agencies with the time and information necessary to conduct an extensive review.[72] HSR required corporations who were party to a proposed merger or acquisition to notify the DOJ's Antitrust Division and the FTC, provide those agencies with details about the proposed transactions and refrain from completing the transaction until a required thirty-day waiting period had expired. During that period, the Antitrust Division's staff and economists would review the transaction details, contact the parties' customers and competitors and determine whether the transaction raised questions of antitrust violation. If the Division decided that the transaction could raise competitive problems, they could issue a request for additional information and receive another thirty-day waiting period to review the new information. If, at that point, the Antitrust Division decided they needed to block an anti-competitive merger or acquisition, they filed suit in federal court to argue that the proposed transaction violated the Clayton and Sherman Acts.[73]

The 1970s also saw the rise of a group that greatly influenced antitrust regulation and enforcement for decades: the Chicago School of antitrust. It began at the University of Chicago in the 1970s, when members of the law school, along with members of the business and economics departments, began questioning and studying antitrust theory and practice. Robert H. Bork, former attorney general and judge for the US Court of Appeals for the District of Columbia Circuit, encapsulated the concerns of the time that sparked the revolution in antitrust:

> Modern antitrust has so decayed that the policy is no longer intellectually respectable. Some of it is no longer respectable as law; more of it is not respectable as economics; and now I wish to suggest that, because it pretends to one objective while frequently accomplishing its opposite, and because it too often forwards trends dangerous to our form of government and society, a great deal of antitrust is not even respectable as politics.[74]

The model developed by the Chicago School is known as the market efficiency model, and it advocates incorporating economic expertise in the evaluation and analysis of alleged or potential antitrust violations. That is not to say that economics had not been previously incorporated in antitrust law and regulation, rather that the Chicago School was the first to develop an approach that relied almost exclusively on economics.[75]

The Chicago School had two primary characteristics: (1) the exclusive goal of antitrust law, and the primary consideration the judge needs to bear in mind, is the maximisation of consumer welfare; (2) economic analysis should be applied to understand the impact of business behaviour on consumer welfare. Consumer welfare should not be weighed against any other goal, such as 'the supposed social benefits of preserving small businesses against superior efficiency'.[76] That meant that judges should privilege the efficiencies that could be provided for consumers by a larger corporation rather than the preservation of small businesses by limiting the size and power of larger corporations. Although the Chicago School developed their approach to antitrust in the 1970s, it was not until the 1980s that it took hold in antitrust enforcement. When Ronald Reagan was elected President, his administration believed, as did the Chicago School, that antitrust interventions in the economy had become overly zealous and obstructed innovation, so they took steps to address the matter. In the most practical sense, antitrust enforcement was weakened by the fact that the number of lawyers in the Justice Department's Antitrust Division was reduced by half over the decade, and its appropriations cut by 30 per cent. FTC personnel and antitrust activities also declined.[77] For example, between 1981 and 1992, antitrust agencies only prosecuted a total of three cases involving misconduct by dominant firms. That was the smallest number of cases since the adoption of the Sherman Act in 1890.[78] While in the 1960s and 70s the DOJ never lost an antitrust case in court, in the 1980s they almost never won because the courts had become much less receptive to the DOJ's opposition to mergers.

In analysing mergers, the DOJ's approach is outlined in their Merger Guidelines. They issued their first Merger Guidelines in 1968, and revised versions were subsequently released in 1982, 1984, 1992, 1997 and 2010. In 2006, the DOJ also released the 'Commentary on the Merger Guidelines'.[79] Those periodic revisions allowed the Merger Guidelines to 'reflect any significant changes in enforcement policy or to clarify aspects of existing policy'.[80] Rather than simply reflecting changes that had already taken place in Agency enforcement and practice, however, the new Merger Guidelines released in the 1980s changed the DOJ's enforcement practices. The Guidelines of the 1980s grounded merger policy solely in considerations of economic efficiency. For example, the 1984 Guidelines stated, 'The primary benefit of mergers to the economy is their efficiency-enhancing potential, which can increase the competitiveness of firms and result in lower prices to consumers.'[81] The Guidelines were not only used in merger policy; they also influenced the questions posed by the courts in antitrust analysis. One of the most significant ways that antitrust regulation and enforcement evolved was through the decisions of the federal courts. Life-tenured judges, appointed by presidents and approved by Congress, ultimately control the interpretation and application of antitrust doctrine. During their time in office, Ronald Reagan and George H. W. Bush appointed two-thirds of the nation's federal judges and five Supreme Court Justices. Those judges were often selected because their ideologies mirrored those of the administration, namely that they believed in the Chicago School views of antitrust and doubted the ability of the government to efficiently intervene in the market.

Shifts in antitrust policy and enforcement during the 1980s parallelled (and perhaps encouraged) a sharp increase in merger activity in the film industry. The mergers resulted in the film studios becoming part of global conglomerates, and created industrial alliances between film, television, cable, publishing, home video, music, merchandising and theme parks. This structural convergence consisted of a mixture of vertical and horizontal integration and conglomeration whose goal was to create synergy between previously distinct industries as well as between production, distribution and exhibition outlets.[82] Whereas vertical integration consisted of control of different stages of a supply chain, such as production, distribution and exhibition of film, horizontal integration is a process wherein a conglomerate owns companies that create or acquire products or services that are complementary or increase market share, such as a conglomerate like 21st Century-Fox, which owns television networks and film studios so that its content can be used synergistically and flow easily across its different media channels. These mergers, and the global and structural convergence that resulted, played a sort of chicken and egg game with antitrust policy. As economist Paul Krugman observed: 'At first, arguments against policing monopoly power [in the 1980s] pointed to the alleged benefits of mergers in terms of economic efficiency. Later, it became common to assert that the world had changed in ways that made all those old-fashioned concerns about monopoly irrelevant.'[83] That assertion was reflected in another significant revision and expansion of the Merger Guidelines in 1997. Those changes reflected an appreciation that mergers could promote competition by enabling efficiencies, and that those efficiencies could be great enough to reduce or reverse adverse competitive effects that might arise in their absence.[84] As the DOJ's Makan Delrahim explained in 2003, 'Our approach to merger enforcement is premised on the idea that competition should be preserved because consumers benefit from it through lower prices and better products, services, and innovation.'[85]

Those attitudes and approaches in antitrust enforcement continued through the administration of President George W. Bush. When the Obama administration came into office, it promised to actively enforce antitrust laws. However, as a result of the 2008 financial crisis and resulting economic recession, no significant antitrust action was taken until Obama began his second term in office.[86] While no important changes were made to antitrust policy between 2008 and 2012, some minor modifications were made. In 2009, the DOJ withdrew a Bush administration policy that 'favored caution by regulators and the development of safe harbors for companies that controlled a given market'.[87] In 2010, it issued revised Merger Guidelines that emphasised the fact that merger analysis does not consist of uniform application of a single methodology.[88] As Sharis Pozen, Assistant Attorney General for the DOJ's Antitrust Division, explained, 'Because mergers "come in a variety of shapes and sizes", effective remedies "also come in a wide variety of shapes and sizes". The touchstone principle, of course, is that "a successful merger remedy must effectively preserve competition in the relevant market"'.[89]

Comcast and General Electric's Merger to Form the Joint Venture NBCUniversal

One of the most significant mergers to test the antitrust policies of the first Obama administration (2009–12), and one of the most significant mergers in contemporary Hollywood, began on 3 December 2009 when Comcast Corporation, General Electric Company, NBCUniversal, Inc. (NBCU) and Navy, LLC announced plans for a new joint venture that merged NBCU's properties with Comcast's regional sports networks, programming networks and certain online businesses. A joint venture (JV) is a short-term business partnership wherein two or more parties agree to pool their resources, intellectual property and assets to develop some kind of business transaction for mutual profit. A joint venture is different from an acquisition because there is no transfer of ownership in the deal. For GE's and Comcast's JV, GE owned 49 per cent of the new company, and Comcast held majority control of and managed the new company: NBCUniversal.[90]

Founded in 1912, Universal Studios is one of the oldest film studios in Hollywood. Starting in the 1960s, the ownership of Universal Studios passed through a number of hands as the result of a variety of mergers and acquisitions. Those included the takeover by MCA in 1962, acquisitions by Matsushita, Seagram and Vivendi in the 1990s and 2000s, and the sale to General Electric in 2004. GE renamed the media conglomerate NBCUniversal, and its film subsidiary retained the name Universal Studios. By combining Universal's film content and distribution outlets, which included Universal Studios, Universal Pictures, Focus Features and Illumination Entertainment, with the television content and cable channels of NBC, GE became a dominant force in the entertainment industry. The new proposed JV between Comcast, GE

Comcast ad promoting the proposed merger with NBCU that ran in the Washington, DC, inside-the-Beltway publication *The Hill* (*MediaPost* www.mediapost.com/publications/article/132436/comcast-pitches-hollywood-pols-on-nbc-merger.html?edition=)

and NBCUniversal combined NBCU's broadcast TV, cable programming, movie studio and theme park business with Comcast's video programming channels and cable service, thereby extending the reach of the company across all traditional and digital platforms.

NBCU was a major content provider, while, as the leading multichannel video programming distributor (MVPD) and broadband internet access provider in the USA, Comcast mainly operated as a distributor of that content.[91] Comcast had nearly 23 million, or a quarter, of MVPD subscribers nationwide and more than 40 per cent of subscribers in seven of the ten largest metropolitan areas.[92] As Brian Roberts, Chairman and CEO of Comcast, argued in the hearing on the merger held by the Congressional Subcommittee on Antitrust, Competition Policy and Consumer Rights:

> This transaction puts two great American communications companies under one roof. It will help to preserve traditional broadcast television, a business that faces serious challenges. And it will also help to accelerate a truly amazing digital future for consumers. Together, Comcast and NBCU can help to deliver the anytime, anywhere, multi-platform video experience Americans want. In combination, we will be a more creative and innovative company that will meet customer demands. And our success will stimulate our competitors to be more innovative, too. So this joint venture should be good for consumers, innovation, and competition.[93]

Roberts repeatedly appealed to the ways the proposed merger would increase efficiency, encourage innovation and benefit the public, principles that had been clearly delineated by the Chicago School as benefits that should outweigh concerns about possible abuses of market power. Clearly, the heads of these corporate giants had become fluent in the language of antitrust.

Soon after the JV was announced, the DOJ began an investigation of the potential implications of the transaction. The DOJ also consulted extensively with the Federal Communications Commission (FCC), who, as the regulating body with jurisdiction over telecommunications policy, held expertise in the economics of the media industries. Although the DOJ and FTC have the primary enforcement responsibility for antitrust law, the FCC shares oversight responsibilities with the DOJ and FTC in regard to any merger involving a regulated communications company.[94] In particular, in this case, the DOJ was concerned about the potential power Comcast would have gained through the merger to restrict competition from online video distributors (OVDs).[95] On 4 February 2010, there was a hearing before the Senate Subcommittee on Antitrust, Competition Policy and Consumer Rights of the Committee on the Judiciary on the effects on competition and consumers of the proposed Comcast NBCUniversal merger. Committee Chairman Herb Kohl opened the hearings by remarking:

> The combination of NBC's content holdings with Comcast's distribution power would create a media powerhouse of unmatched size and scope which, if approved, will have far-reaching consequences for competition and consumers. … We are witnessing the creation of a media conglomerate which is likely to greatly impact both what consumers pay for cable television and the ability of other pay television companies to compete fairly in the market.[96]

As Senator Orin Hatch noted in his opening statement, this was a merger that was primarily about vertical integration, which was, perhaps ironically, the foundation of the offences that the Paramount consent decrees were meant to remedy a half-century earlier.[97] Brian Roberts agreed with Hatch's observation and asserted, 'The combination of NBCU and Comcast, with no significant overlap between the assets of the companies, is primarily vertical, which generally poses fewer antitrust concerns.'[98] Roberts further argued that the programme access and programme carriage rules Congress enacted in 1992 addressed potential risks from vertical integration and ensured that a company which owned cable content and distribution could not treat competitors unfairly.[99] Comcast had been arguing for years, however, to overturn the programme access rules based on the contention that the marketplace was sufficiently competitive and, therefore, no longer required them. Prior to the hearing before the Senate Subcommittee on Antitrust, Competition Policy and Consumer Rights, Comcast had pledged to adhere to a number of commitments with respect to the merger.[100] These included providing more local programming, children's programming and diverse programming on more platforms. They also committed to reassuring competitors that they would compete fairly in the marketplace by volunteering not to apply programme access rules to retransmission consent negotiations and adding at least two new independently owned cable channels to their systems every year.[101]

On 18 January 2011, the USA, along with a group of states, filed a civil antitrust complaint seeking to enjoin the proposed merger because they had determined the:

> Likely effect would be to lessen competition substantially in the market for timely distribution of professional, full-length video programming to residential customers in major portions of the United States in violation of Section 7 of the Clayton Act. The transaction would allow Comcast to disadvantage its traditional competitors (direct broadcast satellite ['DBS'] and telephone companies ['telcos'] that provide video services), as well as competing emerging OVDs. This loss of current and future competition likely would result in lower-quality services, fewer choices, and higher prices for consumers, as well as reduced investment and less innovation in this dynamic industry.[102]

The DOJ proposed a Final Judgment outlining terms upon which they would allow the merger to proceed. Some of the most significant terms included requiring Comcast to fairly license its programming to emerging OVD competitors, and preventing Comcast from interfering with an OVD's ability to obtain content or deliver its services over the internet. The Judgment established a system of arbitration to resolve any disputes that arose regarding alleged violations of those requirements.[103] The Judgment also contained provisions designed to protect Comcast's traditional video distribution competitors by prohibiting any discriminating against or punishing of a content provider for supplying programming to a rival OVD. Further, it required Comcast to treat all internet traffic the same and to ensure that traffic from competing OVDs was treated no worse than other traffic on Comcast's internet access service.[104]

Since the FCC takes its mandate from the Communications Act of 1934, their evaluation of the merger was primarily concerned with determining whether it was in the public interest, convenience and necessity.[105] They considered not only the effects of the merger on competition, but also whether it supported other communications policy objectives. Comcast claimed that the merger would enhance their ability to innovate, and lead to reduced costs for consumers. The FCC found those claims to be 'plausible in principle, but in some respects speculative, overstated, or unsubstantiated'.[106] On 18 January 2011, the FCC adopted a Memorandum Opinion and Order related to the merger, which approved the transaction subject to certain conditions. One of those conditions was that Comcast agreed to follow the FCC's net neutrality guidelines, which required Comcast, as an ISP, to treat all data on the internet equally. That meant that they could not slow down the delivery speeds of, or charge more to, their rival content providers. Another of the most significant requirements was that the new JV was required to license content on reasonable terms to OVDs. It also provided for arbitration for the resolution of disputes over access to programming.[107] That requirement was similar to the one in the DOJ's Final Judgment, and the DOJ had agreed to defer to the FCC's commercial arbitration process to resolve such disputes. The Court approved the DOJ's Final Judgment and FCC's Order on 1 September 2011, and both the Order and the Judgment were set to expire seven years from their dates of entry unless the Court chose to extend them.

Approval of the merger was due in part to the extensive lobbying efforts of Comcast who had more than a hundred registered lobbyists in Washington alone. The FCC also received letters in support of the merger from over fifty-four different groups who benefited from contributions made by Comcast's charitable foundation.[108] Having a network of non-profit groups was particularly helpful when seeking approval from a commission like the FCC, which in making their decisions gave consideration to a corporation's commitments to diversity and local communities. The relationship between gifts and support for deals extended beyond charitable organisations, however. Shortly after the FCC approved the merger in 2011, Meredith Attwell Baker, one of the Commissioners of the FCC who voted to approve the Comcast merger, left the FCC to help lead Comcast's internal lobbying office in Washington. Ninety-one of the ninety-seven members of Congress who signed a letter of support for the merger had received contributions during that election cycle from Comcast's political action committee or executives.[109] Although corporations have always worked to exert their power and influence in politics for their own gain, it is no coincidence that the growth of lobbying forces in Washington over the last few decades has coincided with the explosion of mergers, the tremendous growth of massive media conglomerates and the return to corporate structures and practices that had once been deemed unlawful.

Conclusion

The merger of Comcast's and GE's properties to form a new joint venture in NBCUniversal provides an excellent example of the contemporary relationship between antitrust enforcement and the media industries. It also highlights the extent to which both antitrust and Hollywood have evolved since their beginnings in the 1890s. The examples of the MPPC, Paramount and Comcast provide a roadmap through that evolution, and demonstrate that in each case the companies involved aimed to dominate the industry in the wake of some form of disruption. For the MPPC, it was the company's attempts to control the young industry and create some order in the relative chaos. For the vertically integrated studio system of the 1930s and 40s, the studios worked to maximise profits by insuring and controlling a constant supply and demand in the wake of the Depression and the introduction of sound film. With recent mergers, film and television conglomerates are working to attain and maintain dominance after the introduction of digital media.

What is clear is that, in the wake of legal, technological, political, or industrial disruptions, windows of time open in which monopolistic behaviours are allowed or unnoticed. During those periods of transition, the industry and regulatory agencies like the FCC, FTC and DOJ must grapple with the ramifications of innovation. As the rate of change exponentially increases in the increasingly complex, global media industry, regulators must first answer basic questions of what should be regulated and by whom. Debates over the regulation of the internet and net neutrality serve as a case in point wherein regulators have struggled to keep pace and strike a balance between promoting efficient competition and curbing anti-competitive behaviours. Assistant Attorney General Sharis Pozen also recognised this tendency and predicted:

> In the future, media sectors will witness new periods of rapid or revolutionary change, with new technologies or other innovations challenging reigning paradigms. We can also expect, if the past supplies any lessons, that incumbents will react in different ways, sometimes responding to the new competitive challenge with their own innovations, sometimes with anti-competitive stratagems, sometimes in both or other ways. The Antitrust Division stands ready to police any efforts to short-circuit the competitive process, applying sound principles of antitrust enforcement.[110]

Although this chapter has focused on Hollywood and its relationship to the antitrust laws and enforcement in the USA, one of the next big disruptions in antitrust may come about as a result of the increasingly global nature of the media industries and potential conflicts between international regulatory agencies and policy. The European Union's (EU) antitrust authorities regulate corporations worldwide and adopted merger review guidelines in the Merger Control Regulation which took effect in September 1990. In 2001, the USA's Antitrust Division and the FTC helped found the International Competition Network (ICN), which includes members from over eighty antitrust agencies around the world, and aims to make the merger review process around the world more efficient and effective.[111] Adding to the already complex international web of regulation and enforcement, in 2014 regulators and investigators from the three agencies tasked with enforcing antitrust law in China, the State Administration for Industry and Commerce, Ministry of Commerce and National Development and Reform Commission, indicated their interest in more strictly policing multinational corporations doing business in China.[112] As the media industry becomes an increasingly global and digital enterprise, the relationship between the antitrust law and merger guidelines of the EU, ICN, China and the USA will become increasingly important, and it will be necessary to expand the concept of antitrust to activities that restrict competition worldwide rather than just in American markets.

Notes

1. Janet Staiger, 'Combination and Litigation: Structures of US Film Distribution, 1896–1917', *Cinema Journal* vol. 23 no. 2 (Winter 1984): 41–72.

2. Ibid.

3. Ernest Gellhorn, William E. Kovacic and Stephen Calkins, *Antitrust Law and Economics in a Nutshell*, 5th edn (St Paul, MN: Thomson/West, 1994), pp. 17–21.

4. See Carl Shapiro, 'The 2010 US Horizontal Merger Guidelines: From Hedgehog to Fox in Forty Years', *Antitrust Law Journal* vol. 77 no. 1 (2010).

5. Jack C. High and Wayne E. Gable, 'Introduction', in Jack C. High and Wayne E. Gable (eds), *A Century of the Sherman Act: American Economic Opinion, 1890–1990* (Fairfax, VA: George Mason University Press, 1992), p. viii.

6. Gellhorn, Kovacic and Calkins, *Antitrust Law and Economics in a Nutshell*, p. 23.

7. High and Gable, 'Introduction', p. vii.

8. See Makan Delrahim, 'Antitrust Enforcement in the Entertainment and Media Industries', Remarks Presented at the Recording Artists' Coalition, Los Angeles, 18 December 2003.

9. Ibid.

10. *Standard Oil Co. v. US*, 221 US, 1, 66.

11. Quoted in: 'Brief for the United States'. *The United States of America, v. Motion Picture Patents Company et al.*, 247 US 524; 38 S. Ct. 578; 62 L. Ed. 1248; 1914 US Dist., 8.

12. Delrahim, 'Antitrust Enforcement in the Entertainment and Media Industries'.

13. Ibid.

14. The inclusion of the Méliès Manufacturing Company as a defendant is a strange case of its own. Although the French production company, run by George and Gaston Méliès, was named the Star Film Company, in 1908 Gaston had contracted with J. J. Lodge to create the George Méliès Company in order to carry on and extend the Méliès brothers' business in the USA. Both George and Gaston held a licence from the Edison Manufacturing Company that allowed them to import their film negatives from Paris to the USA, where they produced positive prints for US distribution and exhibition. On 18 September 1908, those licences were formally transferred to the George Méliès Company. Around that same time, the MPPC was established and the George Méliès Company, as an Edison licensee, was made a part of the MPPC. The MPPC warned Lodge that he should not sell shares of the George Méliès Company to any film exchanges, but he went ahead and sold a significant number of shares to an owner of a Chicago film exchange. When the

Méliès brothers and the MPPC found out what Lodge had done, the MPPC cancelled the licence of the George Méliès Company, and the Méliès brothers attempted to sever their ties with Lodge and his company. Lodge refused to accept the Méliès' resignations and brought suit against the MPPC to reinstate the licence of the George Méliès Company. Meanwhile, Gaston Méliès started another company called the Méliès Manufacturing Company in order to produce his own films, and he and his son Paul continued to be involved in the General Film Company as members of the Board of Directors. The complexity and timing of this history of the Méliès' dealings in the USA led to the inclusion of the Méliès Manufacturing Company as a defendant in the antitrust case against the MPPC, but the judge later found that the evidence supported the fact that neither the Méliès Manufacturing Company nor Gaston Méliès had been closely involved in the business of the MPPC and dismissed the charges against them.

15. John C. Swartley, 'Original Petition'. *The United States of America, v. Motion Picture Patents Company et al.*, 247 US 524; 38 S. Ct. 578; 62 L. Ed. 1248; 1912 US Dist., 1.

16. Staiger, 'Combination and Litigation', pp. 41–72.

17. 'Brief for the United States', *The United States of America, v. Motion Picture Patents Company et al.*, 247 US 524; 38 S. Ct. 578; 62 L. Ed. 1248; 1914 US Dist., 120-121.

18. Ibid., 123–4, 131–3.

19. Ibid., 40, 43, 83.

20. Swartley, 'Original Petition', 9–10.

21. 'Brief for the United States', 135–8.

22. Ibid., 3–5.

23. Ibid., 4, 60–6, 146.

24. William Fox started the Greater New York Film Company around 1906 and functioned as a rental exchange and distributor of films, projectors and other appliances for exhibition. Fox became a licensee with Edison, but objected to the terms of the MPPC agreement for two main reasons. First, it stipulated that Fox would lease the films rather than purchase them outright and, second, it gave the MPPC the right to cancel Fox's licence for any reason and without explanation. The MPPC was unwilling to negotiate their terms, so Fox eventually capitulated and became a MPPC licensee. The General Film Company began operations in 1910; by the autumn of 1911, the only licensed rental exchanges left in New York were the Greater New York Film Rental Company and the General Film Company. In September 1911, the GFC offered to buy out the Greater New York Film Company, but Fox refused because his business was doing well. Then, in November of that same year, he received a notice of cancellation without explanation from the MPPC. While there was no explanation given, it was clear that the GFC wanted to eliminate the competition from Fox one way or another. If he wasn't going to sell his company to them, then they were going to run him out of business by cancelling his licence. Fox tried to get his licence reinstated, but was unsuccessful and, finally, agreed to sell. The GFC did not want to buy his company with an expired licence (apparently this caused a great deal of extra paperwork), so the GFC got the MPPC to reinstate Fox's licence on 1 December 1911. Once Fox had his licence reinstated, he again refused to sell. A week later, he received his second notice of cancellation from the MPPC. At that point, he filed an injunction against the MPPC to prevent them from discontinuing their service of film. Fox was in litigation with the MPPC for years, and it was only in late 1913 that the courts finally turned down his appeals because the terms of his contract with

the MPPC did, in fact, allow them to cancel his licence for any reason. Although Fox's case against the MPPC is often conflated with the DOJ's antitrust suit against the MPPC, they were different cases; however, Fox's struggles with the MPPC undoubtedly called the monopoly power of the MPPC to the attention of the DOJ and influenced the DOJ's decision to bring an antitrust suit against the MPPC.

25. Swartley, 'Original Petition', 29–30.
26. District Judge Dickinson, 'Opinion'. *United States v. Motion Picture Patents Co. et al.*, 247 US 524; 38 S. Ct. 578; 62 L. Ed. 1248; 225 F. 800; 1915 US Dist. Lexis 1314.
27. Swartley, 'Original Petition', 40–1.
28. Dickinson, 'Opinion'.
29. 'Brief for the United States', 78–9.
30. Philipp and Homer, 'Memorandum', 62–3.
31. Dickinson, 'Opinion'.
32. Ibid.
33. Ibid.
34. Ibid.
35. Ibid.
36. Ibid.
37. 'Brief for Appellees Motion Picture Patents Company and Edison Manufacturing Company'. *George Méliès Company, Appellant, vs. Motion Picture Patents Company, et al.*, Appellees. F. (3d Cir. 1912).
38. 'Opinion'. *Motion Picture Patents Company et al., Appellants, v. United States*, 247 US 524; 38 S. Ct. 578; 62 L. Ed. 1248; 1918 US Lexis 1945. 3 June 1918.
39. For more information on these factors, see Jeanne Thomas, 'The Decay of the Motion Picture Patents Company', *Cinema Journal* vol. 10 no. 2 (Spring 1971): 34–40.
40. Gellhorn, Kovacic and Calkins, *Antitrust Law and Economics in a Nutshell*, p. 34.
41. Ibid., pp. 35–6.
42. Delrahim, 'Antitrust Enforcement in the Entertainment and Media Industries'.
43. Yvette F. Tarlov, 'Competitive Impact Statement', *United States of America, et al. v. Comcast Corp., et al.*, United States District Court for the District of Columbia 1:11-cv-00106. (18 January 2011).
44. *West's Encyclopedia of American Law*, 2nd edn (The Gale Group, Inc., 2004).
45. Tarlov, 'Competitive Impact Statement'.
46. 15 USCA § 45.
47. Gellhorn, Kovacic and Calkins, *Antitrust Law and Economics in a Nutshell*, p. 51.
48. Michael Conant, *Antitrust in the Motion Picture Industry: Economic and Legal Analysis* (Los Angeles: University of California Press, 1960), pp. 84–8.
49. 'Amended and Supplemental Complaint', *United States of America, v. Paramount Pictures, Inc. et al.*, Civil Action No. 87-273. District Court of the United States for the Southern District of New York. 14 November 1940.
50. 'Dept. of Justice Reopening Verbal Approval of Warner-1st Nat'l Buy, Like Fox-Loew', *Variety*, 3 July 1929; 'Gov't Picks on Pictures', *Variety*, 4 December 1929.
51. 'US Sharpening Pic Axe: Renewed Prosecution by Justice Dept. Vs. Fox-WC Mentioned in Wash.', *Variety*, 16 January 1934.
52. 'Amended and Supplemental Complaint'.

53. Ibid.
54. Augustus N. Hand, 'Opinion'. *United States v. Paramount Pictures, Inc., et al.*, United States District Court for the Southern District of New York. 66 F. Supp. 323. 11 June 1946.
55. Ibid.
56. Justice Douglas, 'Opinion of the Court'. *United States v. Paramount Pictures, Inc. et al.*, Supreme Court of the United States. 334 US 131; 68 S. Ct. 915; 92 L. Ed. 1260. 3 May 1948.
57. Hand, 'Opinion'. 1946.
58. Douglas, 'Opinion'.
59. Hand, 'Opinion'. 1946.
60. Ibid.
61. Ibid.
62. Ibid.
63. Ibid.
64. Ibid.
65. Ibid.
66. Ibid.
67. Ibid.
68. Ibid.
69. Douglas, 'Opinion'.
70. Hand, 'Opinion'. *United States v. Paramount Pictures, Inc. et al.*, District Court for the Southern District of New York. 85 F. Supp. 881. 25 July 1949.
71. Ibid.
72. Delrahim, 'Antitrust Enforcement in the Entertainment and Media Industries'.
73. Ibid.
74. Robert H. Bork, *The Antitrust Paradox: A Policy at War With Itself* (New York: Free Press, 1993), p. x.
75. Herbert Hovenkamp, 'Antitrust Policy After Chicago', *Michigan Law Review* vol. 84 no. 2 (November 1985): 213–84.
76. Bork, *The Antitrust Paradox*, p. xi.
77. Phillip Areeda, 'Antitrust Policy', in Martin Feldstein (ed.), *American Economic Policy in the 1980s* (Chicago: University of Chicago Press, 1994), pp. 573–4.
78. Gellhorn, Kovacic and Calkins, *Antitrust Law and Economics in a Nutshell*, p. III.
79. Shapiro, 'The 2010 US Horizontal Merger Guidelines'.
80. United States Department of Justice, '1984 Merger Guidelines' (1984).
81. Ibid.
82. For an in-depth look at the structural convergence of the 1980s, see Jennifer Holt, *Empires of Entertainment: Media Industries and the Politics of Deregulation, 1980–1996* (New Jersey: Rutgers University Press, 2011).
83. Paul Krugman, 'Barons of Broadband', *The New York Times*, 16 February 2014.
84. Shapiro, 'The 2010 US Horizontal Merger Guidelines'.
85. Delrahim, 'Antitrust Enforcement in the Entertainment and Media Industries'.
86. Jad Mouawad, 'US, Filing Suit, Moves to Block Airline Merger', *The New York Times DealBook*, 13 August 2013, accessed 18 December 2013, http://dealbook.nytimes.com
87. Ibid.

88. United States Department of Justice and Federal Trade Commission, 'Horizontal Merger Guidelines' (2010).

89. Sharis Pozen, 'Insights into Antitrust Enforcement in Media Industries', *Competition Law International* (January 2012): 20.

90. In 2013 Comcast purchased GE's remaining 49 per cent stake in the JV for $16.7 billion. In 2014 they moved to further expand their reach by announcing a deal to acquire Time Warner Cable for about $45 billion.

91. Comcast wholly owned national cable networks, including E! Entertainment, G4, Golf, Style and Versus, and it had partial ownership in Current Media, MLB Network, NHL Network, PBS Kids Sprout, Retirement Living Television and TV One. It owned controlling and partial interests in regional sports networks, and owned digital properties such as DailyCandy.com, Fandango.com and Fancast, its online video website. GE was a global infrastructure, finance and media company. GE owned 88 per cent of NBCU, which wholly owned NBC and Telemundo, as well as ten local NBC-owned and -operated television stations, sixteen Telemundo O&Os and one independent Spanish-language television station. NBCU also owned national cable networks Bravo, Chiller, CNBC, CNBC World, MNBC, mun2, Oxygen, Sleuth, SyFy and USA Network. They partially owned A&E Television Networks (including the Biography, History and Lifetime cable networks), The Weather Channel and Shop NBC. NBCU also owned Universal Pictures, Focus Films and Universal Studios. NBCU produced approximately three-quarters of the original prime-time programming shown on the NBC broadcast network and the USA cable network. NBCU was also a founding partner and 32 per cent owner of Hulu (Tarlov, 'Competitive Impact Statement').

92. Jonathan B. Baker, 'Comcast/NBCU: The FCC Provides a Roadmap for Vertical Merger Analysis', *Antitrust* (Spring 2011): 36.

93. 'The Comcast/NBC Universal Merger: What Does the Future Hold for Competition and Consumers?' Hearing Before the Subcommittee on Antitrust, Competition Policy and Consumer Rights of the Committee on the Judiciary. United States Senate. One Hundred Eleventh Congress, Second Session. US Government Printing Office. 4 February 2010, p. 9.

94. For more information about the boundaries between the FCC's regulatory jurisdiction and antitrust law, which have been hotly debated in regard to net neutrality, see Babette E. L. Boliek, 'FCC Regulation Versus Antitrust: How Net Neutrality is Defining the Boundaries', *Boston College Law Review* vol. 52 no. 1627 (2011).

95. Pozen, 'Insights into Antitrust Enforcement in Media Industries': 18.

96. 'The Comcast/NBC Universal Merger', p. 1.

97. Ibid., p. 3.

98. Ibid., p. 9.

99. Ibid.

100. Ibid., p. 2.

101. Ibid., p. 9.

102. Tarlov, 'Competitive Impact Statement'.

103. Ibid.

104. Ibid.

105. Ibid.

106. Baker, 'Comcast/NBCU': 38.

107. Tarlov, 'Competitive Impact Statement'.

108. Eric Lipton, 'Comcast's Web of Lobbying and Philanthropy', *The New York Times*, 20 February 2014.

109. Ibid.

110. Pozen, 'Insights into Antitrust Enforcement in Media Industries': 21.

111. Delrahim, 'Antitrust Enforcement in the Entertainment and Media Industries'.

112. Neil Gough, Chris Buckley and Nick Wingfield, 'China's Energetic Enforcement of Antitrust Rules
      Alarms Foreign Firms', *The New York Times*, 10 August 2014.

References

'Amended and Supplemental Complaint'. *United States of America, v. Paramount Pictures, Inc. et al.*, Civil
      Action No. 87–273. District Court of the United States for the Southern District of New York.
      14 November 1940.

Areeda, Phillip, 'Antitrust Policy', in Martin Feldstein (ed.), *American Economic Policy in the 1980s*
      (Chicago: University of Chicago Press, 1994).

Baker, Jonathan B., 'Comcast/NBCU: The FCC Provides a Roadmap for Vertical Merger Analysis', *Antitrust*
      (Spring 2011).

Boliek, Babette E. L., 'FCC Regulation Versus Antitrust: How Net Neutrality is Defining the Boundaries',
      Boston College Law Review vol. 52 no. 1627 (2011).

Bork, Robert H., *The Antitrust Paradox: A Policy at War With Itself* (New York: Free Press, 1993).

'Brief for Appellees Motion Picture Patents Company and Edison Manufacturing Company'. *George
      Méliès Company, Appellant, vs. Motion Picture Patents Company, et al.*, Appellees. F. (3d Cir. 1912).

'Brief for the United States'. T*he United States of America, v. Motion Picture Patents Company et al.*, 247
      US 524; 38 S. Ct. 578; 62 L. Ed. 1248; 1914 US Dist.

'The Comcast/NBC Universal Merger: What Does the Future Hold for Competition and Consumers?'
      Hearing Before the Subcommittee on Antitrust, Competition Policy and Consumer Rights of the
      Committee on the Judiciary. United States Senate. One Hundred Eleventh Congress, Second
      Session. US Government Printing Office, 4 February 2010.

Conant, Michael, *Antitrust in the Motion Picture Industry: Economic and Legal Analysis* (Los Angeles:
      University of California Press, 1960).

Delrahim, Makan, 'Antitrust Enforcement in the Entertainment and Media Industries', Remarks Presented
      at the Recording Artists' Coalition, Los Angeles, 18 December 2003.

Dickinson, District Judge. 'Opinion'. *United States v. Motion Picture Patents Co. et al.*, 247 US 524; 38 S. Ct.
      578; 62 L. Ed. 1248; 225 F. 800; 1915 US Dist. Lexis 1314.

Douglas, Justice, 'Opinion of the Court'. *United States v. Paramount Pictures, Inc. et al.*, Supreme Court of
      the United States. 334 US 131; 68 S. Ct. 915; 92 L. Ed. 1260. 3 May 1948.

Gellhorn, Ernest, William E. Kovacic and Stephen Calkins, *Antitrust Law and Economics in a Nutshell*,
      5th edn (St Paul, MN: Thomson/West, 1994).

Hand, Augustus N. 'Opinion'. *United States v. Paramount Pictures, Inc., et al.,* United States District Court
      for the Southern District of New York. 66 F. Supp. 323. 11 June 1946.

Hand, Augustus N. 'Opinion'. *United States v. Paramount Pictures, Inc. et al.*, District Court for the
      Southern District of New York. 85 F. Supp. 881. 25 July 1949.

High, Jack C. and Wayne E. Gable. 'Introduction', in Jack C. High and Wayne E. Gable (eds), *A Century of the Sherman Act: American Economic Opinion, 1890–1990* (Fairfax, VA: George Mason University Press, 1992).

Holt, Jennifer, *Empires of Entertainment: Media Industries and the Politics of Deregulation, 1980–1996* (New Jersey: Rutgers University Press, 2011).

'Opinion'. *Motion Picture Patents Company et al., Appellants, v. United States*. 247 US 524; 38 S. Ct. 578; 62 L. Ed. 1248; 1918 US Lexis 1945. 3 June 1918.

Philipp, M. B. and Francis T. Homer, 'Memorandum for the Motion Picture Patents Company and the General Film Company Concerning the Investigation of their Business by the Department of Justice'. 20 July 1912, 62–3.

Pozen, Sharis, 'Insights into Antitrust Enforcement in Media Industries', *Competition Law International* (January 2012).

Shapiro, Carl, 'The 2010 US Horizontal Merger Guidelines: From Hedgehog to Fox in Forty Years', *Antitrust Law Journal* vol. 77 no. 1 (2010).

Staiger, Janet, 'Combination and Litigation: Structures of US Film Distribution, 1896–1917', *Cinema Journal* vol. 23 no. 2 (Winter 1984): 41–72.

Standard Oil Co. v. US, 221 US, 1, 66.

Swartley, John C., 'Original Petition'. T*he United States of America, v. Motion Picture Patents Company et al.*, 247 US 524; 38 S. Ct. 578; 62 L. Ed. 1248; 1912 US Dist.

Tarlov, Yvette F., 'Competitive Impact Statement'. *United States of America, et al. v. Comcast Corp., et al.*, United States District Court for the District of Columbia 1:11-cv-00106. 18 January 2011.

Thomas, Jeanne, 'The Decay of the Motion Picture Patents Company', *Cinema Journal* vol. 10 no. 2 (Spring 1971): 34–40.

United States Department of Justice and Federal Trade Commission. 'Horizontal Merger Guidelines' (2010).

West's Encyclopedia of American Law, 2nd edn (The Gale Group, Inc., 2004).

5 CONTROLLING CONTENT
GOVERNMENTAL CENSORSHIP, THE PRODUCTION CODE AND THE RATINGS SYSTEM

LAURA WITTERN-KELLER

As this book makes clear, Hollywood has left fingerprints all over the law. This chapter looks at one area where we might expect Hollywood to have made a big legal impression: censorship. Under today's First Amendment jurisprudence, government control of movie content would be nearly impossible.[1] But in the early years of the twentieth century, and well into the early 1960s, censorship of movies by governmental authorities went nearly unquestioned by the moviegoing public and much of the industry itself. We might reasonably assume that moviemakers would have demanded the freedom to make movies their way, leading a fight against such governmental control of their product, but they did not. Indeed, throughout much of its history, Hollywood has worked hand in hand with state and local censorship regimes as well as with various pressure groups intent on dictating acceptable content. It has even censored itself. It all started with the law.

This chapter looks at the law and movie censorship. Starting with the onset of movie censorship in the early twentieth century, it moves to early challenges to those laws, then examines the movie industry's highly effective self-censorship, the government's interest in movie content during World War II and mid-century changes to both the industry's discipline and state control. A case study of the 1948 Italian film *The Miracle* examines the landmark decision by the Supreme Court in 1952 to include movies as speech protected by the First Amendment. The chapter then moves to ever-increasing attacks on all forms of movie control, culminating with the end of industry and governmental control in the mid-1960s, the subsequent creation of today's ratings system and the ineffective legal challenges to that new regime. The chapter concludes with a second case study, looking at how the release of the Spanish production *Tie Me Up! Tie Me Down!* (1990) by the distributor Miramax challenged the MPAA's ratings system.

The Onset of Censorship

Seven states and hundreds of municipalities censored publicly exhibited films within their borders for much of the first two-thirds of the twentieth century.[2] In many areas of the USA, all films – whether American or foreign made – were examined by bureaucrats for moral fitness before public viewing. On top of this legally enforceable layer of control, the American film industry created another layer when it instituted its own censoring apparatus in 1934, a system that lasted until 1966. Two years after the demise of that system, the industry created an arbitrary (albeit voluntary) age-classification process that remains in place today. So, movies have had no less than three control mechanisms – one buttressed with all the power of the law and two with the power of a monolithic trade organisation. Along the way, the exigencies of World War II created yet another.

Underlying all these layers of control is the seemingly unshakeable belief that movies are business rather than art. Looking at movies as business first and artistic endeavour second makes regulation by law quite sensible. If, however, we reverse that order and see movies primarily as art or expression – a view that would gain credence after World War II – legal control loses much of its justification. The process by which the American legal culture moved from movies-as-business to movies-as-art (and speech) forms the focus of this chapter.

The idea that law should be used to control dangerous or threatening film content arose almost immediately, as soon as movies burst onto the cultural scene around the turn of the twentieth century. The first statutory control came in 1907, when Chicago empowered its police chief to examine movies before exhibition. This ordinance, like all those that would follow, contained no escape clause for movies of artistic merit. However, it did recognise that although some movies might be harmful to children, there was no reason to keep them from everyone. So, a special permit could be issued by the police chief for exhibition only to those over twenty-one. As we will see, this age-appropriate provision, which would be adopted widely around the world, would not be copied in succeeding American censorship statutes.

The first-in-the-nation Chicago ordinance survived a first-in-the-nation legal challenge two years later. Disgruntled that the city's police chief need not justify his decision to ban a film, exhibitor Jake Block brought suit, unknowingly foreshadowing legal arguments that would continue to be made long after he was dead and gone. Block argued that the ordinance delegated discretionary and judicial powers to the chief, that it took a film owner's property without due process of law (required by both the Fifth and Fourteenth Amendments), that it was 'unreasonable' and 'oppressive' and that it should be voided for vagueness because the statute carried no standards or guidelines for the chief's decision-making. In response, Illinois' chief justice, Justice James H. Cartwright, also foreshadowed the response to similar arguments to come later. He found no problem with the ordinance's lack of guidelines, writing that 'the average person of healthy and wholesome mind knows well enough what the words "immoral" and "obscene" mean and can intelligently apply the test to any picture'.[3]

Fearing for the artistic freedom of the movies, some Progressives formed a film reviewing organisation called the National Board of Censorship (later the National Board of Review). They hoped that if they could convince film-makers to restrain objectionable content, they could keep other localities from copying Chicago. But when this National Board failed to mollify some critics, calls became loud and insistent for increased governmental control.[4] First to answer that call was Pennsylvania, enacting state-wide censorship in 1911. Ohio and Kansas followed in 1913, Maryland in 1916 and dozens of cities and towns in between. In 1921, moviemakers became increasingly alarmed when, in the aftermath of several high-profile Hollywood scandals – notably the Fatty Arbuckle trial for the rape and murder of starlet Virginia Rappe, the murder of director William Desmond Taylor and the drug overdose of matinee idol Wallace Reid – they found thirty-two more states flirting with censorship statutes. Desperately trying to quell a legislative groundswell for censorship in New York, film producer William A. Brady testified as president of the National Association of the Motion Picture Industry, representing 90 per cent of the state's film producers, promising 'a clean sweep from coast to coast' of 'salacious movies' if movie-makers could have one more year.[5] That plea failed, and the vast New York market fell to state-wide censoring in 1921, followed the next year by Virginia. Cities like

Atlanta, Seattle, Memphis and Providence also joined the censoring bandwagon. Within a span of fifteen years, the nation had covered itself in a crazy quilt of censoring bodies.

Each state's censorship statute was remarkably similar. All (except one) were framed in the negative – films would *not* be allowed if they contained anything 'indecent', 'immoral', 'inhuman', 'obscene', 'sacrilegious', or would be likely to 'incite to crime'.[6] Only Ohio's law was positive, calling for movies to be approved if they were 'of a moral, educational, or amusing and harmless character'.[7] All also expected the costs of review to be borne by the distributor, not by the state. The censoring business thus proved lucrative, with each state taking in more in licensing fees than expending in reviewers' salaries and projector bulbs.[8] And none provided for age-segregation of audiences as Chicago's had.[9] No special permits for adults-only movies would come from these censoring bureaucracies: if it was not fit for children, it was not to be seen by anyone.

Although statutorily similar, every board functioned differently and, in those states whose censors were political appointees, the fate of a film might depend upon which party happened to be in power. Only New York and Ohio required their censors to be civil servants. In those two states, the censor staff did not fluctuate frequently, as often happened on the local boards. Susannah Warfield censored Ohio's films for thirty-one years. Several New York censors (who served under the education department) served as long as sixteen years. Although the staff may have been more consistent, the censors' qualifications were slim everywhere: not even in Ohio or New York was any film background or other special expertise needed.

So, most of the censors knew little of film art. Moreover, because they had nothing to go by but vague words in the statutes like 'immoral' or 'indecent', most censor boards adopted internal regulations to guide their examinations. These, however, were in-house documents, so movie-makers could only wonder what the censors would object to. Files kept by the censors are full of letters from distributors pleading for some guidance. As some critics began to note by the 1930s, the censors' lack of movie experience and their nearly unlimited latitude resulted in movies being cut so deeply that the final product might be an undecipherable plot with unexplained gaps.[10] According to one source, a scriptwriter admiring a comedy in a Kansas theatre later learned that the film was actually what was left of a drama he himself had written after it had passed through ten different censor boards.[11]

Although their statutory marching orders were remarkably similar, and even though the censor boards shared information on a regular basis, what they objected to was far from consistent. Movies banned outright in Kansas might be approved in Pennsylvania. Any depiction of African-Americans other than as servants or criminals was usually banned in Virginia but played elsewhere.[12] Ohio banned a re-release of *Frankenstein* (1931) in 1946 and again in 1952 even though all the other states had approved it.[13] Some state and local boards were known for their leniency, some were strict; but all changed over time. New York, one of the tougher boards in the 1920s and 30s, became one of the more 'enlightened' by the late 1940s.[14] Ohio's board became so concerned that it remained in step with public opinion that it frequently used temporary advisory boards for films with particularly troublesome subject matter.

Beyond the statutes' vague wording and inconsistent application lay a more significant legal feature: each reversed the normal burden of proof of Anglo-American law. Where normally the state must prove its case against a defendant, in the movie-censoring world, the distributor had to prove his case against the state: he had to show that his film was *not* 'immoral' or 'indecent', or any of the other terms the censors had decreed. Statutes did provide for an appeals process – usually first to the head of the censor board, then to that board's direct supervisors, which varied from state to state, and then to the courts. But such a process was both slow and expensive. For film distributors, it was usually easier and cheaper to edit the film prior to its release to meet the censor demands. In the majority of cases, that is what happened.

Mutual Film Challenges the Censors

Not only was the challenge process slow and expensive, distributors were playing against a stacked deck in the form of an overly solicitous judiciary. In 1915, when the Supreme Court considered the constitutionality of movie control for the first time, the legal scales tipped decidedly towards the censors. The case came to the Court when the Mutual Film Corporation, an annoyed national distributor with tentacles in many censoring states, mounted a full-bore attack, throwing every possible argument against the censors of Ohio, Pennsylvania and several localities. In a legal tour-de-force in both state and federal courts, Mutual contended that movie censorship violated the company's right to due process of law. But it did not stop there. It added six more legal arguments: that movie censorship violated the free speech protections of the Ohio Constitution; that movies should be considered part of the press and thus freed from prior restraint; that laws empowering censor bodies unconstitutionally transferred power that belonged to the legislative branch to the censoring agency; that the state censorship laws unduly burdened interstate commerce (over which only the US Congress could exercise authority); that the licensing fee was a tax that far exceeded the necessary cost; and that the examination process prior to release would cause 'irreparable injury' to Mutual's business by causing unnecessary delay.

Despite this dazzling display of legal forensics, the Supreme Court Justices unanimously rejected Mutual's claims and ignored its free speech constitutional argument entirely. The unanimous Court reflected the tenor of the times, the state of the film-making art and the state of free speech jurisprudence when it found that movies were not part of the press or part of any legitimate art, but were 'a business, pure and simple' – more importantly, one that 'may be used for evil'.[15] The *Mutual* case set a precedent that would last for thirty-seven years – that movies were neither protected speech nor part of the press and that society should be able to protect itself from pernicious influences through governmentally empowered experts (even if they had no particular expertise). Censorship of movies could continue virtually unchecked.

The *Mutual* opinion had a long career. Cited in 300 subsequent cases, it kept movie censorship sacrosanct until 1952.[16] In the early twentieth century, judges routinely accepted the opinions of statutorily empowered bureaucrats, and with *Mutual* as precedent, film distributors did not stand a chance. Thus, it was not until the 1950s that judges began to question the judgment of the so-called experts chosen by state agencies, all the while accepting arguments about the constitutionality of laws that restricted all sorts of speech rights.

Hollywood's Self-censorship

Beyond state and local censorship, what really worried industry leaders were the dual, continuing threats of impending federal censorship and incessant pressure-group demands. Attempts to keep the federal government out of the censoring business led the movie industry to adopt a series of *mea culpa*s and promises to self-regulate.[17] In 1921, the year that so many state censorship bills were introduced, the industry created the 'Thirteen Points', a list of what the industry piously claimed it would no longer allow into its product. In reality, the list was a compilation of what state and local censors were objecting to, intended as a warning to producers of potentially troublesome content. Five years later, after three more federal censorship bills had been considered, Hollywood introduced another list, its 'Don'ts and Be Carefuls'. Neither list succeeded very well at protecting movie producers or mollifying moral critics. State and local boards continued to censor all movies shown within their jurisdictions.

Dealing with the threat of expanding censorship kept Hollywood leaders busy, but it was not their only challenge. They also had to respond to religious leaders. Almost immediately at their introduction at the turn of the century, religious leaders had perceived movies as a threat. Movies completely bypassed the traditional communal filters – clergy, teachers and parents – putting the decision about what children could see into the hands of the unknown strangers who were making the movies.[18] Even more threatening, movie theatres were dark; they indiscriminately mixed previously separated classes, ages and sexes; and their screens voyeuristically depicted scenes that many believed should remain private.

At first it was Protestant leaders who led the charge against immoral or dangerous movies, favouring governmental censorship boards. In the 1920s and 30s, Catholic leaders stepped forward, becoming the most vocal force for 'clean' movies. Unlike their Protestant counterparts, Catholic clergy were less interested in legal censorship than they were in convincing the moviemakers to clean up their products at the source. So Catholic leaders launched a lengthy pressure campaign that convinced the Motion Picture Producers and Distributors of America (MPPDA, later the Motion Picture Association of America, or MPAA) to create yet another list of taboos – this one written by part-time movie consultant and full-time priest Father Daniel Lord and trade press publisher Martin Quigley in 1930.[19] It was called the Production Code and it was another list of prohibited content.

Like its predecessor lists, the Code did not work. The Great Depression had caused a drop in attendance in the early 1930s and, rather than adhering to the Code, Hollywood ramped up the sex and violence content. Catholics finally got the movie moguls' attention in 1934 when they threatened a nationwide boycott through a newly created mass-membership organisation they called the Catholic Legion of Decency. The prospect of losing the nation's Catholic audience finally convinced the leaders of the industry that lists were not going to cut it; they needed to create an enforcement arm with real muscle. Hiring a devout Catholic, Joseph Breen, the MPPDA set up the Production Code Administration (PCA) to enforce the Code. Breen began work in 1934, approving scripts before shooting, watching during production and reviewing the final product. From this point, Hollywood studios paid homage to the Code or their films could not be shown in major theatres owned by the MPPDA's members.[20]

Henceforth, the PCA became a powerful force, dictating what could and could not be seen in American movie theatres. From 1934 through the onset of World War II, the PCA influenced movie content so thoroughly that governmental censors had much less to cut. In New York State in 1932, for example, the censors refused to license without concessions fully 19 per cent of all the movies they saw. By 1936, a bit more than a full year after the boot-up of the PCA, that percentage dropped to 9.7, and in 1937 fell further to 6.8, reaching a low of 3.23 per cent in 1941.[21] But the PCA had no legal standing – it was a trade group. Censorship laws in states and municipalities, along with pressure from organisations like the Catholic Legion of Decency, drove this self-censoring regime. The result was a powerful extra-legal influence on movie content for three decades.

Already encouraged by the Legion of Decency, the PCA got even more support when the USA entered World War II and created the Office of War Information in 1942. A subsidiary, the Bureau of Motion Pictures, had one major goal: to make and support films that would boost American morale. To that end, the Bureau of Motion Pictures created a list of questions to guide movie-making, capped off with, 'Will this picture help win the war?'[22] Hollywood was so accommodating that, between 1943 and 1944, the industry complied with 71 per cent of the government's requests.[23]

In those same years and until 1958, more governmental agencies got into the act. The FBI, the House Un-American Activities Committee (HUAC) and an anti-communist industry group called the Motion Picture Alliance succeeded in scaring off most political messages from American-made films.[24] So successful were Breen, the Bureau of Motion Pictures, the federal agencies and the Motion Picture Alliance at controlling movie content that there were no new calls for federal censorship for ten years.[25]

Challenges to Movie Censorship

Through the end of World War II, the MPPDA's member studios largely abided by the PCA (popularly known as the Hays Office), and their movies went almost untouched by governmental censors. But there were some independent producers and distributors whose movies ran into trouble. Disgruntled by the expense, time delay and interference of governmental censorship, some appealed and then sued.[26]

Authority to review a publication before it is released is called prior restraint. Such laws were normally considered anathema in the British and American legal tradition, but the Progressive-era legislators who authored the censorship statutes had satisfied themselves that prior restraint was justified because movies were so potentially dangerous to society and morality and that, by providing the ability to challenge the censors in court, fairness would prevail. However, any challenge to censorship arrived at the courthouse door severely handicapped: this was an era that valued bureaucratic expertise and judges were reluctant to substitute their judgment for the judgment of governmentally empowered 'experts' like the state and local censors. This was also an era that valued 'judicial restraint': the idea that judges should defer to legislatures. So, censorship challenges in the 1920s and 30s took the only avenue open to them: they argued that the censors were wrong in their application of the statute to the film in question. The challenges brought to the courts not questions of law – *is this censorship law wrong* – but questions of fact – *is this censorship law applied incorrectly to my film?* Because judges would not substitute their judgment for that of the bureaucrat, every censorship challenge brought before 1930 (except one minor case) lost.[27] After 1930 and before World War II, only three of fourteen challenges succeeded and of those only one substantially reversed a censor determination.[28]

Before 1925, anyone looking to the First Amendment for help in challenging such laws had been out of luck. No federal court could intervene against speech-repressive state laws: after all, the First Amendment restricts only *Congress* from making any law 'abridging the freedom of speech'. If states wished to abridge freedom of speech, the legal culture held that the First Amendment offered no remedy. But change was coming in the legal culture, tilting gradually in favour of free speech rights for individuals and against the power of the states to infringe rights in the name of the common good, exactly the type of law that movie censorship represented.

There was a powerful weapon at the Supreme Court's disposal if it chose to restrain states from infringing free speech. That weapon had lain mostly dormant since its 1868 ratification: the Fourteenth Amendment. Although intended to assist former slaves by protecting them against discriminatory state action, the Fourteenth Amendment also said that states could no longer infringe any individual's 'liberty' without due process of law. By 1925, when it became clear that some states were doing exactly that – seriously infringing speech and press rights in all sorts of ways – the Supreme Court decided that free speech was part of what the Fourteenth Amendment meant when it used that word 'liberty', and so state statutes infringing free speech without some pressing need were arguably unconstitutional. But what exactly constitutes *speech*? That was a question the Supreme Court would tease out over the next four decades.

In a process that legal scholars call *incorporation*, the Court gradually added new forms of communication to the list of speech that states could no longer infringe without the due process of law required by the Fourteenth Amendment. First came picketing and picket signs, then phonographs, loudspeakers, leafleting, magazines and radio. The mid-twentieth century saw an extraordinarily powerful intersection between the freedoms listed in the Bill of Rights and the Fourteenth Amendment that would drive much of the rights revolution of the 1950s and 60s.[29] Those who loathed prior restraint on movies were watching.

The Supreme Court was not only shifting significantly – towards greater protection of individual liberties – but the movie culture was also shifting rapidly. As World War II ended in Europe, foreign films returned to the American screen, bringing with them a gritty realism new to American audiences. Pressures were mounting on movie companies to leave behind formulaic happy endings and respond to the societal changes wrought by the war.[30] Moreover, starting in 1948, the major studios lost their near-monopoly of theatres. In a major antitrust case (see Chapter 4), the Supreme Court forced the major studios to sell off their theatres.[31] This meant that the studios were no longer able to force-feed movies to the theatres; instead, they would have to compete for theatre bookings and produce what the public wanted. And the public, led by movie critics, was coming to demand more realistic, less stylised, predictable plots.

Normally, in business, companies try to adapt their products to public appetites. But movies, as we have seen, were a legal anomaly: censors had been put in charge to make sure that exactly this type of change did not occur. Legislators intended movie censors to act as brakes on cultural change. So the scene was set for a clash that would play out in America's courts – audiences who wanted greater realism, movie producers who needed to meet that demand and censors who had been legally empowered to keep a lid on threats to the status quo – and it was up to the courts to determine who won.

As anti-censorites watched the Supreme Court shift, they could take heart in a by-product of the major antitrust case mentioned above. In the opinion written at the conclusion of that case, Justice William O. Douglas dropped a big hint that some of the Justices were having a change of heart about the 1915 *Mutual* precedent. Douglas wrote, 'we have no doubt that moving pictures, like newspapers and radio, are included in the press whose freedom is guaranteed by the First Amendment'.[32] Here were the words anti-censorites had waited thirty-three years to hear. But this was a monopoly case and Douglas's comment was an aside – what legal scholars call *dictum* (a statement made that does not directly bear on the issues of the case), so the statement carried no real legal weight. But it hinted that a major change might be coming.

With this mid-century convergence – a legal culture growing ever more solicitous of individual liberties, audience demand for greater realism, movie-makers pressed for product change and distributors growing increasingly fed up with the delay and expense of censorship – censors across the nation found themselves ever more besieged. Although many censors did adapt somewhat to changing social mores, anti-censorites found liberalisation was moving too slowly. Emboldened by profit, demand and the evolving legal culture, distributors began challenges in many locales. At the start of the 1950s, three cases angled for Supreme Court review. Distributors were gambling that the time was right to overturn the stranglehold of the *Mutual* precedent. In that quest, their legal arguments against censorship shifted from the previous 'censorship of this movie is wrong' to 'censorship of all movies is wrong'.[33] Henceforth, the details of each censor board's findings about a particular film became less important as the constitutionality of the censor laws themselves came to the forefront. One of the cases came from the distributor of a movie called *Lost Boundaries* (1949), the story of a black family passing as white in a New Hampshire town. This topic was too much for the censors of Atlanta, and the American Civil Liberties Union (ACLU) saw this movie as a possible vehicle to get the censorship issue before the Supreme Court. A second case came from Marshall, Texas, whose censors objected to another race-themed film, *Pinky* (1949)

A *Miracle* at the Supreme Court

About the same time, a major new censorship controversy was emerging in New York City. Catholics erupted in furore over a short Italian import called *Il Miracolo* (1948) or *The Miracle*; it was this case that the Justices would accept for hearing, finally agreeing to revisit *Mutual* and its denial that movies deserved any rights of expression.

The story began at the 1949 Venice Film Festival when Joseph Burstyn, a Polish-American with a small film importation business, saw the forty-one-minute *Il Miracolo*, made by Roberto Rossellini, co-written with Federico Fellini (who also appears briefly in the film) and starring Anna Magnani. The film tells the story of a demented peasant woman who meets a man she believes to be her favourite saint, St Joseph. Recognising an easy mark, the stranger (Fellini) plies the innocent woman with wine, and then all fades to black. The woman is impregnated by the stranger, and when her neighbours learn that she believes she is carrying the child of St Joseph, they taunt and ridicule her. Cast out by her village, she retreats, alone, to a mountain top church where she gives birth to a son and is seemingly returned to sanity by the love for her child.

Like many artistic films, *The Miracle* was open to various interpretations. Rossellini said he intended the film to be a morality tale about man's inhumanity to man. Whatever its intent, Burstyn loved *The Miracle*. Such passion about a movie was his way of life. His former partner,

Arthur Mayer, described him as 'overwhelmingly and monogamously (temporarily) enamoured of [a film] to the exclusion of everything else in the world'.[34] Burstyn enthusiastically acquired the US distribution rights and proudly brought the film to his adopted hometown, New York City. Then he did what he had done many times before: he submitted the film to the New York State Motion Picture Division for licensing. It passed not just once, but twice. Burstyn next contracted with a fine New York City art-house theatre, the Paris, to open the film.

Critics were mixed with their reviews: some, like Bosley Crowther of *The New York Times*, thought it exceptionally good; others worried that its religiously loaded theme might offend some Catholics. And offend it did. Where Burstyn saw beauty and art, the city's Catholics saw sacrilege and a debasement of the biblical story of the virgin birth. The Catholic Legion of Decency condemned it, and the City's licence commissioner (a Catholic) threatened to rescind the theatre's licence. In a statement delivered at St Patrick's Cathedral in New York, Cardinal Spellman denounced the film from the pulpit as 'a subversion to the very inspired word of God' and 'a viscous insult to Italian womanhood'.[35] Pickets from the Catholic War Veterans surrounded the theatre each night, and Catholics bombarded the state censors with a letter-writing campaign, hoping to get *The Miracle*'s exhibition licence revoked. Some Protestant leaders, writing their own letters, were incensed that Catholics would try to dictate what others could see. New York City had a full-blown controversy pitting Catholics against Protestants and Jews, censors against free speech advocates, city officials against the state censors, and one Polish immigrant film importer against the prior restraint power of the state.

In an unprecedented move, the state Board of Regents, which supervised the censors, bowed to public pressure, rescinding the movie's licence in February 1951 by categorising the movie as 'sacrilegious', something the state censors had not seen when they reviewed the movie.[36] Burstyn hired attorney Ephraim London and, together with just *amicus curiae* (friend of the court) briefs from the ACLU, set off to demand artistic freedom for movies by asking the courts to overturn the thirty-seven-year-old precedent of the *Mutual* decision. Burstyn lost in both rounds of the New York state appellate courts. When the Supreme Court agreed to hear the case in 1952, no one was sure which way it would go. Four years earlier, Justice Douglas had hinted that the Court might be ready to see movies as artistic works worthy of First Amendment protection, but changes in personnel had shifted the Court in a more conservative direction. American culture was leaning towards greater artistic freedoms, and the Supreme Court had been slowly expanding individual rights since the 1930s, but movies had always been seen as different from other media – as more dangerous, especially for children – thus justifying legal restrictions.

As oral arguments began, court watchers and industry insiders believed the decision could go either way. Although the motion picture industry would benefit from a decision striking down governmental censorship, the MPAA declined to help. Worried that the Court could decide to uphold censorship and fearing the growing profitability of foreign films, the MPAA left Burstyn and London to face the Justices alone with only moral support from some liberal organisations like the ACLU and the National Lawyers Guild.

London and Burstyn had more on their agenda than just freeing *The Miracle* for viewing in New York. They wanted the Court to declare movie censorship unconstitutional to overturn *Mutual*. To get the Justices to that point, they argued that censoring standards were so vague as to offend the Fourteenth Amendment's guarantee of due process, that New York's statute authorising censors to search for 'sacrilege' violated both freedom of religion and freedom from the establishment of religion, and that the statute violated the First Amendment's guarantee of free expression. At oral argument, London gave the Justices an out: instead of arguing for total movie freedom, he maintained that prior restraint of movies – that reverse burden of proof – was unconstitutional. On the other side, New York maintained that prior restraint was neces-sary since states needed the power to regulate the potential dangers of movie content and that such a longstanding precedent as *Mutual* should not be overturned.

Four weeks later, Burstyn, London and the State of New York had their answer. As Justice Tom Clark read the opinion, it became clear that a surprisingly unanimous Court was over-turning *Mutual*. All nine Justices agreed that movies did indeed fall under the free speech and free press protections of the First Amendment, but that did not mean, the opinion warned, 'that the Constitution requires absolute freedom to exhibit every motion picture of every kind at all times and all places'. 'Sacrilege', however, for which *The Miracle* had been banned, was far too vague a term to pass constitutional muster and had to go.

So far, all was going the anti-censorites' way. But then Clark's opinion became murky:

> Since the term 'sacrilegious' is the sole standard under attack here, it is not necessary for us to decide … whether a state may censor motion pictures under a clearly drawn statute designed and applied to prevent the showing of obscene films. That is a very different question.[37]

Following the Supreme Court decision, the Paris proudly promoted the return of *The Miracle* (1948). *The New York Times*, 15 June 1952, X4

But what did that mean? Could governments now only censor for obscenity? Or was that just an example, meaning that states could continue censoring under their other terms like 'immoral' and 'indecent' provided they did so under a clearly drawn statute? And if movies were now under the First Amendment's protections, how could they be restrained before exhibition? Such ambiguities bothered Justice Stanley Reed, who added a brief, prescient concurring opinion: the pragmatic Reed foresaw that, without definitive standards in the decision, the Court was setting itself up as super-censor; that because of the lack of clarity in Clark's majority opinion, the Court would need to serve as final arbiter on every problematic movie whose distributer sued on constitutional grounds.[38] Indeed, he was correct, for over the next thirteen years the Court would do exactly that.

So movies had moved from a business totally unworthy of First Amendment protection to a medium partially worthy of such protection. To the anti-censorites, it was a coup, but it was clearly not a total victory. It did, however, leave the censors wounded and vulnerable to the attacks that started coming with greater frequency.

Pushing Back the Censors and the Code

Just one week after *The Miracle* decision, the next major challenge came from that case in Marshall, Texas. Without explaining why, the Court overturned Marshall's ban on *Pinky*. The Justices issued a *per curiam* opinion (an unsigned opinion for the court as a whole) which only cited *The Miracle* case as its reason.[39] Once again, the censoring of a movie had been overruled, but still there was no clarity as to what the censors could restrict.

Hopes arose yet again when New York State banned the French film *La ronde* (1950) because it was 'immoral'. After getting nowhere in the New York State courts, *La ronde*'s distributor petitioned for a Supreme Court hearing. In 1954 the Supreme Court agreed to hear the case and bundled it with another case coming from Ohio's ban of *M* (1951), the US remake of Fritz Lang's 1931 thriller about a child murderer. Agreeing to take both cases at the same time, it seemed that the Court might be ready to clarify the mud left behind in *The Miracle* case. But that was not to be. The two cases resulted in another *per curiam* decision that overturned both the New York ban on 'immorality' and the Ohio ban on 'harmfulness', but without explaining why.[40]

At the same time, Hollywood producers were growing restive under the dictates of the Production Code, and several producers challenged the dominance of Joseph Breen and his pre-filming and pre-exhibition interference with their work. Hollywood was now facing a triple whammy of competition from the new medium of television, pressure to match the creativity of foreign films and rapid suburbanisation that was taking ticket buyers away from the big urban movie theatres. By the mid-1950s, ticket sales had plummeted 50 per cent.[41] Hoping to capitalise on the audience desire for realism in their movies, some producers strained to get away from the happy endings of 1940s movies engendered by the PCA, the Bureau of Motion Pictures and the Motion Picture Alliance. Otto Preminger led the way, releasing *The Moon is Blue* in 1953 through United Artists without the benefit of a Production Code seal, but still managing to make the list of top-grossing films for the year. Preminger's film was a blow that undermined the Code.

Flush from this successful defiance, two years later Preminger made *Man with the Golden Arm* (1955), another film which did not receive Code approval, in this case because of its realistic treatment of drug addiction. Other independents were watching Preminger and they too bypassed the PCA.[42] Responding to these challenges in late 1956, the MPAA reworked its twenty-six-year-old Code a bit. Drug addiction, childbirth and abortion were no longer entirely prohibited, but were not set entirely free. Miscegenation disappeared from the Code, but warnings about brutality, violence and torture were stiffened. Homosexuality ('sex perversion') was still completely forbidden in any Code-approved film. More important than the Code's words, though, was a steadily increasing liberalisation of interpretation.[43]

Even with the relaxation in standards, by 1962, three-quarters of all the films released into the New York market arrived bearing no seal of approval from Hollywood.[44] The Production Code was clearly dying. Calls for an age-related system, which would allow adults to see more mature content while still protecting children, came from within the MPAA and from such groups as the General Federation of Women's Clubs, the National Congress of Parents and Teachers, and some Protestant groups.[45] Ohio, Maryland and New York considered age-classification statutes and, by 1968, even the US Senate held hearings debating a federal age-classification agency.[46]

Nor were the governmental censors feeling optimistic: as more court cases came, they wondered, what could they legally ban? Both the free speech advocates and the censors hoped for some sort of clarity each time a new challenge case arose, but, in four cases that arose between 1955 and 1961, no such vision became clear. In 1955, the Justices heard a challenge to the Kansas board's refusal to allow *The Moon is Blue* because of its 'too-frank bedroom dialogue'. The Court handed down yet another *per curiam* opinion against the censors. Since the only question before the Supreme Court was the constitutionality of the Kansas statute, this should have ended censorship in that state permanently, but a legal quirk kept the state in the censoring business for another ten years.[47] Two years later, a Chicago ban on the French film *Le blé en herbe* (1954) (*The Game of Love*) was overturned by the Supreme Court, but with another frustrating *per curiam* opinion and no revelation as to why.[48]

One definitive ruling did come, however, although even that arrived with five different opinions. This involved the 1959 US release of French production *L'amant de lady Chatterley* (1955), a nearly totally expurgated version of the infamous D. H. Lawrence 1928 novel, *Lady Chatterley's Lover*, which New York's censors had slapped down for its supposed immorality.[49] Censoring for something defined as 'immoral', the Court said, was an impermissible attempt by the state to control an idea; in this case, the idea that sometimes adultery may be acceptable.[50] As the 1960s dawned, to all intents the only thing left was obscenity.

But the Justices were not willing to abandon all movie control. In 1961, the Times Film Corporation strategised a test case that they hoped would end all movie censorship. The company paid a licence fee but refused to submit an innocuous version of *Don Juan*.[51] But Times Film was disappointed when a divided Court refused to go along because voiding Chicago's ordinance would have meant 'complete and absolute freedom to exhibit, at least once, any and every kind of motion picture'.[52] While the Court may have been willing to chip away at the words of the censorship statutes, its majority was clearly not ready to free all movies.

As the Supreme Court incrementally allowed greater artistic freedom by axing terms like 'sacrilege' and 'immorality', state courts joined in. In 1955, the highest courts of both Ohio and Massachusetts declared their censoring unconstitutional. Pennsylvania followed in 1956; disgruntled legislators there reinstated censorship three years later only to have their high court overturn it yet again in 1961.[53] That left only New York, Kansas and Maryland, but they and several large cities like Chicago, Detroit and Providence were not about to give up or give in.[54]

End of the Code

By 1962, movie censorship was weakened but holding on when a Maryland exhibitor decided that he had enough of the board of censorship telling him what he could show in his movie theatre. Ronald Freedman decided to sacrifice himself legally by exhibiting *Revenge at Daybreak*, a completely unobjectionable film about the Irish revolt of 1916, without bothering to ask the Maryland censors if he could. He was arrested, and as he was hauled off to arraignment, he instructed his employees to re-sign the marquee to read, 'Fight for Freedom of the Screen'. Like many of the independent distributors who had challenged censorship before him, Freedman was a principled First Amendment warrior.[55] He had the support of another arch anti-censorite, the Times Film Corporation. When their challenge of Chicago with *Don Juan* had failed the year before, the Justices suggested that they might have prevailed had they actually exhibited the film. They had been listening. This time, their plan was to go straight to the constitutionality of the statute by exhibiting a non-reviewed film.

At the same time, another exhibitor had been arrested in Ohio. Nico Jacobellis had lost both rounds in the Ohio courts and his defence team, which included the ACLU, got the Supreme Court to hear the case. In a significant decision for movie freedom, the Justices found that movies had to be judged by the same standards as other media. Building off a 1957 print obscenity case, *Roth v. United States* – which had set up a five-part test of obscenity in written materials – the opinion in *Jacobellis* established a very high bar for a film to be deemed obscene. *Jacobellis* applied a six-part test: (1) the film had to lack artistic value, (2) exceed the customary limits of candour, appeal to an (3) average person's (4) prurient interest when viewed (5) in its entirety and by (6) standards of the national community.[56]

This was clearly a good sign for Freedman and Times Film. Again hopes ran high that the Supreme Court would hand down a definitive decision. To get the Court to move in that direction, Freedman argued that, in its zeal to find unprotected speech (obscenity), Maryland's statute unfairly delayed constitutionally protected speech. It worked, at least partially. This argument persuaded the Justices that the reverse burden of proof in all governmental censorship statutes since 1907 was unconstitutional. But it did not convince them to strike down movie censorship entirely. Justice William Brennan, writing for the unanimous court, shifted the burden of proof from the distributors to the censors: henceforth, instead of a *distributor* convincing a judge that his film *was not obscene*, the *censors* would have to convince a judge that a film *was obscene*. Brennan also bought Freedman's argument that the state's attempt to control unprotected speech unduly delayed speech that was protected. Any attempt by the censors to deny an exhibition licence had to be done quickly. Although Brennan did not specify exact timing, he did suggest something along the lines of one day for censor review and two days for judicial review.[57]

Prior restraint could go on; it just had to move more quickly and include legal proof that a film was unworthy. Maryland's Attorney General called the decision 'the Armageddon of motion picture censorship'.[58] Although that may sound like hyperbole, he was not far off the mark: the *Freedman* decision overturned the censor statutes of Maryland, New York, Virginia, Kansas, Chicago, Ft Worth, Providence and Detroit. If those areas wished to continue censoring movies, they could, but only for obscenity, and only after they had redrawn their statutes to comply procedurally. That the Court never completely struck down movie censorship should not surprise us: obscenity has always been an exception to the free speech protections of the First Amendment, and denying the state its police powers to protect against obscenity was a step the Court was not willing to take.[59]

Although the Supreme Court declined the request to knock out governmental censorship entirely, sentiment against movie control was running parallel courses in Hollywood and in the courts. Rebellion among the ranks in Hollywood continued curtailing the clout of the PCA. A much-publicised battle over some foul language in the script of *Who's Afraid of Virginia Woolf* (1966) further weakened the PCA.[60] And it was clear the reign of state censorship was coming to a close. Since 1952, when movies had come under the First Amendment, governmental censors had had a nearly perfect losing streak, winning fewer cases in state courts as the years went by and only one at the Supreme Court. In fact, on obscenity determinations, their losing streak was perfect: lower courts had overturned eighteen of eighteen challenges based on the finding that a movie was obscene.[61] And the PCA enforcers faced increasingly obstreperous producers. By 1966, even with some modernisations, the Code seemed a dead letter: 41 per cent of all American-made movies arrived at theatres without bothering to get a Code seal.[62]

The Code's impotence, coupled with the demise of most state and local censors in the wake of the *Freedman* decision, left a vacuum that was quickly filled by local governments instituting age-classification systems to keep clearly adult content from children. When a distributor challenged Dallas's classification of the French/Italian co-production *Viva Maria!* (1965) as 'not suitable for children under sixteen', the Supreme Court upheld, by an eight-to-one vote, the constitutionality of such age-classification boards.[63] Worrying that other classification boards would sprout elsewhere, and facing federal age-classification rumblings from the US Senate, the MPAA's new president, Jack Valenti, announced that he was working on a 'voluntary' industry classification system.

In this way, the MPAA's Code and Rating Administration (CARA) was born in 1968. An idea first proposed in the first censorship law – the 1907 Chicago ordinance – had finally come to pass. Long after many other countries had adopted age classification – the recognition that not all movies need be suitable for everyone – the USA finally dropped its one-type-fits-all movie control system. Originally called the Code and Rating Administration, but later changed to the Classification and Rating Administration, the new system gave film-makers freedom to make virtually any film they wanted. The industry scrapped the old pre-production system of examination and bargaining. Henceforth, those film-makers who opted to have their final products reviewed would find them rated as a guide for parents. Valenti repeatedly emphasised that this was not legal censorship; it was voluntary, and the findings of the raters were meant to serve only as a resource for parents in this new age of movie freedom.

Issues quickly arose because of who was doing the rating. Then, as now, the CARA ratings board comprises a chair selected by the president of the MPAA, anonymous parents who serve as raters and senior raters selected by the chair.[64] Other than being parents of children under twenty-one, the raters' only qualification is that they believe they can determine what the average American parent would think of a film's content. Like their censoring counterparts before them, they need no expertise in film, social science or psychology to inform their decision-making. And like the censoring bureaucrats who came before, the process is secret. A simple majority vote determines the final rating. Senior raters communicate with the film-maker, who then can adjust the film's content to get a different rating. Or the film-maker can appeal. Most members of the Appeals Board come from inside industry. A rating can only be changed if a two-thirds majority determines that the original rating was 'clearly erroneous'. Dissatisfied film distributors can request binding arbitration, but there the matter is supposed to rest. According to CARA, only about four ratings are overturned each year out of the 800–900 films reviewed.[65]

Reflecting the move towards the age-based classification of the governmental boards, the original CARA ratings were G (general audiences), M (mature audiences), R (restricted: no one under sixteen – later seventeen – admitted without parent or guardian) and X (not suitable for anyone under sixteen – later seventeen – for sex, violence, or language). These categories were gradually changed – the M was later divided into PG and PG-13 – but the most problematic was the X. This was the only rating not copyrighted by the MPAA, so film-makers hoping to attract a certain audience could self-designate their films as X, sometimes even a double X or a triple X, and the rating soon became synonymous in the public mind with hard-core pornography. Many mainstream theatres refused to book X-rated films and most newspapers refused their ads. For the film-maker hoping to attract a large audience then, an X rating meant financial disaster – few theatres, few ads, small box office.

Since 1970, the ratings system has faced two types of legal action: challenges to statutory reliance on the ratings, and challenges to the ratings system as applied to individual films. Courts have not been friendly to statutory use of the ratings system. Three times since 1970 courts have struck down statutes that rely on the MPAA's ratings because those ratings have no standards behind them. Only one, a school district regulation, was upheld: the court found a reasonable pedagogical concern that children see only movies rated less than R at school-sponsored activities.[66]

In the category of direct challenge to the rating of an individual film, only three distributors have sued the MPAA. Just as Hollywood had earlier accepted the PCA, for the most part it accepted the ratings system. Instead, it is from among the independents that the challenges have come. The first of these was in 1970 when a federal district court judge found that while the X rating may have had some negative consequences for film distributors, the plaintiff had not proven that the X rating was necessarily at fault for his movie's low profitability. The judge also refused to confront the ratings system itself, arguing that 'at the very least [it] gives the public some information about the content of the films offered for their viewing'.[67]

Miramax Films Gets Tied Up with the Ratings System

The second challenge arose from an X rating on a Miramax-distributed film called *Atame!* (*Tie Me Up! Tie Me Down!*). A dark comedy about obsessive love, this was the 1989 product of Spanish director Pedro Almodóvar. The plot revolves around Ricki (Antonio Banderas), a

Tie Me Up! Tie Me Down! (1989) (BFI)

recently released mental patient who kidnaps a soft-porn actress and ties her to a bed in the conviction that she will eventually learn to love him. She does.

Although CARA did not consider the film pornographic, it applied the X because its reviewers unanimously found two sex scenes and some language unsuitable for anyone under seventeen. Miramax promptly appealed but failed to convince the necessary two-thirds of the Appeals Board to overturn the original rating.[68] Miramax said the X rating was a mistaken application of CARA's rules. As we have seen, the earliest censorship challenges questioned the application of the censoring standards to particular movies. After World War II, the challenges then shifted to questions of law and free speech issues; now, in 1990 when Miramax filed a suit, the challenge shifted back to the fairness of the application. Miramax's principals, brothers Bob and Harvey Weinstein, loved a good controversy to stir up publicity, so they hired famous crusading attorney William Kunstler to sue the MPAA over *Atame!*'s X rating. A year later, when the litigious Miramax also sued television stations that refused to carry ads for *The Pope Must Die* (1991), Harvey Weinstein admitted, 'We looked at those legal expenses as our advertising budget.'[69]

Suing a voluntary membership organisation like the MPAA is never easy, and Miramax had an additional problem: it was not a member. But New York State's civil code provided a way: a section of that code requires that both public *and* private organisations (like MPAA) apply their standards equally and without prejudice. Arguing that Hollywood member companies' films received less draconian ratings for similar violence or sexual content, Kunstler charged that the X rating was 'arbitrary, capricious, and unreasonable' in violation of that New York law and that the MPAA was 'motivated by a prejudice toward foreign films … and independent distributors'.[70] In response, MPAA President Jack Valenti expressed 'total confidence' that the ratings system would be upheld in court and, dismissively rejecting the complaints of non-MPAA studios like Miramax, stated such lawsuits 'mainly come from producers who want publicity for their films'.[71]

The famous Kunstler faced the equally famous First Amendment attorney Floyd Abrams, representing the MPAA. Before New York State Supreme Court Judge Charles E. Ramos, the two put on a 'spirited and often witty' debate over whether the MPAA had violated New York State law by applying its ratings 'arbitrarily or capriciously'.[72] To prove his point that member studios were favoured in this rating game, Kunstler submitted a nine-minute videotape of scenes from five graphically sexual American movies that had been rated R rather than X. Abrams countered that the scenes had been taken out of context and that *Atame!*'s rating was based not just on the sex scenes but also on bondage, drug use and a beating in the film. However, the original MPAA review shows that it was indeed the sex matter that caused the X rating. Echoing an unsuccessful 1970 challenge of arbitrary ratings, Kunstler claimed that an X rating killed potential profitability.[73] He called for a new rating between R and X, an idea which had been championed by some film-makers and many critics for years.[74] A new rating, he maintained, could be applied to films that were intended for mature audiences but were not pornographic.

Justice Ramos listened intently and then ruled against Miramax, but gave the MPAA no cause for celebration. Although Ramos refused to agree that the X rating was either 'arbitrary' or 'capricious', and he concurred with the MPAA that the case had been brought merely to generate publicity, he spent much of his opinion berating the ratings system. 'Censorship is anathema to our Constitution and to this court,' he began, and there was no doubt, he said, that the MPAA's ratings system was censorship. Although the ratings were meant to warn parents, he questioned how well these could work when (1) the raters had no qualifications beyond being parents and (2) violent content was 'condoned to a greater extent than displays of sexual activity'. Only 'excessive and sadistic violence' merited an X rating, a fact that led Ramos to characterise the CARA system as 'hypocritical' in its claim of child protection. He finished with a swipe at the industry, concluding 'that the rating system's categories have been fashioned by the motion picture industry to create an illusion of concern for children, imposing censorship, yet all the while facilitating the marketing of exploitive and violent films with an industry seal of approval'. The industry had better, he warned, revise its ratings system to attain a 'rational and professional' system, or 'cease the practice altogether'.[75]

The *Miramax* case was not an isolated incident: 1990 saw a rash of X ratings from CARA as nine other productions (eight from independents) found themselves in the same situation. CARA refused to budge when the distributors of *The Cook, the Thief, His Wife, and Her Lover* (1989) and *Henry: Portrait of a Serial Killer* (1986) argued for R ratings before the Appeals Board. The third challenge came from Maljack Productions, suing the MPAA because its failure to grant *Henry* an R rating represented the breach of 'a covenant of good faith and fair dealing'.[76] At its first trial in 1992, the court refused Maljack's arguments, but a second court ordered the case to be reheard in 1995. Maljack declined to continue. All this controversy breathed new life into the debate over the need for an intermediate category, something that would indicate to parents that a movie had sexual content but nothing like the level of pornography. Valenti was opposed, but two months after the *Miramax* case, the X rating was gone, replaced by the current NC-17.[77] Today, there is still no intermediate rating. Neither has Justice Ramos's contention about violent content caused any CARA soul-searching for a new rating.

While the MPAA was dealing with Miramax and Maljack, movie-makers found themselves the target of a different kind of interference: pressure-group activity. Mainstream movies like *Dressed to Kill* (1980) and *The Last Temptation of Christ* (1988) that sailed through the CARA ratings process still ran into trouble and aroused major protests.[78] Although resulting in few legal challenges, such high-profile activity was intended to interfere with artistic freedom in the name of public morality, and the arguments were strikingly similar to those of the Progressive reformers seventy years earlier. One protest, however, did lead to legal action: the case surrounding Oliver Stone and *Natural Born Killers* (1994). This movie about a murderous rampage supposedly inspired a young couple to shoot two people, killing one and crippling the other, Patsy Byers. She sued Stone, arguing his film was a direct incitement to the violence that led to her attack and subsequent paralysis. After numerous rounds in court, in 2002 the Supreme Court of Louisiana threw out Byers's claim and ruled that Stone's film was protected speech under the First Amendment.[79]

Conclusion

Movies are a free speech legal conundrum in the USA: business or art? The Supreme Court was likely half right when it said, back in 1915, that movies were a business. The difference today is that we would leave off the 'business pure and simple' part of that original characterisation. Businesses they may be, but movies also communicate and so, many argue, they should be free from all regulation. That argument was made forcefully and repeatedly after World War II. Between 1952, when the Court first responded positively and brought movies under the protections of the First Amendment, and 1965, when the Court removed the last vestiges of the reversed burden of proof on movies, legal challenges abounded to remove all regulation.

So, who brought American governmental movie censorship down? It was the combined but uncoordinated efforts of some independent movie distributors, directors and exhibitors, their lawyers, free speech advocates and Supreme Court Justices, all aided by the liberalising attitudes of a society opting for more open communication and greater freedom of expression. The MPAA played no role beyond encouraging a few postwar films to challenge local censors and filing a few amicus briefs. Since the demise of governmental censorship and the Production Code, the only control of movie content has been the ratings system and the market. In this unofficial yet powerful system, we see the same conundrum we started with in 1907 – are movies a product that can be regulated, or are movies a public art which should be controlled only by the market? That question remains unanswered. Considering the overall quiescence of the movie industry, however, with only three legal challenges to CARA, it seems American movie-makers – at least the MPAA-member studios – have accepted the ratings system as good for business.

Notes

1. In 2011, the US Supreme Court overturned California's ban on the sale of violent video games to minors as a violation of the First Amendment. See *Brown v. Entertainment Merchants Ass'n*, 131 S. Ct. 2729 (2011). Similar state laws were overturned by lower federal courts in Michigan, Minnesota, Oklahoma and Washington; and local ordinances were overturned in St Louis and Indianapolis. See James Dunkelberger, 'The New Resident Evil? State Regulation of Violent Video Games and the First Amendment', *Brigham Young University Law Review* no. 5 (2011): 1659–92.

2. Municipal censor boards came and went and there is no way to have an accurate count of how many cities and towns set up censor boards at any given time. Gregory D. Black estimates that there were 200 (*The Catholic Crusade Against the Movies 1940–1975* [Cambridge: Cambridge University Press, 1997], p. 100). In 1957, Ira Carmen estimated that there were about ninety (*Movies Censorship and the Law* [Ann Arbor: University of Michigan Press, 1966], p. 184).

3. *Block v. Chicago*, 239 Ill. 251, 87 NE 1011 (1909). The Chicago ordinance survived until 1961. To learn more about this case, see John Wertheimer, 'The Mutual Film Reviewed: The Movies,

Censorship and Free Speech in Progressive America', *American Journal of Legal History* vol. 37 no. 2 (1993): 168.

4. To learn why some people clamoured for motion picture censorship, see Nancy J. Rosenbloom, 'Between Reform and Regulation: The Struggle over Film Censorship in Progressive America, 1909–1922', *Film History* vol. 1 (1987): 307–25; Gregory D. Black, *Hollywood Censored: Morality Codes, Catholics and the Movies* (Cambridge: Cambridge University Press, 1994); Andrea Friedman, *Prurient Interests: Gender, Democracy, and Obscenity in New York City, 1909–1945* (New York: Columbia University Press, 2000); Alison M. Parker, *Purifying America: Women, Cultural Reform and Pro-Censorship Activism, 1873–1933* (Urbana: University of Illinois Press, 1997); Garth Jowett, 'Moral Responsibility and Commercial Entertainment: Social Control in the US Film Industry, 1907–1968', *Historical Journal of Film, Radio and Television* vol. 10 no. 1 (1990): 3–32.

5. 'Producers Offer to Clean Up Movies', *The New York Times*, 6 April 1921, p. 17.

6. Records of the New York censors (the Motion Picture Division of the Department of Education) are housed at the New York State Archives in Albany. This archive contains the largest collection of American film scripts. Other censor board records can be found in the state archives of Virginia, Maryland, Kansas, Ohio and Pennsylvania.

7. Ohio Division of Film Censorship collection, Ohio Historical Society, Columbus.

8. The licensing and examination fees collected were greater than the expense of salaries and overheads. For details, see Laura Wittern-Keller, *Freedom of the Screen: Legal Challenges to State Film Censorship, 1915–1981* (Lexington: University of Kentucky Press, 2008), p. 26.

9. Jowett, 'Moral Responsibility and Commercial Entertainment': 3–32.

10. For example, in his review for the 1940 US release of the 1935 French film *Remous* (released as *Whirlpool*), Bosley Crowther wrote, 'whatever emotional impact this tortured psychological drama may have possessed before the public's guardians had at it has been manifestly impaired by the most tantalising interruptions, cuts of critical scenes and a consequent series of blank transitions which leave one groping desperately for the thread'. '"Whirlpool", French Film, Is Presented at the Opening of Art Theatre – "Cuore Napoletano" Here', *The New York Times*, 8 October 1940, p. 31.

11. Benjamin De Casseres, 'Film Censorship as a Sport', *The New York Times*, 5 June 1921, p. 42.

12. Douglas Smith, 'Patrolling the Boundaries of Race: Motion Picture Censorship and Jim Crow in Virginia, 1922–1932', *Historical Journal of Film, Radio and Television* vol. 21 no. 3 (2001): 273, 277.

13. Ohio Historical Commission, Ohio Historical Society, Series 1441 box 50,744 – General Correspondence, box 1.

14. Norman Nadel, review of *Bitter Rice* in *Columbus Citizen*, 26 April 1951, vol. 7: 1.

15. *Mutual Film Corporation v. Industrial Commission of Ohio*, 236 US 230 (1915).

16. Of the fourteen challenges filed against state censorship between the end of the 1920s and World War II, nearly half were filed against the powerful New York State board and none won. Interestingly, none made any constitutional challenges of prior restraint. Instead of challenging the law itself, the challengers limited themselves to squabbling over definitions and application of the law.

17. Between 1916 and 1948 Congress entertained proposals for a national motion picture commission no fewer than eleven times: 1916, 1919, 1922, 1924, 1925, 1927, 1929, 1930, 1937, 1938 and 1948.

18. Garth Jowett, *Film: The Democratic Art* (Boston: Little, Brown and Company, 1976), p. 12.

19. Thomas Patrick Doherty, *Hollywood's Censor: Joseph I. Breen & the Production Code Administration* (New York: Columbia University Press, 2007), pp. 41–6.

20. On the PCA, see Black, *Hollywood Censored*; Black, *The Catholic Crusade Against the Movies*; Frank Walsh, *Sin and Censorship: The Catholic Church and the Motion Picture Industry* (New Haven: Yale University Press, 1996); Leonard J. Leff and Jerold L. Simmons, *The Dame in the Kimono: Hollywood, Censorship, and the Production Code from the 1920s to the 1960s* (New York: Grove Weidenfeld, 1990).

21. Annual Reports, Motion Picture Division records, New York State Archives, see note 6.

22. Clayton R. Koppes and Gregory D. Black, *Hollywood Goes to War: How Politics, Profits and Propaganda Shaped World War II Movies* (Berkeley: University of California Press, 1990), pp. 66–7.

23. Ibid., p. 323.

24. John Sbardellati, *J. Edgar Hoover Goes to the Movies: The FBI and the Origins of Hollywood's Cold War* (Ithaca: Cornell University Press, 2012), p. 185.

25. There were no calls for federal censorship for the ten years after 1938 and before 1948. By contrast, in 1932, no less than forty organisations had been clamouring for federal control of movies; after that there were no serious efforts to set up federal censorship until an age-classification board was contemplated in 1968.

26. Between 1927 and 1940, at least fourteen distributors challenged governmental censors in court, the majority in New York and Pennsylvania. They included a challenge to the censoring of dialogue in the new talkies in Pennsylvania (whose Supreme Court had no trouble extending the censoring of language to the spoken word in 1929), several cases questioned the censoring of political messages in Ohio and Pennsylvania, and, perhaps most famously, a six-year-long battle to show the Czechoslovak-German production named *Ecstasy*. For more, see chapter 4 of Wittern-Keller, *Freedom of the Screen*.

27. The minor case involved New York's ban of a Hal Roach short comedy called *Good Riddance* (1923). The censors worried that some scenes might incite to crime. One editorial noted the 'scenes were plainly humorous, and the producers have taken the case to the courts to see if Judges are as dull as the censors'. 'Incitement to Crime', *The New York Times*, 15 May 1923, p. 18.

28. Two of the cases were procedural reversals; the one substantive reversal came in 1940 and concerned Virginia's ban of the film *The Birth of a Baby* (1938).

29. In 1938, the Court announced that it would closely scrutinise all laws which inhibited personal freedoms. *United States v. Carolene Products*, 304 US 144 (1938).

30. For more, see Tino Balio, *The Foreign Film Renaissance on American Screens, 1946–1973* (Madison: University of Wisconsin Press, 2010).

31. *United States v. Paramount Pictures*, 334 US 131 (1948).

32. Ibid.

33. I have previously discussed this shift using these words. See Wittern-Keller, *Freedom of the Screen*, p. 89.

34. Arthur Mayer, *Simply Colossal: The Story of the Movies from the Long Chase to the Chaise Longue* (New York: Simon and Schuster, 1953), p. 216.

35. Quoted in 'Spellman Urges "Miracle" Boycott', *The New York Times*, 8 January 1951, p. 14.

36. Records of the struggle over the licensing of *The Miracle* can be found at the New York State Archives, series A1420.

37. *Burstyn v. Wilson*, 343 US 495 (1952).

38. Ibid.

38. *Gelling v. Texas*, 343 US 960 (1952).

40. *Superior Films v. Ohio*, 346 US 587 (1954). The New York case and the Ohio case were decided together under the name of the Ohio case.

41. Clayton Koppes, 'Movie Censorship Considered as a Business Proposition'. Paper presented at the Economic and Business History Association Annual Meeting, Columbus, Ohio, 16 April 2011.

42. Geoffrey Shurlock, who replaced Breen as head of the PCA, tried to abandon the Code in 1954 but failed to convince studio executives, worried about possible audience loss, to go along. See Jowett, *Film: The Democratic Art*, p. 419.

43. Peter Lev, *The Fifties: Transforming the Screen, 1950–1959* (Berkeley: University of California Press, 2006), pp. 93–4.

44. Walsh, *Sin and Censorship*, p. 321.

45. William D. Romanowski, *Reforming Hollywood: How American Protestants Fought for Freedom at the Movies* (New York: Oxford University Press, 2012), p. 260.

46. Vincent Canby, 'Plan to Classify Movies Debated', *The New York Times*, 12 June 1968, p. 36.

47. *Holmby Productions v. Vaughn*, 350 US 870 (1955). For more on this and the other 1950s and 60s cases, see Wittern-Keller, *Freedom of the Screen*, chapter 8.

48. *Times Film Corp. v. City of Chicago*, 355 US 35 (1957).

49. *Kingsley International Pictures Corp. v. Regents of the University of the State of New York*, 360 US 684 (1959).

50. Ibid.

51. Given the number of films which have taken the title *Don Juan*, and because court documents reveal only the title as submitted by the distributor in these cases, it is not possible to know for sure which specific film this might be, where it was made, or its original title. Considering the date of the case, it is likely this was the Austrian 1955 production *Don Giovanni*, which was released in the USA by Times Film.

52. *Times Film v. Chicago*, 365 US 43 (1961).

53. *Hallmark Productions v. Carroll*, 384 Pa. 348 (1956); *William Goldman Theatres v. Dana*, 405 Pa. 83 (1961).

54. Richard S. Randall, *Censorship of the Movies: The Social and Political Control of a Mass Medium* (Madison: University of Wisconsin Press, 1968). Randall has a most useful chart on municipal censors on page 79.

55. Author's interview with Ronald Freedman, 11 September 2002.

56. *Jacobellis v. Ohio*, 378 US 184 (1964).

57. This time frame was suggested, but not required. *Freedman v. Maryland*, 380 US 51 (1965).

58. Finan, as quoted in the *Baltimore Sun*, 2 March 1965.

59. Although obscenity remains the only type of movie expression not protected by the First Amendment, today any such prosecution can occur only after exhibition. Moreover, since the advent of VHS technology in the 1980s and the rise of the internet in the 1990s, production of obscene movies has been so decentralised (to use historian Whitney Strub's term) that there have been only a handful of such prosecutions and none since the end of the George W. Bush administration in 2008. For more, see Whitney Strub, *Obscenity Rules: Roth v. United States and the Long Struggle over Sexual Expression*, Landmark Law Cases & American Society (Lawrence: University Press of Kansas, 2013), epilogue.

60. See Leff and Simmons, *The Dame in the Kimono*, chapter 11.

61. For the list of cases, see Randall, *Censorship of the Movies*, p. 254n.54.

62. Black, *Catholic Crusade Against the Movies*, p. 221.

63. *Interstate Circuit v. Dallas*, 390 US 676 (1968).

64. *Classification and Rating Rules* (Motion Picture Association of America and National Association of Theatre Owners, 1 April 2007).

65. *The Movie Rating System: Its History, How it Works and Its Enduring Value*, Classification and Rating Administration (CARA), available online at FilmRatings.com (http://www.filmratings.com/filmRatings_Cara/#/about/, accessed on 27 July 2012). To learn more about the workings of CARA, see Jason K. Albosta, 'Dr Strange-rating or: How I Learned That the Motion Picture Association of America's Film Rating System Constitutes False Advertising', *Vanderbilt Journal of Entertainment and Technology Law* vol. 12 no. 1 (2009): 115–46.

66. Colin Miller, 'A Wolf in Sheep's Clothing: Wolf v. Ashcroft and the Constitutionality of Using the MPAA Ratings to Censor Films in Prison', *Vanderbilt Journal of Entertainment Law and Practice* vol. 6 no. 2 (2004): 265–90.

67. *Tropic Film Corp. v. Paramount Pictures Corp, Paramount Film Distributing Corps and the Motion Picture Assn. Of America, Inc.*, 319 F. Supp. 1247 (1970).

68. Glenn Collins, 'Almodóvar Film's X Stands', *The New York Times*, 25 April 1990, C15. The original CARA vote that branded *Atame!* with the X was six to six, clearly indicating that the rating was far from necessary.

69. Ronald Grover, 'Crying All the Way to the Oscars', *Business Week*, 15 March 1993, p. 38. Neither suit succeeded unless we consider their publicity value.

70. As quoted by Kevin Sandler, *The Naked Truth: Why Hollywood Doesn't Make X-rated Movies* (Piscataway: Rutgers University Press, 2007), p. 102.

71. Ibid.

72. Andrew L. Yarrow, 'Judge to Rule in July on X Rating for "Tie Me Up!"', *The New York Times*, 22 June 1990, C4.

73. *Tropic Film Corp. v. Paramount Pictures Corp, Paramount Film Distributing Corps and the Motion Picture Assn. Of America, Inc.*, 319 F. Supp. 1247.

74. Kari Granville, 'Judge Asked to Overturn Film Rating System', *Los Angeles Times*, 22 June 1990, F10.

75. *Miramax Films Corp. v. MPAA*, 148 Misc. 2d 1; 560 NYS2d 730 (1990).

76. *Maljack Productions v. MPAA*, 52 F.3d 373 (1995).

77. Alisa Perren, *Indie, Inc.: Miramax and the Transformation of Hollywood in the 1990s* (Austin: University of Texas Press, 2012), p. 45. For more on the shift from X to NC-17, see Sandler, *The Naked Truth*, pp. 100–15.

78. For more, see Charles Lyons, *The New Censors: Movies and the Culture Wars* (Philadelphia: Temple University Press, 1997).

79. See Laura Wittern-Keller and Raymond J. Haberski Jr, *The Miracle Case: Film Censorship and the Supreme Court*, Landmark Law Cases & American History (Lawrence: University Press of Kansas, 2008), pp. 186–91.

References

Albosta, Jason K., 'Dr Strange-rating or: How I Learned That the Motion Picture Association of America's Film Rating System Constitutes False Advertising', *Vanderbilt Journal of Entertainment and Technology Law* vol. 12 no. 1 (2009): 115–46.

Balio, Tino, *The Foreign Film Renaissance on American Screens, 1946–1973* (Madison: University of Wisconsin Press, 2010).

Black, Gregory D., *Hollywood Censored: Morality Codes, Catholics and the Movies* (Cambridge: Cambridge University Press, 1994).

Black, Gregory D., *The Catholic Crusade Against the Movies 1940–1975* (Cambridge: Cambridge University Press, 1997).

Block v. Chicago, 239 Ill. 251, 87 NE 1011 (1909).

Brown v. Entertainment Merchants Ass'n, 131 S. Ct. 2729 (2011).

Burstyn v. Wilson, 343 US 495 (1952).

Carmen, Ira H., *Movies, Censorship and the Law* (Ann Arbor: University of Michigan Press, 1966).

Doherty, Thomas Patrick, *Hollywood's Censor: Joseph I. Breen & the Production Code Administration* (New York: Columbia University Press, 2007).

Dunkelberger, James, 'The New Resident Evil? State Regulation of Violent Video Games and the First Amendment', *Brigham Young University Law Review* no. 5 (2011): 1659–92.

Freedman v. Maryland, 380 US 51 (1965).

Friedman, Andrea, *Prurient Interests: Gender, Democracy, and Obscenity in New York City, 1909–1945* (New York: Columbia University, 2000).

Gelling v. Texas, 343 US 960 (1952).

Hallmark Productions v. Carroll, 384 Pa. 348 (1956).

Holmby Productions v. Vaughn, 350 US 870 (1955).

Interstate Circuit v. Dallas, 390 US 676 (1968).

Jacobellis v. Ohio, 378 US 184 (1964).

Jowett, Garth, *Film: The Democratic Art* (Boston: Little, Brown and Company, 1976).

Jowett, Garth, 'Moral Responsibility and Commercial Entertainment: Social Control in the US Film Industry, 1907–1968', *Historical Journal of Film, Radio and Television* vol. 10 no. 1 (1990): 3–32.

Kingsley International Pictures v. Regents, 360 US 684 (1959).

Koppes, Clayton, 'Movie Censorship Considered as a Business Proposition'. Paper presented at the Economic and Business History Association Annual Meeting, Columbus, Ohio (2011).

Koppes, Clayton R. and Gregory D. Black, *Hollywood Goes to War: How Politics, Profits and Propaganda Shaped World War II Movies* (Berkeley: University of California Press, 1990).

Leff, Leonard J. and Jerold L. Simmons, *The Dame in the Kimono: Hollywood, Censorship, and the Production Code from the 1920s to the 1960s* (New York: Grove Weidenfeld, 1990).

Lev, Peter, *The Fifties: Transforming the Screen, 1950–1959* (Berkeley: University of California Press, 2006).

Lyons, Charles, *The New Censors: Movies and the Culture Wars* (Philadelphia: Temple University Press, 1997).

Mayer, Arthur, *Simply Colossal: The Story of the Movies from the Long Chase to the Chaise Longue* (New York: Simon and Schuster, 1953).

Miller, Colin, 'A Wolf in Sheep's Clothing: Wolf v. Ashcroft and the Constitutionality of Using the MPAA Ratings to Censor Films in Prison', *Vanderbilt Journal of Entertainment Law and Practice* vol. 6 no. 2 (2004): 265–90.

Miramax Films Corp. v. MPAA, 148 Misc. 2d 1; 560 NYS2d 730 (1990).

Mutual Film Corporation v. Industrial Commission of Ohio, 236 US 230 (1915).

Parker, Alison M., *Purifying America: Women, Cultural Reform and Pro-Censorship Activism, 1873–1933* (Urbana: University of Illinois Press, 1997).

Perren, Alisa, *Indie, Inc.: Miramax and the Transformation of Hollywood in the 1990s* (Austin: University of Texas Press, 2012).

Randall, Richard S., *Censorship of the Movies: The Social and Political Control of a Mass Medium* (Madison: University of Wisconsin Press, 1968).

Romanowski, William D., *Reforming Hollywood: How American Protestants Fought for Freedom at the Movies* (New York: Oxford University Press, 2012).

Rosenbloom, Nancy J., 'Between Reform and Regulation: The Struggle over Film Censorship in Progressive America, 1909–1922', *Film History* vol. 1 (1987): 307–25.

Sandler, Kevin, *The Naked Truth: Why Hollywood Doesn't Make X-rated Movies* (Piscataway: Rutgers University Press, 2007).

Sbardellati, John, *J. Edgar Hoover Goes to the Movies: The FBI and the Origins of Hollywood's Cold War* (Ithaca: Cornell University Press, 2012).

Smith, J. Douglas, 'Patrolling the Boundaries of Race: Motion Picture Censorship and Jim Crow in Virginia, 1922–1932', *Historical Journal of Film, Radio and Television* vol. 21 no. 3 (2001): 273–91.

Strub, Whitney, *Obscenity Rules: Roth v. United States and the Long Struggle over Sexual Expression*, Landmark Law Cases & American Society (Lawrence: University Press of Kansas, 2013).

Superior Films v. Ohio, 346 US 587 (1954).

Times Film Corp. v. City of Chicago, 355 US 35 (1957).

Times Film v. Chicago, 365 US 43 (1961).

Tropic Film Corp. v. Paramount Pictures Corp, Paramount Film Distributing Corps and the Motion Picture Assn. Of America, Inc., 319 F. Supp. 1247 (1970).

United States v. Carolene Products, 304 US 144 (1938).

United States v. Paramount Pictures, 334 US 131 (1948).

Walsh, Frank, *Sin and Censorship: The Catholic Church and the Motion Picture Industry* (New Haven: Yale University Press, 1996).

Wertheimer, John, 'The Mutual Film Reviewed: The Movies, Censorship and Free Speech in Progressive America', *American Journal of Legal History* vol. 37 no. 2 (1993): 158–89.

William Goldman Theatres v. Dana, 405 Pa. 83 (1961).

Wittern-Keller, Laura, *Freedom of the Screen: Legal Challenges to State Film Censorship, 1915–1981* (Lawrence: University Press of Kentucky, 2008).

Wittern-Keller, Laura and Raymond J. Haberski Jr, *The Miracle Case: Film Censorship and the Supreme Court*, Landmark Law Cases & American History (Lawrence: University Press of Kansas, 2008).

6 HOLLYWOOD EMBASSIES, LABOUR AND INVESTMENT LAWS AND GLOBAL CINEMA EXHIBITION

ROSS MELNICK

Despite the oft-repeated narrative that Hollywood 'lost' control over its exhibition chains after the consent decree, which compelled their divestiture, the Department of Justice made no effort to force the major US film companies to sell off their cinema chains in Canada, South America, Europe, Australia, or other international territories. While Hollywood experienced vertical disintegration in its domestic market through the divorcement of exhibition from distribution and production, it was, nevertheless, able to maintain vertically integrated supply chains overseas through its operation and ownership of cinemas. In fact, Hollywood's global exhibition empires expanded their sometimes fraught, often lucrative, and politically complex relationship with audiences, distributors, exhibitors and politicians around the world after 1948. These US-run cinemas were, after all, not merely outposts for the exhibition of Hollywood films; they also acted as what I call 'cultural embassies', designed to attract local audiences to American films and moviegoing practices. As new cinemas opened around the world, Hollywood not only dominated the content on the screen, but also owned a growing number of the screens, securing distribution *and* exhibition revenues in increasingly profitable territories.

This chapter examines what happened when national laws, movie theatres and Hollywood's investments collided by focusing on two case studies that highlight some of the key legal issues that impacted US exhibition operations overseas in two very different market contexts: Cuba before the 1959 Communist revolution; and political and economic transformations in China at the end of the twentieth century and the start of the twenty-first century. In particular, the chapter focuses on how the exhibition operations of one major studio – Warner Bros. – negotiated the legal terrain of these territories during these periods.

Laws of Exhibition

Theatrical exhibition is, at face value, a seemingly stable business that operates rather simply for patrons: customers pay exhibitors for access to one space/seat for a specified period of time for one or more films and/or live entertainment. This simple description, however, does not begin to address the complex set of relationships and systems involved, and the vast set of local, state, regional, provincial and/or national laws that must be followed for commercial movie theatres built, leased and/or operated by independent exhibitors or national and multinational chains.

Much of the previous writing on 'Hollywood' motion picture exhibition and the law centres on issues of control, ownership and the conduct of the studios in the domestic market: subjects elaborated in Chapter 4 in this collection. These include the legal cases around the Motion

Picture Patents Company between 1908 and 1915, Hollywood and its increasing vertical integration and market power, the control by the studios from the 1910s through the 40s of cinema exhibition and distribution in major urban markets and, of course, the impact of the 1948 consent decree (which was not completed until the official separation of Loew's and MGM in 1959). Previous to that, Paramount and other studios engaged in the anti-competitive practice of block booking, in which exhibitors were required to take an entire slate of releases in order to receive a distributor's product, and blind bidding, so that exhibitors were forced to rent a given picture sight unseen without 'trade screenings'. Such practices aided the 'Big Five' vertically integrated film companies (Paramount, 20th Century-Fox, Warner Bros., RKO and Loew's) in their efforts to consolidate market power and control through film production, distribution and exhibition. Franchise agreements, master agreements and blanket deals,[1] coupled with block booking, also gave these companies a contracted group of exhibitors for their production and distribution units. Vertically integrated companies also kept 100 per cent of the net revenue when their films were booked in their own cinema chains. Meanwhile, an elaborate system of runs (first, second, third, etc.), zones (set geographical areas) and clearances (in which competing cinemas in the same zone could not show the same feature in the same run) further maintained and consolidated the power of vertically integrated film studios (see also Chapter 4).

These practices, many becoming illegal after 1948 in the USA, were large-scale, top-level issues for exhibitors. Like all other retailers, though, the operation of chain and independent movie theatres was also governed by a wide set of intersecting local, state, national and international laws concerning patent, real estate, labour, trademark, tax, finance, banking, bankruptcy, securities, environmental and many other regulations. Each stage of cinema building and film renting was also predicated on a series of contracts and agreements: land purchases or leases; the hiring of architects, designers and builders; and purchase agreements between exhibition companies and lighting, projection, sound, seating, concession and numerous other vendors and installers. Building codes and fire and municipal laws also governed the construction of cinemas, especially during the era of nitrate film, by which fire marshals and other safety inspectors required strict adherence to local laws for film projection and storage. Revenues collected also required extensive accounting and auditing to abide by numerous tax laws, as discussed in Chapter 7.

Labour and employment laws were among the most important for exhibitors (as well as Hollywood production lots), especially for deluxe motion picture theatres that employed anywhere from a hundred to nearly 600 workers each during the pre-1948 halcyon days of downtown moviegoing in the USA. Thus, global exhibition companies like Loew's and 20th Century-Fox kept a stable of in-house attorneys in the USA (and hired others to litigate or settle specific cases) and local attorneys abroad for its foreign movie theatre chains in order to avoid or defend against litigation, investigation, or possible seizure of its cinemas in foreign countries. Overseas, box-office revenue was also subject to local, regional and national constraints that changed from city to city and country to country. And, in numerous cases – in countries such as South Africa, Egypt and Israel – only a portion of those revenues could legally be repatriated to the USA.

In the 1960s, US movie theatres were also key sites of racial tensions and debate over legalised racial exclusion. Like many other retailers/leisure operators during this period, movie theatres in the southern USA were slow to integrate black patrons. These pre-1964 practices were often enforced by exhibitors, who simply pointed to local/state official and/or unofficial racial laws in places like Alabama, Texas and Mississippi and, half a world away, in South Africa, Southern Rhodesia and Kenya, where 20th Century-Fox operated Africa's largest cinema chain that often barred black, Asian and 'coloured' patrons from entering before 1960. (Fox sold its African film exhibition operations in 1969 but South African exhibitors retained their racial policies until the late 1980s.)

More recently, the relationship between law and theatrical exhibition can also be seen in the USA in the impact that the Americans with Disabilities Act (ADA) has had on cinema entrances, restroom facilities, employment practices, box-office and concession placement/accessibility, the 'path of travel' within cinemas and, most importantly, on auditorium design and size.[2]

Global Film Exhibition Research

Film exhibition has become the subject of increasing academic study over the past two decades.[3] However, the US motion picture companies' large-scale operation of movie theatres overseas from 1925 to 2013 has remained under-researched. While scholars such as Ian Jarvie, Kristin Thompson and John Trumpbour have contributed invaluable research on transnational distribution, the growth and importance of multinational cinema circuits operated by Fox, Paramount, Warner Bros. and Loew's/MGM in Europe, Asia, Africa, Australia and South America before 1986 has escaped significant attention.[4] One reason for this lacuna is the limits on the preservation of primary documentation on US film exhibition overseas. Of the five major cinema chains in the USA during the pre-1948 era, for instance, only the Warner Bros.' archives have remained somewhat intact and accessible, while international exhibition records from Fox, MGM and Paramount are much more elusive.

What follows, then, are two specific case studies of the overseas exhibition strategies of one company – Warner Bros. – in two countries during key moments of political, social and economic change: Cuba, in the years immediately before the Communist revolution; and the political and economic reforms witnessed in China from the 1990s onwards. While reflective of strategies and practices adopted by US exhibitors in other foreign markets, these case studies also reveal aspects that were unique to Warner Bros.' international presence in these territories and time periods. Cuban and Chinese exhibition practices and their related laws changed dramatically during their more capitalist phases and during Communism's legal, economic, political and social application. Both, however, demonstrate the importance of 'grounded histories' of this aspect of international theatrical exhibition that examine the interrelationships between the Hollywood studios and their international markets.

Cuba and US International Exhibition

In the late 1910s, Paramount forged a distribution deal with the Caribbean Film Co. to distribute its motion pictures in Cuba, Venezuela, Puerto Rico, 'all the other islands of the West Indies' and 'a large part of Central America'. In addition to Caribbean's distribution of Paramount films throughout these regions, Caribbean also controlled sixty-five cinemas in Puerto Rico, as well as 300 more cinemas in Cuba.[5] The agreement was 'direct evidence of the influence of

Americanization in the West Indies and Central America', *Moving Picture World* wrote. The Paramount–Caribbean deal also enabled the new distribution-exhibition company to set up a system of runs, zones and clearances for films 'in the same manner as they are booked in [the USA]'.[6]

Paramount maintained its cosy relationship with Caribbean throughout the 1920s and, finally, bought its own Cuban cinemas in 1929 through the purchase of US-based Saenger Theatres, which owned and/or operated more than 150 cinemas in fifty locations, including cinemas in Panama, Cuba 'and many important Central American cities'.[7] Paramount's newly acquired Havana cinema was the largest in the city, and the company expanded further in Cuba during the 1930s, becoming full distribution and exhibition partners with the Caribbean Film Co.[8] Warner Bros. also hoped to become a Cuban distributor-exhibitor, completing plans in 1930 for a 3,000-seat shop window cinema in Havana, but which, for reasons unknown, was never built.[9]

Prior to and during World War II, Latin America grew exponentially as an important foreign market for US companies. As the war ended, revenues in Central and South America and the Caribbean became a key focus for Paramount, Loew's, Warner Bros. and Fox. US distributors also wanted to open new cinemas in Cuba, but local exhibitors fought against US expansion by refusing to sell their cinemas to US film companies, while Cuban officials discouraged new cinema construction because of the lack of building materials.[10]

In September 1944, Rafael Ramos Cobián, who operated twenty-two cinemas in Puerto Rico, manoeuvred his way around Cuban opposition to selling cinemas to outsiders, and ongoing material shortages, by leasing both the Smith Circuit, with eight cinemas in Havana, and the Manuel Ramon Fernandez Circuit, with four cinemas in Camaguey. Peter Colli, who was also Warner Bros.' Cuban manager, became the treasurer of the new Cobián circuit in Cuba.[11] Warner Bros. negotiated with Cobián to purchase a share of the company but, despite Colli's relationship with both Warner Bros. and Cobián, the negotiations failed and Warner Bros., for the second time, was left without theatres in Cuba (and without a booking deal with Cobián).

The end of the Cobián–Warner Bros. negotiations left an opening for Paramount to not only distribute their films to Cobián's Cuban cinemas, but also to become equal partners in Circuito Cobián of Cuba, SA, with a new capitalisation of $1 million. The contract, signed by John W. Hicks Jr, president of Paramount International Films, Inc., and by Cobián, president of the new Cuban corporation operating the circuit, outlined an agreement whereby the partners would 'participate equally' in the operation of the chain's eleven cinemas in Havana and Camaguey, and a new venue under construction.[12] Paramount now operated, among others, the first-run Encanto, Fausto and Alcazar, the second-run Florencia, Favorito, Strand and Universal cinemas in Havana and additional cinemas in Camaguey.[13]

Warner Bros. had finally opened its first foreign cinema in 1938, when it built the Warner West End in London's Leicester Square – a highly prestigious central London location. Three years later, Warner Bros. invested over £2 million in the UK-based ABC Cinemas circuit in order to gain greater access to the British market[14] and then leased the Teatro Central in Lima, Peru, in 1943 and, later, the Teatro San Jorge in Bogota, Colombia, in 1946.[15] Its next target, once again, was Cuba.

Warner Bros. Pictures, Inc. Board of Directors met on 27 July 1945 and voted to approve an agreement with Radio Centro that called for Goar Mestre and his Radio Centro SA to purchase a lot at Calle L and Avenida 23 in the Vedado borough of Havana and build a 1,600–1,700-seat cinema that Warner Bros. would subsequently lease and operate. The Warner Theatre became the company's first Cuban cinema and was to be built by 1 August 1947 according to plans and specifications approved by both Warner Bros. Pictures, Inc. and Warner Bros. First National South Films, Inc. The theatre was part of the Radio City-inspired radio–film–entertainment complex named 'Radio Centro' that also housed the offices and studios for the CMQ network. Warner Bros. agreed to pay Radio Centro SA a minimum rental of $30,000 per year against 15 per cent of the gross receipts, purchased $75,000 of preferred stock from Radio Centro SA and then deposited these shares as security for the eventual payment of the lease.[16]

Loew's International also sought a Cuban cinema as part of its $9 million overseas 'theatre building and remodeling program' in Latin America. By January 1946, Loew's began work on a ten-storey air-conditioned office building to house all the US film exchanges, with a 1,500-seat cinema and another smaller 400-seat cinema at an estimated cost of $1.25 million.[17] Paramount, meanwhile, also followed the postwar boom in Cuba as Rafael Ramos Cobián resigned from the Smith Circuit in late 1945 and Paramount International acquired Cobián's stock holdings in the newly reorganised and renamed Circuito Teatral Paramount.[18] This, of course, gave Paramount control of some of the most popular cinemas in Havana.

Cuban labour policies during President Ramón Grau San Martín's tenure (1944–8) reset some of Fulgencio Batista's more capital-friendly policies. Grau's Partido Auténtico, with its 'Cuba para los Cubanos' ('Cuba for the Cubans') mantra, set a firmer tone for his administration's relationship with local and foreign management operating in Cuba, but this did little to quell the strife between the nation's exhibitors and their workers. In 1946, a Cuban Supreme Court ruling that seemed to favour workers – forcing exhibitors to rehire employees who had been recently laid off – sparked new tensions among Payret Theatre employees in Havana, where recently laid-off workers had just been replaced and now refused to quit. In June, hundreds of Havana cinema employees walked out of their jobs in solidarity with labour leaders who had been arrested for organising an 'illegal strike' against the Payret Theatre, keeping it closed for several weeks.[19] Cuban labour leaders, meanwhile, outraged at low wages and cosy US–Cuban business and political relationships, protested further against Cuban and American exhibitors and the Cuban government. And when labour leaders weren't fighting exhibitors, the Moving Picture Union's communist and non-communist members were also fighting each other. Clashes within the larger Cuban Confederation of Workers, of which the MPU was a member, left four dead and more wounded. Due to the violence, general strikes and the possibility of martial law remained, further straining the reliability of exhibition workers and cinemas to stay open.[20]

In 1947, Cuban cinemas were still dominated by American product from Paramount Films of Cuba, Inc., Fox Films de Cuba, Metro-Goldwyn-Mayer, RKO-Radio Pictures of Cuba, SA, Warner Bros. First National South Films, Inc. and other American companies.[21] According to a report by the Motion Picture Association of America (MPAA), of Cuba's 484 cinemas (with a total seating capacity of over 308,000), over 95 per cent were exhibiting US product 'in full or in part'.[22] The US companies dominated some of the most important cinemas in Havana, as well as the content on their screens. In Havana alone, Paramount operated the Alcazar (1,700 seats), the Encanto (1,150 seats), the Fausto (1,609 seats), the Favorito (1,528 seats), the Florencia (1,163 seats), the Strand (1,000 seats) and the Universal (1,048 seats).[23] These seven cinemas contained almost 9,200 seats or 10 per cent of Havana's total seating capacity.

US control over Havana's key exhibition outlets only increased with the construction of the Warner Theatre at Calle L and Avenida 23.[24] Radio Centro SA and Warner Bros. First National South Films, Inc. approved drawings and specifications for the cinema on 25 April 1946 and Warner Bros. Pictures, Inc. delivered a $100,000 surety company bond to begin construction. Luis Augusto, Abel and Goar Mestre concurrently delivered a $25,000 personal bond to Warner Bros. Their updated 3 July 1947 lease agreement called for Warner Bros. to equip the cinema and for Radio Centro SA to furnish and install the equipment. Funds to pay, insure and ship the equipment, along with other related costs for the Warner Theatre, were deducted from the $100,000 bond to be deposited. Radio Centro SA was also responsible for footlights, switchboards and other equipment as stated in the revised lease agreement.[25]

Warner Bros. also added another cinema when Harry M. Kalmine, president and general manager of Warner Theatres, announced the lease of the 800-seat Plaza Theatre in Havana from Enrique Gaston in September 1947. The cinema was then completely renovated with new seats and a new cooling system.[26] Charles J. Bachman, Warner Bros.' sound supervisor, travelled to Cuba in late October 1947 to oversee the installation of new sound equipment in both the new Warner Theatre and the renovated Plaza.[27]

The Warner Theatre opened on 23 December 1947, with American films and local and international performers (Cab Calloway was an early visitor),[28] but a formal lease agreement between Warner Bros. and Radio Centro SA was not signed until 7 January 1948. The twenty-year agreement contracted Warner Bros. to pay Radio Centro SA $20,000 per year in rent.[29] Two months later, the full complex, Radio Centro, described by its founders as 'a miniature Radio City', opened on 12 March 1948 at a cost of $3 million.[30] That spring, Warner Bros. sent Pat Notaro, manager of the Stanley Warner Bromley Theater in Philadelphia, to become the manager for both Warner Bros. cinemas in Havana. Notaro reported directly to Herbert Copelan, zone manager for Warner Bros.' Latin American theatres, which now included the Plaza and Warner in Cuba, the Teatro Central in Lima and the San Jorge Teatro in Bogota.[31]

Throughout the 1940s and 50s, labour issues plagued the transnational relationship between US distribution and exhibition managers in New York and Havana and their Cuban labour force. The local labour union and Cuba's Labor Ministry were increasingly persistent about wage increases, employment practices, hirings and rehirings and other issues – especially since American wages for Cuban cinema workers were still 'below general average comparable work [in] any other American industry', a letter to MPAA foreign managers noted, whether they toiled in 'sugar, railroad, beer, bus, banks, restaurants and many other Cuban industries'.[32]

Government intervention began almost immediately after Warner Bros. took over the Plaza Theatre as the Labor Minister ordered Warner Bros. to retain the cinema's checkers so there would be no worker displacement. Internally, Warner Bros. executives were frustrated by the government edict, but eventually relented, worried that this restriction might soon be placed on the Warner Theatre as well (which had no previous employees and thus skirted this

requirement).[33] While American companies were finally able to acquire and/or build cinemas in
Cuba, local employment was retained and regulated by the Cuban government. As Cuban labour
unions and labour ministers forced local employees and salary increases on American-operated
cinemas – and similar laws were also passed with respect to Cubans working for US distributors
– rifts grew between American companies and Cuban workers. Megan Feeney writes that US
companies were also convinced that Cuban cinema checkers were misreporting grosses at
Cuban-operated cinemas, while 'Hollywood companies with new cinemas, like Paramount and
Warner Brothers, complained that such local biases also led cinema doormen to let friends in
without tickets, depriving them of their rightful earnings.'[34] During this period, there were numerous cases adjudicated before the Ministry of Labor that impacted Warner Bros.' ability to hire and
fire employees and impose their will in regards to wages and bonuses, amid numerous other regulations. Cuban labour laws, for instance, made it impossible to fire an employee without filing for
and receiving an 'expediente' from the Ministry of Labor. Despite meeting with and appealing to
the Under Secretary of Labor for the ability to lay off some of the Plaza's staff and disregard the
30 per cent raise required by a new labour law enacted in May 1948, Warner Bros. was forced
to keep all of its current employees on the payroll and to pay the 30 per cent raise. Warner Bros.
executive Pat Notaro was unsuccessful in removing even one employee: the sign painter, Julio
Ponce, who was implicated by Warner Bros. in a robbery at the theatre. Following the company's
failed attempts to fire him and the ensuing lawsuit, Ponce filed a new petition with the Ministry
of Labor to keep his job (and receive the back pay owed).[35]

As Feeney notes, faced with successive losses – and more legal hassles to come – US companies attempted to reduce these labour problems by funnelling money to Assistant Minister
of Justice Jorge Casuso and 'inside informants within the Cuban justice system to advise them
on decisions before they were announced, thus allowing them time to offer minimal settlement
offers' instead of waiting for a more financially deleterious ruling.[36] The brother of Warner Bros.'
Cuban attorney, Dr Francisco Espino, was reportedly close to the Supreme Court Justices in
Cuba and could, therefore, learn the results of their decisions in advance of the public, thus
enabling the company to settle financial matters before the court publicly rendered a verdict.[37]
Rather than settling with its employees for less, Warner Bros. executives in New York routinely
chose to try and procure privileged information instead. And, storing up future trouble, Feeney
adds, Warner Bros.' New York management still 'tended to deny all raises not regulated by the
Cuban state, ignoring the recommendations of their local managers'. The studios, the Cuban
Cinema magazine wrote, 'practic[ed] the policy of good neighbour with only their own house
in mind'. Feeney argues that Warner Bros. and others short-sightedly 'undermined their Havana
representatives, who had to ask permission of "papa" like children every time they want[ed] to
solve a problem'. Further enraging the local union and Cuban cinema employees, United Artists
also decided to discontinue Christmas bonuses for its distribution employees in Havana, while
Warner Bros. cut all raises for its distribution and exhibition workers throughout the country.[38]
While the America, Radio Cine, Campoamor, Marti and even Paramount's Fausto and Encanto
cinemas had all given their theatre's stage electricians a raise in salary, Warner Bros. refused the
local union's request. The company, then, was the only exhibitor unwilling to support the
union's pay hike, relenting only after numerous union delegates appealed to the company to
avoid complications by paying up.[39]

By June 1950, two and a half years after its debut, the Warner Theatre had grossed over $1 million, while the Plaza had grossed less than $300,000 since the lease had begun at the start of 1948.[40] Whatever its net profits might have been, they were being actively curtailed by the rising cost of labour, legal fees, concerns over admissions irregularities and distrust of its local workers. Still, Warner Bros. renewed their Warner Theatre lease in February 1950 with Radio Centro SA, agreeing to an auditing system whereby Warner Bros. produced a Statement of Account for all income generated by the theatre (and then shared with Radio Centro) and an agreement that granted Radio Centro the right to examine the theatre's and the company's ledgers and vouchers whenever it wanted to verify reported statistics. This was, of course, of great interest to Radio Centro as it pertained to their revenue-sharing agreements.[41]

International labour relations, though, remained a constant source of tension. In February 1951, Warner Bros.' Christmas bonus policy caused new conflicts between the company, its employees and the unions. The General Syndicate of Movie Workers launched a protest with the company after Warner Bros. had paid a bonus to some of its distribution workers but not others. (RKO, MGM, Columbia and other Hollywood companies had all paid the bonus to their workers.) This discriminatory policy, the union reminded the company, was punishable by Cuban law.[42]

The labour situation – and the laws set up to protect workers from foreign *and* indigenous exploitation – may have been one of the reasons MGM, which opened cinemas in nearby Puerto Rico and throughout Latin America, balked at operating cinemas in Cuba. Loew's retained their Cine Metro shop windows in more than half a dozen other Latin American countries (Argentina, Brazil, Chile, Colombia, Peru, Uruguay and Venezuela), but never ventured into Cuba.

As 1951 drew to a close, Warner Bros. decided to abandon the Warner Theatre and the Mestre brothers prepared a series of closing documents for the transfer of the Warner Theatre lease. The agreement forbade Circuito Teatral Radio Centro, SA, from using the Warner or Warner Bros. name or the W or WB symbols. The circuit was also forced to remove the Warner Bros. neon sign from the façade. Radio Centro now assumed all obligations and future liabilities for the theatre, while Warner Bros. transferred all of its previous agreements to the circuit.[43]

On 10 March 1952, Fulgencio Batista organised a military-backed coup, deposing current President Carlos Prío Socarrás and cancelling the country's upcoming elections. The coup rattled the country and especially Havana, immediately affecting movie theatres and all other public amusements and venues. Warner Bros.' Plaza Theatre specifically felt the impact of the coup, since it was close to the Presidential Palace, now occupied by the military.[44] Amid the country's political turmoil, Warner Bros. later unsuccessfully tried to offload the Plaza in 1954 when Nena Bénites, music critic for the *Diario de la Harina* newspaper, hoped to use the venue to present musical concerts featuring the Philharmonic Orchestra; however, the plan fell through.[45]

Warner Bros.' legal entanglements in Cuba did not necessarily scare off all US exhibition investment. Following vertical disintegration, the separated theatre company, Stanley Warner Corporation (SWC),[46] was left without the counsel of its once corporate cousin, and waded directly into Cuba's growing political and social unrest. After removing Cinerama equipment from its Warner Theatre in Oklahoma City in early 1957 – SWC had invested in Cinerama in 1953 and gained a controlling interest in 1958[47] – SWC sent the three-projector system to be installed in the former Warner Theatre in Havana, now Teatro Radio Centro. Cinerama's Cuban debut on 24 February 1958 was greeted with both fanfare and phosphorous bombs thrown by a 'rebel group' into the cinema, ending the premiere abruptly.[48] The attack took place less than nine months after another bomb exploded in the balcony of the Radio Centro, injuring nearby moviegoers. The attacks on Radio Centro were among several by the 26th of July Movement, headed by Fidel Castro, against prominent symbols of the economic, cultural, legal and political relationships between US cultural and material products or businesses and Batista's military dictatorship and sympathetic business leaders.[49]

In January 1959, Batista fled Cuba after years of repression and corruption, all of which helped usher in support for Fidel Castro and the Cuban Revolution that nationalised private businesses. By 1960, the nation's movie theatres were under the control of the Instituto Cubano del Arte e Industria Cinematográficos (Cuban Institute of Cinematographic Art and Industry). All Warner Bros. operations ceased in Cuba and Herb Copelan and Pat Notaro exited the country, like many other Hollywood executives. Goar Mestre also left after the Cuban government commandeered his $25 million broadcasting business in Cuba, departing for Argentina, where he established new television businesses, as well as in Venezuela and Peru.[50]

Warner Bros. exited the Peruvian and Colombian markets of its own accord, but Cuba represented one of the first nations to nationalise its cinemas in ways that would prove deleterious to foreign investment. Warner Bros.' experience in Cuban exhibition represents one of the more fraught examples of Hollywood's attempt to manage the political complexities of local and national laws alongside its overseas exhibition practices. Cuba was a stark reminder of the difficulties of investing in foreign real estate ventures where legal and political systems were either in flux or increasingly hostile to unfettered US investment and control.

China and Warner Bros. International Cinemas

In the 1990s, nearly a half-century after Warner Bros. left the Cuban market – or, more accurately, the Cuban market left Warner Bros. – the company, now part of the multinational media conglomerate Time Warner, waded into another difficult territory where foreign investment laws and real estate partnerships shifted dramatically in response to political, cultural and economic change. Time Warner's interests in expanding its cinema holdings in Asia (beyond Taiwan and Japan) aimed to help position Warner Bros. International Theatres (later Cinemas) as a dominant global player in late twentieth-/early twenty-first-century international film exhibition. Warner Bros.' exhibition initiatives, of course, were coupled with Time Warner's larger efforts to invest in China's media production, distribution and exhibition businesses and expand its presence in a highly lucrative, previously closed market with roughly 20 per cent of the world's population.

Before examining Time Warner's Chinese expansion, it is necessary to briefly look back at Hollywood's turbulent relations with China over the past century and the efforts of US film companies to become players in Chinese theatrical exhibition. China was an enormously under-screened market in the 1910s and 20s – a problem that would plague the nation for the next century – limiting revenues that could otherwise have boosted the indigenous film indus-try. European cinema had dominated Chinese screens before World War I. Afterwards, as wit-nessed in other international markets, US film companies made significant inroads in distribution in cities like Beijing and Shanghai. The local admissions boom was largely financed by ticket sales from US, not domestic, product. Of the 250 cinemas operating in China by 1930, nearly 200 specialised in American films, while US cinema comprised 75 per cent of all motion pictures shown in China. In growing, cosmopolitan cities like Shanghai that figure was closer to 90 per cent.[51] Shanghai had the largest number of cinemas of any city in China in the 1930s (roughly forty) and the American film companies and their motion pictures dominated the screens of those first-run, downtown houses. After premiering there, US films – accumulating scratches, dirt and other imperfections – would trickle down through the subsequent run market in second-, third- and fourth-run venues while the quality of these cinemas and their ticket prices notched lower and lower with each rung. Shanghai's four most opulent movie palaces, the Grand, Nanking, Metropolis and Cathay, were all in the best and most prosperous locations, tempting middle- and upper-class patrons with plush seats, top-notch service, ornate décor and air conditioning throughout the hot summer months. All four cinemas were operated by the same exhibition company, the Asia Theater Group, whose Chinese-born founders, He Tingran and Zhu Bo-Quan, had registered their very Chinese corporation in Delaware, USA, to take advantage of the Delaware General Corporation Law that has lured businesses there for decades for the state's ease of incorporation and its favourable income tax policies.[52]

American film executives made frequent visits to this increasingly important market during the 1930s, adding Shanghai to the list of Asian cities that were fast becoming part of an American network of distribution and exhibition capitals. However, following the Japanese occupation of China and the USA's entrance into World War II, American distribution offices were closed, Shanghai managers fled or were interned and affiliated cinemas like the Roxy in Shanghai, which had been MGM's shop window, were turned over to Japanese films.

The Chinese market reopened to American film companies immediately after Japan's sur-render in 1945. A bilateral business covenant was quickly signed between the US and Chinese governments that enabled American products, including film, to flow back in.[53] US distributors quickly reopened their local branches and their affiliations with local cinemas. (MGM, for exam-ple, inked a new contract with Shanghai's Dahua Theater.)

The end of the Chinese Civil War (fought intermittently between 1927 and 1950), and the establishment in 1949 of the People's Republic of China, once again abruptly ended American supremacy over Chinese movie houses. By July 1950, China's borders were closed to American films, personnel and theatre ownership and/or operation, and nearly a half-century passed before another attempt was made to exploit this enormous market. 'Hollywood's interest in the Chinese market never faded away,' Ting Wang writes. 'Up until the end of the 1970s, US firms made some tentative inquiries about the possibility of re-launching their businesses in China, but they were turned down invariably by the state-run China Film Corporation.'[54]

By the early 1990s, China began to embrace limited economic and cultural reforms that included boosting the national film industry through foreign investment in domestic distribution, co-productions, new technology and a wide-ranging campaign to build cinemas around the country. In so doing, the government hoped to cultivate a larger middle class that would also help embrace and ultimately expand the domestic and international market for Chinese films, thus bolstering a foundering cultural export and industry. The China Film Corporation lowered their drawbridge for foreign investment by allowing Golden Harvest, based in pre-unification Hong Kong, to distribute films across China through a revenue-sharing deal that would become the blueprint and siren song for Hollywood.[55]

After the landmark deal with Golden Harvest, Warner Bros. began discussions with Chinese officials in September 1994, one of the first American media conglomerates to open such negotiations. Through its revenue-sharing agreement, *The Fugitive* (1993) was exhibited in fifty-seven cinemas in six Chinese cities and grossed over $3 million, a relatively modest but promising figure. A new market had opened and any extra yuan from China was a new revenue stream for Warner Bros.[56] 'This historic deal between Warner Bros. and China Film was an epoch-making step not only in China's film reform, and in Sino-US film relations, but also in Hollywood's global expansion,' Ting Wang writes.

> It opened up the Chinese market once again to Hollywood after the latter's absence for 45 years, bringing the major Hollywood studios closer to realizing their long-awaited ambition of cracking the vast, largely untapped and potentially lucrative Chinese market, one of the few remaining distribution and exhibition gold mines in the world.[57]

After departing the Peruvian, Colombian and Cuban exhibition markets in the 1950s, Warner Bros.' sole overseas cinema in the 1960s and 70s was, once again, its flagship Warner West End in London. Warner Bros. did not re-enter global exhibition (beyond London) until 1987 under the guidance of exhibition industry veteran Salah Hassanein, who convinced Warner Bros. that building new multiplexes abroad through a new company, Warner Bros. International Theatres (WBIT), would transform underperforming markets through new exhibition venues. WBIT's model for expansion was to operate multiplexes with joint partners, thus allowing local investors to assuage indigenous concerns about US domination and also helping to clear legal and other regulatory hurdles. This was partly a response to the company's Japanese expansion that, Philip Turner writes, 'had suffered several "teething troubles" arising from cultural insensitivity' and 'other inattention to indigenous planning applications at [the] local level'.[58]

Millard Ochs succeeded Hassanein in 1994 and, by 1998, WBIT operated seventy-four multiplexes around the world, with 654 screens. This included twenty-eight multiplexes in Austria, eighteen in the UK, thirteen in Japan, five in Portugal, four in Germany, three in Italy, two in Spain and a new venture in Taiwan.[59] These joint ventures (JVs) included collaborations with Nichii and Mycal in Japan (Warner Mycal Cinemas), Filmes Lusomundo in Portugal (Warner-Lusomundo) and additional partnerships with the Sogecable Corporation in Spain, Morgan Creek and Chargeurs for planned ventures in the Netherlands and with Metronome for new Warner Bros. cinemas in Denmark. A most prominent partnership, though, was developed with the Australian exhibitor-distributor-producer Village Roadshow, which, Turner notes, formed 'a unified international network of cinemas trading under the aegis of Warner-Village Cinemas'. Warner Village would eventually operate WBIT and Village Roadshow's cinemas in the UK, Germany, Italy and Australia.[60]

In January 1998, WBIT made its first foray into Asia with the new Warner Village Multiplex in the Hsin Yi district of Taipei – a seventeen-screen 'state-of-the-art multiplex' that was the first in the region to offer digital sound, stadium seating and computerised ticketing (and auditing) systems. Michael Curtin writes that the new Taipei multiplex was 'More than a theater complex' with 'thirty shops, restaurants, and related entertainment activities'.[61] The cinema's opening week generated $666,000, which, Warner Bros. noted at the time, was 'believed to be the single biggest opening of any cinema anywhere in the world'. The Warner Village generated over $756,000 in its second week as demand for tickets grew. The cinema's technological and architectural innovations, as Hassanein had once predicted, did indeed create a larger market for Hollywood films, with nine out of the eleven films in its seventeen screens imported from the USA. 'In the face of much negative news about the Asian economy,' Ochs noted at the time, 'we have been able, with the participation of our long-term partners, Village Roadshow, to remain profitable in our expansion in these markets.'[62] In its first year, Warner Village sold roughly 3 million tickets, 25 per cent of the local market and 13 per cent of the country's total ticket sales. Warner Village would later open five more multiplexes in Taiwan, grabbing more than half of all Taiwan's ticket sales in these six venues.[63]

The success of WBIT's international cinemas – and especially the opening of the Warner Village in Taipei – encouraged Warner Bros. and Ochs to try and expand into China with its untapped market of over a billion potential moviegoers. One impediment to Chinese domestic and international growth remained its woefully outdated exhibition industry. Between 1990 and 1994, 10,000 of the country's 14,000 'authorised' cinemas were closed due to their age and/or lack of efficacy.[64] Even with the growth of some new multiplexes, China not only remained extremely under-screened, but its cinemas also failed to attract the country's growing middle class and those looking for an alternative to the widespread availability of pirated DVDs and VCDs and other forms of media access to domestic and international films. Chinese officials, hoping to generate interest in building new venues for Chinese films, removed the prohibition against foreign investment in theatrical exhibition.

In 1997, Hong Kong-based United Artists Cinema Circuit (UACC) built China's first six-screen multiplex in Wuhan. By 1999, UACC operated four multiplexes in China, including a new six-screen cinema in Shanghai.[65] Against the background of UACC's Chinese expansion and the ongoing trade negotiations between the US and Chinese governments, Time Warner's CEO Gerald Levin wrote a letter, in March 1999, to Chinese Premier Zhu Rongji, laying out the company's plan for its 'comprehensive cooperation' with China. These objectives included JVs for media co-productions, distribution operations, ancillary revenue streams and 'other movie-related businesses, such as movie theaters and theme parks'.[66] On 19 November 1999, the USA and China announced a bilateral trade agreement, which was followed by a similar accord between the European Union and China on 19 May 2000. By 19 September 2000, the US Congress had granted China Permanent Normal Trading Rights.[67] At the same time, China's State Administration of Radio, Film and Television (SARFT) – later known as the State Administration of Press, Publication, Radio, Film and Television (SAPPRFT) – and the Ministry of Foreign Trade and Economic Cooperation (MOFTEC) issued new regulations that year, which encouraged more foreign investment in multiplex construction and management. The new Foreign-Invested Enterprise (FIE) regulations set out numerous legal stipulations for new cinema construction based on foreign investments, including that: (1) foreign-invested movie theatres could not be singly owned by foreign companies but had to be part of equity joint ventures (EJVs) or contractual joint ventures (CJVs); (2) foreign-invested theatres could extend terms for no more than thirty years; and (3) Chinese partners had to retain at least a 51 per cent share in an EJV or the primary management rights in a CJV.[68] New multiplexes had to follow all FIE Theater Regulations for construction and approvals and agree to 'profit allocation and timing for return on investment', James M. Zimmerman writes, 'notwithstanding the require-ment that the Chinese party or parties control the operation'.[69]

Global exhibition companies like WBIT salivated at the opportunity to expand into a largely untapped market amid overbuilding in the USA and Western Europe and the impending Chapter 11 bankruptcy protections of North American exhibitors like Loews Cineplex, General Cinema, Regal Cinemas, Edwards Theatres and others. The foreign market – in Asia and Latin America – was and remains the leading growth opportunity for venture capital and expansion in exhibition, with China among the most lucrative in terms of potential. (A 2014 report noted, for instance, that while 'box office in developed markets remained relatively flat' with a 0.4 per cent compound annual growth rate [CAGR] between 2010 and 2013, '[o]verall industry growth was driven primarily by rapid growth in emerging markets, including Latin America (16.8%) and Asia Pacific (7.7%)', with a total 11.3 per cent CAGR for all emerging markets'.[70]) A decade earlier, as executives forecasted the next decade of global expansion, Peter Dobson of WBIT told a March 2000 audience at ShoWest – then the annual trade con-vention for motion picture exhibitors – that the lucrative Chinese market was 'just sitting there waiting for the taking'.[71] In addition to its vast investment potential, Warner Bros.' development of Chinese exhibition was also a key part of its anti-piracy strategy. 'We're cooperating with the government to fight piracy by being inside,' Ochs later noted, 'not standing outside and talking about it.'[72] On 11 November 2001, China officially joined the World Trade Organization and would now have to tackle piracy in a more meaningful way while regulating new foreign invest-ments in its domestic cinemas.[73]

The first WBIT project in China, the 'Shanghai Paradise Warner Cinema City', was a nine-screen multiplex in Shanghai, announced in March 2002, as a JV between Shanghai Paradise Co. Ltd and WBIT, operating as Shanghai Paradise Warner Cinema City Co., with financing also pro-vided by Broadband Investment Limited of Hong Kong, a local restaurant and leisure opera-tor.[74] (Shanghai Paradise's relationship with Warner Bros. stretched back to 1986, when the company co-produced *Empire of the Sun* [1987].)[75] At the time, Shanghai Paradise was the region's top distributor-exhibitor, garnering roughly 80 per cent of the city's total box office from domestic and international films. Shanghai Paradise offered WBIT its 'in-depth knowledge of the audience and marketing techniques'[76] derived from controlling fifty-seven local cinemas with 126 screens, accounting for roughly 75 per cent of the venues in Shanghai.[77] Following the creation of the FIE laws, the JV represented an investment of 28 million yuan (roughly $4.5 mil-lion in 2015 dollars), with Shanghai Paradise Co. owning 51 per cent of the shares, while WBIT controlled the remaining 49 per cent.[78] Shanghai Paradise, not WBIT, applied to the central gov-ernment in Beijing and the municipal government in Shanghai to approve the cinema's design, investment and construction plans.

The new cinema, located in one of Shanghai's largest shopping malls in the Xujiahui district, the Grand Gateway, was, 'designed as a completely immersive Warner Bros. entertainment experience', a WBIT press release noted, 'with numerous scenic and design elements featuring the stars of Warner Bros.' world-class library of movie and animation properties'.[79] The cinema was slated to have a 'large mural of the Bund (the historic Zhongshan Road) in which Chinese movie stars Jackie Chan and Gong Li stand shoulder-to-shoulder with the likes of legends Humphrey Bogart and Clark Gable'. The union of Hollywood's past (Bogart and Gable) and China's present (Chan and Li) paid homage to Warner Bros.' legacy, its production and distribution history in Shanghai and the WB-branded cinemas that would soon exhibit films starring global Hollywood and local Chinese stars. Shanghai Paradise received final approval from the Chinese government to open the new 1,490-seat, nine-screen cinema on 12 July 2003, with *The Matrix Reloaded* (2003).[80]

Following the successful launch of the Shanghai Paradise Warner Cinema City, the Shanghai Cinema Group announced a new 200 million yuan plan in October 2003 to build ten new joint WBIT cinemas throughout China, including a 2,200-seat multiplex in Nanjing and another in Wuhan. The new agreement had one significant change: SARFT had agreed to relax local laws in Beijing, Shanghai, Guangzhou, Chengdu, Xi'an, Nanjing and Wuhan that would now allow Warner Bros. to control 51 per cent of their new investments in these cities, rather than holding only a minority stake.[81] WBIT also announced a new venture with the Dalian Wanda Group to build and operate thirty Warner Wanda International Cinemas in 2003, with the first cinema to open in the Tianjin Municipality in January 2004. The agreement called for Wanda to invest in their construction 'while Warner Bros. will provide overall technical, operational and management services'. Over the next four years, Warner and Wanda planned to open twenty-nine more cinemas in Beijing, Shanghai, Harbin, Dalian, Shenyang, Wuhan and Zhenghou. 'China's cinema market is young and full of opportunities,' Ochs buoyantly observed.[82] The law firm of O'Melveny & Myers LLP helped Warner Bros. International Cinemas (WBIC – WBIT changed its corporate name from 'Theatres' to 'Cinemas') negotiate terms with the Dalian Wanda Group. Warner Bros.' Shanghai attorney and O'Melveny & Myers LLP partner Walker Wallace and Yu Aihong negotiated the 'largest co-development deal for cinemas in China to date' and 'the first of its kind between a Chinese property developer and a Hollywood studio'.[83]

WBIT's optimism, meanwhile, was further boosted by a new law passed in September 2003, Temporary Regulation on Foreign Enterprises' Investment in Chinese Cinemas, that now allowed foreign investors like Warner Bros. to hold a 75 per cent stake in 'joint venture cinemas in seven of China's largest cities' beginning 1 January 2004.[84] Zhang Pimin, vice director of SARFT's Film Bureau, observed that the new more flexible law made China 'a more attractive place for foreign cinema giants' and hoped that 'the coming of Warner Bros. is just a prelude of the foreign inflow in China's movie market' which could help reverse China's 'poor cinema conditions'. At the time, the country still had only 1,200 cinemas with roughly 2,000 screens – a profoundly minute average of one screen for every 650,000 citizens.[85] (By comparison, the USA had over 6,000 cinemas with more than 36,000 screens in 2004.[86])

Warner Bros. also applied for government approval for new multiplexes in Wuhan and Nanjing as the majority partner in a JV with Shanghai United Circuit and for an agreement with Guangzhou Performance Co. for a new WBIC multiplex in Guangzhou.[87] WBIC became the

first western cinema investor to hold a majority interest in a Chinese multiplex through its new
JV with Shanghai United Circuit in Nanjing that offered WBIC a 51 per cent interest, following
the new SARFT guidelines and those of China's Ministry of Commerce and Ministry of Culture
(by comparison to the stipulations regarding opening cinemas in the seven previously mentioned cities). Millard Ochs noted at the time that the revised ownership rules and the approval
given to Warner Bros. was 'a great honor'.[88]

By the end of 2005, the Paradise Warner Cinema City had been the country's most profitable movie theatre for the previous three years, while WBIC cinemas grossed over 120 million
yuan (US$15.2 million) that year alone.[89] WBIC now planned to increase the number of
screens it operated in Shanghai to 170 by the end of 2007.[90] With its UK circuit sold and its
European holdings dwindling, WBIC announced plans to move its theatre design unit from
London to Shanghai 'as part of a continuing expansion into the Chinese market'. From there,
executives would handle all multiplex design work for the company's remaining circuits in
China, Japan and Italy, and for future partnerships in India and Vietnam.[91] The cinema design
employees would join the forty-six staffers already working in Warner Bros.' Shanghai offices.[92]

In July 2005, SARFT had released yet another new set of laws titled Several Opinions in
Foreign Investment in Culture Industry, which retracted the ability of foreign companies to hold
majority positions in Chinese exhibition ventures. Once more, reporter Zhang Rui noted,
Chinese mainland investors had to 'own at least fifty-one percent or play a leading role in their
joint ventures with foreign investors'.[93] After exploring its legal options for the law's repeal, and
'After looking at all possible solutions for the past year', Warner Bros.' China publicist Gao Ming
announced WBIC's immediate and unexpected exit from the Chinese exhibition market in
November 2006. 'While we are disappointed that we must stop our investments in cinemas
due to significant regulatory changes,' Ming added, 'Warner Bros. remains committed to its
other businesses in China including local language film production, a home video joint venture,
consumer products and studio stores all of which have different legal structures, business
models and regulatory requirements.'[94] (SARFT officials refused to comment on the reasons
for the legal change.[95])

All of WBIC's Chinese partnerships quickly came to an end and the company began selling
its stake in operating and uncompleted cinemas.[96] The Los Angeles Times noted that the 'about-
face' highlighted 'Hollywood's long-standing tensions with China' that had been papered over
during Time Warner and WBIC's historic four-year expansion in the country. Yu Guoming, vice
dean at Renmin University's School of Journalism and Communication, observed that WBIC
may have tried to go too fast in its exhibition expansion: 'For global media companies to enter
China, you should have more patience to gradually penetrate into the market. Warner and
many other foreign media giants want to make progress by leaps and hit some milestones. …
This is against the rules of the game in China.'[97]

The country remained heavily under-screened but Warner Bros. was unwilling to chance
the next regulatory or legal challenge. Once more, it was film exhibition – not production or
distribution – that most challenged issues of nationalism and foreign investment. As Xing Yan,
a public relations officer for Beijing's Hua Xing Cinema, noted in 2004, a 'foreign capital influx
into China's cinema market' would ultimately serve to 'erode the interests of local cinemas'
even if it boosted the country's box office.[98] Film production was transient, contingent, tem-

porary and did not create a sustainable industrial base. Film distribution remained largely invisible and still dependent on domestic exhibitors. It was foreign ownership and/or operation of
local cinemas, though, which had long spelled trouble for Hollywood overseas, from economic
boycotts of American exhibitors in the UK to political violence in Egypt. WBIC reasoned that
without clear legal protections, its real estate investments and its exhibition operations in China
would be conducted without control, assurance, or according to conventional Hollywood
wisdom. David Wolf, a media consultant in Beijing, remarked that these new 'hostile regulations
and uncertainties of the future' forced foreign media companies to reconsider their business
plans. 'They're really beginning to question the assumptions of coming here in the first place.'[99]

WBIC's planned circuit of forty Chinese cinemas quickly vanished.[100] Between 2006 and
2008, WBIC sold all of its remaining shares in these JVs to their partners. According to Chinese
law, Equity Transfer Agreements (ETA) also had to be approved by the government.[101] The ETA
between Shanghai Film Group and WBIC was signed on 12 February 2007, with WBIC selling
their 49 per cent stake in the enormously popular Shanghai Paradise Warner Cinema City and
their 51 per cent stake in Nanjing SFG-Warner Cinema City.[102] WBIC was not the only company affected by SARFT's change in the investment laws. The Golden Harvest–Village
Roadshow JV in China also came to an end amid the difficult environment for foreign investors
and operators. 'So multiplexing is here to stay, but the day of the foreign joint venture is over,'
Scott Rosenberg wrote (erroneously) in *Film Journal International*. 'Multiplexing has gone indigenous,' and 'local investors now take all the risk and profit'.[103]

Since 2007, Warner Bros. has actively maintained JVs in film, television and other media
enterprises in China but has strictly avoided theatrical exhibition. 'China is developing methods
for consumers to view movies outside the cinema in a legitimate fashion,' Jim Wuthrich,
President of International Home Video and Digital Distribution for Warner Bros. Home
Entertainment Group stated in 2011. Through new Blu-ray, DVD and VoD deals, he added, 'millions of potential consumers will be able to view our films'.[104] Gala openings for WBIC cinemas,
though, were long gone from the cityscapes of Beijing and Shanghai, even if the company's films
could still easily be found in private homes and public cinemas.

In the end, Warner Bros.' abrupt exit from operating cinemas in China caused the media
conglomerate to miss out on a massive exhibition boom as 'millions of people' visited 'modern
cinemas for the first time', David Pierson wrote in March 2011. 'State-of-the-art theaters are
replacing dilapidated movie houses not only in wealthy urban centers like Beijing and Shanghai
but in outposts like Shengzhou … which has grown into a bustling city of about 800,000.'[105]
Two years later, China became the world's second largest exhibition market, surpassing the EU
and Japan.[106] In 2014 alone, China added 1,015 cinemas and 5,397 screens, bringing the country's screen count up to 23,600. 'On average,' Zhang Hongsen, SAPPRFT's film bureau chief,
noted, '15 more screens were added each day.'[107]

The maximum 49 per cent foreign investment, determined by the revised FIE laws, did not
scare off all exhibitors/investors. Canada's IMAX Corporation opened hundreds of screens
across China, while South Korean companies like Lotte, CJ CGV and Megabox also built new
cinemas.[108] In January 2014, for example, CJ CGV announced intentions to build an additional
nineteen cinemas in China to add to its then current count of twenty-seven cinemas, with 210
screens in sixteen Chinese cities.[109] WBIC, it seems, was early to market and early to exit.

For Warner Bros., its interest in film exhibition overseas appears to be over at the present time. In December 2012, Warner Bros. announced that the Japanese AEON Group (formerly Mycal) would purchase Warner Bros.' remaining 50 per cent stake from its partner in the Warner Mycal chain. This purchase enabled AEON to merge its wholly owned exhibition chain with its Warner Mycal properties (sixty cinemas with 496 screens) to become that country's largest exhibitor.[110] Paul Hastings, a global law firm with offices in the USA, Europe and Asia, negotiated the deal on behalf of AEON.[111] At the close of these negotiations, with its European cinemas long gone and even its flagship property in Leicester Square no longer part of its inventory, Warner Bros. effectively ended its three-quarters of a century in international theatrical exhibition in all markets.

The erosion of Warner Bros.' Japanese chain was part of the overbuilding that plagued mature markets like Japan and the USA – another reason why the opportunities for expansion in China had been so vast and attractive. Alongside the sale of Warner Bros.' last circuit in 2013, Millard Ochs announced his own retirement from WBIC. Asked to summarise the net effect of the company's foray into China and the legal barriers that stopped its progress, Ochs noted that the global scene had dramatically changed in less than a decade. 'When the government changed rules we moved out of China, but we left them with that knowledge base and they've improved upon it,' he told *Screen Daily* in June 2013. 'Now China is the number one international box office territory outside the US and by 2020 China will be the number one box office territory in the world.'[112]

Contracts for international trade between media conglomerates like Time Warner and Chinese firms and producers will continue to grow in the coming years, but movie theatres no longer appear to be in the US media conglomerate playbook. Future deals, instead, may look something like the $50 million investment Time Warner made in June 2013 in China Media Capital to grow the company's interest in homegrown Chinese film and television content. 'Increasing our global presence is one of Time Warner's strategic priorities,' the conglomerate's Chairman and Chief Executive Jeff Bewkes commented at the time, 'and China is one of the most attractive territories in which we operate'.[113] Attractive, indeed, for Warner Bros.' many other operations but not for the ownership of theatrical exhibition.

That's All Folks: Closing Arguments

In advantageous moments, US-operated movie theatres abroad can generate tremendous revenues and brand awareness and engagement. In more politically, financially and legally problematic periods, though, their embodiment of 'Hollywood' and American cultural exportation reverses this appeal and can become a target of local resentment.

During the 1940s and 50s, Warner Bros. sought to expand its burgeoning international exhibition operations in the fraught Cuban market where labour issues and growing political and economic turmoil coincided with rising anti-US sentiment. The Warner and Plaza theatres (and other US-operated cinemas there) represented the latest manifestations of US political, cultural and economic expansion. While moviegoers from across Havana were attracted to these cinemas because of their American operation and film offerings, they also attracted the negative attention of local labour leaders and others opposed to foreign and unfettered control of local labour and capital in Cuba.

Half a century later, Warner Bros.' experience in China also reflected this complicated relationship between global investment, national identity and the shifting nature of law as it sways with political and cultural winds. Warner Bros.' twenty-first-century cinemas in China also attempted to lure moviegoers through the company's brand legacy but their geographical location in city centre areas and the homogeneity between numerous multiplexes – whether they were WBIC, Wanda, or CJ CGV – made their corporate branding less important and susceptible to changing political motivations and legal constraints. Media-related theme parks like Hong Kong Disneyland (and the forthcoming Shanghai Disneyland Park) may be more insulated from these fluctuations because local visitors go precisely because of their Hollywood identity and the branded experiences they offer inside. These parks and the brands and attractions they employ are not easily reproducible by local operators. Dalian Wanda, Warner Bros.' former Chinese partners and the owner of US-based AMC Cinemas, recently opened Wanda Movie Park in December 2014, however, 'to compete with Disney, DreamWorks and Universal, which', *The Hollywood Reporter* noted, 'all have theme park ambitions in China'.[114] While media-related theme parks are routinely tied to branded characters, franchises and specific to its conglomerate affiliation, movie theatres are far more agnostic, forced by their contemporary screen counts to show films from numerous companies. While the Warner Theatre in Havana was a Warner Bros. 'shop window', WBIC cinemas played numerous non-Warner Bros. films. In the end, Warner Bros. films could be seen in numerous multiplexes around China. Movie theatres without Warner Bros. are inherently viable; Disneyland without Disney is not.

As the media business – film, television, music, video games, publishing, etc. – grows more and more digital, the need for US-based multinational media conglomerates to take on the expense and the (legal) risks of international exhibition has decreased, although the challenges of international trade law remain even with digital products. Time Warner has drawn up numerous agreements with international producers, distributors and exhibitors over the past decade, but it has not re-entered global exhibition. Eschewing the need for its own cinemas in China and many other markets, Time Warner, like other multinational media conglomerates, is working steadily and successfully within the laws of the land without having to build any new theatres upon it.

Acknowledgments

Thank you to Jonathan Auxier at the Warner Bros. Archives at the University of Southern California; Kathy McLeister, Janine Pixley and Richard Fosbrink at the Theatre Historical Society; Jeremy Megraw at the New York Public Library for the Performing Arts; the Wisconsin Historical Society; the Media History Digital Library; Yongli Li; and Emily Carman, Philip Drake, Eric Hoyt and Paul McDonald for their editorial guidance. A Thomas R. DuBuque Research Fellowship from the Theatre Historical Society of America and a Faculty Research Grant from the University of California, Santa Barbara Academic Senate both generously funded this research.

Notes

Please note: THS – Theatre Historical Society of America; WB-USC – Warner Bros. Archives, University of Southern California.

1. Simon N. Whitney, 'Antitrust Policies and the Motion Picture Industry', in Gorham Kindem (ed.), *The American Movie Industry* (Carbondale: Southern Illionois University Press, 1982), pp. 166–9.

2. Following the implementation of the ADA in 1990, all new cinemas have had to be constructed with wheelchair and companion seating with the following stipulations: two required wheelchair spaces for auditoria of fifty seats or less; four spaces and four companion seats for auditoria containing fifty-one to 150 seats; five wheelchair spaces and five companion seats for 151 to 300 seats; and six spaces and six companion seats for 301 to 500 seats. In auditoria with more than 300 seats, these six wheelchair spaces and six companion seats *cannot* be in the same row. Thus, many US exhibitors, concerned about having to build two rows of wheelchair and companion spaces, have opted, instead, to build auditoria with less than 300 seats. The placement of these seats must also be 'comparable' with those provided for non-disabled patrons. 'Justice Department Sues Major Movie Theater Chain For Failing To Comply With ADA', ADA.gov (Americans with Disabilities Act), http://www.ada.gov/archive/amcpress.htm (accessed 9 January 2014).

3. In addition to my own book, *American Showman: Samuel 'Roxy' Rothafel and the Birth of the Entertainment Industry* (New York: Columbia University Press, 2012), several excellent books have appeared over the past decade on exhibition including Kathryn H. Fuller-Seeley (ed.), *Hollywood in the Neighborhood: Historical Case Studies of Local Moviegoing* (Berkeley: University of California Press, 2008) and Richard Maltby, Melvyn Stokes and Robert C. Allen (eds), *Going to the Movies: Hollywood and the Social Experience of Cinema* (Exeter: University of Exeter Press, 2007).

4. Charles Acland's *Screen Traffic* examines the proliferation of transnational film exhibition from 1986 to 1998. Charles Acland, *Screen Traffic: Movies, Multiplexes, and Global Culture* (Durham, NC: Duke University Press, 2003).

5. 'Central America Deal', *Variety*, 14 December 1917, p. 50.

6. 'Paramount-Artcraft Expands in South', *Moving Picture World*, 29 December 1917, p. 1923; Caribbean Film Company advertisement, *Cine-Mundial*, January 1920: 57.

7. 'Richards Is President of Saenger Theaters', *The Film Daily*, 19 March 1929, p. 9.

8. Phil M. Daly, 'Along the Rialto', *The Film Daily*, 22 December 1931, p. 4.

9. 'Warner Havana Theatre', *Motion Picture News*, 22 February 1930, p. 15.

10. Mary Louise Blanco, 'Forecast Post-War Cuban Theaters for Majors', *The Film Daily*, 18 April 1944, pp. 1, 6.

11. 'Cuba Decorates Three Warners', *The Film Daily*, 27 September 1944, p. 3; 'Cobian Leases Smith, Ferenandez Circuits', *The Film Daily*, 18 September 1944, p. 1; 'WB, Fox in Cobian Deal? May Join in Cuban Circuit Operation', *The Film Daily*, 20 September 1944, p. 1.

12. 'Paramount and Cobian in Partnership Deal', *The Film Daily*, 30 October 1944, p. 5; 'Paramount and Cobian Partners in Cuba', *Paramount International News*, 3 November 1944, n.p.; 'Chatter: Havana', *Variety*, 22 November 1944, p. 43.

13. 'Mexican "Freeze Out" in Cuba', *The Film Daily*, 10 November 1944, pp. 1, 6.

14. Allen Eyles, *ABC: The First Name in Entertainment* (London: BFI, 1993), pp. 64, 65, 68.

15. 'Warners Buy Lima House, Theater Site in Sydney', *The Film Daily*, 16 March 1943, p. 2, 'Bogota Deluxe to WB; More SA Deals Pending', *The Film Daily*, 18 September 1946, p. 1.

16. Untitled Agreement, 27 July 1945, Box 2713, FO11185, WB-USC.

17. 'Pictures: Loew's Sets $9,008,000 Program For Theatres in Latin America', *Variety*, 5 September 1945, p. 7; Mary Louis Blanco, 'Loew's Building Two; WB Reported Leasing House Being Erected by CMQ', *The Film Daily*, 16 January 1946, p. 1.

18. Mary Louise Blanco, 'Cobian Out of Cuban Circuit', *The Film Daily*, 5 November 1945, pp. 1, 10.

19. 'Havana Theater Workers Walk Out', *The Film Daily*, 8 July 1946, p. 6.

20. Excerpt from *Cuba's Weekly Business Report*, 5 April 1947, in 'CUBA-PAYROLL', Box 16671B, Cuba Labor Laws #2, WB-USC.

21. Motion Picture Association of America, Inc., 'Important Local Offices and Personnel', *Theatre Directory – Cuba* (New York: MPAA, 1947), 90, 91, THS.

22. MPAA, 95, THS.

23. Ibid., 16, 18–20, 28, 29, THS.

24. Megan J. Feeney, 'Hollywood In Havana: Film Reception and Revolutionary Nationalism In Cuba Before 1959', PhD dissertation, University of Minnesota, 2008: 30, 244.

25. 'Proposed Theatre-Havana, Cuba, Modification of Agreement to Lease', Warner Bros. First National South Films, Inc. to Radio Centro, S.A., 3 July 1947, Box 2713, FO11184, WB-USC.

26. Feeney, 'Hollywood In Havana': 26; 'Warners Gets Prado As Havana Showroom', *The Film Daily*, 16 September 1947, p. 1.

27. 'Coming and Going', *The Film Daily*, 24 October 1947, p. 2.

28. R. Hart Phillips, 'Carnival In Havana: Parades and Other Spectacular Events Start This Week and Last Into March', *The New York Times*, 1 February 1948, X17; 'Cab Calloway to Cuba and Europe', *Washington Afro-American*, 21 June 1955, p. 17.

29. 'Warner Theatre, Havana, Cuba, Translation of Lease', 7 January 1948, Box 16671A, F581, WB-USC; Proposed Theatre, Havana, Cuba, Indemnity Bond to Radio Centro, S.A., 3 July 1949, Box 16671A, 581, WB-USC.

30. 'The News of Radio: Teen-Agers to Be Featured on CBS Network on Saturdays in "Accent on Youth"', *The New York Times*, 4 March 1948, p. 50.

31. 'Notaro Set as Warner Havana Theatre Manager', *The Film Daily*, 19 March 1948, p. 2.

32. Quoted in Feeney, 'Hollywood In Havana': 246.

33. John Jones to Wolfe Cohen, 9 February 1948. Box 16671B, WB-USC.

34. Feeney, 'Hollywood In Havana': 245.

35. Pat Notaro to Herbert Copelan, 19 April 1949, 16671B, Julio Ponce Case, WB-USC.

36. Feeney, 'Hollywood In Havana': 245, 246.

37. 'Telephone Call from Herb Copelan – Havana', 14 March 1951, Box 16671B, Esnard Case, WB-USC.

38. Feeney, 'Hollywood In Havana': 248.

39. Pat R. Notaro to John J. Glynn, 12 May 1950, Box 16671B, Cuba Labor Laws #2, WB-USC.

40. Wolfe Cohen to Gabriel Alarcon, 15 June 1950, Box 2713, FO11186, WB-USC.

41. Warner Bros. First National South Films, Inc. to Radiocentro, S.A., 21 February 1950, Box 2713, FO11185, WB-USC.

42. General Syndicate and Its Different Sections to Manager of Warner Bros. First National, 8 February 1951, Box 16671B, Cuba Labor Laws #2, WB-USC. Geza Polaty wrote to John Glynn that the company had tried to hide its selective bonus policy but word had leaked out to other employees. Geza Polaty to J. J. Glynn, 9 February 1951, Box 16671B, Cuba Labor Laws #2, WB-USC.

43. 'Report of Transfer of Lease of WARNER THEATRE, HAVANA at the Office of Goar Mestre, in Radio Centro Building, Havana, Cuba', 10 January 1952, Box 2713, Folder FO11188, WB-USC; 'Memorandum of Transfer,' 15 January 1952, Box 2713, FO11188, WB-USC.

44. Geza Polaty to J. J. Glynn, 15 March 1952, Box 16671B, 17-Misc., WB-USC.

45. Juan Falcon to Karl G. Macdonald, 5 October 1954, 16771B, 17-Misc., WB-USC.

46. Warner Bros. divested its theatre division in 1951 and the separated company was renamed the Stanley Warner Corporation, itself a prior merger of the Stanley Company of America and Warner Bros.

47. Peter Lev, *The Fifties: Transforming the Screen, 1950–1959* (Berkeley: University of California Press, 2006), p. 114.

48. 'Cinerama Quits Oklahoma', *International Projectionist*, February 1957: 36; 'Argentine Driver Released', *The New York Times*, 25 February 1958, p. 14.

49. '15 Cuban Rebels Seized By Army', *The New York Times*, 2 July 1957, p. 9.

50. Michael B. Salwen and Bruce Garrison, *Latin American Journalism* (Hillsdale, NJ: L. Erlbaum Associates, 1991), p. 148.

51. Ting Wang, 'Hollywood's Pre-WTO Crusade in China', *Jump Cut* no. 49 (Spring 2007), http://www.ejumpcut.org/archive/jc49.2007/TingWang/text.html (accessed 27 October 2013).

52. Poshek Fu, *Between Shanghai and Hong Kong: The Politics of Chinese Cinemas* (Redwood City, CA: Stanford University Press, 2003), pp. 32, 33, 36. Financier Zhu Bo-Quan, also known as Percy Chu, studied business administration and economics at NYU and Columbia University. Connie Fan and April Ma, 'Percy Chu, 1898–2001', *Rotary International* (December 2006), http://www.rotary-first100.org/global/asia/images/Percy%20Chu.pdf (accessed 4 January 2015).

53. Wang, 'Hollywood's Pre-WTO Crusade in China.'

54. Ibid.

55. Ibid.

56. Ting Wang argues that this enthusiasm for American films 'came to its peak when *Titanic* swept the entire nation in 1998 with a magic box office of 360.1 million yuan RMB (US$43.5 million), a figure that more than tripled that of the second most successful film, *True Lies*'. Ibid.

57. Ibid.

58. Philip Turner, *Warner Cinemas* (St Paul's Cray: Brantwood Books, 1997), pp. 12, 16, 17.

59. Time Warner, 'Warner Bros. and Village Roadshow Open Their First Multiplex in Taiwan to Blockbuster Attendance', 12 February 1998, http://www.timewarner.com/newsroom/press-releases/1998/02/Warner_Bros_Village_Roadshow_Open_Their_First_Multiplex_02-12-1998 (accessed 5 November 2013).

60. Turner, *Warner Cinemas*, pp. 8, 17.

61. As Michael Curtin notes, Warner Bros. distributors had 'no special deals' with Warner Village and each film was negotiated picture by picture as each did with their other partners. It was, then, Time Warner that profited most from these kinds of investments, rather than the individual divisions, which competed for yearly profits and internal reputation. Michael Curtin, *Playing to the World's Biggest Audience: The Globalization of Chinese Film and TV* (Berkeley: University of California Press, 2007), pp. 85, 101.

62. Time Warner, 'Warner Bros. and Village Roadshow Open Their First Multiplex in Taiwan to Blockbuster Attendance'.

63. Curtin, *Playing to the World's Biggest Audience*, pp. 85, 101.

64. James M. Zimmerman, *China Law Deskbook: A Legal Guide for Foreign-Invested Enterprises, Volume 1* (Chicago: American Bar Association, 2010), pp. 175, 176.

65. Wang, 'Hollywood's Pre-WTO Crusade in China'.

66. Ibid.

67. Penelope B. Prime, 'China Joins the WTO: How, Why, and What Now?', *Business Economics* vol. 37 no. 2 (2002): 28–9.

68. Zimmerman notes that foreign ownership could be 'up to 75 percent in some pilot city markets including Beijing, Shanghai, Guangzhou, Chengdu, Xi'an, Wuhan, and Nanjing'. Zimmerman, *China Law Deskbook*, pp. 175, 176.

69. Ibid., p. 176.

70. Redwood Capital, *Cinema Operator Industry Sector Review*, May 2014, http://www.redcapgroup.com/media/1035a448-73ff-4295-b83d-46d24aee8a73/ Sector%20Reports/2014-05-07_Cinema%20Operator%20Industry%20Report%20May %202014_pdf (accessed 4 January 2015).

71. Quoted in Wang, 'Hollywood's Pre-WTO Crusade in China'.

72. 'Warner Bros. Lands in China; Opens First Phase in Pirate War', *Taipei Times*, 21 July 2003: 10, http:// www.taipeitimes.com/News/biz/archives/2003/07/21/2003060268 (accessed 5 November 2013).

73. Prime, 'China Joins the WTO': 28–9.

74. 'Warner's First Cinema in China Operational', *People's Daily Online*, 13 July 2003, http://english. peopledaily.com.cn/200307/13/eng20030713_120100.shtml (accessed 5 November 2013).

75. Time Warner, 'Warner Bros. International Theatres to Open Multiplex Cinema in Shanghai with Local Partners', 4 March 2002, http://www.timewarner.com/newsroom/press-releases/2002/03/Warner_Bros_International_Theatres_to_Open_Multiplex_03-04-2002 (accessed 5 November 2013); Time Warner, 'Chinese Government Approves Warner Bros. International Cinemas' Multiplex In Shanghai', 10 July 2003, http://www.timewarner.com/news-room/press-releases/2003/07/Chinese_Government_Approves_Warner_Bros_International_07-10-2003 (accessed 5 November 2013)

76. Time Warner, 'Warner Bros. International Theatres to Open Multiplex Cinema in Shanghai with Local Partners'.

77. 'Warner's First Cinema in China Operational'.

78. Ibid.

79. Time Warner, 'Warner Bros. International Theatres to Open Multiplex Cinema in Shanghai with Local Partners'. Millard Ochs later recalled that, '[W]e assisted Shanghai Paradise from the early stages with the complex's design and technical specifications, as well as with training of management and operations personnel.' Time Warner, 'Chinese Government Approves Warner Bros. International Cinemas' Multiplex In Shanghai'.

80. Ibid.

81. 'Warner Bros. Taps China's Cinema Market', *People's Daily Online*, 15 October 2003, http://english. peopledaily.com.cn/200310/15/print20031015_1 (accessed 5 November 2013).

82. Press Release, 'Warner Brothers Marches into China's Cinema Market', Consulate-General of the People's Republic of China in Houston, 18 January 2004, http://houston.china-consulate.Org/ eng/zt/t58722.htm# (accessed 5 November 2013); Zhang Rui, 'Warner Bros.

Pulling Out from China's Cinema Business', *China.org.cn*, 8 November 2006, http://www.china.org.cn/english/entertainment/188323.htm (accessed 6 November 2013).

83. 'O'Melveny & Myers Represents Warner Bros. International Cinemas In China Entertainment Venture', *PR Newswire*, 29 January 2004, http://www.thefreelibrary.com/O%27Melveny+%26+Myers+Represents+Warner+Bros.+International+Cinemas+In...-a0112663193 (accessed 6 November 2013).

84. 'Warner Brothers Marches into China's Cinema Market'; Rui, 'Warner Bros. Pulling Out from China's Cinema Business'.

85. 'Warner Brothers Marches into China's Cinema Market'.

86. National Association of Theatre Owners, 'Number of US Movie Screens', http://natoonline.org/data/us-movie-screens/ (accessed 5 January 2014); National Association of Theatre Owners, 'Number of US Cinema Sites', http://natoonline.org/data/us-cinema-sites/ (accessed 5 January 2014).

87. WBIC Press Release, 'Wanda Group and Warner Bros. International Cinemas to Build Some 30 Multiplexes in China', 21 January 2004, http://cinematreasures.org/blog/2004/1/21/wanda-group-and-warner-bros-international-cinemas-to-build-some-30-multiplexes-in-china (accessed 5 November 2013).

88. Time Warner, 'Warner Bros. International Cinemas Becomes First Western Cinema Investor Approved to Hold Majority Ownership in Chinese Cinemas Under New Sarft Guidelines', 30 January 2004, http://www.timewarner.com/newsroom/press-releases/2004/01/Warner_Bros_International_Cinemas_Becomes_First_Western_01-30-2004 (accessed 5 November 2013).

89. Rui, 'Warner Bros. Pulling Out from China's Cinema Business'.

90. 'Warner Brothers to Build Digital Cinema in Beijing', *China.org.cn*, 26 December 2005, http://www.china.org.cn/english/features/film/153221.htm (accessed 5 November 2013).

91. Levent Ozier, 'Warner Bros. Moves Cinema Design Center to Shanghai', *Dexigner*, 7 January 2006, http://www.dexigner.com/news/6527 (accessed 5 November 2013).

92. Time Warner Inc.: Cinema Building-Design Center Will Be Relocated to Shanghai', *The Wall Street Journal*, 9 January 2006, A8; Josh Friedman and Don Lee, 'Time Warner Quits China Cinema Deal, Citing Rules', *Los Angeles Times*, 9 November 2006, http://articles.latimes.com/print/2006/nov/09/business/fi-chinafilm9 (accessed 5 November 2013).

93. Rui, 'Warner Bros. Pulling Out from China's Cinema Business'.

94. Gao Ming, quoted in Rui, 'Warner Bros. Pulling Out from China's Cinema Business'; Friedman and Lee, 'Time Warner Quits China Cinema Deal, Citing Rules'.

95. Geoffrey A. Fowler, 'Time Warner Decides to End Theater Run in China', *The Wall Street Journal*, 9 November 2006, B2.

96. Rui, 'Warner Bros. Pulling Out from China's Cinema Business'; Friedman and Lee, 'Time Warner Quits China Cinema Deal, Citing Rules'.

97. Friedman and Lee, 'Time Warner Quits China Cinema Deal, Citing Rules'.

98. 'Warner Brothers Marches into China's Cinema Market', Consulate-General of the People's Republic of China in Houston, 18 January 2004, http://houston.china-consulate.Org/eng/zt/t58722.htm# (accessed 5 November 2013).

99. Friedman and Lee, 'Time Warner Quits China Cinema Deal, Citing Rules'.

100. 'Warner Brothers Exits From China's Movie Theatre Mkt', *The Economic Times*, 10 November 2006, http://articles.economictimes.indiatimes.com/2006-11-10/news/27431867_1_theatres-china-beijing-news (accessed 5 November 2013).

101. Time Warner, 'China Film Group Taking Over Three WBIC Cinemas in China', 1 March 2007, http://www.timewarner.com/newsroom/press-releases/2007/03/China_Film_Group_Taking_Over_Three_WBIC_Cinemas_in_China_03-01-2007 (accessed 5 November 2013); Li Fangfang, 'Warner Bros Offloads Theaters', *China Daily*, 3 February 2007: 13, http://english.people daily.com.cn/200703/02/print20070302_353671.html (accessed 5 November 2013).

102. Time Warner, 'Shanghai Film Group Taking Over Two WBIC Cinemas in China', 10 April 2007, http://www.timewarner.com/newsroom/press-releases/2007/04/Shanghai_Film_Group_Taking_Over_Two_WBIC_Cinemas_in_China_04-10-2007 (accessed 5 November 2013).

103. Scott Rosenberg, 'Plex Drive: Asian Multiplexes Celebrate a New Era of Success', *Film Journal International*, 30 November 2007, http://www.filmjournal.com/filmjournal/esearch/article_display.jsp?vnu_content_id=1003679840 (accessed 5 November 2013).

104. Time Warner, 'Warner Bros. Entertainment to Become First Studio to Offer Films on Demand Nationally via Television Sets in the People's Republic of China', 15 June 2011, http://www.timewarner.com/newsroom/press-releases/2011/06/Warner_Bros_Entertainment_to_Become_First_Studio_to_06-15-2011 (accessed 5 November 2013).

105. David Pierson, 'China is on a Cinema-building Binge', *Los Angeles Times*, 6 March 2011, http://articles.latimes.com/2011/mar/06/business/la-fi-china-cinema-20110306

106. Wayne Ma, 'American Movies Lose Market Share in China; Local Filmmakers Step Up Their Game in Fast-Growing Market', *The Wall Street Journal*, 23 October 2013, http://online.wsj.com/news/articles/SB10001424052702304682504579153241399905968 (accessed 5 November 2013).

107. Clifford Coonan, 'China's Box Office Surges 36 Percent in 2014 to $4.76 Billion', *The Hollywood Reporter*, 1 January 2015, http://www.hollywoodreporter.com/news/chinas-box-office-surges-36-760889 (accessed 1 January 2015).

108. Ibid.

109. Jean Noh, 'CJ CGV to Open 19 More Cinemas in China', *Screen Daily*, 9 January 2014, http://www.screendaily.com/news/cj-cgv-to-open-19-more-cinemas-in-china/5065190.article (accessed 9 January 2014).

110. 'Aeon Buys Out Warner Mycal Cinemas', *Film Business Asia*, 20 December 2012, http://www.film-biz.asia/news/aeon-buys-out-warner-mycal-cinemas (accessed 5 November 2013); Mark Schilling, 'Warner Exits Japan Exhib Market', *Variety*, 19 December 2012, http://variety.com/2012/film/news/warner-exits-japan-exhib-market-1118063823/ (accessed 5 November 2013).

111. Press Release, 'Paul Hastings Advises AEON on Buyout of Warner Mycal from Warner Bros.', 1 March 2013, http://www.paulhastings.com/news/details/?id=437C2F26-8AA5-6986-8B86-FF00008CFFC3 (accessed 5 November 2013).

112. Jeremy Kay, 'Millard Ochs, Warner Bros.', *Screen Daily*, 20 June 2013,

http://www.screendaily.com/features/millard-ochs-warner-bros/5057576.article (accessed
   5 November 2013).

113.   Amol Sharma and Melodie Warner, 'Time Warner Invests $50 Million in China', *The Wall Street
      Journal*, 6 June 2013, http://online.wsj.com/news/articles/SB10001424127887
      324299104578529594007840524 (accessed 6 November 2013).

114.   Patrick Frater, 'China's Wanda Opens First Movie Theme Park in Wuhan', *The Hollywood Reporter*,
      19 December 2014, http://variety.com/2014/biz/news/chinas-wanda-opens-first-movie-theme-
      park-in-wuhan-1201384159 (accessed 4 January 2015).

References

Acland, Charles, *Screen Traffic: Movies, Multiplexes, and Global Culture* (Durham, NC: Duke University
   Press, 2003).

'Aeon Buys Out Warner Mycal Cinemas', *Film Business Asia*, 20 December 2012, accessed 5 November
   2013, http://www.filmbiz.asia/news/aeon-buys-out-warner-mycal-cinemas

Blanco, Mary Louise, 'Cobian Out of Cuban Circuit', *The Film Daily*, 5 November 1945, pp. 1, 10.

Blanco, Mary Louise, 'Forecast Post-War Cuban Theaters for Majors', *The Film Daily*, 18 April 1944,
   pp. 1, 6.

Blanco, Mary Louise, 'Loew's Building Two; WB Reported Leasing House Being Erected by CMQ', *The
   Film Daily*, 16 January 1946, p. 1.

'Bogota Deluxe to WB; More SA Deals Pending', *The Film Daily*, 18 September 1946, p. 1.

Caribbean Film Company Advertisement, *Cine-Mundial*, January 1920: 57.

'Central America Deal', *Variety*, 14 December 1917, p. 50.

'Chatter: Havana', *Variety*, 22 November 1944, p. 43.

'Cinerama Quits Oklahoma', *International Projectionist*, February 1957: 36.

'Cobian Leases Smith, Ferenandez Circuits', *The Film Daily*, 18 September 1944, p. 1.

'Coming and Going', *The Film Daily*, 24 October 1947, p. 2.

Coonan, Clifford, 'China's Box Office Surges 36 Percent in 2014 to $4.76 Billion', *The Hollywood Reporter*,
   1 January 2015, accessed 1 January 2015, http://www.hollywoodreporter.com/news/chinas-box-
   office-surges-36-760889

'Cuba Decorates Three Warners', *The Film Daily*, 27 September 1944, p. 3.

Curtin, Michael, *Playing to the World's Biggest Audience: The Globalization of Chinese Film and TV* (Berkeley:
   University of California Press, 2007).

Daly, Phil M., 'Along the Rialto', *The Film Daily*, 22 December 1931, p. 4.

Eyles, Allen, *ABC: The First Name in Entertainment* (London: BFI, 1993).

Fangfang, Li, 'Warner Bros Offloads Theaters', *China Daily*, 3 February 2007, p. 13, accessed 5 November
   2013, http://english.peopledaily.com.cn/200703/02/print20070302_353671.html

Feeney, Megan J., 'Hollywood In Havana: Film Reception and Revolutionary Nationalism In Cuba Before
   1959', PhD dissertation, University of Minnesota, 2008.

Fowler, Geoffrey A., 'Time Warner Decides to End Theater Run in China', *The Wall Street Journal*,
   9 November 2006, B2.

Frater, Patrick, 'China's Wanda Opens First Movie Theme Park in Wuhan', *The Hollywood Reporter*,
   19 December 2014, accessed 4 January 2015, http://variety.com/2014/biz/news/chinas-wanda-
   opens-first-movie-theme-park-in-wuhan-1201384159

Friedman, Josh and Don Lee, 'Time Warner Quits China Cinema Deal, Citing Rules', *Los Angeles Times*, 9 November 2006, accessed 5 November 2013, http://articles.latimes.com/print/2006/nov/09/business/fi-chinafilm9

Fu, Poshek, *Between Shanghai and Hong Kong: The Politics of Chinese Cinemas* (Redwood City, CA: Stanford University Press, 2003).

Fuller-Seeley, Kathryn H. (ed.), *Hollywood in the Neighborhood: Historical Case Studies of Local Moviegoing* (Berkeley: University of California Press, 2008).

'Havana Theater Workers Walk Out', *The Film Daily*, 8 July 1946, p. 6.

Katz, S. D., 'Welcome to the Chinaplex', *Millimeter*, July/August 2008: 20–6.

Kay, Jeremy, 'Millard Ochs, Warner Bros.', *Screen Daily*, 20 June 2013, accessed 5 November 2013, http://www.screendaily.com/features/millard-ochs-warner-bros/5057576.article

Lev, Peter, *The Fifties: Transforming the Screen, 1950–1959* (Berkeley: University of California Press, 2006).

Ma, Wayne, 'American Movies Lose Market Share in China; Local Filmmakers Step Up Their Game in Fast-Growing Market', *The Wall Street Journal*, 23 October 2013, accessed 5 November 2013, http://online.wsj.com/news/articles/SB10001424052702304682504579153241399905968

Maltby, Richard, Melvyn Stokes and Robert C. Allen (eds), *Going to the Movies: Hollywood and the Social Experience of Cinema* (Exeter: University of Exeter Press, 2007).

Melnick, Ross, *American Showman: Samuel 'Roxy' Rothafel and the Birth of the Entertainment Industry* (New York: Columbia University Press, 2012).

'Mexican "Freeze Out" in Cuba', *The Film Daily*, 10 November 1944, pp. 1, 6.

Motion Picture Association of America, Inc. *Theatre Directory – Cuba* (New York: MPAA, 1947).

National Association of Theatre Owners, 'Number of US Movie Screens', accessed 5 January 2014, http://natoonline.org/data/us-movie-screens/

Noh, Jean, 'CJ CGV to Open 19 More Cinemas in China', *Screen Daily*, 9 January 2014, http://www.screendaily.com/news/cj-cgv-to-open-19-more-cinemas-in-china/5065190.article

'Notaro Set as Warner Havana Theatre Manager', *The Film Daily*, 19 March 1948, p. 2.

Ozier, Levent, 'Warner Bros. Moves Cinema Design Center to Shanghai', *Dexigner*, 7 January 2006, accessed 5 November 2013, http://www.dexigner.com/news/6527

'Paramount and Cobian in Partnership Deal', *The Film Daily*, 30 October 1944, p. 5.

'Paramount and Cobian Partners in Cuba', *Paramount International News*, 3 November 1944, n.p.

'Paramount-Artcraft Expands in South', *Moving Picture World*, 29 December 1917: 1923.

Prime, Penelope B., 'China Joins the WTO: How, Why, and What Now?', *Business Economics* vol. 37 no. 2 (2002): 26–32.

'Pictures: Loew's Sets $9,008,000 Program For Theatres in Latin America', *Variety*, 5 September 1945, p. 7.

Redwood Capital, *Cinema Operator Industry Sector Review*, May 2014, accessed 4 January 2015, http://www.redcapgroup.com/media/1035a448-73ff-4295-b83d-46d24aee8a73/Sector%20Reports/2014-05-07_Cinema%20Operator%20Industry%20Report%20May%202014_pdf

'Richards Is President of Saenger Theaters', *The Film Daily*, 19 March 1929, p. 9.

Rosenberg, Scott, 'Plex Drive: Asian Multiplexes Celebrate a New Era of Success', *Film Journal International*, 30 November 2007, accessed 5 November 2013, http://www.filmjournal.com/filmjournal/esearch/article_display.jsp?vnu_content_id=1003679840

Rui, Zhang, 'Warner Brothers Marches into China's Cinema Market', *China.org.cn*, 8 November 2006, accessed 6 November 2013, http://www.china.org.cn/english/entertainment/188323.htm

Salwen, Michael B. and Bruce Garrison, *Latin American Journalism* (Hillsdale, NJ: L. Erlbaum Associates, 1991).

Schilling, Mark, 'Warner Exits Japan Exhib Market', *Variety*, 19 December 2012, accessed 5 November 2013, http://variety.com/2012/film/news/warner-exits-japan-exhib-market-1118063823/

Sharma, Amol and Melodie Warner, 'Time Warner Invests $50 Million in China', *Wall Street Journal*, 6 June 2013, accessed 6 November 2013, http://online.wsj.com/news/articles/SB10001424127887324299104578529594007840524

'Time Warner Inc.: Cinema Building-Design Center Will Be Relocated to Shanghai', *The Wall Street Journal*, 9 January 2006, A8.

Turner, Philip, *Warner Cinemas* (St Paul's Cray: Brantwood Books, 1997).

Wang, Ting, 'Hollywood's Pre-WTO Crusade in China', *Jump Cut* no. 49 (Spring 2007), accessed 27 October 2013, http://www.ejumpcut.org/archive/jc49.2007/TingWang/text.html

'Warner Brothers Exits From China's Movie Theatre Mkt', *The Economic Times*, 10 November 2006, accessed 5 November 2013, http://articles.economictimes.indiatimes.com/2006-11-10/news/27431867_1_theatres-china-beijing-news

'Warner Brothers to Build Digital Cinema in Beijing', *China.org.cn*, 26 December 2005, accessed 5 November 2013, http://www.china.org.cn/english/features/film/153221.htm

'Warner Havana Theatre', *Motion Picture News*, 22 February 1930, p. 15.

'Warners Buy Lima House, Theater Site in Sydney', *The Film Daily*, 16 March 1943, p. 2.

'Warners Gets Prado As Havana Showroom', *The Film Daily*, 16 September 1947, p. 1.

'WB, Fox in Cobian Deal? May Join in Cuban Circuit Operation', *The Film Daily*, 20 September 1944, p. 1.

Whitney, Simon N. 'Antitrust Policies and the Motion Picture Industry', in Gorham Kindem (ed.), *The American Movie Industry* (Carbondale: Southern Illinois University Press, 1982), pp. 161–82.

Zimmerman, James M., *China Law Deskbook: A Legal Guide for Foreign-Invested Enterprises, Volume 1* (Chicago: American Bar Association, 2010).

PART 3
NEGOTIATION AND LABOUR

7 ASSET OR LIABILITY?
HOLLYWOOD AND TAX LAW

ERIC HOYT

In 1952, director John Huston gave up his American citizenship and migrated to Ireland. He became an Irish citizen because of one thing about the USA that he could no longer tolerate: his taxes.[1] In the USA, Huston was one of many highly compensated Hollywood creative workers who paid marginal income tax rates as high as 80 to 90 per cent.

By migrating to Ireland, Huston saved substantially on his taxes. But he also had to change the types of films he made. Earlier in his career, Huston showed an affinity for making films set in the urban underworld, such as *The Maltese Falcon* (1941) and *The Asphalt Jungle* (1950). But in 1955, Huston explained to his agent, Paul Kohner, why he could not make movies about American gangsters and shoot them abroad:

> I would have to confess that [shooting the picture away from the USA] was only to avoid paying taxes, as there isn't a single other reason that would hold water. I wouldn't like saying this, Paul, nor, I think, would people like to hear me say it ... So long as I make pictures outside the United States I shall have to limit myself to material that doesn't call for a modern day, American setting. We should consider this a rule.[2]

Huston opted to only direct movies that he claimed could be 'more easily made away' from the USA. These included films with international settings, such as *Moulin Rouge* (1952) and *Beat the Devil* (1953) and classics of American literature, such as *Moby Dick* (1956), which Huston justified because 'the little Irish town, which served as the location for the only dry land sequence, is more like old New Bedford than anything in New England today'.[3] Still, certain types of movies couldn't be made. Huston's desire to 'avoid paying taxes' ruled out the possibility of him telling stories with 'a modern day, American setting'.

From income taxes to foreign tariffs, from box-office admissions taxes to production incentives, Hollywood has encountered taxation in many forms. The results of these encounters have influenced the course of film history and altered the history of policy-making and governance as well. John Huston provides just one example of how laws of taxation have influenced creative and business decisions in the Hollywood film industry. In the years since the 1950s, few high-profile actors or directors have gone so far as to change nationalities simply to avoid taxes (French actor-turned-Russian citizen Gerard Depardieu offers one notable exception).[4] Yet the relationship between Hollywood and tax law remains as significant and fraught as ever. In the contemporary era, film producers make decisions about how to finance projects and where to shoot them based on tax incentives offered by American states and foreign governments.

Increasingly, though, state governments are reaching the conclusion that the lost tax revenue outweighs the benefit to the state by hosting film productions.

This chapter offers a survey of the history of Hollywood's relationship with tax laws. The chapter is structured in four main sections. The first section surveys how film exhibition, film distribution and physical reels of film have been taxed. The second section analyses how taxes on the income of highly paid actors and directors changed their behaviour and, in the process, changed film history. The desire to escape high income tax rates encouraged top talent to work less in the 1930s, form corporations in the 1940s and live and work abroad in the 1950s. As a case study, we explore Charles Laughton's successful 1939 defence of his 'loan-out' corporation. Laughton's victory against the US Commissioner of Internal Revenue inspired other movie stars, along with people in other industries, to lower their tax liabilities through the creation of personal corporations.

The third section explores the significant role tax laws (and tax shelters) have played in contemporary film finance and international location shooting. In the 1980s, savvy lawyers pioneered the 'sale and leaseback' model of financing, allowing British and Australian investors to write off their tax liabilities and simultaneously subsidise Hollywood budgets. As a case study, we examine the Australian Tax Office's controversial decision to deny Australian investors a tax write-off on the film *Moulin Rouge* (2001) – the Baz Luhrman musical, not the movie directed by American Irishman John Huston. The fourth section explores the current debates over the efficacy and sustainability of US state tax incentives.

This chapter necessarily covers a great deal of ground – much of it involving policies, percentages and numbers. Although these policies and numbers may seem like dull accounting details, the reality is that they have a significant impact on the Hollywood entertainment industry and the economies of cities, states and nations. When the state of Michigan awards $39.96 million in tax credits to a single film – *Oz: The Great and Powerful* (2013) – it has consequences for the tax payers of the state, the recipients of services from the state of Michigan and the film crews in Los Angeles who sit and watch more and more productions move to other locations for tax reasons.[5] Hollywood's lobbying arm, the MPAA, trumpets the 'multiplier effect' that tax incentive-hungry Hollywood productions have on local businesses – such as restaurants and dry cleaners – and tourism, wherever they shoot. But money going to Hollywood productions can also mean trade-offs – less revenue available to pay for schools, law enforcement and other government services, as well as contributing to the shrinking middle class of media professionals in southern California. To study the history of film and tax law is to study how policies change human behaviour, and how those changes in behaviour hold creative, social and economic stakes.

Taxing the Cinema: Exhibition, Distribution and Property

As Peter Decherney explains in Chapter 1 in this collection, on copyright law, the US courts in the early twentieth century grappled with the question of how to define film. Was it a form of photography? Or was it closer to live theatre? These sorts of questions about the nature of the medium also shaped early tax policies towards film. Should the presentation of films be taxed? The distribution? Or the reels of films themselves?

When, in 2013, the state of North Carolina passed an admissions tax on movie theatres, it was reviving a century-old policy.[6] The first significant tax policies to focus on the motion picture industry concerned the exhibition of films. An admissions tax on exhibitors was a natural target for legislators. Like a sales tax, it is fairly simple for governments to audit and collect an admissions tax. Additionally, because the public frequently perceives motion pictures as a glamour industry awash in money, legislators can argue that the industry suffers very little from such a tax. And there was yet another assumption held by some of the officials who passed the early admissions tax laws: going to the movies put the public at moral danger, and moviegoing was a form of behaviour to be discouraged.[7]

The mid-1910s witnessed the motion picture industry's first major grappling with an admissions tax. Motion picture distributors and exhibitors grew concerned when politicians in the state government of New York proposed such a tax. As film historian Kia Afra has shown, the threat of taxation served as a rallying point to bring different wings of the industry closer together.[8] The industry and its allies successfully defeated the tax on the grounds that it discriminated against one industry. The episode marked an early victory for motion picture trade organisations (in this case, the National Association of the Motion Picture Industry, or NAMPI).[9] Less than a year after defeating the New York tax, however, the federal government levied a 10 per cent admissions tax on film theatres as part of the War Revenue Act of 1917, a law passed by Congress to finance the USA's entry and participation in World War I.[10]

US federal admissions taxes were again in effect during World War II. This was an era before newspapers immediately reported the weekend's box-office results. In the absence of such centralised and immediate reporting, the tax collection figures reported by the Internal Revenue Service (IRS) were the industry's best way of monitoring the overall health of the box office (simply divide the tax collected by the tax rate, as a percentage, and you arrive at the total box-office revenue). During the war years, the American box office boomed, and the government needed as much revenue as possible to fund the war, so Congress increased the admissions tax on movie theatres to 20 per cent.[11] The year following World War II's end, 1946, marked the industry's richest year ever, generating $2.29 billion. The government saw no reason to reduce the 20 per cent tax and happily collected $458 million in revenue from the box office.[12]

Unfortunately, admissions to US movie theatres fell dramatically over the next several years, from an average weekly attendance of 90 million in 1946 to an average of 45.9 million in 1953.[13] The industry's decline was the result of a combination of factors – suburbanisation, the baby boom and competition from other services and products, especially television. Although the IRS saw evidence of this decline every three months when it collected the taxes, the government took no action to reduce or eliminate the 20 per cent tax. As hundreds of movie theatres closed for business in the late 1940s and early 50s, exhibitors attempted unsuccessfully to persuade Congress to eliminate the tax, which, even if it was not the source of their troubles, certainly contributed to the red ink bleeding from their balance sheets. Finally, in 1953, Congress exempted movie theatres from the 20 per cent admissions tax.[14] For the owners of the roughly 4,500 theatres that closed between 1946 and 1953, however, the exemption from the tax marked a case of too little, too late.[15]

In addition to taxing exhibition, governments have found a number of ways to tax the distribution of films. In the early twentieth century, numerous American state governments passed what the industry angrily referred to as 'censorship taxes' – fees charged by state censorship offices on a per foot or per print basis (for more on censorship laws, see Chapter 5). Hollywood's greatest adversaries in taxing their distribution operations, though, have been foreign governments, who have enacted numerous censorship and import restrictions in attempts to protect local film industries and/or limit the perceived ideological and linguistic influences of Hollywood films. Some of the protectionist measures take the form of quotas, limiting the number of film imports. Other measures are forms of taxation – for example, a customs tariff paid upon importation and calculated on the quantity of film footage – or an excise tax paid at the point of sale within the country.[16]

Hollywood's most dramatic battle against tariffs occurred in the UK in the late 1940s. For a long time Hollywood's biggest foreign market, the UK had imposed a quota law to protect its domestic market in 1927. World War II brought a new urgency for regulating imports – not so much to reduce the number of imports but to reduce the outflow of Sterling currency to the USA. In 1947, as the nation recovered from war, Britain imposed a 75 per cent duty on imported films. The major Hollywood studios immediately launched a boycott, cutting off the export of newly produced films to the UK until the British government agreed to new terms. Finally, some eight months later in 1948, the British caved in and the boycott ended. As Ian Jarvie explains in his excellent analysis of the boycott, Britain agreed to remit revenues of up to $17 million per year, plus whatever amount British films had earned in the USA.[17]

Whereas, in the 1940s, the UK was Hollywood's most important foreign market, the global film marketplace of the twenty-first century looks very different. In 2012, China generated $2.7 billion in box-office revenue, making it the world's second largest movie market by revenue (the USA is still number one, Japan ranks third and the UK and France tie for fourth place).[18] Hollywood's attempts to woo China – by self-censoring content, casting Chinese actors and various publicity stunts – have received extensive attention in news coverage of the media industries.[19] However, the revelation in 2013 that China's state-run distributor, China Film Group, was charging a new government tax on foreign producers' shares of the box-office gross was a reminder that the taxation of film distribution continues to matter. The Hollywood studios currently only receive a 25 per cent share of the Chinese box office. China Film Group's application of the new tax could lower the studios' anticipated theatrical revenue from China by 8 per cent.[20] In this case, though, a Hollywood boycott is nearly impossible to imagine – the studios lack sufficient leverage, too many substitutes for Chinese movie screens exist and Hollywood does not want to alienate the world's fastest-growing film market.

Taxing exhibition treats movies as a performance or event; taxing distribution treats movies as a commodity that moves across state or national boundaries. From the 1930s to the 60s, however, the state of California applied yet another tax treatment towards film: *film as property*.[21] Los Angeles County, empowered by the state of California, levied a personal property tax on the amount of film that individuals or corporations had on hand as of 1 March each year. Film producers were taxed on the *intangible value* of their film negatives, rather than the film's *material value*. In other words, the county assessor recognised that the negative was worth far more than those same rolls of celluloid if they had not been exposed. *Los Angeles Times* columnist Philip Scheuer summarised how the tax was calculated: 'If a picture's budget is expected to reach $1 million, the assessment figure is one fourth or $250,000. If the picture was that day finished and in the can, the county says the producer owes it the full amount or $25,000. If the picture is considered only one-tenth finished the price would be as "low" as $2,500.'[22] The local community tax rates shifted the equation a bit, but the basic calculation was: TAX = (Budget) × 25% × (7 to 10%) × (1 to 100% – the percentage of the completed film that has been shot). Essentially, once a year, the state of California taxed the production of intellectual property.

The tax assessors in Los Angeles that applied the personal property tax to film negatives did not intend to alter production schedules or promote inefficient behaviour. Unfortunately, this is exactly what happened. 'The film capital has long adopted a policy that the fewer pictures started, the better, during the month of February unless they can also be finished before the end of the month,' reported the Los Angeles Times in 1952.[23] Many other postwar reports echoed the same sentiment that 'production was depressed in the months prior to the [1 March] assessment date' and, as a result, film workers found themselves unemployed more frequently in the early part of the year.[24] Industry lore also exists that, as 1 March approached each year, some studios loaded up railcars with reels of film and rushed them over to the neighbouring state of Nevada, then moved them back to California days later. I have yet to find any evidence from studio archives documenting this process, but it is plausible that the scheme was used. All the ingredients were there: a monetary incentive to alter behaviour; a form of property that, unlike real estate, was transportable; a predictable tax assessment date; and an industry that has innovated far bolder and more roundabout tax shelters.

In late 1960s, the property tax on film received its most extensive coverage yet. In April of 1968, California's State Senate passed a bill that 'prevent[ed] the county assessor from levying property taxes on film distribution rights and other intangibles'.[25] The tax exemption was strongly championed by the major studios and Hollywood labour unions, which blamed the property tax as one of the causes of high unemployment among Los Angeles film industry workers and runaway production (a topic discussed in greater depth later in this chapter).[26] Not everyone was convinced. The Los Angeles Times ran an editorial entitled 'Film Tax Exemption Unwarranted' in which the paper's editors expressed scepticism that the property tax had a significant impact on the runaway production problem. 'The motion picture industry may, indeed, have problems,' wrote the Times' editors, 'but the solution does not lie in shifting a part of its burden to the rest of the taxpayers.'[27]

Fortunately for the Hollywood studios and unions, they had an old ally in Sacramento. In the summer of 1968, former Hollywood actor and then California Governor Ronald Reagan signed into law the Senate bill. The tax exemption, valued as a $2.3 million saving to the movie industry, 'limit[ed] the assessment of processed film for tax purposes to hard cash value of the material rather than the intangible value of motion pictures on the film'. Reagan proudly declared, 'we are hereby canceling out a discriminatory tax that penalized only one business and literally made the production of motion pictures a seasonal industry'.[28]

When Reagan served as President of the USA in the 1980s, he passed far more sweeping tax policies – lowering the nation's highest income tax rate from 50 per cent to 28 per cent. As Reagan claimed in his memoirs, his fervency to lower income taxes began when he was a Hollywood actor, who, like many of his peers, was paying an extremely high marginal tax rate.[29]

It is to this history of high tax rates paid by Hollywood's top talent that we now turn. As we will see, Hollywood's top talent, aided by savvy lawyers and advisors, innovated numerous methods to reduce their income taxes.

Income Taxes of the Stars

Any government must decide how to divide its tax burden across citizens. Sales taxes and theatre admissions taxes are *regressive;* they place a greater burden on the poor than the rich. The rich person and poor person pay the same 25 cents in admissions tax, but the 25 cents absorbs significantly more of the poor person's wealth. A graduated income tax, on the other hand, is *progressive* – the tax rate increases as an individual's income increases.

The history of how the USA established its federal income tax is long and complicated, but here are the essential facts. In 1913, the US Congress passed the Sixteenth Amendment of the Constitution, legalising a federal income tax.[30] The Sixteenth Amendment came after decades of political and legal fighting to achieve a progressive system of taxation in the USA. The government raised tax rates in 1916 to finance US involvement in World War I, but only a small fraction of the US population was taxed on their income and Hollywood's top talent did not

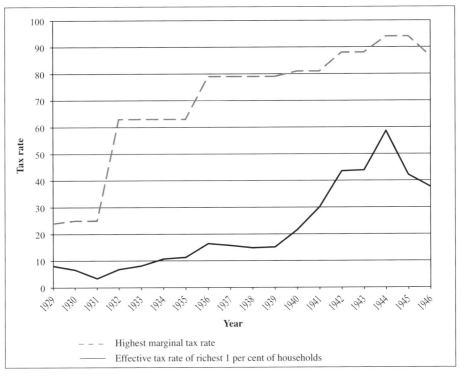

Marginal and Effective Tax Rates, 1929–46

(Sources: Robert A. Wilson, *Personal Exemptions and Individual Income Tax Rates, 1913–2002,* Internal Revenue Service Data Release (Spring 2002), p. 219, accessed 20 October 2008, www.irs.gov/pub/irs-soi/02inpetr.pdf; W. Elliot Brownlee, 'Historical Perspective on US Tax Policy Toward the Rich', in Joel B. Slemrod (ed.), *Does Atlas Shrug? The Economic Consequences of Taxing the Rich* (New York: Russell Sage Foundation, 2000), pp. 45, 51, 60.

confront significantly high taxes until the 1930s. During the 30s – in the midst of the Great Depression and after numerous silent film stars had earned millions of lightly taxed dollars – the US Congress raised the highest marginal tax rate from 25 per cent at the beginning of the decade to 79 per cent by 1939.[31] The highest marginal tax rates of each year from 1929 to 1946 are illustrated on the preceding page. This was the context of high tax rates that influenced Reagan's political ideology, John Huston's move to Ireland and Charles Laughton's use of a loan-out corporation.

Looking at the highest marginal tax rates only tells part of the story. A marginal tax rate does not tax the individual's entire income, only the amount that exceeds a particular threshold. If an individual earned an income above the highest marginal tax rate (above $200,000 in 1942, for instance), he or she would actually be taxed at an escalating marginal tax rate, encompassing twenty-four surtax brackets.[32] In the tax code during this time, the 'surtax' was the higher marginal tax that was added to the 'normal tax' that someone paid (usually either 4 per cent or 8 per cent). One way to imagine the escalating surtax brackets is that a dollar earned in January would be taxed much more lightly than a dollar earned in December. Because the surtax was broken into twenty-four different brackets, there were many incentives and opportunities to lower one's taxable income and wiggle into a lower tax bracket. By contrast, the US tax code today only has seven different brackets, none of which top 40 per cent.[33]

Additionally, the highest marginal rates only tell part of the story because they leave out the *effective* tax rates – that is, what people actually paid in taxes. The chart on page 188 also illustrates the effective tax rates of the richest 1 per cent of households over these years, revealing the large disparity between the highest marginal tax rates and what the rich actually paid. In his 1941 sociological study of the Hollywood industry, Leo Rosten found that while talent complained loudly about their high tax brackets they quietly paid much lower rates. Sampled from the 1938 incomes and tax payments of a handful of actors, writers, directors and producers, Rosten's data reveals that in all sixteen cases the effective tax rate paid by talent in federal, state and property taxes fell significantly below the commensurate marginal rate.[34] How, then, did talent manage to pay lower effective tax rates?

Hollywood's top talent utilised many strategies to reduce their taxable income, the most common of which was to aggressively deduct business expenses. Actors and directors had every right to deduct legitimate business expenses, such as legal fees and the commissions paid to agents. The wardrobes of actors, however, reveal how the distinction between a deductible business expense and a non-deductible personal expense could be blurry. Ronald Colman's 1935 contract with 20th Century-Fox required the actor to 'provide, at his own expense, such modern wardrobe and wearing apparel as may be necessary for any and all parts' that he portrayed (the studio granted an exception for period films).[35] In this case, Colman could legitimately deduct the expense of acquiring the clothes that he wore on screen. But what about clothing worn off-screen? Some stars argued that appearing fashionable was essential to maintaining their image and earning power. Actress and model Adrienne Ames explained that she 'could wear a dress but two or three times if it was distinctive, and never more than six or twelve times if not a distinctive dress'.[36] These types of arguments tended to fall on unsympathetic government ears. *Dinner at Eight* (1933) actress Madge Evans deducted $2,350 for a mink coat she used on a 1934 trip to New York, reasoning that the industry figures, reporters and adoring public would expect to see her in the sharpest winter clothing. Internal Revenue agents clamped down on her mink coat deduction and disallowed other expenses she wrote off related to the trip. The government's logic was simple; the trip was fundamentally a vacation, not a business trip, and the mink was a warm coat, not a necessary business expense.[37] Movie stars and the government continue to this day to clash over wardrobe deductions.

Deducting business expenses was an important way that top talent in the 1930s reduced their taxable income. But there was another, even more basic way to reduce taxable income – simply working less. Actresses Irene Dunne and Claudette Colbert both reduced their workload in the late 1930s, a move made possible by agent Charlie Feldman's skill in negotiating short-term contracts.[38] The reduced workload offered multiple advantages, including higher project selectivity and a more flexible schedule. But the steep marginal tax rates of the time were a major factor, providing little incentive to sign on for more than one or two projects per year. If stars like Dunne or Colbert, earning up to $150,000 per picture, agreed to make a third picture in a given year, they would find themselves facing a steep marginal tax for each additional dollar earned. By 1941, several stars were cutting back on their workloads for tax reasons.[39]

After entering World War II in 1941, the USA overhauled the federal income tax – expanding the number of tax payers required to file an income tax from 3.9 million in 1939 to 42.6 million in 1945.[40] Feature films, cartoons and, especially, radio programmes participated in the campaign to teach Americans about the income tax and inspire them to pay their taxes.[41] Meanwhile, clever film producers found a new way to use corporations to reduce their tax liabilities. Producers Samuel Goldwyn and Lester Cowan, and stars such as Gary Cooper, James Cagney and James Stewart, all utilised 'collapsible corporations' to receive modestly taxed capital gains rather than heavily taxed earned income. A November 1945 *Time Magazine* article succinctly explained the basics of how the capital gains tax shelter operated:

> A corporation can hold its picture for six months, then sell it and call the profit a capital gain, taxable at 25% instead of 85–95%, the top tax on ordinary income. A producer can either 1) sell his interest as a stockholder in the corporation; or 2) dissolve the company that made the picture. An example: Independent Producer Lester Cowan, who made *Story of GI Joe* and *Tomorrow the World*, sold his interest as a stockholder at a net profit of $1,000,000. By paying only a 25% capital gains tax, he pocketed $750,000 as compared to the mere $100,000 he would have had if he had paid an income tax.[42]

Film historians Tino Balio and Thomas Schatz have both identified the capital gains tax shelter as one the major causes for the 1940s boom in independent productions.[43] Hollywood's top producers, directors and stars seized the opportunity to gain more creative control over their productions and retain significantly more income. In 1946, the Bureau of Internal Revenue declared the capital gains tax shelter to be illegal and, in 1950, Congress amended the tax code in a way that removed the shelter's financial benefit.[44] Writing in 1953, Duke University Law Professor Charles L. B. Lowndes noted: 'Hollywood, which frequently takes the lead in tax fashions, produced some of the most bizarre examples of incorporated pocket-books.'[45] Lowndes called the capital gains tax shelter 'another Hollywood super-colossal production' and wrote, 'the collapsible corporation which originated in the motion picture industry … spread to other fields of endeavor, such as the building industry, before the 1950 Act caught up with it'.[46] Lowndes' analysis highlights how tax schemes pioneered by the Hollywood film industry have influenced other businesses and industries. One of the most important of these innovations involved the income taxes of actor Charles Laughton.

The Cases of Charles Laughton

The most influential and long-lasting tax reduction strategy utilised by Hollywood talent has been the formation of personal corporations. The precedent-setting case starred Charles Laughton in the role of defendant. In 1937, the US Treasury Department identified Laughton as a 'tax dodger' who had used a foreign corporation as a way of reducing his income. These were not criminal charges, but they arrived with bad publicity and a hefty price tag – Laughton owed a $104,431 tax deficit for the years of 1934 and 1935.[47] Laughton's tax woes were the result of Motion Picture and Theatrical Industries Ltd, a corporation he formed in 1934 in England. Ostensibly, the company was formed to produce motion pictures. A board of directors of which Laughton was not a member managed Industries Ltd. In reality, however, Industries Ltd served as Laughton's corporate shell. Laughton was the sole owner of outstanding stock and benefited from the flexible payment schemes inherent in this structure.

Here is how the corporate structure and Laughton's arrangement worked. Laughton entered into a contract with Industries Ltd, granting the corporation his sole and exclusive services. Industries Ltd then 'loaned out' Laughton to different Hollywood studios. In late 1934, for instance, Paramount contracted with Industries Ltd for Laughton to star in *Ruggles of Red Gap* (1935), Leo McCarey's comedy about a Brit who crosses the Atlantic and discovers the American dream. Paramount paid Industries Ltd around $6,000 per week for Laughton's serv-

ices. Industries Ltd, on the other hand, only sent Laughton a weekly cheque for $750. Was Laughton's company giving him a bad deal? Far from it. By having the corporation only pay him a fraction of his regular acting fee and holding on to the rest, Laughton greatly reduced his taxable income and dropped into a significantly lower tax bracket. Additionally, the arrangement provided more long-term income stability to the notoriously volatile profession of acting. If, two years later, Laughton fell out of public favour and could not find acting work, then Industries Ltd could still pay him from its funds in the bank. The personal service cor-

The US Treasury Department labelled actor Charles Laughton as a 'tax dodger'. Laughton fought back in court and established an important precedent (BFI)

poration offered other benefits too – covering a number of Laughton's expenses and, most notably, loaning Laughton $78,625 in 1935 for the purpose of purchasing a property lease in London and acquiring valuable art work.[48]

The US Treasury Department saw Industries Ltd as an off-shore tax avoidance scheme, pure and simple. Laughton fought back against the charges – albeit at a safe distance. As the actor was residing back in England in 1938, Laughton's tax advisor, A. T. Chanalls, and lawyer, Lloyd Wright, appeared on his behalf at a hearing of the US Board of Tax Appeals. Chanalls explained Laughton's reason for forming the corporation. It was done not to evade taxes, he argued, but based on Laughton's firm belief that actors die poor while producers die rich, a fate he wanted to avoid. Like Madge Evans arguing for a wardrobe deduction, Laughton was essentially appealing to the unique circumstances of his profession. Unfortunately, IRS agents and federal judges found Laughton's rationale equally unpersuasive. The counsel for the Board of Appeals objected to Chanalls' testimony, saying he merely offered Laughton's opinion and no substantive argument.[49]

Fortunately for Laughton, his team of advisors one year later presented a more convincing argument. In 1939, *Laughton v. Commissioner of Internal Revenue* came before Judge William W. Arnold in the US Board of Tax Appeals. Emotional appeals about the plight of the poor actor were set aside in favour of a cool, clear-headed logic of corporations and the studio system. Laughton's legal team argued that Industries Ltd was created not to avoid taxes but to make movies. The judge agreed, ruling in Laughton's favour and stating that Industry Ltd's 'failure to engage extensively in the production of motion pictures during the taxable years was reasonably explained as due to a lack of capital'.[50]

As further reason to support Laughton's claim, the judge called attention to the business practices of other corporations in Hollywood. In his opinion, Judge Arnold wrote: 'The loan agreement whereby petitioner [Laughton] was to act for Hollywood producers were in accordance with the general practice of the industry, where one studio or producer had a long-term contract for the services of an actor.'[51] Warner Bros. loaned its actors under contract to RKO. MGM loaned its contract players to Columbia. Why should Industries Ltd be treated any differently under the law when it loaned Laughton to Paramount? The judge considered the fact that Laughton and Industries Ltd were British to be 'immaterial so far as the present question of law is concerned'.[52] Previous tax appeals centred on the unique circumstances of Hollywood – the way the industry compounded business and personal matters, or the boom and bust nature of stardom – had failed. But courts were receptive to a corporate logic, one acknowledging the unique circumstances of how motion picture corporations frequently loaned contracted talent to one another.

In 1940, the US Ninth Circuit Court of Appeals reversed the decision in part, but the Court upheld the validity of Industries Ltd as a corporation.[53] In the following years, many more actors formed their own corporations, which, until the tax code was amended, allowed them to turn their personal income into less heavily taxed corporate income.[54] In 1942, Errol Flynn formed Thomson Productions, Inc. and, in 1943, Bette Davis formed BD, Inc. The corporate logic of loan-outs was built directly into Flynn's and Davis's arrangements. The agreements contracting Flynn and Davis to their respective companies both used contracts nearly identical to the agreements binding their companies to Warner Bros. The deals represented a studio-sanctioned form of star incorporation, offering Flynn and Davis increased creative control, profit participation and potential tax savings (see Chapter 8, 'Doing the Deal', for more on the history of talent contracts).[55] Significantly, the legacy of *Laughton v. Commissioner of Internal Revenue* reached beyond the motion picture industry, providing legal armour to individuals in other fields, such as sales, medicine and law, seeking to form personal service corporations and reduce their tax liabilities. The US tax code has changed many times since 1939, making personal service corporations at various points more or less valuable as tax-saving devices, but Laughton's lawsuit remains an important moment in the history of personal service corporation case law.[56]

Runaway Production, Tax Shelters and Film Finance

From the post-World War II era onward, the most significant impact of tax policy upon Hollywood has been as a driver of runaway production. 'Runaway production' refers to the wide-scale production of what we think of as Hollywood movies in locations far away from southern California. To be sure, the causes for runaway production are not limited to taxation. Additional economic motives for runaway production include labour costs, advantageous exchange rates and monetary remittance policies (in the postwar era, the UK and many western European nations limited the amount of currency that US companies could remit home; Hollywood studios could spend their 'frozen funds' by producing movies in those countries).[57] Also, numerous Hollywood productions have travelled outside of LA for creative reasons. Location shooting can provide realistic or spectacular settings that are impossible to create in southern California. Historically, Hollywood unions and industry commentators have distinguished between 'economic runaways' and 'creative runaways', reserving their harshest scorn for the former.[58] However, as the example of John Huston declining to make any movie with a contemporary US setting demonstrates, the reasons for making a 'creative runaway' are often inseparable from the economic benefits that can be gained from shooting outside of LA.

The importance of tax as a causal factor in runaway production has shifted over time, but we can see that it played an especially important role during two periods – the 1950s and the contemporary era. First, in the early 1950s, Hollywood actors and directors actively sought to make movies abroad to escape from their high income tax rates. The movement started in 1951 after Congress amended Section 116 of the Tax Code. The amendment exempted income taxes on monies earned if the tax payer resided abroad for seventeen out of eighteen consecutive months. Congress intended the so-called 'eighteen months exemption' to be an incentive for construction and oil engineers working abroad in the postwar years. But top Hollywood talent quickly discovered ways to utilise the exemption for their own advantage – travelling abroad to make movies either with independent financing or the 'frozen funds' of studios. Galvanised by the prospect of earning hundreds of thousands of dollars in untaxed earnings, Kirk Douglas, Alan Ladd, Gene Kelly and William Wyler all travelled to Europe in the early 1950s to make films.[59] The US government eventually responded by limiting the amount of earned income that could go untaxed, but not before the production of numerous films abroad that might not otherwise exist, including William Wyler's classic, *Roman Holiday* (1953).[60]

Our contemporary era marks a second, longer and more consequential period of tax policies influencing runaway production decisions. No longer is the process driven by stars seeking to reduce their income taxes, which have gone down substantially since the 1950s. Instead, over the last thirty years, the most important impact of tax policy upon Hollywood has been in the area of film finance – especially, studios' and producers' embrace of tax shelters and incentives as a means of financing films and lowering production costs. Significantly, these tax incentives have typically been tied to shooting in a particular nation or state, thus impacting both the film crews left behind in southern California and the local populations that host the shoots and pay out generous tax benefits. The first significant case of such tax shelter exploitation occurred in the early 1980s in the UK. Utilising a loophole in the British tax code that allowed an investor to write off the cost of acquiring a film asset, a system developed known as 'sale and leaseback' in which the studio or producer would sell a qualifying movie to a group of British investors and then lease the movie back from them at a below-market interest rate for a fifteen-year period.[61] Britain's Inland Revenue Office shut down sale and leaseback in 1985, but permitted it in a different form in the 1990s. A similar model of sale and leaseback developed in Germany until the German government clamped down and closed the loopholes that made this possible. Where there are ambiguously written tax laws involving motion picture production, Hollywood's sharpest minds are never far behind.[62]

In the 1990s, Australia became one of the preferred locations for runaway Hollywood productions. Sound stages, locations and labour could all be obtained far more inexpensively than in the USA. As the value of the Australian dollar dropped 15 per cent against the US dollar during the 1990s, the number of runaway productions to Australia increased by 26 per cent over the course of the same decade.[63] Two Hollywood studios, Warner Bros. and 20th Century-Fox, invested in building sound stages and production facilities in Australia, further incentivising them to take runaway productions 'down under' and amortise the costs of studio construction. Meanwhile, Australian film-makers and policy-makers struggled to maintain a sense of Australian national cinema. In the 1970s and 80s, Australia's tax-based film incentives emerged out of the desire to promote a distinctively Australian national cinema. Without government support, argued film-makers and policy-makers, Australia would have neither the population nor the language barrier to resist complete market domination by imported Hollywood movies. The first significant Australian film-oriented tax policy occurred in 1978, when 'tax laws under section 10B of the Tax Assessment Act were re-drafted, to allow film investment to be written off over two years, allowing investors considerable savings on their tax bills'.[64]

Numerous Australian film producers utilised the 10B tax shelter to help finance their films. But large-budget films without any distinctively Australian content, such as the sci-fi action movie *The Matrix* (1999) and sci-fi noir *Dark City* (1998), also employed the 10B deduction. In 2001, the Australian Taxation Office (ATO) increased its scrutiny on the 10B deduction and the convoluted, inefficient tax shelters that had become commonplace. The timing coincided with the release of a movie musical that was filmed in Australia, set in France and a celebration of show business artifice.

Moulin Rouge and the Australian Taxation Office

When *Moulin Rouge* was released in the summer of 2001, audiences and critics debated the aesthetic merits of Luhrmann's postmodern audiovisual style. At that same moment, however, an altogether different debate was taking place among studio executives, financiers and Australian policy-makers. Director Baz Luhrmann and his production team had shot *Moulin Rouge* on the Fox Studios Australia sound stages and financed the movie with money borrowed as part of a 10B tax shelter. To their great surprise, however, the ATO denied *Moulin Rouge*'s Australian investors the two-year tax write-off they were expecting.[65] The case prompted a discussion about national film identity and became a turning point for Australian tax policy in regards to film production.

To understand the complex financing deal at the centre of the tax dispute, we should look closely at the film itself. As Felicity Collins and Therese Davis point out, *Moulin Rouge* is a postmodern film that is filled with 'layers of audiovisual sampling and citation'.[66] The most recognisable moments of citation reference Elton John, Marilyn Monroe and *The Sound of Music*. But there is a moment in this postmodern backstage musical that offers a citation – albeit unintentional most likely – of the complex financing arrangement behind the film. In *Moulin Rouge*, the core group of characters requires funding before they can mount their production of 'Spectacular, Spectacular'. Enter the character of the Duke – the oblivious, curly moustached British millionaire, played by actor Richard Roxburgh. In a scene of great narrative importance but probably less memorable than any of the musical numbers, the Duke and Zigler, the show's producer-director, hammer out the terms of the Duke's investment in the production of 'Spectacular, Spectacular' and the renovation of the Moulin Rouge from a club into a

The tax shelter used to finance *Moulin Rouge* (2001) mirrors aspects of the film itself (BFI)

theatre. The Duke demands that Satine, the object of his affection and the reason for his foray into show business, be bound under contract directly to him.

However, there is an even more important component to the Duke's deal. 'Naturally, I shall require some security,' the Duke says. 'I shall require the deeds to the Moulin Rouge.' This line of dialogue offers an entry point to understanding the tax scheme used to finance *Moulin Rouge*. Like many other large-budget movies previously shot in Australia, *Moulin Rouge* was financed through a series of deals and agreements between the film-makers, Australian investors and the studio 20th Century-Fox. These agreements were designed to reduce the cost of production for the film-makers and the studio and to reduce the amount of taxable income for the investors. The financial gurus intended to utilise section 10B of the Australian Tax Act to achieve these benefits.

Here is how the 10B tax scheme worked. A group of Australian investors form a special-purpose company for the sole reason of investing in a particular motion picture. Let's assume the picture's budget is AUS$100 million – very close to the actual budget of *Moulin Rouge*.[67] The special-purpose company raises 20 per cent of the picture's budget or AUS$20 million in equity. This AUS$20 million is the only cash contribution the investors will put up. The remaining 80 per cent of the budget, or AUS$80 million, is obtained through a bank loan. The special-purpose company is backed by an AUS$80 million guarantee that the film-makers or studio place with the bank or an independent guarantor. The bank loans the special-purpose company the AUS$80 million against this guarantee, and it is the studio – not the investors' special-purpose company – that ultimately pays back the loan. The special-purpose entity has raised AUS$100 million through a 20/80 split of equity and debt, and can take a tax deduction on the total budget, not simply the equity portion. That means the company realises a AUS$100 million deduction instead of simply a AUS$20 million deduction. The deductions transfer to the investors under group loss transfer provisions, and the investors can write off their investments over a two-year period. For any individual investor, this arrangement brings the benefit of tax savings greater than the amount of equity he or she invested.[68]

However, it is not enough for the special-purpose entity to merely invest in the picture; the company needs to own or partially own the copyright for at least a short period of time. The section 10B tax deduction 'applies to capital expenditure incurred in acquiring rights in or under copyrights relating to an Australian film'.[69] The investors pay the AUS$100 million to the film-makers to purchase the film's rights. With this purchase, the special-purpose entity becomes eligible for the 10B tax deduction. And it is here we can return to the Duke's control of the Moulin Rouge deeds. His ownership mirrors the special-purpose entity's control of *Moulin Rouge*'s copyright, which enables the investors to qualify under division 10B and realise large tax write-offs over a two-year period. *Moulin Rouge* proves to be a film packed with quotes and allusions not simply to cultural works, but to the culture industries that produce and finance them.

After the Duke obtains the deeds, things do not go as he planned. He loses Satine – first to the idealistic writer Christian, then to something graver. Much like the Duke, *Moulin Rouge*'s investors found themselves in a position they had never expected to be in. The 10B tax shelter scheme described above had routinely been used since 1996 to finance large-budget international movies.[70] However, in August of 2001, the ATO denied the investors in *Moulin Rouge* the right to qualify for deductions under division 10B.[71] The ATO ruled that the film's investors entered into a 'tax avoidance agreement', which is forbidden under section 82KL of the Income Tax Assessment Act of 1936. The ATO questioned the legitimacy of even calling this practice an 'investment'. By definition, shouldn't an investment entail the assumption of risk on the part of the investor? However, due to the advantageous mix of debt and equity, and the studio's loan repayment guarantees, the ATO found the investors had 'little or no commercial exposure to the success or failure of the film'.[72]

Additionally, the ATO took issue with the assignment of copyright from the film-makers to the investors' special-purpose company. In the ATO's 2002 ruling on division 10B tax avoidance schemes, the ATO noted: 'the transfer of the rights from the film maker to the special purpose company is conditional on the disposal of those rights to the distributor'.[73] In other words, Baz Luhrmann's production company sold the rights to the investors' special-purpose company, only to have those rights immediately transfer to the studio 20th Century-Fox. Commenting that 'there is never a measurable period of time during which the special purpose entity possesses the rights', the ATO used the transfer of copyright as one of the key reasons for rejecting *Moulin Rouge* and future pictures utilising the same tax scheme for qualifying under 10B.[74]

As a film, *Moulin Rouge* recognises and celebrates the artificiality that is central to the musical genre and, on a more significant level, cinema as a whole. In the financial arrangement that made the film possible, a similar game of smoke and mirrors was at play – one that enabled the investors to make an 'investment' without taking any risk, one that conveyed the copyright to the investors' company only nominally and never for any measurable period of time. The ATO pulled back the red curtain and rejected *Moulin Rouge*'s deduction claims as a tax avoidance scheme.

Many members of the Australian press and government, however, perceived the matter differently. The Australian Broadcasting Corporation's news programme *Lateline* described *Moulin Rouge* as a 'hit Australian film' and 'Australia's most expensive film'. *Lateline* pointed out that *Moulin Rouge* had an Australian leading actress and Australian director and questioned why 'the tax office has decided not to allow *Moulin Rouge* Australian tax concessions. This is despite the tax office approving concessions in the past for Hollywood films such as *The Matrix*.'[75] For the tax office, this was a simple matter of income tax evasion. However, *Lateline*'s coverage of the story transformed this issue of tax evasion into an issue of nationalism and national cinema. *Lateline* echoed other Australian journalists and critics who defended *Moulin Rouge* as a non-American blockbuster and claimed the film arrived at a 'cinematic language' that was 'particularly Australian'.[76] Though the film's narrative does not take place in Australia and none of the lead characters speak with Australian accents, these critics hold that *Moulin Rouge* reflects the production location of 'Sydney not as a place but a sense of style'.[77]

The arguments defending *Moulin Rouge*'s aesthetic Australian-ness are precarious at best. *Moulin Rouge* is a pastiche that draws from a range of international traditions, including, as Marsha Kinder puts it, 'globalizing postmodernist spin-offs like music video'.[78] Moreover, the notion of a 'particularly Australian' cinematic language presents further problems. There is little aesthetically that links the hallmark films of Australian cinema, such as *Picnic at Hanging Rock* (1975), *Mad Max* (1979), *Breaker Morant* (1980) and Luhrmann's own *Strictly Ballroom* (1993).[79] *Moulin Rouge* could not and did not usher in a new era where the aesthetic borders of Australian national cinema were any better defined than they were before. *Moulin Rouge* blurs the clear boundaries between Australian cinema, Hollywood cinema and globalised media. The film is a transnational production that unites entertainment capitals, international labour and global finance, and depends on the international marketplace to recoup its invest-ment and realise a profit.

However, the message of the Australian media was not simply pro-Australia and anti-America. ABC's *Lateline* broadcast displays a tension between, on the one hand, the valuing of Australian cinema over Hollywood and, on the other hand, the fear of alienating Hollywood and driving away future productions. Sometimes, this tension takes the form of a split between policy-makers in the federal government and state governments. Policy-makers at the federal level are more likely to support the objectives that have traditionally been aligned with national cinema, namely creating movies that are culturally significant and serve as ambassadors for Australian life. State and regional governments, however, tend to be more interested in the eco-nomic growth that high-budget film-making can bring to a region.[80]

The case of *Moulin Rouge* proved to be a turning point for Australian tax policy, Hollywood runaway productions shot in Australia and hybrid Australian-Hollywood-transnational films, such as *Moulin Rouge*. Following the ATO's decision, the Hollywood studios lost their ability to finance movies shot in Australia using division 10B. In late 2001, however, the Australian government – under lobbying pressure from Fox and other companies – passed a new 'refundable film tax offset'.[81] This new programme was designed to be cleaner and simpler, eliminating the middle-men of Australian 'investors' and paying out rebates directly to producers at a rate of 12.5 per cent for qualifying expenditures.[82] In 2007, the Australian government increased the offset to 15 per cent – a response to shifting exchange rates and more governments worldwide com-peting to attract film productions. That same year, the Australian government granted Baz Luhrmann and Fox a 40 per cent offset for their expensive epic, *Australia* (2008).[83] This time, no one questioned the Australian-ness of the film. However, the press did question why Australian tax payers were paying for so much of the budget of Luhrmann's film.[84] A global arms race of tax incentives aimed at film productions was underway. US states would soon offer equally generous incentives to producers and generate even more controversy in the process.

US Production Tax Incentives in the Twenty-first Century

In the twenty-first century, film producers have been able to capitalise on highly advantageous tax policies without leaving the USA. From the period of 2002–10, American states enacted tax incentives for film and television productions at a blistering pace. In 2002, the state of Louisiana enacted the Louisiana Motion Picture Incentive Act, which offered productions that shot in the state a transferrable tax credit ranging from 30 per cent to 40 per cent of approved budget costs.[85] Using a middleman, the producer could then sell the tax credit at a discounted rate to one of the state's companies or wealthy individuals in the oil industry. Louisiana's gen-erous tax credit caused the annual spending on film production to skyrocket in the state – from $3.5 million the year before the credit went to effect to over $674 million by 2010.[86]

Other states that moved early and aggressively to pass film production tax legislation included New Mexico, Michigan and North Carolina – all of which offer expenditure-based rebates and not transferrable credits (like Louisiana). After the film or television production shoots, the state pays out a rebate to producers based on the budget items that qualify for the tax rebate. Although the rebate check generally does not arrive until after the movie wraps, a producer can borrow money from a lender against the expected rebate and use the loan to help fund the film.

In 2012, *Variety* described the prevailing Hollywood attitude about tax incentives: 'The vast majority of industryites seem to agree on one thing: Production incentives are good news both for them and the local communities that host the shoots.'[87] One argument is that incentives are vital for the production of smaller, artistically challenging films in the $1 million–$10 million range – particularly in the contemporary era of studio blockbusters. *Dallas Buyers Club* (2013), for example, was not shot on location in Dallas, Texas. Instead, the producers financed the Oscar-winning drama, set during the AIDS epidemic of the 1980s, by shooting in Louisiana and using the state's tax credit to finance roughly $1 million of its $5.6 million budget. Would this powerful American film have been produced without access to state tax incentives?[88] Potentially, the answer is no.

Film-makers may praise tax incentives for the types of movies they enable them to make, but the lobbyists advocating for state production tax incentives tend to focus their arguments on economics. The Hollywood motion picture industry has used research sponsored by its trade organisation, the MPAA, to argue that film incentives benefit the states that offer them.[89] The growth of taxable revenue in related sectors, along with the establishment of new community infrastructure, allegedly offset the money the state is giving away in the form of tax credits and rebates. Supporters of incentive legislation cite a 'multiplier effect' and increases in employment, tourism and the revenue of local businesses – such as restaurants, hotels and dry cleaners – when productions come to town.[90]

Unfortunately, a larger body of evidence suggests that it is state tax payers who are being taken to the cleaners.[91] Proponents of state tax incentives argue that such policies benefit the state through the creation of new jobs. However, the state of Massachusetts calculated that every job directly created through its film incentive programme in 2009 cost the state $129,130. And, if you only counted Massachusetts residents who obtained new jobs, then the cost to the state was a whopping $324,838 per job.[92] Moreover, the Massachusetts study found that for every $100 spent on its film tax credit programme, the state lost $86. The MPAA has disputed the findings of Massachusetts' critical reports, but studies of the Louisiana and Michigan incentive programmes have similarly found that the cost per direct job is extremely high – $193,333 per job in Michigan in 2009 and over $60,000 per job in Louisiana.[93] Moreover, as the Louisiana Budget Project noted, 'in order to keep many of those jobs in Louisiana, the state must continue to pay year after year'.[94] Additionally, most empirical studies of states with generous and uncapped tax incentives find that the aggregate boost to economic activity – the so-called multiplier effect – cannot compensate for the lost tax dollars, which could otherwise go towards funding education, infrastructure and other state services.

After the financial recession took hold in 2008, numerous state governments realised that they were losing valuable tax dollars on film incentive programmes and they adapted accordingly. The state to which I pay taxes, Wisconsin, was one of several US states to drastically scale back the amount of tax credits and reduce the total payout for any given year.[95]

The state of Iowa discovered fraud in its incentive programme, with producers padding budgets and using state dollars to pay for personal cars and luxury goods. Amid the ensuing scandal, an Iowa judge sentenced one film producer to ten years in prison.[96] For most states, though, the problem was not bad producers; the problem was bad policy. States had offered film productions a way to realise enormous budget savings, and entrepreneurial producers did exactly what one would expect, capitalising on the tax rebates and tax credits to the fullest extent possible.

When states cut back tax incentives, producers also behaved exactly as one would expect – they found other places to make movies. In 2011, Marvel moved shooting on its blockbuster, *The Avengers*, from Michigan to Ohio after Michigan's governor proposed cuts to the state's extraordinarily generous incentive programme.[97] The speed at which Marvel and other producers fled Michigan demonstrates, in the words of attorney Adrian H. McDonald, that 'any hope that film and television production will remain in states with no history in the industry once the production incentives cease is wishful thinking'.[98]

Is there a better tax policy solution? Runaway production remains a significant issue for the Hollywood film industry – particularly as post-production and visual effects contract work migrates from Los Angeles to foreign territories, such as Vancouver, Canada, that offer generous tax benefits. Adrian H. McDonald forcefully and persuasively argues:

> If the United States has a national interest in preventing runaway production to foreign nations, then having all fifty states competing with each other is not only counterproductive, but it is financially devastating to numerous state governments unable to sustain the huge amount of funds needed to pay for production incentives.[99]

The better solution, McDonald suggests, lays in federal policy that focuses on keeping the USA competitive in global film production and harnesses the strengths of its deep and talented production communities in Los Angeles and New York, not trying to invent new production communities and industries in Michigan, Wisconsin, Ohio and other states at a heavy cost to tax payers. However, in light of the US Congress's intense partisanship and inability to perform even the most basic tasks (such as passing a budget and avoiding a government shut-down), the prospect of comprehensive federal tax policy oriented towards film production seems unlikely any time soon.

In the meantime, as Hollywood earns more and more of its box-office revenue each year from markets outside of North America, and as studios pursue co-production arrangements with the world's fastest-growing market, China, it may become increasingly difficult to claim that productions belong in the USA in the first place. Michael Bay reduced his usual directing fee to keep production on *Transformers* (2007) in California.[100] For the fourth installment of the franchise, *Transformers: Age of Extinction* (2014), though, Bay and his team shot significant portions of the film in China. Paramount, in turn, collected millions of dollars in product placement fees to feature a Beijing hotel and Wulong tourist destination in the movie.[101] The questions about national identity that emerged in the Australian *Moulin Rouge* tax debates will become more common for Hollywood and could further complicate the passing of federal US tax incentive policies.

Conclusion

This chapter has surveyed a hundred-year history of the Hollywood film industry's engagement with numerous tax laws, ranging from admissions taxes, to star income taxes, to Australian tax shelters and US state tax incentives. Like doing one's own taxes, the study of Hollywood and tax law can, at times, feel like an exercise in accounting minutiae. Why do these policies matter? Why does this history matter? I will conclude by suggesting three reasons why the historical and contemporary relationships between Hollywood and tax law are important.

First, tax policy has influenced how the American motion picture industry has organised itself. In the mid-1910s, New York's proposed tax on exhibition brought together different wings of the film industry to fight the legislation and demonstrated the value of a coordinated trade organisation. The industry's long-running trade organisation, the MPAA, both historically and today devotes a great deal of energy towards fighting taxes and tariffs that foreign nations levy against Hollywood imports. Additionally, if we look at how above-the-line workers in the film industry organise themselves, tax laws exert a profound influence. Thanks to Charles Laughton's successful appeal, Hollywood actors, directors and other workers can form personal corporations, 'loan out' their services to studios and producers and retain more income after taxes.

Second, tax policy has significantly influenced the production process for Hollywood movies – the when, where, what, who and how of film production. After Laughton's tax victory, more movie stars formed their own corporations, contributing to the post-World War II rise in independent productions. For John Huston, the desire to escape his taxes prompted him to move to Ireland and fundamentally change the types of screen stories he was willing to tell. There are numerous other examples of creative choices being made for tax reasons. In 2009, producer Ingo Volkhammer boasted to the *Los Angeles Times* that he reduced the $25 million budget of an action thriller to a mere $15 million by attaching a German director and changing the story's setting from Texas to Madrid to Berlin and, finally, Montreal.[102]

However, we should not focus our understanding of the production process simply on screen stories, locations, producers, directors and stars. The people that location shooting impacts most are below-the-line film workers – especially the grips, electricians, set decorators and other mid- to lower-level crew members who, unlike the director of photography and other key department heads, are unlikely to be flown and boarded at an out of town location. Instead, the job that they would otherwise fill will go to a worker in whatever city or state has successfully lured the production. Southern California has the world's largest concentration of skilled film and television crews and post-production vendors. This dense talent cluster is essential for the continued success of a highly collaborative creative industry, and it is this population of workers that feels the impact of runaway production especially acutely. We should also acknowledge, however, that there are now crews and production vendors clustered in Vancouver, Detroit and Baton Rouge. Ultimately, the point is not that Los Angeles has some divine right to host film and television productions. The point is that world-class media production requires concentrations of skilled workers, and those workers deserve more respect and stability than is currently afforded. Better tax policies can help stabilise the below-the-line production sector and make Hollywood's production process more efficient and globally competitive.

Third, and perhaps most importantly, the relationship between Hollywood and tax law is important because its influence reaches far beyond Hollywood and impacts society and the economy more broadly. Charles Laughton's personal corporation inspired high-paid professionals in other industries to form their own corporations. Ronald Reagan credited his Hollywood years as the catalyst for his aggressive tax reform philosophy, which he later implemented as US President. American states that pay out tens of millions of dollars in tax credits to individual films can find they have less money left over to fund education, infrastructure and other public services.

On the micro level, tax policy provides incentives for individuals and firms to alter their behaviour, to choose one path over another. On the macro level, tax policy impacts what the government can fund, employment numbers, the size of the national debt and how the tax burden is split among rich, poor and those in the middle. The interplay between the micro and macro – between policy, cultural production and social and economic effects – lies at the core of the ongoing relationship between Hollywood and tax law. Shortly before I completed writing this chapter, in September 2014, California's Governor, Jerry Brown, announced an expansion of the state's film and television production tax credit policy. The new policy offers a tax credit of 20 per cent for qualifying expenditures, an annual programme cap of $330 million (more than triple the previous annual cap of $100 million) and a more predictable system for awarding credits based on job creation, rather than the previous lottery system, which made it impossible for producers to predict if they would receive a credit and sent many packing for Louisiana.[103] LA's production community welcomed the expanded programme, which will most likely have a positive effect on their lives and southern California's film industry. But what will it mean for the rest of the state? As we have seen, it is a tightrope that all tax incentive policies have to walk between, on the one hand, strengthening the production sector and growing the state economy and, on the other hand, not unfairly damaging the rest of the state's tax base and public services. If Governor Brown can pull it off, he deserves an Oscar – along with the thanks of an industry and base of tax payers.

Notes

1. Axel Madsen, *John Huston* (Garden City: Doubleday & Company, 1978), p. 134. Axel Madsen discusses Huston's move to Ireland and acknowledges the tax motivations behind it.
2. John Huston to Paul Kohner, 25 October 1955, John Huston Papers, 1162, AMPAS.
3. Ibid.
4. Alan Cullison and Inti Landauro, 'French Actor Gets Star Treatment – and Job Offer – in Russia', *The Wall Street Journal*, 1 July 2013, A8.
5. Adrian McDonald, 'Down the Rabbit Hole: The Madness of State Film Incentives as "Solution" to Runaway Production', *University of Pennsylvania Journal of Business Law* vol. 14 no. 1 (2011): 141.
6. David Ranii, 'NC Tax Changes Mean New Admission Charges for Arts and Sporting Events', *News & Observer* (North Carolina), 24 November 2013, accessed 9 June 2014, http://www.ncspin.com/nc-tax-changes-mean-new-admission-charges-for-arts-and-sporting-events/
7. For more on early American cinema and moral reformers, see Lee Grieveson, *Policing Cinema: Movies and Censorship in Early-Twentieth-Century America* (Berkeley: University of California Press, 2004).

8. Kia Afra, 'Hollywood's Trade Organizations: How Competition and Collaboration Forged a Vertically-Integrated Oligopoly, 1915–1928', PhD dissertation, Brown University, 2011: 152–5.

9. Ibid.

10. Kia Afra, '"Seventeen Happy Days" in Hollywood: Selig Polyscope's Promotional Campaign for the Movie Special of July 1915', *Film History* vol. 22 no. 2 (2010): 212, 217; *Exhibitors Herald*, 'Film Industry Feels Pinch of War Tax Nov. 1', 27 October 1917, p. 15, accessed 27 July 2014, http://lantern.mediahist.org/catalog/exhibitorsherald05exhi_0855

11. *The Film Daily*, 'Illinois UTO Attacks 20% Admissions Tax Proposal', 23 November 1943, accessed 6 January 2014, http://lantern.mediahist.org/catalog/filmdail84wids_0397; *The Film Daily*, 'Oct. Admish Tax Collections Highest in History', 23 November 1943, accessed 6 January 2014, http://lantern.mediahist.org/catalog/filmdail84wids_0397

12. *Variety*, '2 Billion Gross Reached by Show Biz for 1st Time in '46; Pix Alone Top Mark', 5 March 1947, p. 2.

13. Jack Alicoate (ed.), *The 1955 Film Daily Year Book of Motion Pictures* (New York: Wid's Films and Film Folk, 1955), p. 141.

14. *Variety*, 'Push Repeal of 20% Tax Via Proof of Exhib Losses', 19 November 1952, pp. 4, 21; John D. Morris, 'Mixed 1953 Record Built by Congress', *The New York Times*, 4 August 1953, p. 13.

15. Alicoate, *The 1955 Film Daily Year Book*, p. 145.

16. For more on the history of these international distribution policies, see Ian Jarvie, *Hollywood's Overseas Campaign: The North Atlantic Movie Trade, 1920–1950* (Cambridge and New York: Cambridge University Press, 1992); Kristin Thompson, *Exporting Entertainment: America in the World Film Market, 1907–1934* (London: BFI, 1985); Ruth Vasey, *The World According to Hollywood, 1918–1939* (Madison: University of Wisconsin Press, 1997).

17. Jarvie, *Hollywood's Overseas Campaign*, pp. 213–46.

18. MPAA, 'Theatrical Market Statistics 2012', 2012, accessed 6 January 2014: 5, http://www.mpaa.org/wp-content/uploads/2014/03/2012-Theatrical-Market-Statistics-Report.pdf

19. Michelle Kung, '"Odd Couple" China Meets Hollywood', *The Wall Street Journal*, 17 April 2012, p. 1; Amy Qin, 'The Return of Transformers', *The New York Times*, 15 June 2014, accessed 14 July 2014, http://www.nytimes.com/2014/06/16/arts/international/The-Return-of-Transformers-shanghai-festival.html?_r=0

20. *The Wall Street Journal*, 'China Film Tax Rankles Hollywood', 28 April 2013, B3.

21. Edwin Schallert, 'Isa Miranda, Novarro Probable Co-Stars', *Los Angeles Times*, 3 March 1939, A19.

22. Philip K. Scheuer, 'Studios Facing Tithe That Binds', *Los Angeles Times*, 22 February 1966, 21.

23. Edwin Schallert, 'Movie Will Explore Raid Effect, Cause; Awards' Fete Set', *Los Angeles Times*, 27 January 1952, D10.

24. *Los Angeles Times*, 'Job Dearth Laid to Tax, Freight Rates', 30 April 1950, B1; *The Film Daily*, 'Production Tempo to Jump in March', 26 February 1948, accessed 6 January 2014, p. 5, http://lantern.mediahist.org/catalog/filmdaily93wids_0309

25. *Los Angeles Times*, 'State Senate OKs Property Tax Cut for Movie Makers', 25 April 1968, p. 3.

26. Ibid.

27. *Los Angeles Times*, 'Film Tax Exemption Unwarranted', 24 April 1968, A4.

28. *Los Angeles Times*, 'Reagan Signs Measure Giving Tax Break to Film Industry', 2 August 1968, p. 3.

29. Ronald Reagan with Richard G. Hubler, *Where's the Rest of Me?* (New York: Duell, Sloan and Pearce,

1965), p. 245; Ronald Reagan, *An American Life* (New York: Simon and Schuster, 1990), p. 117. For more on the influence of Reagan's Hollywood career on his tax reforms, see my earlier article: Eric Hoyt, 'Hollywood and the Income Tax, 1929–1955', *Film History* vol. 22 no. 1 (2010): 5–20.

30. W. Elliot Brownlee, *Federal Taxation in America: A Short History*, 2nd edn (New York: Woodrow Wilson Center Press and Cambridge University Press, 2004), p. 53; Richard J. Joseph, *The Origins of the American Income Tax: The Revenue Act of 1894 and Its Aftermath* (Syracuse, NY: Syracuse University Press, 2004).

31. Robert A. Wilson, 'Personal Exemptions and Individual Income Tax Rates, 1913–2002', Internal Revenue Service Data Release (Spring 2002): 219, accessed 20 October 2008, www.irs.gov/pub/irs-soi/02inpetr.pdf

32. *Cumulative Changes in Internal Revenue Codes of 1939 and Tax Regulations Under the Code* (Englewood Cliffs: Prentice-Hall, 1960), Sec. 29.12-2.

33. Internal Revenue Service, 'Tax Guide 2013 for Individuals', 26 November 2013: 262, accessed 14 July 2014, http://www.irs.gov/pub/irs-pdf/p17.pdf

34. Leo Rosten, *Hollywood: The Movie Colony, The Movie Makers* (New York: Harcourt Brace and Co., 1941), p. 92.

35. Agreement between Ronald Colman and 20th Century-Fox, 7 November 1935, private collection.

36. William M. Pinkerton, 'Glamour Girls Regard Mink as Business Necessity', *St Petersburg Times*, 25 February 1939, p. 11.

37. Ibid.

38. Tom Kemper, *Hidden Talent: The Emergence of Hollywood Agents* (Berkeley: University of California Press, 2010), p. 82.

39. In a 24 July 1941 column, *Los Angeles Times* columnist Edwin Schallert wrote that an Audience Research Institute poll of theatre audiences shows 'that movie luminaries who limit their appearances to one or two annually, because of high taxes on their stipends, do serious damage to their marquee value. And quite a few of the stars are following that course today, because of the tax situation.' According to the Audience Research poll, the ideal number of appearances each year was three. The study is hardly convincing as scientific fact, but Schallert's article makes it clear that, by 1941, numerous stars were working less for tax reasons. Edwin Schallert, 'High Salaries Prove Boomerang to Stars', *Los Angeles Times*, 24 July 1941, p. 8.

40. Brownlee, *Federal Taxation in America*, p. 115.

41. Carolyn C. Jones, 'Class Tax to Mass Tax: The Role of Propaganda in the Expansion of the Income Tax during World War II', *Buffalo Law Review* vol. 37 (1989): 718.

42. 'Independent Income', *Time*, 5 November 1945, p. 84.

43. Tino Balio, *United Artists: The Company Built by the Stars* (Madison: University of Wisconsin Press, 1976), p. 190; Thomas Schatz, *Boom and Bust: American Cinema in the 1940s* (Berkeley: University of California Press, 1997), p. 181.

44. Lloyd Norman, 'Treasury Acts to Halt Movie Stars' Racket', *Chicago Daily Tribune*, 27 July 1946, p. 10; Charles L. B. Lowndes, 'Taxing the Income of the Close Corporation', *Law and Contemporary Problems* vol. 18 no. 4 (1953): 578.

45. Lowndes, 'Taxing the Income of the Close Corporation': 572.

46. Ibid.: 572, 578.

47. 'Seven Called Tax Dodgers by Treasury', *Los Angeles Times*, 19 June 1937, p. 1; 'Actors Plan Tax Appeals', *Los Angeles Times*, 24 July 1937, p. 3.

48. *Laughton v. Commissioner of Internal Revenue*, 40 B.T.A. 101 (B.T.A. 1939), rev'd in part, 113 F.2d 103 (1940).

49. 'Actor's Film Production Venture Told in Tax Court', *Los Angeles Times*, 28 June 1938, p. 2.

50. *Laughton v. Commissioner of Internal Revenue*, 40 B.T.A., 107.

51. Ibid., 106.

52. Ibid.

53. *Commissioner of Internal Revenue v. Laughton*, 113 F.2d 103 (9th Cir. 1940).

54. Lowndes, 'Taxing the Income of the Close Corporation': 572.

55. Warner Bros.' 1943 BD, Inc. deal was modelled on the 1942 Thomson deal. Contracts and legal correspondence on the BD, Inc. agreement can be found in the Bette Davis legal folder, 2828, Warner Bros. Archive, School of Cinematic Arts, University of Southern California.

56. Many tax-oriented law review articles cite *Laughton v. Commissioner of Internal Revenue*. For an article that discusses Laughton's case in the context of other personal service corporations, see Stuart M. Lewis and Mary B. Henever, 'Attribution of Income in Personal Service Corporations', *Virginia Tax Review* vol. 1 (Autumn 1981): 327.

57. Thomas H. Guback, 'Hollywood's Foreign Market', in Tino Balio (ed.), *The American Film Industry*, rev. edn (Madison: University of Wisconsin Press, 1985), pp. 477–8.

58. For an excellent overview of the discourse surrounding runaway production, including the distinctions drawn between 'creative runaways' and 'economic runaways', see Camille Yale, 'Runaway Film Production: A Critical History of Hollywood's Outsourcing Discourse', PhD dissertation, University of Illinois at Urbana-Champaign, 2010: 84–133.

59. Edwin Schallert, '30 Actors in Foreign Land Now', *Los Angeles Times*, 15 March 1953, D1.

60. Thomas M. Pryor, 'Tax Exodus Seen Cutting Film Jobs', *The New York Times*, 3 June 1953, p. 39.

61. Bill Baillieu and John Goodchild, *The British Film Business* (Chichester: John Wiley and Sons, 2002), p. 119.

62. Edward Jay Epstein, 'How to Finance a Hollywood Blockbuster: Start with a German Tax Shelter', *Slate*, 25 April 2005, accessed 4 December 2014, http://www.slate.com/id/2117309/

63. Toby Miller, Nitin Govil, John McMurria and Richard Maxwell, *Global Hollywood* (London: BFI, 2001), p. 63.

64. Lisa French, 'Patterns of Production and Policy: The Australian Film Industry in the 1990s', in Ian Craven (ed.), *Australian Cinema in the 1990s* (London: Frank Cass, 2001), p. 20.

65. Michaela Boland and Don Groves, 'Oz Investors Seeing Red After "Rouge" Tax Ruling', *Variety*, 1 August 2001, accessed 9 June 2014, http://variety.com/2001/biz/news/oz-investors-seeing-red-after-rouge-tax-ruling-1117850645

66. Felicity Collins and Therese Davis, *Australian Cinema After Mabo* (Cambridge: Cambridge University Press, 2004), p. 30.

67. Ibid., p. 28.

68. Australian Taxation Office, 'Taxation Ruling TR 2002/13', 26 June 2002: 5–7, accessed 8 June 2014, http://law.ato.gov.au/atolaw/view.htm?docid=TXR/TR200213/NAT/ATO/00001

69. Australian Taxation Office, 'Taxation Ruling No. IT 2629', 21 March 1991: 2, accessed 8 June 2014, http://law.ato.gov.au/atolaw/view.htm?docid=ITR/IT2629/NAT/ATO/00001

70. Fox Studios Australia. 'Refundable Film Tax Offset Scheme 2006 Review of the Income Tax Assessment Act of 1997', 2006, accessed 18 November 2007, http://www.dcita.gov.au/__data/assets/pdf_file/51676/Fox_Studios_Australia.pdf (website no longer live).

71. Don Groves, 'Australia: "Rouge" Investors Aren't Done Yet', *Variety*, 24–30 September 2001, p. 13.

72. Australian Taxation Office, 'Taxation Ruling TR 2002/13': 1.

73. Ibid.: 11.

74. Ibid.: 7.

75. Margot O'Neill, 'ATO Tax Ruling Sends Film Industry into Frenzy', *Lateline*, Australian Broadcasting Corporation, 1 August 2001, online television transcript, accessed 18 November 2014, http://www.abc.net.au/lateline/content/2001/s339353.htm

76. Collins and Davis, *Australian Cinema After Mabo*, p. 30.

77. Ibid., p. 31.

78. Marsha Kinder, Review of *Moulin Rouge*, dir. by Baz Luhrmann, *Film Quarterly* vol. 55 no. 3 (2002): 52–9.

79. For more on this point, see Tom O'Regan, *Australian National Cinema* (London: Routledge, 1996), p. 2.

80. Ben Goldsmith and Tom O'Regan, *The Film Studio: Film Production in the Global Economy* (Lanham: Rowman & Littlefield, 2005), p. 94.

81. Fox Studios Australia, 'Refundable Film Tax Offset Scheme 2006 Review of Division 376 of the Income Tax Assessment Act of 1997'.

82. Australian Government Department of Communications, Information Technology and the Arts, 'Refundable Film Tax Offset Scheme: Report of the 2006 Review of Division 376 of the *Income Tax Assessment Act 1997*', November 2006, accessed 5 December 2014, http://arts.gov.au/sites/default/files/pdfs/Film_Tax_Offset_06.pdf

83. Michaela Boland, 'Australia Changes Incentives', *Variety*, 5 August 2007, accessed 6 December 2014, http://variety.com/2007/film/news/australia-changes-incentives-1117969724/

84. Christine Sams, 'Why You're Footing the Bill for Luhrmann's Australia', *Sydney Morning Herald*, 14 December 2008, accessed 6 December 2014, http://www.smh.com.au/news/entertainment/film/why-youre-footing-the-bill-for-bazs-epic/2008/12/13/1228585174538.html

85. Vicky Mayer and Tanya Goldman, 'Hollywood Handouts: Tax Credits in the Age of Economic Crisis', *Jump Cut* vol. 52 (2010), http://www.ejumpcut.org/archive/jc52.2010/mayerTax/text.html

86. McDonald, 'Down the Rabbit Hole': 105.

87. Todd Longwell, 'The Biz's Taxing Situation', *Variety*, 8 October 2012, pp. 1, 12.

88. Christopher Palmeri, 'Oscar's Indie Film Financiers Take the Spotlight', *Businessweek*, 20 February 2014, accessed 7 March 2014, http://www.businessweek.com/articles/2014-02-20/oscars-indie-film-financiers-take-the-spotlight

89. See, for example, the MPAA-sponsored report by Ernst & Young, *Evaluating the Effectiveness of State Film Tax Credit Programs*, 2012, accessed 13 July 2014, http://www-deadline-com.vimg.net/wp-content/uploads/2012/05/Motion-Picture-assoc.-film-credit-study__120510071748.pdf

90. Longwell, 'The Biz's Taxing Situation': 1, 12.

91. Robert Tannenwald, *State Film Subsidies: Not Much Bang for Too Many Bucks*, Center on Budget & Policy Priorities, 2010, accessed 14 July 2014, http://arev.assembly.ca.gov/sites/arev.assembly.ca.gov/files/hearings/CBPP_Report.pdf ; McDonald, 'Down the Rabbit Hole'.

92. Navjeet K. Bal, 'A Report on the Massachusetts Film Industry Tax Incentives, Commonwealth of Massachusetts Department of Revenue', January 2011: 17, accessed 14 July 2014, http://www.mass.gov/dor/docs/dor/news/reportcalendaryear2009.pdf

93. David Lieberman, 'MPAA Study says that Massachusetts Film Tax Incentives Boosted Spending and Jobs', *Deadline Hollywood*, 23 May 2013, accessed 16 July 2014, http://www.deadline.com/2013/05/mpaa-study-massachusetts-film-tax-incentive-economy/; David Zin, 'Film Incentives in Michigan', Senate Fiscal Agency, September 2010: 1, accessed 15 July 2014, http://www.senate.michigan.gov/sfa/publications/issues/filmincentives/filmincentives.pdf

94. Tim Mathis, *Louisiana Film Tax Credits: Costly Giveaways to Hollywood*, Louisiana Budget Project, 2012: 4, accessed 14 July 2014, http://www.labudget.org/lbp/wp-content/uploads/2012/08/LBP-Report.Louisiana-Film-Tax-Credits.pdf

95. P. J. Huffstutter and Richard Verrier, 'In Strapped States, Film Subsidies Lose Glamour', *Los Angeles Times*, 22 September 2009: A1; Jay Raith, 'Cut! Wisconsin's Moviemaking Tax Incentive Didn't Get a Fair Chance', *Isthmus*, 7 January 2011, pp. 10–11.

96. Joe Barrett, 'Tax-Credit Fraud Puts Filmmaker in Prison', *The Wall Street Journal*, 18 May 2011, A5.

97. Rachel Abrams, 'H'wood wary of Michigan', *Daily Variety*, 22 February 2011, p. 1; Karen Idelson, 'A State of Disregard: Incentive Cuts Leave Workers Holding the Bag', *Daily Variety*, 13 October 2011, p. 11.

98. McDonald, 'Down the Rabbit Hole': 106.

99. Ibid.

100. Ibid: 120. Michael Bay is quoted.

101. Clifford Coonan, 'Another Chinese Company Mulling Lawsuit Over "Transformers 4" Product Placement', *Hollywood Reporter*, 3 July 2014, accessed 16 July 2014, http://www.hollywoodreporter.com/news/chinese-company-mulling-lawsuit-transformers-716529

102. Lauren A. E. Schuker, 'Local Incentives Play Bigger Role in Creative Decisions for Movies', *The Wall Street Journal*, 27 October 2009, B1.

103. Ted Johnson, 'California Governor Signs Expansion of State Film and TV Tax Credit', *Variety*, 18 September 2014, accessed 6 December 2014, http://variety.com/2014/artisans/news/california-governor-signs-expansion-of-state-film-and-tv-tax-credit-1201308384/

References

Afra, Kia, 'Hollywood's Trade Organizations: How Competition and Collaboration Forged a Vertically-Integrated Oligopoly, 1915–1928', PhD dissertation, Brown University, 2011.

Afra, Kia, '"Seventeen Happy Days" in Hollywood: Selig Polyscope's Promotional Campaign for the Movie Special of July 1915', *Film History* vol. 22 no. 2 (2010).

Alicoate, Jack (ed.), *The 1955 Film Daily Year Book of Motion Pictures* (New York: Wid's Films and Film Folk, 1955).

Baillieu, Bill and John Goodchild, *The British Film Business* (Chichester: John Wiley and Sons, 2002).

Balio, Tino, *United Artists: The Company Built by the Stars* (Madison: University of Wisconsin Press, 1976).

Brownlee, W. Elliot, *Federal Taxation in America: A Short History*, 2nd edn (New York: Woodrow Wilson Center Press and Cambridge University Press, 2004).

Collins, Felicity and Therese Davis, *Australian Cinema After Mabo* (Cambridge: Cambridge University Press, 2004).

Cumulative Changes in Internal Revenue Codes of 1939 and Tax Regulations Under the Code (Englewood Cliffs: Prentice-Hall, 1960).

French, Lisa, 'Patterns of Production and Policy: The Australian Film Industry in the 1990s', in Ian Craven (ed.), *Australian Cinema in the 1990s* (London: Frank Cass, 2001), pp. 15–36.

Goldsmith, Ben and Tom O'Regan, *The Film Studio: Film Production in the Global Economy* (Lanham: Rowman & Littlefield, 2005).

Grieveson, Lee, *Policing Cinema: Movies and Censorship in Early-Twentieth-Century America* (Berkeley: University of California Press, 2004).

Guback, Thomas H., 'Hollywood's Foreign Market', in Tino Balio (ed.), *The American Film Industry*, rev. edn (Madison: University of Wisconsin Press, 1985), pp. 463–86.

Hoyt, Eric, 'Hollywood and the Income Tax, 1929–1955', *Film History* vol. 22 no. 1 (2010): 5–20.

Jarvie, Ian, *Hollywood's Overseas Campaign: The North Atlantic Movie Trade, 1920–1950* (Cambridge and New York: Cambridge University Press, 1992).

Jones, Carolyn C., 'Class Tax to Mass Tax: The Role of Propaganda in the Expansion of the Income Tax during World War II', *Buffalo Law Review* vol. 37 (1989): 685–737.

Joseph, Richard J., *The Origins of the American Income Tax: The Revenue Act of 1894 and Its Aftermath* (Syracuse, NY: Syracuse University Press, 2004).

Kemper, Tom, *Hidden Talent: The Emergence of Hollywood Agents* (Berkeley: University of California Press, 2010).

Kinder, Marsha, Review of *Moulin Rouge*, dir. by Baz Luhrmann, *Film Quarterly* vol. 55 no. 3 (2002): 52–9.

Laughton v. Commissioner of Internal Revenue, 40 B.T.A. 101 (B.T.A. 1939), rev'd in part, 113 F.2d 103 (1940).

Lewis, Stuart M. and Mary B. Henever, 'Attribution of Income in Personal Service Corporations', *Virginia Tax Review* vol. 1 (Autumn 1981): 327–74.

Lowndes, Charles L. B., 'Taxing the Income of the Close Corporation', *Law and Contemporary Problems* vol. 18 no. 4 (1953): 558–83.

Madsen, Axel, *John Huston* (Garden City: Doubleday & Company, 1978).

McDonald, Adrian H., 'Down the Rabbit Hole: The Madness of State Film Incentives as "Solution" to Runaway Production', *University of Pennsylvania Journal of Business Law* vol. 14 no. 1 (2011): 101–81.

Miller, Toby, Nitin Govil, John McMurria and Richard Maxwell, *Global Hollywood* (London: BFI, 2001).

O'Regan, Tom, *Australian National Cinema* (London: Routledge, 1996).

Reagan, Ronald, *An American Life* (New York: Simon and Schuster, 1990).

Reagan, Ronald with Richard G. Hubler, *Where's the Rest of Me?* (New York: Duell, Sloan and Pearce, 1965).

Rosten, Leo, *Hollywood: The Movie Colony, The Movie Makers* (New York: Harcourt Brace and Co., 1941).

Schatz, Thomas, *Boom and Bust: American Cinema in the 1940s* (Berkeley: University of California Press, 1997).

Thompson, Kristin, *Exporting Entertainment: America in the World Film Market, 1907–1934* (London: BFI, 1985).

Vasey, Ruth, *The World According to Hollywood, 1918–1939* (Madison: University of Wisconsin Press, 1997).

Yale, Camille, 'Runaway Film Production: A Critical History of Hollywood's Outsourcing Discourse', PhD dissertation, University of Illinois at Urbana-Champaign, 2010.

8 DOING THE DEAL
TALENT CONTRACTS IN HOLLYWOOD

EMILY CARMAN AND PHILIP DRAKE

Since its inception, the Hollywood entertainment industry has employed contracts to regulate a variety of industry practices that engage with and, in some instances, have helped to shape US law. Put most simply, a contract is a legal agreement, either expressed or implied, between two or more parties. In the USA it is governed by contract law, which varies in each state though much legislation is shared. These laws are part of the US common law system that draws on the body of case law produced by judicial court decisions, and this establishes legal precedents in making future rulings. Hollywood contracts have included minimum guarantees with distributors, block-booking agreements with exhibitors, optioning of scripts, standardised union and guild contracts for workers and individually negotiated contracts for major talent. Contracts and the agreements made by and through agents, managers and lawyers reveal detailed information about the industrialisation of creative processes in Hollywood, highlight the balance of power in negotiating deals between parties and present us with important material through which to analyse the historical development of the Hollywood industry.

Commonplace reports about industry deal-making, as regularly announced in industry trade papers *Variety* and *Hollywood Reporter*, reveal how Hollywood depends on such legal frameworks and how the accumulation of past case law has informed and established contemporary industry practices and norms. Nowhere is this more evident than in the development and evolution of Hollywood contracts and the laws that regulate and enforce them. Contracts exist in every aspect of Hollywood production, distribution and exhibition, from the hiring of below-the-line production labour to the deals that govern the division of revenues between cinema and distributor. This chapter will focus on the industry contract that has attracted the most visibility: the high-profile above-the-line talent contract. Most below-the-line contracts are offered on standardised terms, usually negotiated as set contracts through recognised craft guilds and unions. Even above-the-line talent can draw on such standard contracts – for instance, the minimums ('scale') specified by the Directors Guild of America (DGA), the Screen Actors Guild (SAG) and the Writers Guild of America (WGA) (see Chapter 9).[1] However, above-the-line contracts involving high-profile 'talent', actors, directors, producers and writers, which are commonplace in many Hollywood features, are individually negotiated and have, over time, evolved into large, complex legal agreements, negotiated by agents and lawyers who represent their clients' interests.

Although some scholars have studied film industry contracts, there has been relatively little research on how such contracts, and the processes through which they have been negotiated and contested, enact forms of agency.[2] Contracts formalise promises, helping to codify, hierarchise and publicise the market value for talent, establishing their place in the industry through salary compensation and recognition of status via possessory credits, expense accounts and so on. In short, they provide the necessary legal frameworks to allow Hollywood's industrial processes to function. For example, the agreement to use an 'A-list' actor to perform and promote a particular film requires the licensing of rights (i.e., the use of that actor's services, specified assignment of their image rights) that are negotiated by the actor's agent and lawyer with the studio or production company (which has its own legal representation). Such contracts also spell out in great detail the precise terms of their employment duration and compensation. More recently, 'pay or play' contracts have included the requirement for payment whether or not the film is produced. The contracting of the services of high-profile freelance talent has, since the 1930s, often been via a loan-out agreement with their personal service corporation, done for tax efficiency (see Chapter 7 for more on the practice of loan-out companies). In addition, such an agreement specifies various add-ons (such as travel expenses), possessory screen credits, promotional duties and, crucially, extensive annexes with definitions of the key contractual terms (such as 'net profits', 'break-even' and so on).

Our aim in this chapter is to suggest that the analysis of contracts – and their historical evolution – can offer scholars important historical evidence about the functioning of Hollywood's organisational and industrial processes. First, we trace the evolution of the long-term 'option contract' for talent in the vertically integrated Hollywood studio system. As 'personal service contracts', these exclusive agreements were originally part of the California Civil Code Section 1980 – later transferred to the Labor Code Section 2855 as part of the Industrial Labor Relations Act of 1937 – and were widely used by the studios until they were abandoned in the 1950s in favour of individually negotiated freelance deals.[3] However, even during the zenith of the old studio system, motion picture actors began to contest the legality of these binding option contracts – most famously the Warner Bros. stars James Cagney and Bette Davis – especially after the establishment of their box-office power. The most prominent legal challenge came in 1944, when the actress Olivia de Havilland sued Warner Bros. over their attempt to extend her contract by adding on her cumulative suspension time when she had refused film assignments, even though her seven-year contract had expired. The 'De Havilland Law' (as it is referred to in legal parlance, although the actress's name was misspelled by the Court and henceforth the case was published as 'De Haviland') remains the seminal case that interpreted Section 2855. Moreover, the case reveals how California public policy laws shaped the framework of the talent contract in the studio era.[4]

Second, this chapter will analyse the development of complex and intricate contracts developed through the 1950s to present-day Hollywood, including 'gross' and 'net' profit and 'break-even' definitions, extensive possessory credit demands and – in comparison to union and guild minimum contracts – inflated up-front salaries as well as deferred compensation. The *Buchwald v. Paramount* lawsuit of 1990–2 offers a ground-breaking legal case as it demonstrates not only the complexity of recent Hollywood contracts, but also how the creative accounting routinely adopted in Hollywood since the 1970s developed as a studio response to the increased profit participation demands from freelancing stars, leading to a shift by major A-list talent towards gross rather than net profit participation contracts. We conclude the chapter by assessing the current applications of the *De Haviland* and *Buchwald* decisions in recent contract negotiations and legal disputes in Hollywood.[5]

The Talent Contract in Studio-era Hollywood

From the early days of cinema, the studio contract was a pliable document. The standard studio contract could span anywhere from two to seven years, and for many artists in Hollywood, ranging from character actors to top stars, directors and writers, these contracts guaranteed steady employment and ensured regular film production schedules. As Tom Kemper puts it, a studio contract represented 'an achievement all of its own ... as an object of desire and value for artists' in the studio era.[6] During the 1920s, the typical Hollywood studio contract for actors was limited to a five-year term – until August of 1931, when the California State Senate officially approved Section 1980 statute of the Civil Code that extended personal service contracts to seven years, which enabled film studios and producers to hold exclusive, long-term agreements with talent.[7] The law reads as follows: 'A contract to render personal service ... may nevertheless be enforced against the person contracting to render such service, for a term not beyond a period of seven years from the commencement of service.'[8] The only clue that this law pertained to the film industry was in its definition of personal service: 'to perform or render service of a special, unique, unusual, extraordinary, or intellectual character, which gives it peculiar value'.[9] This language is reminiscent of the terminology used in the studio talent contracts that define the performance of an actor as a commodity.[10] Thus, motion picture actors' labour was legally recognised as a 'master/servant continuous employment agreement' to a specific studio, producer, or corporate entity, bound by contract.[11]

Not surprisingly then, the new seven-year option contract perplexed Hollywood's acting community, and these sentiments were voiced in the industry trades – for example, in 'Objections to the 7-Yr. Contract', in *Variety* in 1931:

> New California law allowing seven-year contracts is not looked on favorably by talent, who see it only as an advantage to the producer. It gives the film company a chance to shake the player at option time, but binds the artist for full length of time, according to the players' side. Present five-year contracts are called only that in name because of the semi-yearly options to be taken at the producer's preference. Adding two years to these would only lengthen the agony, these contractees contend.[12]

Here *Variety* illuminated the clashes over the contract between producers and actors at play in the early 1930s, as both the existing and new law favoured the producer over the actor to exercise renewal options. By this time, Hollywood had weathered financial challenges from the conversion to sound film and the economic hardships inflicted by the Depression, and the major studios used the climate of fiscal uncertainty to subvert the empowered and financially lucrative contracts that popular, money-making stars had enjoyed in the 1920s as they reorganised their business practices to be a vertically integrated, big business oligopoly in the 1930s.

Indeed, the studio long-term option contract was an ingenious legal document that reserved the studio's exclusive right to 'option' the services of talent every six months for up to seven years that usually included an increase in salary raise at each renewal. It especially enabled the studios to develop and promote a stable of stars who epitomised the company's signature style as a visual trademark, like Joan Crawford and Clark Gable of MGM, for example. The 'option' worked in the following ways, as Tino Balio explains: 'Every six months the studio reviewed an actor's progress and decided whether or not to pick up the option. If the studio dropped the option, the actor was out of work; if the studio picked up the option, the actor continued on the payroll for another six months.'[13] Thus, talent did not always have the corresponding authority to opt out of their contracts if they so wished. If there was a dispute about roles or salary, these long-term option contracts enabled the studios to suspend talent without pay if they refused film assignments, disputed the terms of their contracts, or desired to become freelance artists. As Jane Gaines writes,

> Suspension effectively stopped the seven-year contract clock, thus adding more time to the actor's required employment for every day he or she was laid off. Actors who wanted to be free to work for other studios on scripts of their own choice felt trapped by the compulsory extension of their contracts.[14]

Understood in this context, movie stardom appeared to be what Balio characterises as a 'dazzling illusion to the degradations of servitude' during the 1930s.[15] What emerged, then, was a paradox between the stars' 'glamorous' images and their material labour as contractually obligated workers in the film industry; although they were extremely well-compensated employees, stars still had to conform to the decrees of studio bosses and the hierarchies of their oligopolistic business practices.

The key legal disputes over the studio long-term option contracts in the 1930s resulted from its suspension policies, mainly at Warner Bros., with actors James Cagney, Bette Davis and Olivia de Havilland being the demonstrative examples. All attempted to get out of their long-term contract agreements with the studio, but for different rationales and legal justifications. Each lawsuit pertained to California Civil Code Section 1980/Labor Code Section 2855, but only de Havilland's resulted in the setting of a new legal precedent. Cagney brought a lawsuit against Warner Bros. in 1936 to cancel his contract due to the studio's failure to deliver on verbal promises that he appear in no more than four films a year. The actor's original legal argument had been that Warner Bros. over-exposed his image by requiring him to appear in more than four pictures. Ultimately, though, it was a violation of the actor's billing clause in his contract that persuaded Judge Charles L. Bogue to rule in Cagney's favour in Los Angeles Superior Court on 3 March 1936 and nullify his contract, effectively declaring him a free agent.[16] While Warner Bros. appealed the decision to the California Supreme Court, no other major studio risked employing Cagney, in case the court reversed the decision. During this period, the actor made only two films for the independent production company Grand National (both of which lost money and were a great personal financial loss to the actor, since he also produced the films). This adverse experience led to Cagney's return to Warner Bros. prior to the California Supreme Court verdict.[17] Nevertheless, his experience attests to how Hollywood actors used the legal system to attain increased leverage over their celebrity and, in this instance, it indirectly led to a better contract and working terms at Warner Bros. When he returned to the studio in 1938, his new contract specified eleven films in four years, with story approval and star billing, as well as the right to make his own radio appearances and personal endorsements of commercial products.[18]

A similar situation occurred in 1936 with Bette Davis, Warner Bros.' most prominent female star, over her film assignments, which she felt were unjustifiable given her recent Best Actress Oscar for *Dangerous* (1935). She rejected Warner Bros.' new contract offer with only a 'vague promise of better roles', after which the studio placed her on suspension.[19] Davis ultimately fled to England to make a film with Toeplitz Productions. Warner Bros. sued her, citing their suspension policy in their contract with the actress, and the studio won the case in the English courts in October 1936. Davis acquiesced to Warner Bros. and returned to Los Angeles to sign a new contract, but it was still bereft of any star billing or story selection guarantees.[20] Nonetheless, Davis's experience echoes Cagney's in that her recalcitrance with the studio paid off – Jack Warner did give Davis better roles in 'A' pictures, one of which, *Jezebel*, was purchased specifically for her and resulted in a second Best Actress Oscar for her in 1938.

Cagney and Davis, along with other Warner Bros. stars, battled the studio through litigation in order to gain some degree of control over their careers rather than simply to defeat the studio or invalidate their long-term contracts.[21] But, as Kemper notes, these legal battles 'also betray poor management, a dimension that is generally elided in most histories on classical Hollywood' and that 'Cagney and Davis were stuck with bad contracts' from an 'equally bad strategy and bad countermoves' by their agents.[22] Indeed, a long-term contract could be empowering to talent and work to their advantage in studio-era Hollywood, especially with the help of a good agent. Savvy talent agents like Myron Selznick, Charles Feldman, Leland Hayward and others were instrumental in bargaining for and the writing of contracts for their star clients in studio negotiations.[23] As their market value grew, it was customary practice for talent to renegotiate long-term contracts with elements of creative control, including director, cast, crew and/or story approvals, as well as protection from overwork, and innovative financial agreements such as percentage shares that awarded them a cut of their films' box-office profits. In some cases, stars went freelance, working independently at an array of studios on specific film projects of their choosing. For instance, Carole Lombard exited Paramount after a seven-year long-term option contract in 1937 to negotiate two impressive freelance deals with Paramount and Selznick International Pictures that not only made her Hollywood's highest-paid star of that year, but also bestowed to her several contractual provisions that included her choice of director, cinematographer, co-star, producer or screenwriter, story discretion, designer of choice and/or make-up, hairstylist and even her publicist and a 'no loan-out' clause.[24] What's more, these agents regularly requested profit participation deals for their top clients. For example, in 1933 and 1934, negotiated by Selznick and Hayward, Katherine Hepburn signed a series of deals with the studio RKO that allocated her between 5 and 12.5 per cent of the gross receipts (depending on the total box-office takings), plus up-front salary. These contracts, while not widespread, were also not unusual for top talent. For example, Feldman arranged for a lucrative deal for client Irene Dunne in 1933 that gave her 15 per cent of her film's gross receipts once it had recouped twice the amount of the film's budget back in distribution; she collected a respectable salary from the third film that she made in this agreement, *Roberta* (1935), with her percentage earnings reaching a grand total of $157,948.50 by November 1941.[25] A 1934 deal between MGM and the Marx Brothers offered 15 per cent of the gross receipts for *A Day at the Races* (1937) and *A Night at the Opera* (1935). Claudette Colbert, loaned out by Paramount and represented by Feldman, received $65,000 plus 2 per cent of the gross receipts for the 1934 Universal film *Imitation of Life*.[26]

However, the widespread practice of freelancing can be also attributed to another case involving the film industry, that of *De Haviland v. Warner Bros.* in 1944, which resulted from the lawsuit Olivia de Havilland brought against Warner Bros., who tried to apply their suspension policy and prevent the actress from becoming a free agent after the expiration of her seven-year long-term contract. The verdict for de Havilland's case litigated Section 2855 of the CA Labor Code and, in doing so, set a landmark legal precedent for the US entertainment industry that legally recognised artists as free agents.[27]

The De Havilland Law

Although the de Havilland lawsuit is continually cited in American film and legal histories as an important achievement for screen actors' rights, the key details and events leading up to her case and how it pertained to the Section 2855 statute, as well as how the case impacted Hollywood talent contracts thereafter, merits more detailed scrutiny. The actress first entered into a long-term contract with Warner Bros. in 1935 after appearing in their film production of Shakespeare's *A Midsummer Night's Dream* (1935).[28] Her weekly salary began at $250, and rose each time the studio exercised the option in her contract, culminating in $2,500 in 1943. Yet her contract did not give the actress any creative discretion over her film roles, and she found herself typecast as the brunette ingénue at the studio, appearing often as Errol Flynn's love interest in films like *The Adventures of Robin Hood* (1938). De Havilland finally received a career-changing role when she convinced Jack Warner to loan her out for the plum role of Melanie Hamilton Wilkes in David O. Selznick's blockbuster *Gone with the Wind* (1939), for which she received an Academy Award nomination for Best Supporting Actress. De Havilland followed up this success with another Oscar-nominated performance, this time as Best Actress, for *Hold Back the Dawn* (1941), when she was loaned out to Paramount. Back at her home studio, the actress felt that she kept receiving lacklustre material, despite her proven talent and market value; as De Havilland herself recalled:

> I finally began to do interesting work like Melanie, but always on loan out to another studio ... So I realised that at Warner Bros. I was never going to have the work that I so much wanted to have. I knew that I had an audience, that people really were interested in my work, and they would go to see a film because I was in it, and I had a responsibility toward them, among other things. I couldn't bear to disappoint them by doing indifferent work on an indifferent film.[29]

The emboldened actress began declining assigned film roles and, by 1943, she had been suspended by Warner Bros. five times.[30] It is interesting to consider the studio perspective in their handling of de Havilland's career. Although Warner Bros. had a reputation for their careful management of top talent, Jack Warner found the actress's claims of unworthy roles 'ridiculous'. Warner elaborated his position in this studio memo from 1943, noting that de Havilland:

> made no complaint about the pictures that she did make, which were successful, so we certainly know what we were doing equally as much in the pictures we wanted her to do that she would not appear in ... If Miss de Havilland wants to compare all pictures with *Gone with the Wind* I will get David Selznick, Daniel O'Shea, and every other top producer to testify that such a comparison would be absurd.[31]

De Havilland playing second fiddle to Errol Flynn in
The Adventures of Robin Hood (1938) (BFI)

From the point of view of Warner Bros., the actress had unrealistic expectations – not every Warner film in which de Havilland appeared could be of the quality and stature of her loan-out films.

Perhaps the financial success of her Warner Bros. films explains why de Havilland entered into negotiations with the studio to renew her agreement with the studio but this time on a non-exclusive basis. The actress asked for a three-picture deal at a salary of $75,000 per film, with the following rationale, as outlined by producer Steve Trilling:

> She originally preferred to be free at the end of her present contract, but realizes Warner Bros. have been very good for her and probably in some respects it would be best to be tied up with us. But she wants to reserve the right to do at least one outside picture each year, so that when a *Hold Back the Dawn* … role does come along she would be in a position to accept.[32]

Trilling concluded the memo by asking his boss whether he had any interest in pursuing this offer, which Jack Warner rejected, even though he had sanctioned similar deals with freelance talent at the studio.[33] Instead, he elected to extend de Havilland's long-term contract by adding up the cumulative sum of her suspension time to extend her original seven-year contract (approximately nine months).

In response, de Havilland's agents, Phil Berg and Bert Allenberg, had a plan of legal action. They advised the actress to seek a judgment declaring that her prior contract was unenforceable after seven years because it was a violation of the California Labor Code 2855. De Havilland proceeded with the lawsuit and, as expected, Warner Bros. countered that the actress had 'effectively waived the protection of section 2855 by her breaches of the contract', which were due to personal choice, and 'was thus stopped from disputing the validity of the contract extensions'.[34] The actress expected to lose in the Superior Court and planned on appealing for a win in the Appellate Court, but, to her surprise, the Superior Court ruled in her favour, thereby guaranteeing the rights of the employee over the corporation. Warner Bros. immediately appealed to the Appellate Court, which upheld the prior ruling and sided with the actress. Arbitrating Judge Charles S. Burnell ruled that:

> Seven years of time is fixed as the maximum time for which they may contract for their services without the right to change employers. … [T]hereafter they may make a change if they deem it necessary. … As one grows more experienced and skilful there should be a reasonable opportunity to move upward and employ his abilities to the best advantage and for the highest obtainable compensation.[35]

The court's ruling underscored an artist's right to the highest salary possible contingent upon their market value, which in de Havilland's case equated to becoming a freelance artist. At the same time, this ruling did not eradicate the seven-year option contract norm; in fact, the court reaffirmed the legality of it in their interpretation of Section 2855 as a strong public policy that could not be extended beyond the calendar time of seven years because doing so would 'nullify any practical effect of the statute'.[36] Hence, the *De Havilland v. Warner Bros.* verdict upheld the right for Hollywood talent to be free agents and provided a legal path for freelancing in the film industry, but *only after* they had completed the full term of any prior contractual obligations to a maximum of seven years. This was the major legal obstacle that derailed the case brought against Warner Bros. by Bette Davis in 1936; she had signed an exclusive long-term option contract that prevented her ability to work elsewhere.

After the conclusion of her court battles, Olivia de Havilland received multiple freelance offers from other major studios, despite Jack Warner's attempt to bar other major studios and producers from hiring her.[37] The first of these was Paramount's *To Each His Own* (1946), which brought not only critical praise, but also de Havilland's first Best Actress Oscar. The De Havilland Law was part of several larger film industry shifts that occurred in postwar Hollywood that helped to furnish the free agency that largely remains in place for A-list screen talent today. Factors included: the slow-down of film production after the Paramount Decree, which forced the studios to divest themselves of their exhibition chains (for more on the legal impacts of this decision, see Chapter 4), as well as the emergent rival medium of television, which began to chip away at Hollywood's audience – both of which resulted in less predictable demand for product and a decline in film production. Moreover,

it was no longer economically feasible to retain high-priced studio talent on long-term contracts with the downturn in production, as the studios needed to cut their overheads. Thus, it was both cheaper and lower risk for the studios to hire film talent on freelance contracts. Nonetheless, the De Havilland Law continues to be invoked in contractual legal disputes over Section 2855 in entertainment industries, such as the popular music business, as Jonathan Blaufarb has shown in an analysis of the lawsuit that singer Melissa Manchester brought against Arista Records in 1981.[38]

De Havilland as a freelance star in her Oscar-winning role as Jody Norris in *To Each His Own* (1946) (BFI)

Post-Studio System Deal-making and Evolution of the Gross and Net Participation Contract

Freelancing would increasingly become standard practice for A-list Hollywood talent, especially in the postwar years after the 1948 Paramount Decree verdict declared that the vertically integrated practices of the film industry were anti-competitive (see Chapter 4).
Continuing the negotiating tactics established by Selznick, Feldman and Hayward, the agents
Lew Wasserman, Ray Stark, Phil Gersh and Irving 'Swifty' Lazar were instrumental in innovat-
ing contracts for their clients and pushing for deferred compensation via complex profit-sharing deals. By 20 January 1953, industry changes in talent contracts were such that the front
page of The Hollywood Reporter could announce: 'Long-term Deals on the Way Out'. The
accompanying article detailed how only a handful of stars remained under contract with the
studios, citing reasons such as poor box-office returns, studio down-sizing and a preference
by studios for open market bidding for talent. By the end of the 1950s the majority of
Hollywood talent were on non-exclusive freelance contracts, usually contracted on a film-
by-film basis. The change is striking. In 1944 there were 804 actors under contract with the
major studios, by 1961 it had declined to just 164 and it continued to fall throughout the
1960s.[39] As we have established, such structural changes in the industry only increased the
importance of agents in the packaging of talent and the reliance on talent as guarantors of
finance and underwriters of risk. The new freedom for the most powerful star talent allowed
them to negotiate contractual terms in their favour, especially through the development of
more complex participation contracts, where talent was paid a percentage of contractually
defined box-office proceeds, often movable at various points, after contractually agreed
deductions.

Perhaps the most famous net participation contract was MCA agent Lew Wasserman's
deal with Universal for James Stewart's services on Winchester '73 (1950) and Harvey (1950).
Stewart was paid $200,000 for his work on Harvey but on Winchester '73 he substituted his
usual fixed compensation for 50 per cent of the film's net profits, payable only when receipts
in excess of twice the negative costs (i.e., the production cost of the film) had been recouped
and then calculated after various deductions had been made (distribution fees, expenses,
studio overheads).[40] However, the most notable element of this deal was that Stewart effectively became a financial backer of the film, forgoing his up-front salary and instead taking on
a significant risk in anticipation of a larger reward if the film was successful, thus reducing the
overall risk to Universal. If the film failed, he would have received no salary, but box-office success promised a lucrative return. The film grossed approximately $2.25 million, paying Stewart
a reported $600,000 (50 per cent of the net profits, calculated out of the distributor's share
of box-office receipts after deductions).[41] However, it was not a template for the contemporary 'net profits' deals that followed, which, as a rule, do not forgo all up-front compensation,
as this did, and are rarely on such generous terms. Although called a 'net profit' contract, as
Mark Weinstein notes it was really an unusual 'adjusted gross' contract as Stewart was paid a
large percentage of the gross-after-deductions by deferring all his salary.[42] However, the contract was striking in pointing out how a major established star such as Stewart was willing to
underwrite the risk of a film through his deferment of salary, by instead accepting contingent
compensation.

Concepts such as 'gross receipts' and 'net profits' were routinely defined in the annexes of postwar talent deals and, with the ending of long-term contracts, top talent saw themselves as partners rather than employees of the studios, aware of their power in raising finance and promoting the film. Again, it was talent agents who paved the way for the package-unit system in which they and managers became as fundamental to film production as financiers and producers. Wasserman was even prescient enough to recognise the importance of television and residuals for his clients, adding clauses negotiating future television rights, such as Alfred Hitchcock's lucrative franchise contract for the 1950s television series *Alfred Hitchcock Presents*.[43] Wasserman also acted as financial advisor to his clients, developing complex subcontracting and tax-sheltering companies that helped them avoid paying hefty personal income tax. The star independent production trend became more pronounced in the 1950s, with examples such as Kirk Douglas's Bryna Productions, Burt Lancaster and his agent Harold Hecht's Hecht–Lancaster, John Wayne's Wayne–Fellows Productions and The Filmmakers, founded by actress, turned director, producer and writer Ida Lupino, with her husband producer Collier Young and writer Malvin Wald.[44]

Wasserman also persuaded the SAG, via its president (and MCA client) Ronald Reagan, to grant MCA a secret ten-year waiver to both represent talent and make television productions, concealing a major conflict of interest. This gave MCA a substantial advantage over the studios as it could package talent and control contracts. In the 1950s MCA became the leading supplier of prime-time programming to television and was able to package talent and dictate the terms of their contracts to the television networks. This lasted until the 1960s, when MCA bought Universal Pictures and had to relinquish its talent agency. Established through his talent agency as a leading industry powerbroker, Wasserman was highly influential for many years at Universal, being instrumental in installing Jack Valenti at the MPAA and remaining a close friend of US President Ronald Reagan at the White House.[45]

During the 1960s and 70s, building on the negotiating success of Wasserman and others, talent and their agents began to demand both up-front fixed compensation and 'back-end' compensation in the form of profit participation. The weakened studios, and the rise of independent producers, meant that stars often took on producing roles and increasingly worked outside the major studios. Less powerful talent (often writers and producers) were more likely to be rewarded with net participation, which represents a percentage of profits after deductions of costs (including gross participation). Through the 1980s and 90s, higher gross percentage participation for A-list stars became more common, as did the packaging of talent by agencies such as the powerful Creative Artists Agency (CAA), under Michael Ovitz, a former William Morris agent who co-founded CAA in 1975. The clout of CAA during the 1980s and 90s was extraordinary, as they represented major Hollywood talent including actors Tom Cruise, Sylvester Stallone, Kevin Costner, Barbra Streisand and directors including Steven Spielberg and Barry Levinson. However, even for the exclusive A-list, very few of these contracts were true 'first dollar gross' contracts, but were subject to negotiated and agreed 'off the top' deductions of costs by the studio (thus being a form of adjusted gross contract, often expressed as 'gross after recoupment' contracts). Early $10 million plus adjusted gross compensation contracts were struck at the end of the 1980s by Sylvester

Stallone and Arnold Schwarzenegger. The increase in gross participation by the most bankable talent (including Eddie Murphy and Tom Cruise in the 1980s, and Demi Moore, Julia Roberts, Tom Hanks and Jim Carrey in the 1990s) had the effect of further diminishing the likelihood of net profits, and hence receiving any deferred payment through participation in the 'net' for less powerful players. This delineation of power was not limited to actors. Less glamorous, but at times even more well-remunerated, were producers of franchises such as Jon Peters and Peter Guber (from the *Batman* franchise) and top producer-directors such as George Lucas, Steven Spielberg and, in the 2000s, Peter Jackson.[46] The importance of negotiating gross participation in a successful franchise was infamously illustrated by the venerable actor Alec Guinness, who, in the 1970s, chose to defer some of his salary for the initial three *Star Wars* films and instead negotiated to receive 2 per cent of the gross participation that was due to producer, George Lucas. By doing so, he earned more than all his other roles combined: by 2009, a reported £56 million, or approximately $84 million.[47] For *Mission Impossible*, in 1996, Tom Cruise was widely reported as receiving a fixed payment of $20 million plus profit participation of 25 per cent of the gross receipts. According to Edward J. Epstein, for the 2003 film *Terminator 3: Rise of the Machines*, Arnold Schwarzenegger was paid $29.25 million up-front for his role, plus $1.5 million of perks (including use of a private jet) and, once a defined break-even point was reached, 20 per cent of the gross receipts from all worldwide sources including (very unusually) not only theatrical, but also video, DVD, television and licensing revenues.[48]

   Such contracts are, of course, exceptional, and enabled the most powerful talent to become major financial investors in a film or franchise. Successful films that spawn franchises uniquely allow star talent to exploit the monopoly power they hold over their images and performances – they (and the studios) also recognise that successful franchises often spawn lower-risk sequels. The centrality of Schwarzenegger's image to the first two *Terminator* films was such that he could leverage this monopoly power in his remarkable deal for the third film. However, whether this reflects the true bankability of unique talent is less certain, as Arthur De Vany has noted.[49] The reboot of the *Terminator* franchise in 2009, *Terminator Salvation*, with Christian Bale taking the role of John Connor, grossed $371 million worldwide at the box office, a lesser though not dissimilar amount to *Terminator 3*'s $430 million (albeit significantly less after adjusting for inflation).[50] Other than a fleeting appearance in virtual form, Schwarzenegger is absent from the reboot. *Terminator Salvation*, while critically unsuccessful, performed decently at the box office without its previous lead, drawing instead on the box-office lure of Bale, a major star following his lead role in the reboot of the *Batman* film series. Both the *Terminator* and *Batman* franchises demonstrate that the monopoly nature of star power is rarely absolute, and that major star talent for certain films can often be replaced. Franchise reboots, such as the *Amazing Spider-Man* series (2012–), have deployed new talent to potentially successfully reduce the costs associated with above-the-line talent and profit participation, as well as renew a familiar narrative through the casting of new stars. It is also notable that the hierarchies of star talent established by contracts are also gendered, with fewer female stars in recent years negotiating such lucrative contracts – especially in terms of fixed compensation – as their A-list male counterparts, and far fewer women commanding star roles over the age of forty-five.[51]

A consequence of the rise in freelancing talent, and the ongoing evolution of contemporary talent contract forms, has been to gradually shift much of the core emphasis of the Hollywood studios towards the more lucrative and less risky activity of distribution. Deal structures favour the distributor over the producer or net profit participant, as studio distribution charges and overheads are deducted before participation for all but very top 'first dollar' talent. Indeed, gross participation by talent can have the effect of actually *increasing* studio profits, as the costs of gross participation are charged to the film, and the studios are able to add charges and overheads on this charge. With a distribution fee often as high as 30–40 per cent, depending on territory, plus an additional distribution charge, and the deduction of production costs and gross participation, the likelihood of net profits on most studio movies becomes increasingly small. Instead, film costs are inflated, especially by very top A-list talent who, as we have seen, can cost $10–25 million, plus 10–20 per cent 'off the top' gross profit participation, and by large distribution charges, fees and studio overheads that do not reflect actual costs of distribution.[52] As a way of controlling these costs, studios increasingly use a 'cash-break' contract where levels of percentage participation are only triggered when a film moves into positive 'cash-break-even' territory, reducing the potential risk attached to star compensation (similar to the James Stewart deal outlined earlier). Sometimes termed 'creative accounting' or even simply 'Hollywood accounting', this process offers a key explanation for many of the clauses in contemporary Hollywood contracts. Furthermore, the method of allocating video revenues into the participation pot, and, more recently, revenues from online distribution, have been further key points of negotiation by talent. Although rarely on as generous terms as the gross participation deals for theatrical revenues, significant 'back-end' royalties on these revenues can be negotiated by the most powerful talent. In addition, all actors and directors are paid residuals (required by the SAG/American Federation of Television and Radio Artists and the DGA) when a film is released on video or broadcast on television.

Contemporary Hollywood Contracts: Revisiting *Buchwald v. Paramount* (1990)

By the 1980s, as we have outlined, the freelance contracting of talent was well established and agencies such as CAA negotiated lucrative deals on behalf of their star clients. Yet, in January 1984, just thirty years after *The Hollywood Reporter* announced the end of long-term studio deals, the *Los Angeles Herald Examiner* proclaimed that 'Studio–Star Marriages Make a Comeback'.[53] The story went on to detail how three comedy stars – Richard Pryor, Eddie Murphy and Michael Keaton – had signed to long-term contracts with studios that included large up-front fees, plus gross participation: Columbia's multiple film deal with Pryor was reported as being worth $40 million over five years; Paramount offered Murphy, having starred in just two pictures (albeit the hugely successful *48 Hrs* [1982] and *Trading Places* [1983]) the sum of $15 million, plus approximately 15 per cent of the gross, for his next five films (later revised upwards to $8 million per picture); and 20th Century-Fox offered Keaton a deal guaranteeing he could make four from five films with the studio and also direct one.[54] By 26 August 1987 *Variety* reported that, following the success of *Beverley Hills Cop 2*, Murphy's contract with Paramount had again been renegotiated to offer him even greater payment – approximately $15 million per film – in a new open-ended five-picture deal extending into the 1990s.[55] In the article Murphy was quoted as saying:

When you make a deal to … do like five pictures, and the (first) movie did so well, we went back and said, 'Hey, let's renegotiate' … 'This is a business where you renegotiate deals. Do I believe in living up to contracts? Yes. Do I believe in being underpaid for something I do? No.'[56]

In the same article, Paramount President Sidney Ganis proclaimed Murphy the 'bona fide number-one box-office star in all the world' based on the box-office grosses of his Paramount features – totalling more than $632 million domestically to that date, and almost equally lucrative overseas.[57] Following this contract, Murphy's next proposed film was called 'Quest', which was retitled – eventually becoming the hugely profitable 1988 Paramount comedy, *Coming to America*.

Coming to America reunited *Trading Places* director John Landis with Murphy, and went on to gross $288 million worldwide on its initial release.[58] However, it also gave rise to a landmark lawsuit that opened up Hollywood contracts and questioned the routine accounting processes upon which these contracts are based. As we will outline, the high-profile lawsuit *Buchwald v. Paramount* was revealing as it caused major ripples through Hollywood, as Paramount had to disclose both how deals were struck (in particular, nuances of the net profits contract) and to justify how such a film could have made no net profit despite being one of the top box-office hits of the year.

In considering this lawsuit, the details of what underpinned the case need to be briefly outlined.[59] In early 1982, Art Buchwald, a famous American writer and humourist, wrote an eight-page screen treatment for a film, titled 'It's a Crude, Crude World', later renamed 'King for a Day', based on an incident he had witnessed on the state visit of the Shah of Iran to America.[60] The story focused on the visit to the USA of an extremely wealthy, handsome and spoiled young African king. In Buchwald's treatment, the king is taken on a grand tour of

Eddie Murphy, star of, and gross profit participant in, *Coming to America* (1988). Produced by Paramount Pictures and Eddie Murphy Productions; distributed by Paramount Pictures; directed by John Landis

the USA and arrives at the White House, where a remark made by the President infuriates him. While in the USA, he is deposed, deserted by his entourage and left destitute. He ends up in a Washington ghetto, stripped of his clothes and befriended by a woman. He obtains employment as a waiter and, in order to avoid extradition, marries the woman who befriended him and lives happily ever after.[61] Buchwald's friend, a producer named Alain Bernheim (who later also became a plaintiff in the case) registered the treatment with the WGA. Bernheim suggested to Buchwald he reduced the treatment from eight to two to three pages, with the view to a friend – Louis Malle – directing the film.[62] Later that year, Bernheim met Jeffrey Katzenberg, then Head of Production at Paramount, to pitch the story for Eddie Murphy to star, who was under contract with them for the five-film deal mentioned above.[63] By February 1983, Paramount and Bernheim set up a legal agreement for the latter to produce the film – should it be green-lit – that entitled him to payment and, in March that year, Buchwald sold the rights to the story and concept to Paramount.[64] Paramount then engaged another writer, Tab Murphy, to write a script, and budgeted the film at $12 million, with John Landis to direct.[65] A script was delivered in September 1983 but reportedly not well received by the studio. Paramount extended their option on the treatment, while seeking another writer to deliver a further script by October 1984, eventually bringing the development costs to in excess of $418,000.[66] However, by early 1985, progress on the film began to stall. A new writing team had been engaged but then aborted and, in March 1985, Bernheim was informed by Paramount that the project had been abandoned and was in turnaround.[67] After Paramount's option on the treatment lapsed, Buchwald and Bernheim set about selling the idea to Warner Bros. and, in May 1986, optioned the treatment to them.[68]

However, in August 1985 a new idea was developed by Paramount titled 'Ambassador At Large' and, by 1987, this had developed into a film idea, the aforementioned 'The Quest', based on a story by Eddie Murphy and written by two more writers. In November 1987, Buchwald learned that Paramount were planning to shoot a movie with a very similar premise to his treatment, in which Eddie Murphy was to play an African prince who comes to America to find a wife. Paramount insisted that the film was unrelated to Buchwald's original idea; however, despite this Warner Bros. abandoned Buchwald's project once they learned of a film with a similar premise.[69] Outraged by Paramount's denial, Buchwald and Bernheim decided to sue the studio for 19 per cent of the net profits of Coming to America, as would have been their contractual entitlement had their film been made. In the contracts originally agreed, Buchwald was due 1.5 per cent of net profits, plus $65,000 payment, while as producer Bernheim was due 17.5 per cent of net profits, plus $200,000 payment.[70]

The lawsuit was extensive and took over two years. Although the case revolved around a two and a half-page treatment, it produced over 10,000 pages of sworn testimony, 200 pleadings, and – to their discomfort – Paramount was forced to make over a million pages of documents available to the court.[71] From a dispute over a two-page treatment, an estimated $12 million was spent fighting the lawsuit, producing appellate court records running to 37,000 pages.[72] The courts examined at length the legality of the studio's contract with Buchwald and Bernheim, and engaged in a detailed discussion about the definition and calculation of the net profits contract.[73]

The initial stages of the lawsuit resulted in significant wins for Buchwald and Bernheim, rocking the industry. The first stage of the action was to determine if, indeed, the concept for *Coming to America* was based upon a 'material element' within or 'inspired by' Buchwald's treatment. This 'material element' test was received to consider if there was a *prima facie* case to answer – clearly the issue of compensation would have been irrelevant unless it could be proven to have been based on Buchwald's idea. This raised a number of important questions. Despite similarities, the film also had key differences from the treatment. However, case law had established that the 'test for similarity' was lowered if the court could establish that there been access to the treatment, which they duly did. The court also noted that both scripts included key 'gimmicks', such as Eddie Murphy playing multiple characters and the use of a mop to foil a robbery. The Court, however, was clear that this was not a case about Eddie Murphy's own integrity, stating that:

> At the outset the Court desires to indicate what this case is and is not about. It is not about whether Art Buchwald or Eddie Murphy is more creative. It is clear to the Court that each of these men is a creative genius in his own field and each is an uniquely American institution. This case is also not about whether Eddie Murphy made substantial contributions to the film 'Coming to America.' The Court is convinced he did. Finally, this case is not about whether Eddie Murphy 'stole' Art Buchwald's concept 'King for a Day.' Rather, this case is primarily a breach of contract case between Buchwald and Paramount (not Murphy) which must be decided by reference to the agreement between the parties and the rules of contract construction, as well as the principals of law enunciated in the applicable legal authorities.[74]

The court duly established there was, indeed, a 'substantial similarity' between Buchwald's treatment and the final film. After careful consideration of meetings, deal memos and story comparisons, Judge Harvey A. Schneider opined, in Phase 1 of the lawsuit, that the film was based on Buchwald's treatment.[75] He also noted that the eventual director, John Landis, had been sent the treatment and considered as a director for the project. And, despite the court making clear that the case was not about Murphy stealing the idea, his proven access to Buchwald's treatment was used as additional evidence in favour of Buchwald to show that the similarities were not a coincidence. Yet, despite holding that *Coming to America* had been 'based upon' Buchwald's treatment, the court refused to extend this to consider the law of torts – damages that might stem from fraud or acting in bad faith.[76]

The result of Phase 1 of the lawsuit was that it established Buchwald and Bernheim were, indeed, net profit participants in the film, as per their contracts with Paramount. Phase 2 set about determining whether the contracts and business dealings were fair. Paramount's argument was that, as both plaintiffs held net profit participation contracts, they were due no more than their fixed compensation, as they claimed the film had made a net loss of $18 million.[77] Challenged on this, the argument of Paramount's counsel centred on the claim that while talent with power make deals that guarantee them fees and percentages of gross profits, net profits were deals made by the relatively powerless.[78] Murphy, who earned over $20 million from the film, even referred in his deposition testimony to net profit participation points as 'monkey points', so worthless were they usually to their recipients.[79] However, the court examined the net profit deductions, and Buchwald and Bernheim's lawyers contested the studio's justifications and accounting for the costs and revenues of the film. The court revealed that Paramount had charged interest on the film's negative costs, its distribution fee and its fee. It also deducted 15 per cent of the gross for overhead on Eddie Murphy's operational allowance, and a further 15 per cent of this amount on top of the first charge.[80] The court thereby argued that this was, in effect, a double charge, an 'overhead on overhead', that had no correspondence to any actual incurred costs. In response, Paramount attempted to mount a 'risky business' defence, arguing that the Hollywood business relied on winners to compensate for more numerous losses.[81] However, when challenged by an unimpressed Judge Schneider to allow an independent auditor to examine the Paramount accounting books, the studio panicked and withdrew this defence to ensure that finances of all their films were not placed in public view.

In his tentative decision, Judge Schneider called the contracts held by Buchwald and Bernheim 'overly harsh' and 'one sided', forcing the plaintiffs to be 'a party in a vastly inferior bargaining position'.[82] He ruled that the net profits contract was 'unconscionable' on seven provisions and that *Coming to America* did, indeed, evolve from the two-page synopsis presented to Paramount by Buchwald and Bernheim, that Paramount's accounting formula – an industry-wide practice that limited the likelihood of any film ever reaching net profitability – was unconscionable and that the parties had been subject to an unfair 'contract of adhesion'.[83] Phase 3 of the lawsuit then moved to calculate the appropriate compensation for Buchwald and Bernheim. Judge Schneider concluded that the Buchwald–Bernheim synopsis was worth $900,000 ($150,000 to Buchwald and $750,000 to Bernheim), adding in provision for profit participation based on figures arrived at after removing a number of studio deductions from net profits, and thus discounting the studio's claims that the film had made a loss.[84] The case dragged on for two years, with escalating legal costs. Fearing that all their books would be reopened for similar cases, Paramount filed an appeal, but eventually settled with Buchwald and Bernheim for $900,000 just before the appellate court issued an opinion, an attempt (according to industry commentators) to avoid the setting of a legal precedent for future litigation by similarly aggrieved plaintiffs.[85]

The *Buchwald v. Paramount* lawsuit caused ripples across Hollywood as the major studios had never been fully challenged on their accounting deductions in court, and studio executives feared the legal judgment would lead to a rush of lawsuits on similar grounds. It was historically important, then, for a number of key reasons. First, Paramount had to disclose details of the contracts to prove how a film that had grossed over $288 million worldwide had made a net loss, requiring no payment to net profit participants, and they failed to convince the court of this. Second, Paramount were forced to abandon their 'risky business' assertion that movie production was high risk and that wins are needed to offset the studio losses, for fear that audits would further expose the creative accounting and contracting methods revealed in the court-room. The *Buchwald v. Paramount* lawsuit, therefore, usefully scrutinised the contracts and profit definitions that typify contemporary film industry deals, which are subject to the 'creative accounting' practices routinely adopted by Hollywood studios.

So did *Buchwald v. Paramount* change industry contracts? Despite the claims that the case would overturn the way the studios calculate net profits, this is unproven. Further cases, such as *Batfilm Productions, Inc. v. Warner Bros.* (1994) did not reinforce the 'unconscionable contract' judgment made in this case.[86] The relatively low level of payment made to the plaintiffs, when their legal fees ran to over $2.5 million (luckily for the pair, borne by the law firm, who took the case on a contingent fee basis) did not offer emphatic encouragement for future attempts. Nonetheless, it did highlight the unequal nature of contracts in the industry, as well as a greater recognition by talent and their agents of the need to carefully negotiate definitions of net profits. Further cases demonstrate the relative power of Hollywood talent. For instance, another surprising example of a recorded net loss, also leading to a lawsuit, concerned the film *Forrest Gump* (1994). Despite earning $678 million at the box office and $382 million domestically, the studio reported a net 'loss' of $62 million and no net profits for writer Winston Groom, who was contracted for a fixed fee plus 3 per cent of net profits. The film declared this substantial loss despite returning revenues to the studio through distribution ($128.3 million) and finance ($21.3 million).[87]

The *Buchwald v. Paramount* lawsuit is a landmark case, therefore, in that it publicly revealed the disproportionate balancing of profit participation definitions for talent in favour of the studio and the lucky few gross participants. Yet, despite the court declaring that such net profits contracts were unconscionable, such contracts continue to be common currency in Hollywood and the case ultimately failed to transform studio accounting practices, which have grown even more sophisticated. However, the case did reveal the industry machinery of lawyers, accountants and complex contractual clauses that structure contemporary Hollywood deals. Contractual disputes such as those in *Buchwald v. Paramount* can, therefore, be seen as representing a power struggle between talent and the Hollywood studios, articulated through their agents and lawyers.

Hollywood Contracts into the Twenty-first Century

For conglomerate Hollywood today, use of the seven-year option contract is more commonplace in television, where shows have the potential for long-running seasons and years of stable production, than in major feature production, where the freelance deal has supplanted the long-term studio contract. One of the most recent legal uses of the De Havilland Law was by the *Modern Family* sitcom stars – Julie Bowen, Ty Burrell, Jesse Tyler Ferguson, Ed O'Neil, Eric Stonestreet and Sofia Vergara – in July 2012, when table readings for the upcoming fourth season were due to begin.[88] The lead actors brought a lawsuit in LA Superior Court against 20th Century-Fox TV as contract renegotiations for higher salaries with the company came to a stalemate. What is interesting, however, is their reason for bringing a case against their employers: their original contracts, signed with Fox TV, 'violate California's seven-year limit on personal service contracts'. *Variety* made the analogy to de Havilland on 24 July 2012, remarking that this legal precedent 'was established in 1944 after actress Olivia de Havilland waged a long contract fight against Warner Bros.'.[89] The trade journal went on to highlight the precise difference between de Havilland's long-term studio contract and the *Modern Family* stars' TV sitcom deal. 'In common industry practice, actors starting out on a series sign deals that run for *seven television seasons*. Depending on the time an actor is signed up for the pilot, the term often runs *longer than seven years*.'[90] Like Warner Bros.' attempt to tack on the accumulated suspension time on the end of de Havilland's contract in 1943, the TV talent contract based on show seasons as opposed to actual calendar time is a violation of Section 2855, and the lead actors of *Modern Family* argued this point – Vergara had originally signed up with ABC in 2007 to a holding deal before she was assigned to *Modern Family* in October 2008, while Bowen, Burrell, Ferguson and Stonestreet all asserted that their contracts should end in February 2016, as opposed to June 2016.[91]

Ultimately, the case never went to court, as three days later, on 27 July, the actors reached a deal with 20th Century-Fox TV. Cynthia Littleton, for *Variety*, noted that 'the family drama is over', and explained that, although 'details of the deal' were 'sketchy', it was understood that the actors agreed to an additional season, higher salaries and won a key provision – a syndication deal.[92] Although the actors only achieved a quarter point share, the article underscored its significance in the long run, given that the show is expected to 'gross hundreds of millions in syndication': 'Achieving a profit participation stake, however small, had been an important point to the thesps.'[93] She elaborated on this point, stating that the actors had been wrangling with the studio for over a year about getting a cut of *Modern Family*'s syndication earnings. This was the crucial bargaining point for the actors rather than the actual calendar time of their seven season contracts. Nonetheless, this legal technicality established by the De Havilland Law brought 20th Century-Fox TV to the bargaining table; as *Variety* noted in their coverage of the deal, use of that lawsuit was 'a ploy to take the dispute public and force the studio to sweeten its offer'.[94]

Conclusion

This chapter has illuminated the legal terms of the talent contract and considered how the resulting precedents established by California case law have shaped Hollywood's industrial practices, particularly in terms of high-profile above-the-line talent contract negotiations. Both *De Haviland v. Warner Bros.* and *Buchwald v. Paramount* are landmark cases that reveal important and contested aspects of contractual battles in Hollywood's history that are still relevant in the industry today. However, further analysis of Hollywood contract negotiations faces significant research challenges in terms of access to primary sources. Although the *De Haviland v. Warner Bros.* legal materials are available at the USC Warner Bros. Archive in Los Angeles, and the *Buchwald* case is available from the LA Superior Court files, this access remains a novelty for studying contracts and legal dealings of the Hollywood studios. Likewise, there is a paucity of primary documents through which to analyse the media industries of conglomerate Hollywood. The data is not available for researchers, who therefore have to draw on a range of other methods. One key resource for accessing contemporary industry contracts is through litigation in the LA Superior Court, since these documents become public record.[95] Moreover, the major talent agencies – William Morris Endeavor, Creative Artists Agency, United Talent Agency and the contemporary studios – do not make their archives accessible to researchers, presumably for reasons of commercial confidentiality. In addition, the majority of lawsuits are settled before they go to a legal decision, so consequently are unable to establish a precedent in case law, and out-of-court settlements are usually kept confidential. This presents substantial challenges for scholars wishing to produce an accurate history of Hollywood's legal contracts, as most accessible contracts are either concerning contractual disputes (which become matters of legal record) or standard 'boiler plate' contract agreements, such as those negotiated by the major guilds (DGA, SAG and WGA).

We should also note additional issues of method in using secondary sources such as trade journals to examine the brokering of deals. Industry trade and newspaper articles are a vital and valuable resource to trace key events and trends of the business due to the scarcity of access to conglomerate Hollywood contracts and corporate records.[96] Hence, scholars utilise the trades and press in addition to new media outlets like industry insider blogs such as *Deadline Hollywood* and *The Wrap* to study the media industries of today. However, frothy speculation about talent and box office has long been used by agents and studios for creating publicity around their projects, with *Variety* and *The Hollywood Reporter* being important industry journals in this respect, so we also require a critical view of the relationship between the trade papers and the industry they report on.

In this chapter, we have not only analysed Hollywood contracts, but also considered their impact on the talent, as both employees and labourers. In doing so, we have highlighted the importance of comprehending contracts and their clauses and of deciphering Hollywood's creative accounting. Thus, to fully understand these deal structures, we must unpack complex legal documents and digest their numerous pages of clauses. At the same time, we also echo Jane Gaines in being cognisant to what she calls the 'truth status' of contracts, which can become seductive in their apparent authority.[97] Contracts tend to be most relevant when matters reach dispute and go to court. While they rarely reveal simple industry axioms of film authorship or creative decision-making, contracts do inform and regulate the conditions of film production. Nevertheless, as this chapter has illustrated, contracts can also be an instrument of agency and power as well as oppression/control, especially in Hollywood.

Notes

1. Danae Clark, *Negotiating Hollywood: The Cultural Politics of Actors' Labor* (Minneapolis: University of Minnesota Press, 1995).

2. Some economists and lawyers have attempted to address this, including: Darlene C. Chisholm, 'Profit-sharing Versus Fixed-payment Contracts: Evidence from the Motion Pictures Industry', *Journal of Law, Economics, & Organization* vol. 13 no. 1 (1987): 169–201; Darlene C. Chisholm, 'Two-part Share Contracts, Risk, and the Life Cycle of Stars: Some Empirical Results from Motion Picture Contracts', *Journal of Cultural Economics* vol. 28 no. 1 (2004): 37–56; Joe Sisto, 'Profit Participation in the Motion Picture Industry', *Entertainment and Sports Lawyer* vol. 21 no. 2 (2003): 1, 21–8; Mark Weinstein, 'Profit-sharing Contracts in Hollywood: Evolution and Analysis', *Journal of Legal Studies* vol. 27 no. 1 (1998): 67–112. Examples of analysis within film, media and communications include: Emily Carman, '"Women Rule Hollywood": Ageing and Freelance Stardom in the Studio System', *Celebrity Studies* vol. 3 no. 1 (2012): 13–24, and *Independent Stardom: Freelance Women in the Hollywood Studio System* (Austin: University of Texas Press, 2016); Philip Drake, 'Reputational Capital, Creative Conflict and Hollywood Independence: The Case of Hal Ashby', in Geoff King, Claire Molloy and Yannis Tzioumakis (eds), *American Independent Cinema: Indie, Indiewood and Beyond* (London: Routledge, 2012), pp. 140–52; Tom Kemper, *Hidden Talent: The Emergence of Hollywood Agents* (Berkeley: University of California Press, 2010); and Paul McDonald, *Hollywood Stardom* (Malden, MA: Wiley-Blackwell, 2013), in particular, on the inflation of star compensation in conglomerate Hollywood.

3. Jonathan Blaufarb, 'The Seven-Year Itch: California Labor Code Section 2855', *Communications and Entertainment Law Journal* vol. 6 no. 3 (1983–4): 656. We are indebted to Matt Stahl, who pointed us to Blaufarb's essay for his analysis on the evolution of Section 2855 in California and for underscoring the importance of Olivia de Havilland's case as the key litigation for the interpretation of this statute. Stahl's work on recording artist contracts is also exemplary in understanding the struggles between artists and the music industry. See Matt Stahl, *Unfree Masters: Recording Artists and the Politics of Work* (Durham, NC: Duke University Press, 2013).

4. We will use the misspelling of her last name when referring to the case and the actress's correct spelling when referring specifically to her. Additionally, while motion picture contracts are now performed on a freelance basis, option contracts remain for television talent, mirroring the old studio system long-term option contracts.

5. The residual payments from DVD/video, television and online, paid to talent, have become increasingly important as, by the 1990s and 2000s, revenues from ancillary markets provided a much larger proportion of revenues and profit for the Hollywood studios than that produced at the theatrical box office. This ultimately transcends our analysis of contracts in the chapter, but is a compelling subject for further research. See also Chapter 9 in this book, which considers residuals in regard to the Writers Guild.

6. Kemper, *Hidden Talent*, p. 127.

7. In 1872, the term was limited to two years, extended to five in 1919. See Forty-Ninth Session of California State Senate, Chapter 705, Section 1980, approved by the Governor on 10 June 1931, and put into effect on 14 August 1931.

8. Ibid.

9. Ibid.

10. For example, provision number twelve in actor Ronald Colman's 1935 contract with Selznick International Pictures nearly replicates this parlance: 'It is mutually understood and agreed that your services are special, unique, unusual, extraordinary, and of an intellectual character, giving them a peculiar value.' See contract dated 23 July 1935, Ronald Colman Legal file, David O. Selznick Collection (DOSC), Harry Ransom Center (HRC), University of Texas-Austin.

11. Blaufarb, 'The Seven Year Itch': 657.

12. 'Objections to 7-Yr. Contract', *Variety*, 30 June 1931, p. 3.

13. The studio, not the star, had the right to drop or pick up the option. See Tino Balio, *Grand Design: Hollywood as a Modern Business Enterprise, 1930–1939* (Berkeley: University of California Press, 1995), p. 145.

14. Jane Gaines, *Contested Culture: The Image, the Voice, and the Law* (Chapel Hill: University of North Carolina Press, 1991), p. 152.

15. Balio, *Grand Design*, p. 143. See also Richard Jewell, *The Golden Age of Hollywood 1929–1945* (Malden, MA: Blackwell, 2007), pp. 255–7.

16. Cagney's 1932 contract guaranteed star billing and specified that Warner Bros. must obtain consent from the actor if they sought to bill anyone else before the star. Cagney's lawyer found evidence that Pat O'Brien had been billed over Cagney on a downtown Los Angeles theatre marquee for their film *Ceiling Zero* (1936), to which the star had not agreed. See James Cagney legal file, Warner Bros. Archive (WBA), USC. See also Robert Sklar, *City Boys: Cagney, Bogart, Garfield* (Princeton, NJ: Princeton University Press, 1994), p. 53.

17. The CA Supreme Court upheld the earlier decision in 1938.

18. Contract dated 7 July 1939, see James Cagney legal file, folder marked 1939–40, WBA, USC.

19. See Thomas Schatz, '"A Triumph of Bitchery:" Warner Brothers, Bette Davis, and *Jezebel*', in Janet Staiger (ed.), *The Studio System* (New Brunswick, NJ: Rutgers University Press, 1995), p. 81. Schatz's essay remains the best source for Davis's legal battles with Warner Bros., the trial in England with Warner Bros. and its resulting change in her star status at the studio in the 1930s.

20. Ibid. Schatz notes how even the Warner Bros. studio lawyer in London sided with Davis, counselling Jack Warner after the trial that while 'the company "should have the right to suspend" there "should be a limit to the period which the Producer can add on to the existing period of the contract'''. Ibid., p. 81.

21. Other stars include George Brent, Kay Francis and Ann Dvorak. See Thomas Schatz, *The Genius of the System* (New York: Henry Holt and Company, 1988), pp. 217–18, 220.

22. Kemper, *Hidden Talent*, p. 131.

23. See Kemper's *Hidden Talent* for an overview on the important role talent agents played in studio-era Hollywood, in particular chapter 6, 'Sealing the Deal: The Contract Industry', on how agents parlayed their clients' contracts into greater professional autonomy.

24. For information on the A-list freelancers of the 1930s, all of whom had impressive contracts, see Emily Carman's book, *Independent Stardom*, Chapter 2, The [Freelance] Contract in Context.

25. The last percentage earnings statement in Dunne's RKO files is from 1948, which states that her total cut of the profits was $161.969.09. See contract with RKO dated September 1933, Irene Dunne Collection, USC Cinematic Arts Library.

26. See Kemper, *Hidden Talent*, p. 84.

27. See California State court brief dated 23 March 1944. *De Haviland v. Warner Bros. Pictures, Inc.*, 67 Cal. App. 225, 153 P.2d 983 (1944) (her name was misspelled in the Court's final verdict).

28. See contract dated 12 February 1934 (effective 28 February 1935), WBA, USC.

29. Interview, 'The Last Belle of Cinema', Academy of Achievement, 5 October 2006, http://www.achievement.org (accessed 4 January 2015). De Havilland is one of the last living actresses of her generation (born 1916).

30. De Havilland declined to appear in the following four pictures: *Saturday's Children* (1940), *Flight Angels* (1940), *George Washington Slept Here* (1942) and *One More Tomorrow* (1946), also known as *The Animal Kingdom*. The parts she refused pale in comparison to the number of assignments she accepted between 1935 and 1943: twenty-eight in total.

31. Undated Jack Warner memo titled 'Olivia de Havilland Case', circa 1943. The actress's films had all made profits for the studio, and even those that she refused to appear in made a profit, with *George Washington Slept Here* making over $1 million at the box office. Financial information provided by studio figures in Olivia De Havilland legal file, WBA, USC.

32. Memo to Jack Warner from Trilling, dated 20 February 1942, De Havilland legal file, WBA, USC.

33. For example, Warner Bros. had made freelance deals with Carole Lombard, Barbara Stanwyck and Gary Cooper, among others in the 1930s and early 40s. See Carman, *Independent Stardom*, chapter 2, 'The [Freelance] Contract in Context' and chapter 4, 'Independent Stardom Goes Mainstream', in particular.

34. See Blaufarb, 'The Seven Year Itch': 666.

35. *De Haviland v. Warner Bros. Pictures, Inc.*, 67 Cal. App. 2d at 235, 153 p.2d, 988.

36. Blaufarb, 'The Seven-Year Itch': 668.

37. See Olivia de Havilland legal file, WBA, USC as well as 'De Havilland Sues For Work', *Variety*, 14 July 1944, p. 1.

38. See Blaufarb, 'The Seven-Year Itch': 669–75. Manchester attempted to free herself from a series of contracts with Arista Records, and her case relied on the *De Haviland* interpretation of Section 2855 to do so.

39. S. Abraham Ravid, 'Information, Blockbusters, and Stars: A Study of the Film Industry', *Journal of Business* vol. 72 no. 4 (1999): 482.

40. Weinstein, 'Profit-sharing Contracts in Hollywood': 84. See also McDonald, *Hollywood Stardom*, p. 146. For an account of Wasserman's important influence upon the contemporary Hollywood cinema see Douglas Gomery, 'Hollywood Corporate Business Practice and Periodizing Contemporary Film History', in Steve Neale and Murray Smith (eds), *Contemporary Hollywood Cinema* (London: Routledge, 1998), pp. 47–57.

41. Box-office gross figures estimated by authors based on Stewart's earnings from the deal. See also John W. Cones, *The Feature Film Distribution: A Critical Analysis of the Single Most Important Film Industry Agreement* (Carbondale: Southern Illinois University Press, 1996), pp. 21–2, and Dennis McDougal, *The Last Mogul* (New York: Crown, 1998), p. 153, on the particulars of Stewart's earnings.

42. Weinstein, 'Profit-sharing Contracts in Hollywood': 84n26.

43. See Connie Bruck, *When Hollywood Had a King: The Reign of Lew Wasserman, Who Leveraged Talent into Power and Influence* (New York: Random House, 2003) and McDougal, *The Last Mogul*.

44. See introductory chapter of Denise Mann, *Hollywood Independents: The Postwar Talent Takeover* (Minneapolis: University of Minnesota Press, 2008). See also McDonald, *Hollywood Stardom*, pp. 107–16, for more extensive examples from the 1950s to the 90s and 2000s.

45. See Bruck, *When Hollywood Had a King*.

46. For more on Peters and Guber, see Nancy Griffin and Kim Masters, *Hit and Run: How Jon Peters and Peter Guber Took Sony for a Ride in Hollywood* (New York: Touchstone, 1997).

47. Reported in David Stephenson, 'Fortune is Strong with Alec's Estate NINE Years Beyond the Grave, the Force, or Fortune, is Still with the Late Star Wars Actor Sir Alec Guinness', *Daily Express*, 17 May 2009. Exchange rate converted at £1 as $1.5.

48. Edward J. Epstein, *The Big Picture: The New Logic of Money and Power in Hollywood* (New York: Random House, 2005), p. 18.

49. Arthur De Vany, *Hollywood Economics: How Extreme Uncertainty Shapes the Film Industry* (London: Routledge, 2003).

50. Reported worldwide box-office grosses from Internet Movie Database, accessed 15 September 2014, http://www.imdb.com/title/tt0181852/business and http://www.imdb.com/title/tt0438488/business

51. McDonald, *Hollywood Stardom*, p. 28. See also Carman, '"Women Rule Hollywood"', p. 22.

52. For an analysis, see the case-study of the creative accounting of *Forrest Gump* (1994), in Philip Drake, 'Distribution and Marketing in Contemporary Hollywood', in Paul McDonald and Janet Wasko (eds), *The Contemporary Hollywood Film Industry* (Oxford: Blackwell, 2008), pp. 140–52.

53. Aljean Harmetz, 'Studio–Star Marriages Make a Comeback', *Los Angeles Herald Examiner*, 8 January 1984, E4.

54. Ibid.

55. 'Murphy Gets More Cash, Clout in Renegotiated Par Contract', *Variety*, 26 August 1987, pp. 1, 11.

56. Ibid., p. 1.

57. Ibid., p.11.

58. Reported worldwide box-office gross of *Coming to America*, accessed 15 September 2014, http://www.imdb.com/title/tt0094898/business?ref_=tt_ql_dt_4

59. For this and the details that follow, see *Buchwald v. Paramount Pictures Corp.*, 1990 Cal. App. LEXIS 634 (1990); Adam J. Marcus, '*Buchwald v. Paramount Pictures Corp.* and the Future of Net Profit', *Cardozo Arts & Entertainment Law Journal* vol. 9 (1991): 545–85; Pierce O'Donnell and Dennis McDougal, *Fatal Subtraction: The Inside Story of Buchwald v. Paramount* (New York: Doubleday, 1992). The latter's appendix includes the judicial decisions for each of the three phases of the case.

60. *Buchwald v. Paramount Pictures Corp.*, 1990 Cal App. LEXIS 634, *18 [asterisk in original].

61. Ibid., *30.

62. Ibid., *1.

63. Ibid., *3

64. Ibid.

66. Ibid., *16.

67. Ibid., *14–15.

68. Ibid., *14–16.

69. Ibid., *16–18.

70. O'Donnell and McDougal, *Fatal Subtraction*, p. xxv.

71. Ibid., p. 524.

72. Robert W. Welkos, 'Buchwald, Paramount Settle Film Dispute', *Los Angeles Times*, 13 September 1995, accessed 15 August 2014, http://articles.latimes.com/1995-09-13/business/fi-45442_1_paramount-pictures

73. Marcus ,'*Buchwald v. Paramount Pictures Corp.* and the Future of Net Profit', 547.

74. *Buchwald v. Paramount Pictures Corp.*, 1990 Cal App. LEXIS 634, *17–18.

75. Ibid., *39

76. Ibid., *43.

77. Marcus, '*Buchwald v. Paramount Pictures Corp.* and the Future of Net Profit': 559.

78. Ibid.

79. O'Donnell and McDougal, *Fatal Subtraction*, p. 238.

80. 'Tentative Decision (Second Phase)', *Buchwald v. Paramount Pictures Corp.*, Los Angeles Superior Court, Case No. 706083 (21 December 1990), reprinted in the appendix of O'Donnell and Dennis McDougal, *Fatal Subtraction*, p. 550.

81. Ibid., p. 566.

82. Ibid., pp. 550–1.

83. Ibid., pp. 543, 550–1.

84. 'Statement of Decision (Third Phase)', *Buchwald v. Paramount Pictures Corp.*, Los Angeles Superior Court, Case No. 706083 (16 March 1992), reprinted in the appendix of O'Donnell and Dennis McDougal, *Fatal Subtraction*, pp. 558, 560. See also *Buchwald v. Paramount Pictures Corp.*, Cal.Super.Ct., LASC No. 706083 (16 March 1992) [ELR 13:11:3].

85. Nina J. Easton 'Hollywood's Ledger Domain', *Los Angeles Times*, 6 January 1991, pp. 5, 78.

86. *tfilm Productions, Inc. v. Warner Bros.*, Nos. B.C. 051653 & B.C 051654.

(Cal. Super. Ct. Mar. 14, 1994). See also Ronald J. Nessim, 'Profit Participation Claims', in Charles J. Harder (ed.), *Entertainment Litigation* (New York: Oxford University Press, 2007), pp. 426–7.

87. Drake, 'Distribution and Marketing in Contemporary Hollywood', pp. 79–80.
88. Andrew Wallenstein and Cynthia Littleton, '"Modern Family" Battle Leads to Lawsuit', *Variety*, 24 July 2013, accessed 15 August 2014, http://variety.com/2012/tv/news/modern-family-battle-leads-to-lawsuit-1118056976/
89. Ibid.
90. Ibid.
91. On Vergara's holding deal, see Maria Elena Fernandez, 'Sofia Vergara Heats Up ABC's *Modern Family* and Makes us Laugh', *Los Angeles Times*, 6 December 2009, accessed 4 January 2015, http://latimesblogs.latimes.com/showtracker/2009/12/sofia-vergara-heats-up-abcs-modern-family-and-makes-us-laugh.html
92. Cynthia Littleton, '"Modern Family" Actors Reach Deal with 20th TV', *Variety*, 27 July 2013, accessed 15 August 2014, http://variety.com/2012/tv/news/modern-family-actors-reach-deal-with-20th-tv-1118057178/
93. Ibid.
94. Ibid.
95. For an example, see Drake 'Reputational Capital, Creative Conflict and Hollywood Independence', pp. 140–52.
96. As we completed this chapter in autumn 2014, the industry was rocked by the illegal hacking of Sony Pictures Entertainment computers, placing a large volume of contractual documents and confidential emails into the public domain and providing unprecedented access to the industry practices of a contemporary major media conglomerate. Hence, researching the 'Sony hack' presents scholars with additional complex ethical questions about the use of contractual data made public through unofficial or illegal means.
97. See Gaines, *Contested Culture*, p. 146.

References

Balio, Tino, *Grand Design: Hollywood as a Modern Business Enterprise, 1930–1939* (Berkeley: University of California Press, 1995).
Batfilm Productions, Inc. v. Warner Bros., Nos. B.C. 051653 & B.C 051654 (Cal. Super. Ct. Mar. 14, 1994).
Blaufarb, Jonathan, 'The Seven Year Itch: California Labor Code Section 2855', *Communications and Entertainment Law Journal* vol. 6 no. 3 (1983–4): 653–93.
Bruck, Connie, *When Hollywood Had a King: The Reign of Lew Wasserman, Who Leveraged Talent into Power and Influence* (New York: Random House, 2003).
Buchwald v. Paramount Pictures Corp., 1990 Cal. App. LEXIS 634 (1990).
Carman, Emily, *Independent Stardom: Freelance Women in the Hollywood Studio System* (Austin: University of Texas Press, 2016).
Carman, Emily, '"Women Rule Hollywood": Ageing and Freelance Stardom in the Studio System', *Celebrity Studies* vol. 3 no. 1 (2012): 13–24.
Chisholm, Darlene C., 'Profit-sharing Versus Fixed-payment Contracts: Evidence from the Motion Pictures Industry', *Journal of Law, Economics, & Organization* vol. 13 no. 1 (1987): 169–201.

Chisholm, Darlene C., 'Two-part Share Contracts, Risk, and the Life Cycle of Stars: Some Empirical
    Results from Motion Picture Contracts', *Journal of Cultural Economics* vol. 28 no. 1 (2004): 37–56.

Clark, Danae, *Negotiating Hollywood: The Cultural Politics of Actors' Labor* (Minneapolis: University of
    Minnesota Press, 1995).

Cones, John W., *The Feature Film Distribution: A Critical Analysis of the Single Most Important Film Industry
    Agreement* (Carbondale: Southern Illinois University Press, 1996).

Daniels, Bill, David Leedy and Steven D. Sills, *Movie Money: Understanding Hollywood's (Creative)
    Accounting Practices* (Los Angeles: Silman-James Press, 1998).

De Haviland v. Warner Bros. Pictures, Inc., 153 P.2d 983 (Cal. Dist. Ct. App. 1944).

De Vany, Arthur, *Hollywood Economics: How Extreme Uncertainty Shapes the Film Industry* (London:
    Routledge, 2003).

Drake, Philip, 'Distribution and Marketing in Contemporary Hollywood', in Paul McDonald and Janet
    Wasko (eds), *The Contemporary Hollywood Film Industry* (Oxford: Blackwell, 2008), pp. 63–82.

Drake, Philip, 'Reputational Capital, Creative Conflict and Hollywood Independence: The Case of Hal
    Ashby', in Geoff King, Claire Molloy and Yannis Tzioumakis (eds), *American Independent Cinema:
    Indie, Indiewood and Beyond* (London: Routledge, 2012), pp. 140–52.

Epstein, Edward J., *The Big Picture: The New Logic of Money and Power in Hollywood* (New York: Random
    House, 2005).

Gaines, Jane, *Contested Culture: The Image, the Voice, and the Law* (Chapel Hill: University of North
    Carolina Press, 1991).

Gomery, Douglas, 'Hollywood Corporate Business Practice and Periodizing Contemporary Film History',
    in Steve Neale and Murray Smith (eds), *Contemporary Hollywood Cinema* (London: Routledge,
    1998), pp. 47–57.

Griffin, Nancy and Kim Masters, *Hit and Run: How Jon Peters and Peter Guber Took Sony for a Ride in
    Hollywood* (New York: Touchstone, 1997).

Jewell, Richard B., *The Golden Age of Cinema: Hollywood 1929–1945* (Malden, MA: Blackwell, 2007).

Kemper, Tom, *Hidden Talent: The Emergence of Hollywood Agents* (Berkeley: University of California Press,
    2010).

Mann, Denise, *Hollywood Independents: The Postwar Talent Takeover* (Minneapolis: University of Minnesota
    Press, 2008).

Marcus, Adam J., '*Buchwald v. Paramount Pictures Corp.* and the Future of Net Profit', *Cardozo Arts &
    Entertainment Law Journal* vol. 9 (1991): 545–85.

McDonald, Paul, *Hollywood Stardom* (Malden, MA: Wiley-Blackwell, 2013).

McDougal, Dennis, *The Last Mogul* (New York: Crown, 1998).

Nessim, Ronald J., 'Profit Participation Claims', in Charles J. Harder (ed.), *Entertainment Litigation*
    (New York: Oxford University Press, 2007), pp. 403–65.

O'Donnell, Pierce and Dennis McDougal, *Fatal Subtraction: The Inside Story of Buchwald v. Paramount*
    (New York: Doubleday, 1992).

Ravid, S. Abraham, 'Information, Blockbusters, and Stars: A Study of the Film Industry', *Journal of Business*
    vol. 72 no. 4 (1999): 463–92.

Schatz, Thomas, '"A Triumph of Bitchery:" Warner Brothers, Bette Davis, and *Jezebel*', in Janet Staiger
    (ed.), *The Studio System* (New Brunswick, NJ: Rutgers University Press, 1995), pp. 74–92.

Schatz, Thomas, *The Genius of the System* (New York: Henry Holt and Company, 1988).

Sisto, Joe, 'Profit Participation in the Motion Picture Industry', *Entertainment and Sports Lawyer* vol. 21 no. 2 (2003): 1, 21–8.

Sklar, Robert, *City Boys: Cagney, Bogart, Garfield* (Princeton, NJ: Princeton University Press, 1994).

Stahl, Matt, *Unfree Masters: Recording Artists and the Politics of Work* (Durham, NC: Duke University Press, 2013).

Weinstein, Mark, 'Profit-sharing Contracts in Hollywood: Evolution and Analysis', *Journal of Legal Studies* vol. 27 no. 1 (1998): 67–112.

9 WILL WORK FOR SCREEN CREDIT
LABOUR AND THE LAW IN HOLLYWOOD

CATHERINE L. FISK

The glamour of work in film and television production obscures the fact that, although some Hollywood work is creative, well paid and fulfilling, some is underpaid or unpaid, tedious, gruelling, insecure and without realistic prospect of advancement. The stark contrast between the fabulous wealth of some Hollywood workers and the exploitation and poverty of others has long fascinated those who write on film and television production, as Chapter 8 illustrates. Hollywood is a microcosm of the polarisation between 'good jobs' and 'bad jobs' that increasingly characterises the contemporary economy.[1] And, in Hollywood especially, the difference between good and bad jobs depends on the complex and porous web of legal rules and contracts governing terms of employment, rights in copyrightable works, collective bargaining agreements and customs about paying one's dues in order to, perhaps, one day break into the industry. This chapter explores the role of law, especially labour law, in constituting some jobs as good jobs and others as bad ones and the persistent challenge of regulating the Hollywood labour market.

Hollywood film and TV production is largely, though not entirely, unionised. Craft and below-the-line workers belong to unions organised along the lines of technical speciality (musicians belong to the American Federation of Musicians, truck drivers belong to the Teamsters), although many technical employees, ranging from cinematographers to make-up artists, belong to the International Alliance of Theatrical and Stage Employees (IATSE), which is an industry-wide union representing all types of below-the-line workers in film and TV, as well as stage hands and others working in live theatre. Writers belong to the Writers Guild of America (WGA, also referred to here as the Guild). Actors belong to SAG-AFTRA, which was formed from the 2012 merger of the Screen Actors Guild (SAG), which had its origins among film actors, and the American Federation of Television and Radio Artists (AFTRA), with origins among radio and later television actors. Animators belong to the Animation Guild (an affiliate of IATSE) and directors to the Directors Guild of America (DGA). All of these unions bargain collectively on behalf of employees with the Alliance of Motion Picture and Television Producers (AMPTP), which represents hundreds of large and independent production companies, television networks and studios. These collective agreements (known as minimum basic agreements, or MBAs) provide minimum standards of employment for all employees. The conditions that led to de-unionisation across North America and Europe – labour surpluses, repeated industrial restructuring and vitriolic right-wing and managerial attacks on the concept and reality of unionisation – have eroded the strength of the unions and guilds, but have not destroyed them.

In fieldwork conducted in 2013 and 2014, I interviewed dozens of writers working on acclaimed (and less acclaimed) cable and network television shows from the 1970s through the present.[2] Writers almost unanimously praised unionisation for its role in securing decent pay and benefits, in protecting the status of writers, including through Guild control of screen credit designations, and for its administration of the fantastically complex system of foreign copyright royalties and residuals for reuse of writers' material. The Guild agreements for writers, like the similar agreements that SAG-AFTRA and the DGA have negotiated for actors and directors, contain creative, innovative and powerful solutions to vexing problems associated with collaborative creative labour and short-term, episodic work. Union and guild agreements provide pensions and health insurance for their current and retired members, a complex and important function in a labour market characterised by short-term employment punctuated by periods of unemployment.

The first case study in this chapter focuses on one aspect of the law that protects 'good' jobs for talent: the MBA requirement that production companies pay residuals to writers, actors and directors every time a film or TV programme is re-broadcast or, with some exceptions, sold as a DVD or streamed or downloaded from the internet. Residuals are a form of profit sharing, like copyright royalties, under which creators are paid for each qualifying use of their work. Residuals matter because writers, directors, actors, animators, cinematographers and all the other people who might be deemed the 'authors' of movies or TV shows for purposes of copyright law sign away their status as authors as a condition of employment. Under US copyright law and these contracts, movies and TV shows are 'works made for hire'; the production company or studio is the author and copyright owner and, absent the collectively bargained requirement to pay residuals, the studios could profit from endless reuse of the works because their legal status as copyright owners entitles them to keep all the copyright royalties for themselves.[3] Screen credit and payment of residuals to credited writers, actors and directors are significant, even if they offer protection to relatively few and relatively privileged above-the-line workers. The credit and residual provisions in the Guild agreements are innovative pay practices that many other sectors of the knowledge economy – software and video game production, to name two – could emulate. The persistence of unions and their contributions to rationalising the labour market in film and TV production and to ameliorating some of the harsh effects for some workers of highly competitive and episodic labour, together with copyright's work-for-hire doctrine, are a bright side of the sometimes grim tale of labour in the global economy.

But all is not on the bright side. Producers of film, television and, more recently, digital media use the glamour of Hollywood to persuade aspiring entrants to the field to work long hours at low wages or even for free. The conditions of labour in the invisible and unglamorous sectors of media industries are extremely difficult. Globalisation and the drive for corporate profits have driven down pay and eliminated or off-shored jobs in film and TV production. Union organisers and activists in the media industries lament that these pressures have made it all but impossible to unionise, or to improve working conditions in new sectors of the media industries, including the production of video games, YouTube videos, webisodes (TV produced for the internet) and reality TV. The second case study in this chapter examines this facet of media work through the lens of the law and practice of unpaid internships, a pervasive and apparently intractable problem in media production culture.[4]

Hence, this chapter on employment practices and law in Hollywood is divided into five parts. The first is a brief overview of the three regimes of law – employment contracts, statutory wage and hour regulation and collective bargaining agreements – that determine the conditions of labour in Hollywood. The next two parts examine labour at the high end of the pay and prestige scales, focusing on the origins of the Writers Guild control over screen credits for writing and, in particular, the origins of the residuals system for credited writers in the 1940s and early 50s. In addition to explaining the role of the WGA in developing the complex system for crediting and compensating writers, the case study considers the way in which debates over fair compensation and creative control in the classic Hollywood era echo among TV writers today. The remaining sections then look at employment practices at the low end of the pay scale. Section four explores the question of why people are willing to work for free in order to break into the movie and television business, and assesses the strength of the legal regime that attempts to distinguish when free labour is exploitative and when it is an opportunity. The fifth section then analyses the litigation over the use of unpaid internships in film and television production, with a case study of the class action lawsuit arising from the use of unpaid interns on *Black Swan* (2010) and *(500) Days of Summer* (2009).

The Legal *Mise en Scène*

Unless a person to be hired has the bargaining power to insist on contractual protection against arbitrary termination without notice, generous payment and the right to control his or her conditions of work, the regime of employment contracts in the USA accords substantial power to the employer in hiring, firing, pay and promotion. Subject to certain non-waivable statutory minimum wage rules and protections against race, gender and other forms of discrimination, employers can hire on whatever terms the employee will accept.

Individual contracts of employment for talent employed in motion picture and television production typically give employers exclusive rights in their employees' time and effort, and ownership of all intellectual property rights generated by employees' work, apart from top talent, who can negotiate more favourable deals. Under US copyright law, the employer is deemed the author and, therefore, the copyright owner of all works made for hire, which includes works prepared by an employee 'within the scope of his or her employment' or works 'specially ordered or commissioned' from anyone who is not an employee.[5] That the employer is deemed the 'author' of any copyrighted work made for hire is important in film and TV production as it removes any possibility that one who worked on a film or TV programme might claim the rights of a joint author (and thus the ability to block distribution of the work). But it also means that, absent some contract provision altering the default rules of copyright ownership, those who work on films or TV programmes have no right to be paid for later uses of their work, no right to share in the profits of the work, no right to be identified as a contributor to the work and no right to prevent the destruction or alteration of work that they may consider to be their own.

Although today's successful writers may negotiate slightly better terms – the provisions of employment agreements are often contractually stipulated to be confidential – the standard employment contracts for screenwriters now and in the classical era gave studios broad rights to the employee's time and talent in exchange for relatively generous wages. The 1946 six-month employment agreement between Warner Bros. and James R. Webb (the credited writer of *How the West Was Won* [1962] and *Cape Fear* [1962] and a number of westerns and thrillers in the late 1940s and 50s) is illustrative.[6] For the salary of $450 per week for the six-month term (in today's dollars about $5,700 per week, or $138,000 for six months), Webb promised to render whatever services as a writer the studio might require at whatever time and place the studio might demand, and to make television or radio broadcasts for no additional compensation. The agreement entitled Warner Bros. to 'lend the services of the Author to any person, form or corporation in any capacity in which Author is required to render his services'.[7] According to the contract, Warner Bros. held the option to extend the agreement for a maximum of seven years, provided it paid increased compensation (up to a maximum of $1,250 per week in the seventh year). Warner Bros. was granted rights to exhibit any film on 'radio and television and all other improvements and devices which are or may hereafter be used in connection with the exhibition, reproduction and/or transmission of any present or future kind of motion picture production' on which Webb worked. And, importantly, the agreement granted 'all rights whatsoever in and to all and every [sic] the works that he shall write, conceive, compose, or produce during the full term', including 'the motion picture, talking picture, radio, television, phonographic, publication and dramatic rights' in his works. This last provision inscribes by contract the rights under the copyright law that the employer is the author of any work made by an employee for hire absent a written agreement to the contrary.[8] Another standard provision in writers' agreements of that era allowed the studio to lay off the writer, 'without pay, at such times and for such periods as it may elect', although some agreements imposed a maximum length on the lay-off period.[9]

Today, writers working in Hollywood tend to be hired by the job rather than by the week: they are hired to write or revise a script and may be paid a set amount and be required to complete the project in a stipulated time. The collective bargaining agreement between the Writers Guild and the production companies sets the minimum compensation, but individual writers can negotiate (usually through their agent) for payment beyond the Guild minimum. Writers working in television are usually hired for the season, that is, the length of time it takes to write and produce somewhere between nine and twenty-two episodes (the standard number of episodes for a season of US network TV is twenty-two; the standard number on cable is thirteen). They are paid a salary and an additional script fee for each episode for which the writer receives a 'written by' screen credit, and the custom in most writers' rooms is that the showrunner (the head writer who serves as the executive producer as well) will divide the primary responsibility for writing scripts (and therefore the written by credits) equitably among all writers working on the show. These individual employment contracts give the studio the right to terminate the agreement early if, for example, the TV show is cancelled mid-season.

Individual and collective agreements are negotiated against the backdrop of federal and state law regulating conditions of employment. A second important type of law regulating labour in Hollywood is federal and state law controlling wages and hours. The federal Fair Labor Standards Act (FLSA) requires payment of a statutorily prescribed minimum wage (currently $7.25 per hour) and a premium payment of one and a half times the regular rate of pay for hours worked over forty in a week, and the California wage and hour law is more employee-protective.[10] The FLSA applies to almost all private-sector employers and to any person who is employed in any work other than a salaried executive, administrative, or professional capacity, or as an independent contractor or trainee. Every guild and union agreement in film and TV production requires pay far above the federal and state minimum wage and, in addition, the union agreements covering film crews extensively regulate the number of hours worked each day and require premium pay for the long days that are customary when shooting. But, as will be seen below, people often work in violation of individual and collective agreement provisions, or state and federal wage and hour laws. Writers, animators, editors and VFX workers, among others, complain about being asked to do free rewrites or modifications (which is a violation of Guild agreements, the law and their individual employment contracts). And, as will be discussed in the second case study, droves of production assistants work for no pay at all.

A third significant regulatory regime governing work in film and television production is the National Labor Relations Act (NLRA) and the collective bargaining agreements negotiated under its auspices. Since 1935, the NLRA has given all employees the right to form, join or assist a labour union and the right to bargain collectively over terms and conditions of employment.[11] Unlike any other segment of the knowledge economy at almost any period, and unlike the overwhelming majority of American workers today, a significant and influential portion of both talent and craft workers in Hollywood are unionised. The unionisation in the 1930s of talent (e.g., actors, writers, directors, cinematographers) and in the 1920s of craft workers (electrical, set construction, editing) proved to be enormously important for workers.

When workers in the Hollywood film business unionised, some formed unions with those who worked in the same occupation or craft (hence the term 'craft unions') rather than forming one big union to which everyone in the industry could belong. Unlike, for example, autoworkers or steel workers who formed industry-wide unions regardless of the technical, craft or skill divisions of work, Hollywood workers followed the common pattern of nine-teenth-century skilled workers who formed unions limited to those who worked in the same craft (such as in the construction trades). The Writers Guild, the Directors Guild, the Actors Guild, the Federation of Radio Artists (later Television and Radio Artists) and the American Federation of Musicians, as well as the Teamsters (representing drivers), the International Brotherhood of Electrical Workers (IBEW, representing various types of electrical workers) and the Carpenters, are craft unions. Some Hollywood workers formed unions to which anyone working in the industry could belong – for example, IATSE, which, in 1926, became the first union to sign a collective bargaining agreement with the studios.[12]

A union that succeeds in gaining recognition from an employer negotiates an agreement on behalf of all workers within a defined unit (known as a bargaining unit) setting minimum terms of employment. These collective bargaining agreements (or MBAs, as they are known in Hollywood) provide extensive protections on pay and working conditions beyond what state and federal law require. Talent – writers, directors, actors and some cinematographers (or directors of photography [DPs]) – typically have detailed individual employment agreements negotiated by their agent and also benefit from the MBA. Craft workers are more likely to work under standard individual employment contracts drafted by the production company's labour relations lawyer and offered on a take-it-or-leave-it basis, but these agreements cannot be less employee-protective than the applicable MBA. Employees not covered by a union agreement – those employed by companies not signatory to an MBA or employed to work under-the-table (as it were) on a non-union project being done by a company that should be doing all its work by union standards – work under whatever conditions the company offers. This complex and overlapping network of federal and state law, and of individual and collective contracts, makes labour relations law in film and TV production exceedingly complex. But, as will be shown in the two case studies that follow, the most significant source of complexity, at least to outsiders, is the customs in the industry. These norms – concerning what rules are obeyed and which are not, or about which contract terms are important and which are not – are poorly understood by many, including those working in Hollywood, and are important determinants of power, prestige and working conditions.

The Promise: Authors at Work in Hollywood

Film and television production attracts highly educated, skilled and creative people willing to work long hours on short-term projects and at locations all over the world because of the fun of working in the media and with other like-minded people. All of the writers I interviewed in my fieldwork defined success in terms of seeing their words become images on a screen, seeing their name in the credits *and* helping other writers do their best work even if one's contributions are known only to the people who were in the writers' room at the moment a great story idea was born, a plot problem was solved, or a joke hit a chord. Knowing that film and TV are collaborative media in which authorship is collective, they are willing to trade ownership of the copyright in their work for access to the resources and collaborations that will get their ideas made into movies or TV shows.

Writers first agreed to give up the copyright in their work in the very early history of film production because they and the studios envisioned a single use – the script would be made into a film that would show for a certain number of weeks and then would disappear forever. They stuck to that choice when they gained union recognition in the late 1930s because sacrificing their copyrights was the price of gaining legal protection for the right to unionise. Only 'employees' (not 'independent contractors') have the legal right to unionise under the NLRA of 1935, but copyright law deems the employer the author of any work created by an employee, whereas independent contractors lose the copyright in their work only if it was specially commissioned and a written agreement memorialises the commission.[13] For most writers and directors, the trade-off of work-for-hire for the protections of Guild agreements seemed worth it – the Guild salary provisions are generous and the copyright to a film is valuable in proportion to the willingness of the studio to invest in making a good film from the contributions of all the creative people who work on it.

Although the work-for-hire rule is integral to the operation of film and TV production, and is not usually a source of controversy, occasionally it has been criticised and questioned, and this chapter explores some of those moments of rupture. John Caldwell has argued that the high salaries and job security of the studio era 'no longer make sense as a fair trade-off for losing copyright, given the explosion of non-union production, the over-supply of creative labour, and the technological reconfiguration of film and media creation' that – in an 'era of syndication and endless repurposing' – now allows screen content to provide 'a revenue stream for the IP rights holder forever'.[14] Caldwell concedes that, '[t]o be fair, writers and directors went along with this scheme – thus functioning as "contract labour" – in part because they were so well paid for their creations in the classical and network era'.[15] Writers today echo this sentiment, noting that successful writers are well paid but lamenting that they have acquiesced to a legal regime in which they lose all the intellectual property rights in their work. What they do have – contractual rights to screen credit and to bonuses or script fees, and to residuals for shows or films on which they are the credited writer – is important, but it does not represent ownership of their material. The origin of the Guilds is tied to the loss of intellectual property rights.

In 1921, the Screen Writers Guild (SWG) was first organised in Hollywood as a branch of the Authors League of America to promote the interests of writers. The Guild did not obtain the right to represent writers until 1938, after the NLRA of 1935 gave employees legal protection in forming unions and required employers to bargain in good faith with a union chosen by the employees. Between the Guild's formation in 1921 and its first legal recognition in 1938, it went through several changes in structure and leadership, and a total collapse in membership. (The early history of the Screen Actors Guild and the Directors Guild are similar; all were organised in the early 1930s and all three of them went to the National Labor Relations Board in 1937–8 to force the studios to recognise and bargain with them.) Among the Writers Guild's first concerns was to secure fair terms of hiring and fair allocation of credit for writing. Although, by that point, it was already established practice in Hollywood that writers would sell the copyright in their works to studios as part of the contract of employment, authors nevertheless wanted to end some of the most abusive labour practices. In particular, what writers most hoped to gain through unionisation was a higher minimum wage, and an enforceable promise that studios would not ask writers to work 'on spec', whereby they produced work for free with a promise of later compensation if the studio purchased the script or treatment. Writers also wanted labour contracts to protect certain aspects of authorship, including accurate attribution and some creative control.

Writers initially resisted the label 'employee', preferring to think of themselves as contractors because they insisted on independence, the right to control their hours of work and the content of their writing. Most important, if they were independent contractors, under the work-for-hire provision of the 1909 Copyright Act, they rather than their employer would own the copyright in their work, unless a contract of hire specified otherwise. But producers insisted on contract terms assigning copyrights to them, and the New Deal era labour laws (first the National Industrial Recovery Act and the NLRA of 1935) granted only employees (not independent contractors) the right to organise and bargain collectively.[16] Writers eventually realised that only through collective action could they secure acceptable compensation and other terms. Since they had no hope of retaining the copyright in their work even if they were independent contractors, because studios insisted on complete assignments of all intellectual property rights, they agreed to give up their quest for independent contractor status in order to secure legal protection for their right to unionise. Had they been playwrights, short story writers, or novelists, they generally would have retained ownership of their copyrights, as the custom in those sectors is that writers retain ownership and sell options to produce them as films. Short story writers and novelists, of course, worked on their own and sold or licensed their work to magazines or book publishers on whatever terms they and their literary agent could secure. Playwrights, dramaturges, songwriters and lyricists generally worked as independent contractors and, therefore, tended to license rather than sell their work outright.[17]

Leo Rosten's sociological study of Hollywood in the late 1930s identified the writer's status as *employee* as 'the key to many of the problems, dilemmas, and agonies of the writer in Hollywood'.[18] Rosten and others observed that writers were often offended by their lack of creative control, particularly when compared to their experience of writing for the stage, and they were especially galled by their banishment from the set during filming. Many writers were irritated by the penchant of producers to give screen credit that, as the first president of the WGA John Howard Lawson later said, bore 'no relationship to the work accomplished'. 'Hollywood writers were treated with contempt; it was not uncommon for eight or ten writers to work on one script with screen credit whimsically distributed among the producers' in-laws, golf partners, or bookies.'[19] Moreover, as Eric Hoyt has shown, Hollywood talent and studios recognised the value of reissued movies long before television created a huge new market for reissues.[20] Reissuing work made studio ownership of rights even more important because otherwise new licences might have to be obtained from copyright owners for every use after the initial run.

It may never be known whether the discontents of writers about writing on spec, screen credit and creative control could ever have boiled over into action had not the Great Depression caused an epic crisis. But, when the Depression hit hard in 1933, the studios called an emergency meeting of all writers, actors, directors and producers and announced a 50 per cent pay cut.[21] Outraged writers met shortly thereafter at the Hollywood Knickerbocker Hotel to revive the SWG, which had collapsed in the early years of the Depression as writers joined either a quiescent rival union (Screen Playwrights) or determined to remain non-union and negotiate their employment agreements individually.[22] Though the newly revived Writers Guild's first meeting was in a decidedly more plush venue than most union workers ever saw, writers joined the union for the same reasons that workers across the USA turned to unions in the worst years of the Depression: unions seemed to offer the only hope of protection from drastic wage cuts and massive lay-offs.

Since its founding, a core part of the Writers Guild's mission has been helping writers manage reputation, income and intellectual property rights in the highly mobile labour market that has always characterised Hollywood.[23] Deliberations within the Executive Board of the Writers Guild of the 1930s and 40s reveal that even successful screenwriters had serious qualms about the wisdom of giving up the intellectual property rights in their work, even if they were compensated handsomely. Some of the most vocal sceptics about the wisdom of the trade-off – screenwriters John Howard Lawson, Ringgold Wilmer 'Ring' Lardner Jr and Lester Cole – were themselves very well paid. They were also Communists, which makes their insistence on employee ownership of intellectual property both unsurprising – worker ownership of the means of production was a central tenet of Marxism – and a bit ironic, for it was the Communists who urged writers to be more entrepreneurial. Lawson, Lardner and Cole were also three of the Hollywood Ten, the ten writers subpoenaed in 1947 to testify before the US House of Representatives Un-American Activities Committee (HUAC) about their involvement in the Communist Party. When they refused to answer some of the questions posed to them by HUAC, they were held in contempt of Congress and jailed, and were among the first wave of creative professionals to be blacklisted thereafter. While fights over the blacklist consumed the Guild in the late 1940s and the 50s, as they have consumed the attention of schol-

Members of the 'Hollywood Ten' with their families demonstrating before their imprisonment for failure to testify before the House Un-American Activities Committee. Ring Lardner Jr, at the right wearing spectacles, stands under the Adrian Scott sign (with the permission of the Wisconsin Center for Film and Theater Research)

ars since, less well known are the efforts of the Guild to renegotiate the arrangement over writers' compensation for the sale of creative material.

In August of 1947, Lardner published an article in *The Screen Writer* (which for a few years was the magazine of the SWG) with the title 'First Steps in Arithmetic', part of a collectively authored special section '1% of the Gross – An Economic Primer of Screen Writing' discussing the economic and professional welfare of writers.[24] In this, Lardner observed that writers received as payment about 1 per cent of the box-office revenue from films. Lardner asked: 'Does it seem preposterous to argue that we actually provide as much as, say, two per cent of what the movie goer gets for his money?'[25] The question was rhetorical; Lardner argued that Hollywood writers were both underpaid and under-appreciated for their contributions to films. Lardner's argument echoed a complaint writers had made from the earliest days of the film business up to the present. From the beginning, the meaning of authorship and control over intellectual property rights were principal points of contention between writers and film producers. Disputes over copyright, credit, compensation and – especially – profit sharing were at the core of the screenwriters' successful drive for unionisation in the 1930s and have been the source of labour unrest in Hollywood from the early 1930s through the long 2007–8 writers' strike (see also the discussion of the *Buchwald v. Paramount* case in Chapter 8). Today, the two most significant functions of the Writers Guild involve the administration of two forms of intellectual property rights that are unique to Hollywood: the system of residuals – a form of deferred compensation first created by the Guild in 1951–2 that resembles, but is not, a copyright royalty – and the screen credit system, which the Guild has administered since 1941. Residuals and screen credit are understood in their details by relatively few, but are recognised as important by all who work in Hollywood.

The issue of profit sharing as a cornerstone of Hollywood authors' rights emerged most pointedly immediately after World War II as writers prepared to negotiate their second collective bargaining agreement with the studios. The rapid growth of television, the drastic reduction in the number of movies made by the major studios and the growing number of reissues of old films caused widespread unemployment among writers for film. Against these triple financial threats, and in the midst of the existential threat posed by the hunt for Communists among Hollywood writers (compounded by the studios' calculated use of the Red scare as a way to reduce labour costs by firing outspoken and well-paid writers and terrifying the Guild into quiescence), the Guild finally secured collective bargaining agreement provisions requiring payment to credited writers for the reuse of their material in the early 1950s.[26] Those payments – known as residuals – were first required by the 1953 Guild agreement for television writers and only covered the reuse of programmes made for television. Residuals for the reuse of theatrical films shown on television were first required in the 1960 film and television agreements.

The Guild insisted on residual payments in the belief that re-runs reduced employment for writers and, as long as the studios were making money from reuse of a film or TV programme, writers should share in the profit. Residuals have been a cornerstone of writers' compensation and the union's work ever since. It is a sign of their value that every writers' strike has been to secure and extend their rights to residuals. In 1952, writers struck to obtain a contract covering TV and to obtain the right to payment for reuse of TV programmes. In 1959–60, writers struck twice to get residuals for reuse of theatrical films on TV. Writers did not strike in the 1960s and 70s, perhaps in part because no new technologies emerged to challenge the formula by which writers and studios shared the profit from work. But, as new technologies, networks and markets changed the entertainment business model – cable TV, home video, foreign sales for TV programming, Fox and other new networks, DVDs and, finally, the internet – writers struck repeatedly (most recently for a hundred days in 2007–8) to secure compensation for the use of their work in these new forms of distribution.[27]

The Origin of Residuals, 1947–52

With the history of the Writers Guild and writers' longstanding concerns about fair compensation and the copyrights in their work, we can see the importance of the Guild contracts in creating a legal requirement that writers be paid for reuse of their work. As we have seen, because copyright law gives film and TV writers no right to compensation for reuse of their scripts, their only legal protection comes from Guild-negotiated contracts. The following account of the origin of residuals in the early days of television illustrates the Guild's creative use of contract rights to enhance the power, wealth and artistic status of unionised writers.

Writers working in film and TV production today regard their right to be paid residuals for reuse of any material on which they receive screen credit to be so fundamental as to hardly require discussion. When asked 'What do you think of residuals?' writers I interviewed in my fieldwork invariably laughed and responded that residuals are great but are something to which they are entitled. But writers, directors and actors working under Guild agreements in film and TV production are among the very few employees who are entitled as a matter of contract to be paid for reuse of the intellectual property they help create. Video game creators, newspaper writers, advertising agency writers and every other employee who creates copyrighted material has no entitlement under US law or under their employment contract to be paid a percentage of the profits their employer (or former employer) makes for later uses of their work. Musicians credited as songwriters have some rights to royalties under the licensing regimes administered by the American Society of Composers, Authors and Publishers (ASCAP) and Broadcast Music, Inc. (BMI), but musicians typically are not employees of the companies that produce, record, or distribute their work, and thus their working conditions are more akin to freelancers (like novelists) than to employees (like TV writers).[28] This case study on how and why the Writers Guild negotiated for residuals for credited writers shows that the private intellectual property rights regime exists only because of unionisation.

Among the goals articulated at one of the very first Guild meetings was the objective to get writers paid on a royalty basis. John Howard Lawson insisted that as a matter of principle 'writers are the owners of their material'.[29] As Lawson later recalled, this 'could best be done by embodying in a standard writer's contract a minimum percentage of the gross revenues of the picture, the writer to have a specified drawing account against such royalties'.[30] Payment on a royalty basis rather than a salary basis would free writers from the whims of producers and unilateral salary cuts. Moreover, ownership of copyright in the material also would recognise the writers' status; as Lawson declared at the Knickerbocker, 'The *writer* is the creator of motion pictures.'[31]

When the Guild began forming its bargaining strategy in late 1937 and early 1938, it considered various proposals that writers would be paid royalties for the use of their material or would be paid some form of profit sharing.[32] The Guild leadership decided to abandon that provision in its first MBA (which went into effect in January 1942), focusing instead on a minimum wage, advance notice of lay-offs or termination of employment, union security, arbitration of contract disputes and writers' control over screen credit.[33] Copyright ownership and profit sharing were traded for wages, some degree of job security, union strength and writers' control over screen credit.

When World War II ended, the issue of ownership and profit sharing re-emerged as soon as the Guild began planning to negotiate for its second collective bargaining agreement. As the previous chapter outlines, stars and celebrity directors had received contracts entitling them to share a percentage of a film's profits since the 1930s, and writers felt they, too, should share in the profits but could secure such 'percentage' deals only by bargaining collectively through the Guild.[34]

The most serious effort the Guild ever made to eliminate the outright sale of copyright or writing under work-for-hire contracts was in 1946. As chair of the Committee on the Sale of Original Material, Ring Lardner Jr proposed to the Executive Board and to the Authors League that they:

substitute a limited licensing agreement for the current system of outright sale … It is our belief that this action would be one of the major landmarks in the history of the League, and that there is no moral or practical reason why the same general concepts of copyright vested in the author, reversion of rights and control of subsidiary rights should not obtain in the motion picture field as have been won during the past three decades in other fields. Though present practices vary with the type of material purchased and in the bargaining power of the individual author, picture studios remain alone in the extremes of ownership and control which they demand in their purchases. The introduction of television … gives increased urgency to this reform.[35]

The Authors League was sceptical that such a system could be implemented. In reply to Lardner's letter, Elmer Rice, the President of the Authors League, wrote, 'I do not know how many of the members would voluntarily forego a motion picture sale, in the event that the prospective purchaser refused to buy anything but unlimited rights.' But 'the chief problem', thought Rice, would be the Dramatists Guild, which represented playwrights in New York.

Under the Basic Agreement, the manager has an unqualified right to participate in the proceeds of a motion picture sale, and I doubt if the Guild could jeopardize that right by imposing limitations which might result in the loss of a sale and the consequent loss of revenue for the manager.[36]

The Basic Agreement could, of course, be modified,

but I think we would have a very hard time getting the managers to accept it, in view of the fact that there is a time limitation on the manager's participation in motion picture rights and therefore he would have little or nothing to gain in the event of a resale of the rights.[37]

Nevertheless, the Dramatists Guild did endorse a formula proposed by the SWG regarding licensing of material and agreed that it should be included in the proposals when a new Basic Agreement was negotiated.[38] This proposal was also granted by the SWG Executive Board to be submitted for approval at the next general SWG membership meeting.[39] The Radio Writers Guild (also an affiliate of the Authors League) joined the effort, demanding in its 1947 contract negotiations that radio producers agree only to license material for a single performance rather than purchase rights to it, and the SWG endorsed their effort.

Some form of profit sharing, as well as payments for reuse or reissues, emerged as priority issues in late 1946, when the Executive Board began considering its bargaining strategy for a new agreement.[41] The Board appointed a committee to consider Lester Cole's proposal that the Guild ask for a percentage of profits to be paid in addition to salaries and for payments to be made to those receiving screen credit on all reissues and remakes.[42] The issue of compensation for reissues was one that could unite many otherwise opposed groups both in the talent guilds and in the craft unions.[43] Lester Cole reported at a July 1947 meeting of talent guild and craft union representatives that of the 400 films released for exhibition in the previous year, more than a hundred were reissues. Cole estimated that the hundred reissues 'displaced from employment at least two or 300 writers, a couple of hundred directors and producers, and thousands of actors and skilled studio workers'.[44] Insisting that the problem of reissues was not merely about unemployment, but also of fair compensation, Cole was quoted as saying:

> Our industry is one of the few in the world where the talents and skills of its workers, preserved on strips of celluloid, can be used repeatedly without any remuneration to the possessors of those talents and skills. This fact must be recognized, and some plan is called for whereby compensation will be paid for the repeated use of the creative and technical work of those who make our motion pictures.
>
> Compare motion pictures with the book publishing industry. Writers of books are protected by copyright law, and when their books are re-issued, they are compensated for it. Probably the only workers who are not compensated in the reprinting of a book are the original type-setters. If new plates are made, even the type-setters are paid.[45]

At the meeting, all in attendance agreed that Hollywood labour groups deserved to share in the profits from reissues.

In the lead-up to the September 1947 general membership meeting, the Guild published a number of articles in its magazine, *The Screen Writer*, presenting different points of view on the question of royalty payments for reissues, and profit sharing more generally.[46] These articles were invited responses to Ring Lardner Jr's article arguing that writers were paid about 1 per cent of a film's gross profits and deserved 2 per cent.[47] Noted writers generally favoured the idea. Stephen Longstreet scoffed that 'no author in his right mind would work for two percent no matter how hungry', except of course in Hollywood.[48] British author James Hilton, who wrote the novel *Lost Horizon* and won the 1942 Academy Award for his work on the screen-play for *Mrs Miniver*, opined 'Hollywood would be a bigger and certainly a better success if writers had more share in *production* and *responsibility* – as in England. That would make more sense – and probably also more cents.'[49] Not surprisingly, producers saw it differently. Samuel Goldwyn insisted that the proposal that all writers deserve a percentage of the profits did a 'disservice to a great field of art' because it lumped all Hollywood writers with 'the few capable ones'.[50] In Goldwyn's view,

> it is a virtual impossibility in Hollywood to assign a writer to a script and to get from him a work that can be put on the screen. … Hollywood is hungry for new and fresh material and Hollywood still pays the highest monetary reward in the world for creative writing. But let's have more attention paid to fine ideas and vibrant words than to percentage figures.[51]

David O. Selznick agreed: 'the contributions of writers to motion pictures are not sufficiently uniform, in relation to the pictures in their entirety, to warrant any arbitrary allocation of the share of the earnings as the proper share of the writers, either real or merely credited'.[52] Moreover, Selznick argued, 'the earnings on a picture are dependent, to an extraordinary extent, upon such factors as star values, showmanship, presentation, distribution and the effectiveness of and expenditures for exploitation. To none of these does the writer contribute, of course.'

And, he could not resist pointing out, 'the best writing does not necessarily mean the highest earnings'.[53]

The question of what the Guild should demand with respect to payment of percentages on the gross got caught up in the emerging fight between the left and right wings of the Guild that consumed the autumn of 1947. Ring Lardner Jr and Lester Cole, both leftists who shortly thereafter were blacklisted, delivered the report of the Economic Committee urging the membership to adopt as its economic programme in bargaining a demand that writers be paid a percentage of the gross on a film. Emmet Lavery – who at the time was leading the effort to get Executive Board members to sign affidavits of non-Communist affiliation – opposed the report, saying that the Guild should study the matter more fully before acting and that it should determine whether the percentage of the gross be paid to the individual writers or to the Guild, which would distribute it among the members on some basis. While the membership voted 195 to 136 to adopt the committee report, the political controversy hung over the whole matter.[54] Deliberations over how to handle reissues continued through 1948.[55]

Negotiations for a new agreement lasted from 1949 until agreement with the major movie studios was finally reached in February 1951, and an agreement for writers employed in television production followed in 1953. Along with minimum compensation, the most contentious issues were payments for reissue or reuse of work and separation of rights. The Guild finally struck over those three issues. After a hard-fought strike, the Guild secured a provision in the new Basic Agreement requiring that writers be paid residuals.[56] As noted above, at first the Guild secured only the right to be paid for the re-broadcast of television programmes. Later the Guild obtained the right to be paid for the use of theatrical films on television. As new technologies have added to the range of available outlets for the distribution of material – first, cable, satellite and pay-per-view TV, then videocassettes and DVDs and now video-on-demand, and downloading and streaming on the internet – the Guild has fought to obtain the right in its contracts for writers to be paid for each use.

Residuals help writers survive the periods of intermittent unemployment that became endemic in the industry with the demise of the studio system in the 1950s and the move towards the organisation of the industry around contracting creative talent for single film and television projects. When movies or TV programmes have unexpectedly long and lucrative afterlives in re-runs, writers share in the profits. This is particularly important when the business model involves some films or shows being fabulously lucrative and others sinking like a stone.

The Peril: Will Work for Screen Credit (or Nothing)

There are vast inequalities among workers in film and television production, and no account of the law and labour would be complete without noting the situation of those who do not benefit from the basic agreements negotiated by the talent guilds or the craft unions and do not have the labour market power to negotiate a decent individual employment agreement. The fieldwork and writings of John Caldwell, Vicki Mayer, David Hesmondhalgh and Sarah Baker, among others, have emphasised the importance of studying the vast numbers of workers who are not earning a fabulous (or even a modest) living in film, television and digital media production.[57] Although the majority of people employed in film and TV production in Hollywood work for companies with twenty or more employees, most companies in the industry have

fewer than five employees, and government agencies find it extremely difficult to monitor compliance with even the most basic labour law protections in medium-sized or small firms.[58]
Holes in the web of labour law protections partly explain why labour exploitation exists in an
industry where a few earn extraordinarily large salaries. But part of the problem is the lack of
enforcement of the laws that do exist. Workers may be unaware of their rights or unwilling to
alienate future employers by insisting on compliance with wage and other laws, or perhaps
cowed by implicit or explicit threats to move production to lower-wage locations.

One of the most pervasive problems in the low-wage sector and even in the middle rungs
of the economy, is systematic underpayment of wages. Underpayment takes many forms.
Employers sometimes require or encourage employees to 'work off the clock', meaning that
employees work more hours in a day than they report, so they are paid for, say, eight hours but
in fact work nine.[59] Another is 'misclassification', in which the employer incorrectly designates
an employee to be exempt from the protections of the wage and hour laws and, therefore, the
employer refuses to pay premium pay for overtime work or, in egregious cases, pays less than
the statutory minimum wage.[60] Empirical work on video game production suggests that misclassification and rampant violations of overtime laws are endemic in that industry.[61] A third –
one that is particularly common in creative industries and is conceptually related to the first
two – is the practice of hiring unpaid interns to do work that should be a paid job.[62]

All of these practices are illegal. They occur when middle managers feel pressure to reduce
labour costs while achieving productivity targets and have access to a labour force who either
are unaware of their legal rights or are willing to tolerate violations for the sake of getting or
keeping a job. These labour law violations tend to be the most difficult for employee activists
to combat when the entity that effectively controls working conditions in its supply chain has
no direct employment relationship with the workers and, instead, contracts with intermediaries
to supply goods or services at low cost and the intermediary feels pressure to drive down
labour costs by violating the law. This form of top-down budget-cutting and labour cost control
has become common in vertically disintegrated industries, which includes Hollywood film and
TV production. A handful of conglomerated firms control the distribution of Hollywood film
and TV, and they are pressuring production companies to reduce production costs.[63]
Consequently, lawyers and activists have focused their enforcement efforts on the name brand
companies at the top of the chain to cajole or force them to set realistic prices and productivity goals for their suppliers that allow for lawful pay practices all the way down the production
chain. This has been the strategy to address low-wage labour in garment manufacturing,[64] in
Walmart's distribution operations in the USA[65] and, now, in film and TV production.

The social context in which existing labour rights are not enforced is determined not only
by top-down pressures, but also by the willingness of workers to take a job at almost any
cost. The story of the aspirant who gets off the bus at the old terminal near the intersection
of Hollywood and Vine and hopes to make it big has remained an enduring Hollywood legend;
the contemporary version is the smart film school graduate who works for months or years
as an unpaid intern in the hope of one day landing a paying job. As John Caldwell has explained
many times, there is a vast surplus of aspiring producers, writers, actors, directors, VFX artists
and others who are willing to be exploited for a period of months or years in the hope of succeeding.[66] They believe that an internship will enable them to gain skills and connections – and,

ideally, a screen credit to acknowledge their contribution to the art of film-making.[67] A recent variation on the old jokes about the willingness of people to work for nothing but screen credit is a cartoon depicting a Hollywood tour bus driving past a person holding up a sign. The tour guide says: 'And if you look to the left of the bus, you'll see an independent producer at work.' The person's sign says, 'Will give screen credit 4 food'.

Working for free is not a new problem in the film business. One of the major priorities of the Writers Guild from the beginning was to eliminate the practice of writing on spec, in which a studio would ask a writer to write a script or a treatment which the studio might pay for if it met the studio's demands when complete. Yet writers working in television today invariably report that, to get hired onto the staff of a dramatic series, it is essential to present at least one original pilot script for a new series, as well as often a spec script for an existing show, and those works are, of course, written without compensation. Even experienced writers complain about being asked to do free rewrites. VFX artists who obtain a fixed-price contract to do specified work for a film (such as create the effect of rain drops in several scenes) complain when the director decides late in post-production to alter a scene and asks the VFX artists to do substantial additional work for no additional compensation.[68]

Working for free (beyond a carefully circumscribed certain amount of additional work, such as one or two rewrites of a script, for example) violates the collective bargaining agreements governing talent and craft labour, the individual employment contracts of each worker and, as explained in detail below, federal and state law. As Caldwell, Philip Drake, Bridget Conor and others have described, people will do some additional uncompensated work for understandable reasons, including the desire to produce excellent work and to create a reputation as a dedicated and flexible collaborator.[69] Even so, the practice of employing legions of unpaid interns to work on every facet of film and TV production should astonish all but the most jaded.

The FLSA does not contain an express exemption for interns. On the contrary, its definition of workers entitled to be paid at least the minimum wage includes anyone whom the employer permits to work, and the list of enumerated exceptions to that definition (for independent contractors, for salaried executives, administrators and professionals and for specific other workers) does not include trainees or interns. However, the US Supreme Court read an exemption into the statute in a 1947 case involving trainees who shadowed railway employees on the job for one unpaid week. Emphasising that the trainees benefited from the training and that the railway did not, and that it was a longstanding custom in the heavily unionised railway industry to allow the practice, the Court held that the trainees were not 'employees' under the statute and, therefore, not entitled to be paid for that week.[70] Nothing in that fact-specific decision, however, explained whether interns in other types of programmes are also exempt.

Based on that decision, the Wage and Hour Division of the US Department of Labor, which enforces the FLSA, has held that interns or trainees need not be paid if: (1) their work is training similar to that which would be given in an educational setting, including a vocational school; (2) the training is for the benefit of the trainee; (3) the trainees do not displace regular employees, but work under their close supervision; (4) the employer derives no immediate advantage from the trainees' work and, indeed, its operations may actually be impeded; (5) the trainees are not necessarily entitled to a job at the completion of the training; and (6) the employer and the trainees understand that wages will not be paid for the training.[71] The Wage and Hour Division generally regards unpaid internships at governmental and non-profit organisations as permissible, but scrutinises more carefully unpaid internships at for-profit businesses, even where the intern receives academic credit for the internship, unless it is clear from the facts that the intern is not displacing paid employment, is carefully supervised and is learning skills that are not merely firm-specific.[72]

Unpaid Interns on *Black Swan* and *(500) Days of Summer*

A legal challenge to the widespread use of unpaid interns on major motion pictures illuminates the reasons why aspirants to the movie business work for free, providing a snapshot of those who do unpaid work – they aren't all film school students – and also offers an opportunity to consider the film studios' defence of the practice. In 2011, unpaid interns in the Accounting department and the Production Office of a company that produced *Black Swan* – later joined by an unpaid intern in the Art department of a company that made *(500) Days of Summer* – filed a class action lawsuit against Fox Searchlight and Fox Entertainment Group seeking unpaid wages under the FLSA and its state law equivalent.[73] The interns asserted they had performed the same kinds of work as paid workers and had worked alongside them. The accounting intern, Eric Glatt, testified that he handled purchase orders, invoices, petty cash and personnel files, and made photocopies and deliveries. Production intern Alexander Footman set up office furniture, booked lodging arrangements for cast and crew, made photocopies and deliveries and fetched coffee and lunch. Art department intern Kanene Gratts constructed and maintained sets. They all did so in the hope of eventually being hired into paying jobs in the industry,

Interns working on *Black Swan* (2010) filed a class action suit against the film's producers for unpaid wages (BFI)

and Gratts even believed that she would be paid for her work on *(500) Days of Summer*, though she never was.[74] Another intern, who had worked directly for Fox Searchlight in its New York City Publicity department, later joined the lawsuit, asserting claims for unpaid wages for interns who worked in Fox's corporate offices.[75]

In defence, Fox asserted that it had nothing to do with the employment of any of the interns except those who worked for its own corporate offices. As Fox pointed out, those who work on a film are typically hired by separately incorporated companies established specially for the purpose of making a single film. The special-purpose company enters into a production–distribution–finance agreement with a studio under which the studio provides financing for the film, then promotes and distributes it. Under this arrangement, technically, the film is made by people who are not employed by the studio. According to the pleadings filed in the litigation, the interns who sued Fox worked for Lake of Tears and 500 DS Films, single-project companies created for the sole purposes to make *Black Swan* and *(500) Days of Summer*, respectively.[76] Many smaller production companies – including, for example, the production companies controlled by the director or a star or a producer – may have contracts with a studio in connection with a single movie.[77] Other members of the class involved in film production, Fox emphasised, worked for the many different production companies making movies rather than for the distributor. Fox insisted that it 'does not produce motion pictures' and 'does not employ crew members on productions', but rather it only 'finances, distributes and markets films produced by separately incorporated production companies'.[78]

In technical legal terms, Fox's argument is correct; Fox Entertainment Group and Fox Searchlight are separate legal entities from the companies that employed the interns and the paid crew who actually made the movies. Fox finances and distributes movies under its own name, but it does not directly employ the people who make movies. And, in some cases, such as where a company similar to Fox purchases a completed film at a film festival like Sundance and has absolutely no role in its actual production, it is both legally and factually correct to say that the studio should bear no responsibility for the working conditions on the film. However, where a movie studio is involved in the planning and production of a film from pre-production through post-, it may properly bear legal and moral responsibility for the working conditions on the film, as it is not simply a source of funding to pay for the distribution of a movie that other wholly independent movie studios made.

As the judge ruling on the case found, the production agreements under which *Black Swan* and *(500) Days of Summer* were made gave Fox substantial power to control the hiring and firing of all crew on each film, and Searchlight required the companies to provide daily call sheets and wrap reports detailing the crew, including interns, who would work and did work each day and what hours they worked.[79] The judge found that Lake of Tears required Searchlight's permission to have an unpaid intern who was not receiving college credit, and Searchlight withheld employees' pay until they signed employment and confidentiality agreements ('deal memos') that Searchlight approved. Lake of Tears and 500 DS Films do not appear, from the facts the judge found, to be independent production companies that controlled the working conditions. Even a close reading of the promotional material for the films will not uncover Lake of Tears or 500 DS Films, but Fox Searchlight Pictures is identified as the first producer credit on the posters for both films.[80] It matters a great deal, as a practical matter, for workers to be able to sue Fox or one of the actual independent production companies that controlled the production, for only those entities have the contractual power to change the working conditions of the interns and, in the period after a film wraps, only the studio or the independent production companies have any money to pay a judgment for wages.

Fox's alternative defence to the interns' claims for payment as employees was that the entitlement of any intern to pay as an employee must be determined on the facts of the particular case and, therefore, that class action treatment is inappropriate.[81] This would be an advantageous legal argument for any entity that employs interns because it would require each person to file an individual lawsuit claiming unpaid wages, and interns are unlikely to do so for at least three reasons. First, the amount of money at stake in an individual case would not justify a lawsuit. If the job paid $10 per hour for forty hours of work for twenty weeks, the unpaid wages would be $8,000. Most lawyers are unwilling to take a case in which the maximum likely recovery is so small because the cost of researching, filing and proving the claim is too high. Second, many interns are very likely unaware that they are entitled to be paid for work if it benefits their employer and is not genuine training for them. Finally, people who want to work in such a competitive industry rarely have the nerve to begin their career by suing their prospective employers.

On the merits of whether Glatt and the others should to be paid, the federal trial court found that the interns were employees and so were entitled by law to be paid. The opinion emphasised that the interns did not receive formal training during the internship and acquired only those new skills – such as how a production office worked – that any worker would acquire 'simply by being there'.[82] Although the interns received some benefit – 'such as resume listings, job references and an understanding of how a production office works' – these benefits, the court found, 'were incidental to working in the office like any other employee and were not the result of internships intentionally structured to benefit them'.[83] The interns, the court decided 'worked as paid employees work, providing an immediate advantage to their employer and performing low-level tasks not requiring specialized training'.[84] Fox benefited from the unpaid work, the judge found. Their work, 'menial as it was', nevertheless was essential and did not impede Fox's work. Further, the judge found, the interns 'performed routine tasks that would otherwise have been performed by regular employees'.[85] Finally, the court found insignificant the fact that neither the interns nor Fox expected the positions to be paid:

> the FLSA does not allow employees to waive their entitlement to wages. If an exception to the Act were carved out for employees willing to testify that they performed work 'voluntarily', employers might be able to use superior bargaining power to coerce employees to make such assertions, or to waive their protections under the Act.[86]

The court of appeals decided the trial court had given insufficient weight to the question whether Fox or the interns were the primary beneficiary of the interns' work, which the court thought should be the most important consideration, and so it remanded the case to the trial court to reconsider whether Glatt and the others were interns or employees.[87] The court of appeals directed the trial court to consider some factors that were the same as the ones the trial court had considered under the old rule: the expectation of payment, whether the intern's work displaced or complemented the work of paid employees, the extent to which the intern-ship provides training that would be similar to that given in an educational environment. The court of appeals added some new factors to consider: whether the internship is given aca-demic credit, corresponds to the academic calendar, and is limited to the period in which the intern receives 'beneficial learning,' and whether, considering all the factors, the intern or the company was the 'primary beneficiary' of the work. The court of appeals also directed the trial court to reconsider whether to allow the interns to sue as a class under a new legal standard making it more difficult to establish that the questions common to all the interns predominated over questions of fact that might differ from one intern to another.

The court of appeals' decision probably will not significantly change how entertainment companies handle interns if they had already changed their practices in light of the trial court decision, although it will make it more difficult for the plaintiffs in the litigation to obtain a set-tlement of the unpaid wage claims for all interns who would have been in the proposed class and collective actions.

In the years since the *Black Swan* litigation was filed and made news in the entertainment industry, some employers have changed their practices so that the internship offers more train-ing, interns are less likely to be undertaking the type of work which the company would oth-erwise assign to paid employees and that work confers less immediate benefit on the company. Some now pay their interns the minimum wage, or will allow unpaid interns only if the intern is a current student and receives academic credit for the internship. Some claim to have elim-inated intern positions entirely, presumably shifting the work to paid employees. And some apparently continue their internship programmes as if nothing had happened, presumably counting on no one suing them.[88] The improper use of unpaid interns in jobs that should be paid is not unique to the USA, nor to film and television production, and some entertainment industry companies have been accused of misclassifying employees as interns in the UK and Australia in the same manner that the Fox litigation highlights.[89]

Conclusion

Jobs in the contemporary economy can usefully be understood as being either 'good' or 'bad'. A good job pays reasonably well, gives the worker a sense of satisfaction and a degree of autonomy at work and sufficient time away from work, and enables the worker to have a career – that is, some kind of life-long path. A bad job has none of those characteristics. The polarisation between good and bad jobs has grown more acute in recent decades in a way that is structural, not cyclical.[90] Nowhere is that more true than in film and television production. Labour in film and television production exists in a complex web of statutory, contractual and customary practices governing pay, creative control and attribution of work. Hollywood has always had some spectacularly good jobs and many bad ones, but media production studies scholars have documented the growth in such low-paid, unfavourable jobs and the increasingly large gap (in terms of pay, hours, autonomy, stability and career trajectory) between advanta-geous and inferior jobs, and the hollowing out of the middle range. This chapter has argued that law plays a significant role in constituting some media jobs as 'good' and others as 'bad', and that weakening contractual protections and widespread flouting of statutory protections con-tributes to the polarisation.

Notes

1. Arne L. Kalleberg, *Good Jobs, Bad Jobs: The Rise of Polarized and Precarious Employment Systems in the United States, 1970s to 2000s* (New York: Russell Sage Foundation, 2011).

2. Bibliographic note. Interviews with working writers were conducted by the author in Los Angeles between August 2013 and February 2014. The writers' employment contracts during the classical era are available in Warner Bros. Archive at the Library at the University of Southern California in Los Angeles and the Paramount Archive at the Margaret Herrick Library of the Academy of Motion Picture Arts and Sciences in Los Angeles. References to the internal deliberations of the Writers Guild are from the recorded minutes of the Executive Board of the Writers Guild of America, West, which are housed at the Writers Guild in Los Angeles. The WGA minutes are not public documents and the author gratefully acknowledges the permission of the Writers Guild to read and quote from them.

3. *Community for Creative Non-Violence v. Reid*, 490 US 730, 737 (1989) (explaining the significance of employer authorship of copyrighted works made for hire).

4. Vicki Mayer, *Below the Line: Producers and Production Studies in the New Television Economy* (Durham, NC: Duke University Press, 2011); John Thornton Caldwell, *Production Culture: Industrial Reflexivity and Critical Practice in Film and Television* (Durham, NC: Duke University Press, 2008); David Hesmondhalgh and Sarah Baker, *Creative Labour: Media Work in Three Cultural Industries* (London: Routledge, 2011); Ellen Seiter, 'Pennies from Google', paper presented at the annual meeting of the Society for Cinema and Media Studies, Chicago, Illinois, 6–10 March 2013; Matt Stahl, *Unfree Masters: Recording Artists and the Politics of Work* (Durham, NC: Duke University Press, 2013).

5. 17 USC §§ 101, 201.

6. James R. Webb contract, Warner Bros. Archive, USC, # 12591A (4 February 1946). Other accounts of the variety of terms in writers' agreements in the 1930s and 40s are found in biographies of particular writers, such as Larry Ceplair, *A Great Lady: A Biography of Screenwriter Sonya Levien* (Lanham, MD: Scarecrow Press, 1996)

7. See the discussion of talent contracts and loan-out agreements, Chapter 7.

8. 17 USC § 201. See Catherine L. Fisk, *Working Knowledge: Employee Innovation and the Rise of Corporate Intellectual Property, 1800–1930* (Chapel Hill: University of North Carolina Press, 2009).

9. For example, the contract between Arthur Alsberg and Paramount Pictures allowed a lay-off for six weeks out of twenty-six for the first two six-month periods covered by the contract, and twelve weeks out of each year for the second through seventh years of the contract. Arthur Alsberg contract (28 June 1948), 1-f.33, Paramount Collection, Herrick Library.

10. Effective 1 July 2014, the California minimum wage was increased to $9 per hour; effective 1 January 2016, the California minimum wage will be $10 per hour; and in California overtime must be paid for hours worked in a day in excess of eight, even if the work-week does not exceed forty hours. Cal. Lab. Code Section 1182.12. The provisions of the federal Fair Labor Standards Act are clearly summarised on the US Department of Labor's website. See http://www.dol.gov/whd/regs/compliance/hrg.htm (accessed 4 October 2014).

11. 29 USC § 157.

12. Mike Nielsen and Gene Mailes, *Hollywood's Other Blacklist: Union Struggles in the Studio System* (London: BFI, 1995), pp. 6–9; Douglas Gomery, *The Hollywood Studio System: A History* (London: BFI, 2005), chapter 14; Murray Ross, *Stars and Strikes: Unionization of Hollywood* (New York: Columbia University Press, 1941).

13. *Community for Creative Non-Violence v. Reid*, 490 US 730 (1989).

14. John T. Caldwell, 'Authorship Below-the-Line', in Jonathan Gray and Derek Johnson (eds),
    A Companion to Media Authorship (Malden, MA: Wiley-Blackwell, 2013), p. 353.

15. Ibid.

16. The exclusion of independent contractors from legal protections for the right to unionise under
    the National Labor Relations Act was done as a matter of administrative agency practice before
    1947, and the exclusion was quite narrow. When Congress amended the statute in the 1947 Taft–
    Hartley Act, it added a broader exclusion for independent contractors than the agency had
    previously used. Michael C. Harper, 'Defining the Economic Relationship Appropriate for Collective
    Bargaining', *Boston College Law Review* vol. 39 (1998): 329.

17. On the early history of the Writers Guild and the differences between screenwriters and
    playwrights' contracts, see Christopher Dudley Wheaton, 'A History of the Screen Writers' Guild
    (1920–1942): The Writers' Quest for a Freely Negotiated Agreement', PhD dissertation, University
    of Southern California, 1974, pp. 11–14.

18. Leo C. Rosten, *Hollywood: The Movie Colony, The Movie Makers* (New York: Harcourt Brace and Co.,
    1941), p. 306.

19. Gerald Horne, *The Final Victim of the Blacklist: John Howard Lawson, Dean of the Hollywood Ten*
    (Berkeley: University of California Press, 2006), pp. 91–2.

20. Eric Hoyt, *Hollywood Vault: Film Libraries before Home Video* (Berkeley: University of California Press,
    2014), pp. 120–4.

21. Thomas Schatz, *The Genius of the System: Hollywood Filmmaking in the Studio Era* (Minneapolis:
    University of Minnesota Press, 1988), p. 152.

22. Nancy Lynn Schwartz, *The Hollywood Writers' Wars* (New York: Knopf, 1982).

23. On the history of the Guild's creation and administration of screen credit, see Catherine L. Fisk,
    'The Role of Private Intellectual Property Rights in Markets for Labor and Ideas: Screen Credit and
    the Writers Guild of America, 1938–2000', *Berkeley Journal of Employment and Labor Law* vol. 32
    (2011): 215.

24. Ring Lardner Jr, 'First Steps in Arithmetic', *The Screen Writer* vol. 3 no. 4 (1947): 16–20.

25. Ibid.: 16.

26. On the studios' use of the HUAC hearings to strengthen their hand *vis-à-vis* labour, see Jon Lewis,
    Hollywood v. Hard Core: How the Struggle Over Censorship Saved the Modern Film Industry (New York:
    New York University Press, 2000), especially chapter 1, 'How the Blacklist Saved Hollywood'. On
    residuals, see the *Residuals Survival Guide* (revised December 2013), available on the Writer's
    Resources page of the WGA site:
    http://www.wga.org/uploadedFiles/writers_resources/residuals/residualssurvival2013.pdf (accessed
    16 February 2014).

27. Jonathan Handel, *Hollywood on Strike: An Industry at War in the Internet Age* (Los Angeles: Hollywood
    Analytics, 2011), pp. 8–9.

28. I am unaware of a history of the compulsory music licensing system of ASCAP and BMI. However,
    what ASCAP and BMI do in administering licences for music performances is described in Robert P.
    Merges, 'Contracting into Liability Rules: Intellectual Property Rights and Collective Rights
    Organizations', *California Law Review* vol. 84 (1996): 1293.

29. Schwartz, *The Hollywood Writers' Wars*, p. 21.

30. Quoted in ibid., p. 94.

31. Ibid., p. 97 (the emphasis I imagine to be Lawson's).

32. Kurt Newman, 'Cultural Work and the Politics of "Value Incommensurability": John Howard Lawson, the Screen Writers Guild, and the National Recovery Administration, 1933–35', unpublished manuscript: 12; WGA Executive Board Minutes, 31 January 1938.

33. WGA Executive Board Minutes, 31 January 1938.

34. Some of the early percentage deals are described in Tom Kemper, *Hidden Talents: The Emergence of Hollywood Agents* (Berkeley: University of California Press, 2010), p. 150.

35. WGA Executive Board Minutes, 4 March 1946.

36. Ibid., 16 March 1946.

37. Ibid.

38. Ibid., 16 March 1946, 22 April 1946.

39. Ibid., 22 April 1946, 10 June 1946 (approving Ring Lardner Jr's suggestion that the Committee should draft specific proposals for putting the licensing resolution into effect to be submitted to the Authors League and its member Guilds).

40. Ibid., 31 March 1947.

41. Ibid., 18 November 1946.

42. Ibid. The Guild also considered whether or how to urge other Guilds to take action on the problem of reissues at a meeting on 9 June 1947, but referred the matter to committee for further study.

43. This account of the debate over reissues is drawn from and focuses on the Writers Guild Executive Board meetings. A fuller account of the postwar debate over reissues drawing on different sources is in Hoyt, *Hollywood Vault*, pp. 115–24.

44. 'Conference on Reissues', *The Screen Writer* vol. 3 no. 3 (1947): 42.

45. Quoted in ibid.

46. Samuel Goldwyn, James Hilton, Stephen Longstreet, Irving Pichel, Howard Lindsay, David O. Selznick and Millen Brand, 'The Writer's Share: Some Comments on the Contribution of Writers to the Screen Industry, and Vice Versa', *The Screen Writer* vol. 3 no. 4 (1947): 29–33; Ring Lardner Jr, Lester Cole, Martin Field, Paul Gangelin and Philip Stevenson, '1% of the Gross – An Economic Primer of Screen Writing', *The Screen Writer* vol. 3 no. 3 (1947): 16–33.

47. Records do not reveal what formula Lardner used to calculate percentage of the gross, so it is not feasible to assess how his calculation corresponds to contemporary debates over the arcane but hugely important details of accounting of profits from films.

48. Longstreet, in Goldwyn et al., 'The Writer's Share': 29.

49. Hilton, in Goldwyn et al., 'The Writer's Share': 29, emphasis in original.

50. Goldwyn, in Goldwyn et al., 'The Writer's Share': 29.

51. Ibid.

52. Selznick, in Goldwyn et al., 'The Writer's Share': 31.

53. Ibid.: 32.

54. WGA General Membership Meeting, 8 September 1947.

55. WGA Executive Board Minutes, 25 October 1948, 20 December 1948.

56. Ibid., 20 November 1950, strike authorisation resolution approved for submission to membership, stating that three issues on which the Guild finds producers' position unacceptable are separation

of rights, minimum compensation and 'the rights and obligations as between the writers and producers with respect to television'.

57. Mayer, *Below-the-Line*; Caldwell, *Production Culture*; Hesmondhalgh and Baker, *Creative Labour*.

58. Keith Randle, 'The Organization of Film and Television Production', in Mark Deuze (ed.), *Managing Media Work* (Los Angeles: Sage, 2011), p. 148; Mark Deuze, *Media Work* (Cambridge: Polity Press, 2007).

59. Nantiya Ruan, 'Same Law, Different Day: A Survey of the Last Thirty Years of Wage Litigation and Its Impact on Low-wage Workers', *Hofstra Labor & Employment Law Journal* vol. 30 (2013): 355.

60. Bruce Goldstein, Marc Linder, Laurence E. Norton II and Catherine K. Ruckelshaus, 'Enforcing Fair Labor Standards in the Modern American Sweatshop: Rediscovering the Statutory Definition of Employment', *UCLA Law Review* vol. 46 (1999): 983.

61. Toby Miller, 'The New International Division of Cultural Labor', in Mark Deuze, *Managing Media Work* (Los Angeles: Sage, 2011), p. 94.

62. Craig Durrant, 'To Benefit or Not to Benefit: A Mutually Induced Consideration as a Test for the Legality of Unpaid Internships', *University of Pennsylvania Law Review* vol. 162 (2013): 169.

63. Susan Christopherson, 'Connecting the Dots: Structure, Strategy, and Subjectivity in Entertainment Media', in Mark Deuze (ed.), *Managing Media Work* (Los Angeles: Sage, 2011), pp. 182–3.

64. Shirley Lung, 'Exploiting the Joint Employer Doctrine: Providing A Break for Sweatshop Garment Workers', *Loyola University of Chicago Law Journal* vol. 34 (2003): 291.

65. Brishen Rogers, 'Toward Third Party Liability for Wage Theft', *Berkeley Journal of Employment & Labor Law* vol. 31 (2010): 1.

66. John T. Caldwell, 'Stress Aesthetics and Deprivation Payroll Systems', in Petr Szezepanik and Patrick Vonderau (eds), *Behind the Screen: Inside European Production Cultures* (New York: Palgrave Macmillan, 2013), pp. 91–2.

67. Ibid.

68. I am indebted to Michael Curtin and Kevin Sanson for this insight, which they presented in a paper at the UCI Creative Economies Center on 14 February 2014.

69. Caldwell, 'Stress Aesthetics and Deprivation Payroll Systems'. See also Philip Drake, 'Policy or Practice? Deconstructing the Creative Industries', in Petr Szezepanik and Patrick Vonderau (eds), *Behind the Screen: Inside European Production Cultures* (New York: Palgrave Macmillan, 2013), pp. 221–36, and Bridget Conor, 'Subjects at Work: Investigating the Creative Labour of British Screenwriters', in Petr Szezepanik and Patrick Vonderau (eds), *Behind the Screen: Inside European Production Cultures* (New York: Palgrave Macmillan, 2013), pp. 207–20.

70. *Walling v. Portland Terminal Co.*, 330 US 148 (1947).

71. US Department of Labor, Wage and Hour Division, Fact Sheet # 71; Internship Programs Under the Fair Labor Standards Act (April 2010), available at http://www.dol.gov/whd/regs/compliance/whdfs71.pdf (accessed 17 February 2014).

72. Opinion FLSA 2004-5NA (17 May 2004), available at http://www.dol.gov/whd/opinion/FLSANA/2004/2004_05_17_05FLSA_NA_internship.pdf (accessed 17 February 2014).

73. *Glatt v. Fox Searchlight Pictures, Inc.*, 293 F.R.D. 516 (SDNY 2013).

74. Memorandum of Law in Support of Plaintiffs' Motion for Partial Summary Judgment, No. 11- Civ. 6784 WHP, *Glatt v. Fox Searchlight Pictures Inc.*, 3–5.

75. Memorandum of Law in Support of Defendants' Motion for Summary Judgment, No. 11-Civ-6784-WHP-AJP, *Glatt v. Fox Searchlight Pictures, Inc.*, 26.

76. *Glatt v. Fox Searchlight Pictures, Inc.*, 293 F.R.D. 516; Memorandum of Law in Support of Defendants' Motion for Summary Judgment, No. 11-Civ-6784-WHP-AJP, *Glatt v. Fox Searchlight Pictures, Inc.*, 10–23.

77. The *Black Swan* poster stated 'Fox Searchlight Pictures presents in association with Cross Creek Pictures a Protozoa and Phoenix Pictures Production a Film by Darren Aronofsky', while the *(500) Days of Summer* poster likewise gave top producer billing to Fox Searchlight. Neither even mentioned the corporate entities through which the actual production was funnelled. Protozoa Pictures is the production company of Darren Aronofsky, the director of *Black Swan*. Phoenix Pictures is an independent production company; Watermark Pictures is also an independent production company. Note earlier comments on the crediting of Protozoa, Phoenix and Watermark, and the use of 'presents' to acknowledge Fox is the distributor.

78. Memorandum of Law in Support of Defendants' Motion for Summary Judgment, No. 11-Civ-6784-WHP-AJP, *Glatt v. Fox Searchlight Pictures, Inc.*, 4.

79. *Glatt v. Fox Searchlight Pictures, Inc.*, 293 F.R.D. 516.

80. The poster for *Black Swan* identifies the film as a Fox Searchlight, Protozoa and Phoenix production, but makes no mention of Lake of Tears: www.impawards.com/2010/black_swan_xlg.html (accessed 5 October 2014). Similarly, the poster for *(500) Days of Summer* identifies Fox Searchlight and Watermark, but makes no mention of 500 DS Film: www.impawards.com/2009/five_hundred_days_of_summer_xlg.html (accessed 5 October 2014).

81. Memorandum of Law in Support of Defendants' Motion to Strike the Class and Collective Action Allegations/Claims, No. 11-Civ-6784-WHP, *Glatt v. Fox Searchlight Pictures, Inc.*, 4.

82. *Glatt v. Fox Searchlight Pictures, Inc.*, , 293 F.R.D. 516.

83. Ibid.

84. Ibid.

85. Ibid.

86. Ibid. (quoting *Tony & Susan Alamo Foundation v. Secretary of Labor*, 471 US 299, 301 [1985]).

87. *Glatt v. Fox Searchlight Pictures, Inc.*, __ F.3d __, 2015 WL 4033018 (2d Cir. 2015).

88. *The New York Times* coverage of the growth and persistence of unpaid internships illustrates their continued staying power, even as litigation over their legality continues. See Alex Williams, 'For Interns, All Work and No Payoff: Millennials Feel Trapped in a Cycle of Internships with Little Pay and No Job Offers', *The New York Times*, 16 February 2014, ST1; Steven Greenhouse, 'Jobs Few, Grads Flock to Unpaid Internships', *The New York Times*, 6 May 2012, A1; Steven Greenhouse, 'The Unpaid Internship: Legal or Not?' *The New York Times*, 3 April 2010, B1.

89. On the use of interns and efforts to change unlawful practices regarding their employment in the UK, see sources cited on www.internaware.org (accessed 5 October 2014), and in Australia, see Michelle Innis, 'Australia Challenges Use of Unpaid Internships', *The New York Times*, 10 November 2014, B4.

90. Kalleberg, *Good Jobs, Bad Jobs*.

References

Caldwell, John Thornton, *Production Culture: Industrial Reflexivity and Critical Practice in Film and Television* (Durham, NC: Duke University Press, 2008).

Caldwell, John T., 'Authorship Below-the-Line', in Jonathan Gray and Derek Johnson (eds), *A Companion to Media Authorship* (Malden, MA: Wiley-Blackwell, 2013), pp. 349–69.

Caldwell, John T., 'Stress Aesthetics and Deprivation Payroll Systems', in Petr Szezepanik and Patrick Vonderau (eds), *Behind the Screen: Inside European Production Cultures* (New York: Palgrave Macmillan, 2013), pp. 91–112.

Ceplair, Larry, *A Great Lady: A Biography of Screenwriter Sonya Levien* (Lanham, MD: Scarecrow Press, 1996).

Christopherson, Susan, 'Connecting the Dots: Structure, Strategy, and Subjectivity in Entertainment Media', in Mark Deuze (ed.), *Managing Media Work* (Los Angeles: Sage, 2011), pp. 179–90.

'Conference on Reissues', *The Screen Writer* vol. 3 no. 3 (1947): 42.

Conor, Bridget, 'Subjects at Work: Investigating the Creative Labour of British Screenwriters', in Petr Szezepanik and Patrick Vonderau (eds), *Behind the Screen: Inside European Production Cultures* (New York: Palgrave Macmillan, 2013), pp. 207–20.

Deuze, Mark, *Media Work* (Cambridge: Polity Press, 2007).

Drake, Philip, 'Policy or Practice? Deconstructing the Creative Industries', in Petr Szezepanik and Patrick Vonderau (eds), *Behind the Screen: Inside European Production Cultures* (New York: Palgrave Macmillan, 2013), pp. 221–36.

Durrant, Craig, 'To Benefit or Not to Benefit: A Mutually Induced Consideration as a Test for the Legality of Unpaid Internships', *University of Pennsylvania Law Review* vol. 162 (2013): 169–202.

Fisk, Catherine L., 'The Role of Private Intellectual Property Rights in Markets for Labor and Ideas: Screen Credit and the Writers Guild of America, 1938–2000', *Berkeley Journal of Employment and Labor Law* vol. 32 (2011): 215–78.

Fisk, Catherine L., *Working Knowledge: Employee Innovation and the Rise of Corporate Intellectual Property, 1800–1930* (Raleigh: University of North Carolina Press, 2009).

Goldstein, Bruce, Marc Linder, Laurence E. Norton II and Catherine K. Ruckelshaus, 'Enforcing Fair Labor Standards in the Modern American Sweatshop: Rediscovering the Statutory Definition of Employment', *UCLA Law Review* vol. 46 (1999): 983–1164.

Goldwyn, Samuel, James Hilton, Stephen Longstreet, Irving Pichel, Howard Lindsay, David O. Selznick and Millen Brand, 'The Writer's Share: Some Comments on the Contribution of Writers to the Screen Industry', *The Screen Writer* vol. 3 no. 4 (1947): 29–33.

Gomery, Douglas, *The Hollywood Studio System: A History* (London: BFI, 2005).

Handel, Jonathan, *Hollywood on Strike: An Industry at War in the Internet Age* (Los Angeles: Hollywood Analytics, 2011).

Harper, Michael C., 'Defining the Economic Relationship Appropriate for Collective Bargaining', *Boston College Law Review* vol. 39 (1998): 329–64.

Hesmondhalgh, David and Sarah Baker, *Creative Labour: Media Work in Three Cultural Industries* (London: Routledge, 2011).

Horne, Gerald, *The Final Victim of the Blacklist: John Howard Lawson, Dean of the Hollywood Ten* (Berkeley: University of California Press, 2006).

Hoyt, Eric, *Hollywood Vault: Film Libraries before Home Video* (Berkeley: University of California Press, 2014).

Kalleberg, Arne L., *Good Jobs, Bad Jobs: The Rise of Polarized and Precarious Employment Systems in the United States, 1970s to 2000s* (New York: Russell Sage Foundation, 2011).

Kemper, Tom, *Hidden Talent: The Emergence of Hollywood Agents* (Berkeley: University of California Press, 2010).

Lardner, Ring Jr, Lester Cole, Martin Field, Paul Gangelin and Philip Stevenson, '1% of the Gross – An Economic Primer of Screen Writing', *The Screen Writer* vol. 3 no. 3 (1947).

Lewis, Jon, *Hollywood v. Hard Core: How the Struggle Over Censorship Saved the Modern Film Industry* (New York: New York University Press, 2000).

Lung, Shirley, 'Exploiting the Joint Employer Doctrine: Providing a Break for Sweatshop Garment Workers', *Loyola University of Chicago Law Journal* vol. 34 (2003): 291–354.

Mayer, Vicki, *Below the Line: Producers and Production Studies in the New Television Economy* (Durham, NC: Duke University Press, 2011).

Merges, Robert P., 'Contracting into Liability Rules: Intellectual Property Rights and Collective Rights Organizations', *California Law Review* vol. 84 (1996): 1293–393.

Miller, Toby, 'The New International Division of Cultural Labor', in Mark Deuze (ed.), *Managing Media Work* (Los Angeles: Sage, 2011), pp. 87–99.

Newman, Kurt, 'Cultural Work and the Politics of "Value Incommensurability": John Howard Lawson, the Screen Writers Guild, and the National Recovery Administration, 1933–35', unpublished manuscript.

Nielsen, Mike and Gene Mailes, *Hollywood's Other Blacklist: Union Struggles in the Studio System* (London: BFI, 1995).

Randle, Keith, 'The Organization of Film and Television Production', in Mark Deuze (ed.), *Managing Media Work* (Los Angeles: Sage, 2011), pp. 145–53.

Rogers, Brishen, 'Toward Third Party Liability for Wage Theft', *Berkeley Journal of Employment & Labor Law* vol. 31 (2010): 1–64.

Ross, Murray, *Stars and Strikes: Unionization of Hollywood* (New York: Columbia University Press, 1941).

Rosten, Leo C., *Hollywood: The Movie Colony, The Movie Makers* (New York: Harcourt Brace and Co., 1941).

Ruan, Nantiya, 'Same Law, Different Day: A Survey of the Last Thirty Years of Wage Litigation and Its Impact on Low-wage Workers', *Hofstra Labor & Employment Law Journal* vol. 30 (2013): 355–88.

Schatz, Thomas, *The Genius of the System: Hollywood Filmmaking in the Studio Era* (Minneapolis: University of Minnesota Press, 1988).

Schwartz, Nancy Lynn, *The Hollywood Writers' Wars* (New York: Knopf, 1982).

Seiter, Ellen, 'Pennies from Google', paper presented at the annual meeting of the Society for Cinema and Media Studies, Chicago, Illinois, 6–10 March 2013.

Stahl, Matt, *Unfree Masters: Recording Artists and the Politics of Work* (Durham, NC: Duke University Press, 2013).

Wheaton, Christopher Dudley, 'A History of the Screen Writers' Guild (1920–1942): The Writers' Quest for a Freely Negotiated Agreement', PhD dissertation, University of Southern California, 1974.

Writers Guild of America, *Residuals Survival Guide* (revised December 2013), accessed 16 February 2014, http://www.wga.org/uploadedFiles/writers_resources/residuals/residualssurvival2013.pdf

Cases, Statutes and Administrative Agency Decisions

Community for Creative Non-Violence v. Reid, 490 US 730, 737 (1989).

Glatt v. Fox Searchlight Pictures, Inc., 293 F.R.D. 516 (SDNY 2013).

Walling v. Portland Terminal Co., 330 US 148 (1947).

17 USC §§ 101, 201.

29 USC § 157.

California Labor Code § 1182.12.

US Department of Labor, Opinion FLSA 2004-5NA (17 May 2004), available at http://www.dol.gov/
whd/opinion/FLSANA/2004/2004_05_17_05FLSA_NA_internship.pdf

US Department of Labor, Wage and Hour Division, Fact Sheet # 71; Internship Programs Under the
Fair Labor Standards Act (April 2010), available at http://www.dol.gov/whd/regs/compliance/
whdfs71.pdf

INDEX

Page numbers in **bold** indicate chapters dedicated to the relevant subjects; those in *italics* indicate an image or chart

List of Illustrations

While considerable effort has been made to correctly identify the copyright holders, this has not been possible in all cases. We apologise for any apparent negligence and any omissions or corrections brought to our attention will be remedied in any future editions.

Malcolm X, © Warner Bros./© Victor Company of Japan/©Largo International N.V.; Ginger and Fred, © Produzione Europee Associate; Paper Moon, Saticoy Productions/Directors Company; Tie Me Up! Tie Me Down!, El Deseo; Moulin Rouge, © Twentieth Century Fox Film Corporation; The Adventures of Robin Hood, © Warner Bros.; To Each His Own, Paramount Pictures; Coming to America, Paramount Pictures Corporation/Eddie Murphy; Black Swan, © Twentieth Century Fox Film Corporation/Dune Entertainment III LLC.